EUROPEAN BOOKDEALERS
LIBRAIRIES D'OCCASION EUROPÉENNES
EUROPÄISCHE ANTIQUARIATE

Uniform with this volume are:

Pareils à ce tome sont:

Diesem Bande gleich sind:

DEALERS IN BOOKS

A directory of dealers in secondhand
and antiquarian books in the
British Isles

BOOKDEALERS IN NORTH AMERICA

A directory of dealers in secondhand
and antiquarian books in Canada and
the United States of America

BOOKDEALERS IN INDIA
PAKISTAN, SRI LANKA ETC.

A directory of dealers in secondhand
and antiquarian books in the
Southwest Asian sub-continent

EUROPEAN BOOKDEALERS

A DIRECTORY OF DEALERS IN SECONDHAND AND
ANTIQUARIAN BOOKS ON THE CONTINENT OF EUROPE

LIBRAIRIES D'OCCASION EUROPÉENNES

UN RÉPERTOIRE DE MARCHANDS DE LIVRES ANCIENS
ET D'OCCASION DE L'EUROPE CONTINENTALE

EUROPÄISCHE ANTIQUARIATE

EIN ADRESSBUCH DER ANTIQUARIATSBUCHHÄNDLER
IN DEN EUROPÄISCHEN LÄNDERN

1985 – 87

SIXTH EDITION: SIXIÈME ÉDITION: SECHSTE AUSGABE

LONDON: SHEPPARD PRESS

First published: Première édition: Erste Auflage
(1967–9) August 1967

Second edition: Deuxième édition: Zweite Ausgabe
(1970–72) March 1971

Third edition: Troisième édition: Dritte Ausgabe
(1976–78) October 1975

Fourth edition: Quatrième édition: Vierte Ausgabe
(1979–81) April 1979

Fifth edition: Cinquième édition: Fünfte Ausgabe
(1982–84) April 1982

Sixth edition: Sixième édition: Sechste Ausgabe
(1985–87) August 1985

SHEPPARD PRESS LIMITED
RUSSELL CHAMBERS, COVENT GARDEN
LONDON WC2E 8AA

ISBN: 0 900661 36 4
ISSN: 0071 – 2523

© 1985 SHEPPARD PRESS LIMITED

Made in England

Printed by: Imprimeur: Druck:
Unwin Brothers Limited, Old Woking, Surrey.

CONTENTS

v

TABLE DE MATIÈRE

INHALTSANGABE

WARNING

Whilst every care has been taken in compiling this directory, the publishers cannot accept any responsibility for the accuracy of the information given or for the reliability of any dealer included.

ADVERTISSEMENT

Bienque ce répertoire ait été composé avec le plus grand soin possible, les éditeurs ne peuvent garantir ni l'exactitude des renseignements fournis ni la réputation professionelle des marchands cités.

ZUR BEACHTUNG!

Obwohl dieses Adressbuch mit der grössten Sorgfalt vorbereitet wurde, können die Verleger Verantwortung weder für die Genauigkeit der darin enthaltenen Angaben noch für die Verlässlichkeit der aufgeführten Händler übernehmen.

PREFACE

This is the sixth edition of a comprehensive directory of dealers in second-hand and antiquarian books on the continent of Europe and is a companion volume to the well-known directories for the British Isles and North America, which are now in their eleventh and ninth editions respectively.

In compiling it the editors encountered a number of problems, mostly arising from the use of so many different languages. After much experimenting it was decided that the entries for French and German-speaking countries should be in their own languages and all the rest in English. It was thought that most dealers, librarians, and collectors would have a working knowledge of one of these languages, and that by supplying a simple glossary all entries could be easily understood.

In solving orthographical problems and those caused by the amalgamation of several alphabets into one index, due regard was paid to accuracy and convention, but where they seemed to conflict with common sense the latter was allowed to triumph.

Names are usually given in the form used by the person or country to which they belong, so one will find MÜLLER and MUELLER, HELSINKI and HELSINGFORS. Accents and umlauts have been printed, but in indexing they have been ignored, Ø and Ö being included among the O, and LL with L, because it was thought that most people would look for them there.

The publishers would be glad to receive information about any dealers who have not been included, or any alterations or additions that should be made in the next edition.

ix

PRÉFACE

Cette sixième édition d'un répertoire qui comprehend les marchands de livres d'occasion et anciens dans toute l'Europe continentale, se joint à celles, pour les Iles Britanniques et l'Amérique du Nord dont respectivement la onzième et la neuvième édition ont paru.

En composant le répertoire les éditeurs avaient rencontré de nombreux problèmes provenant pour la plupart de l'emploi de tant de langues différentes. Après des tentatives diverses on décida de donner les reseignements pour les pays ou on parle français ou allemand dans ces langues-ci, tandis que tout le reste serait en anglais, puisqu'on pouvait supposer que la plupart des marchands, bibliothécaires et amateurs de livres auraient au moins une connaissance élémentaire d'une de ces trois langues. En outre, pour faciliter la compréhension, un simple glossaire fut ajouté.

Lorsqu'il s'agissait de résoudre des difficultés d'orthographe ou des problèmes créés par l'amalgamation de différents alphabets en un seul index, le plus grand régard fut accordé à la précision ainsi qu'à la tradition orthographique, et ces deux principes ne furent abandonnés que dans le cas ou ils étaient en criant désaccord avec le sens commun.

En général les noms propres sont indiqués dans la forme habituelle dans le pays d'origine. Ainsi on trouvera MÜLLER et MUELLER, HELSINKI et HELSINGFORS. Les accents et les umlauts, bienqu'imprimés sont ignorés dans l'index lui-même, on trouvera alors Ø et Ö parmi O, et LL parmi L, puisque sans doute la plupart des gens seront naturellement portés à les y rechercher.

Les éditeurs seraient très reconnaissants de recevoir des renseignements sur des marchands omis dans cette édition, ou sur les changements ou additions qu'il faudrait faire dans la septième édition.

VORWORT

Dies ist die sechste Ausgabe eines umfassenden Adressbuches von Antiquaren in Kontinentaleuropa. Sie folgt den bereits wohlbekannten Bänden für die britischen Inseln und Nordamerika, deren elfte bzw. neunte Auflage bereits erschienen sind.

Bei ihrer Zusammenstellung stiessen die Herausgeber auf mehrere Schwierigkeiten, die hauptsächlich vom Gebrauch so vieler verschiedener Sprachen herrührten. Nach einigem Hin- und Herexperimentieren wurde beschlossen, Angaben in Bezug auf deutsche und französisch sprechende Länder in der Originalsprache und alles übrige auf englisch abzufassen. Es wurde angenommen, dass die meisten Händler, Bibliothekare und Sammler ausreichende Kenntnisse einer dieser drei Sprachen besitzen. Es gibt ein einfaches Glossar, welches behilflich sein wird, alle Angaben leicht zu verstehen.

Wenn es sich darum handelte, orthographische Probleme zu lösen oder verschiedene Alphabete in einem Index zu vereinen, wurde mit grösster Genauigkeit und im Sinne der Übereinkunft verfahren, ausgenommen dort, wo dies dem gesunden Menschenverstand widersprochen hätte.

Eigennamen sind gewöhnlich in der in dem Herkunftslande üblichen Form eingetragen: so findet man z.B. MÜLLER und MUELLER, HELSINKI und HELSINGFORS. Akzente und Umlaute wurden gedruckt, aber beim Aufstellen der Verzeichnisse nicht beachtet, Ø und Ö sind unter O, und LL unter L zu finden, da man annehmen konnte, dass die meisten Benutzer sie dort nachschlagen würden.

Die Verleger wären dankbar, von Händlern, die in dieser Ausgabe nicht enthalten sind, in Kenntnis gesetzt und über Vorschläge für Änderungen und Addenda für die siebente Auflage unterrichtet zu werden.

TELEGRAPHIC ADDRESSES
ADRESSES TÉLÉGRAPHIQUES
TELEGRAMMADRESSEN

ANTIQVA, GOTEBORG	Thulin & Ohlson
ARDLOWY, PARIS	Edouard Loewy
ARTANCIEN, ZURICH	L'Art Ancien, S.A.
ARTBOOKS, 's-GRAVENHAGE	Martin Veeneman
ARTBRUG, AMSTERDAM	Antiquariaat Broekema
ARTUS, BERN	Kornfeld & Klipstein
ATHBOOKS, AMSTERDAM	Athenaeum Antiquarian Booksellers
BENPER, AMSTERDAM	John Benjamins
BERGBOOKS, AMSTERDAM	Van Berg Antiquariaat
BIBLIOCRAMER, GENÈVE	Galerie Gérald Cramer
BOERNERKUNST, DÜSSELDORF	C. G. Boerner
BOGKUNST, KØBENHAVN	Rosenkilde & Bagger
BOKBOR, OSLO	Børsums Forlag
BOKBORJE, STOCKHOLM	Björck & Börjesson, A.B.
BOOKBUSCK, KØBENHAVN	Arnold Busck
BOOKS, REYKJAVIK	Snaebjorn, Jonnson & Co.
BOOKS, 's-GRAVENHAGE	Martinus Nijhoff
BOOKBEE, UTRECHT	J. L. Beijers, N.V.
BOOKSHOP, BRUXELLES	W. H. Smith & Son
BOUMABOEK, GRONINGEN	Bouma's Boekhuis, N.V.

BUCHWENNER, OSNABRUCK	H. Th. Wenner
BUECHERHAUS, FRANKFURT	Peter Naacher
BUCHERSTUBE, KONSTANZ	S. & P. Neser (Bücherstube am See)
BURCHARD, WUPPERTAL	Friedrich Burchard
CANTABILE, GENÈVE	E. Engelberts, S.A.
CHARAUTOGRAPHE, PARIS	Maison Charavay
CURIOBOOK, BRUXELLES	Louis Moorthamers
DAMMANFIKK, OSLO	Damm's Antikvariat
DEGRAAF, NIEUWKOOP	Antiquariaat de Graaf
DENOBELEF, PARIS	F. de Nobele
DESIDERATA, ZÜRICH	Büchersuchdienst Pinkus & Co.
DOERLINGANT, HAMBURG	F. Dörling
DOMSCH, FIRENZE	Domsch & Cie.
ELWERT, MARBURG	N. G. Elwert'sche Universitäts Buchhandlung
ENNIBOOK, AMSTERDAM	N. Israel
ERASMUS, TORINO	Bottega d'Erasmus
ESMO, ATHENS	Les Amis du Livre
EUROACADEMIC, BRUXELLES	Presses Academiques Europeén, S.A.
FAB, STUTTGART	F. A. Brockhaus
GALBAS, BERLIN	Galerie Gerda Bassenge
GARISENDA, BOLOGNA	Garisenda Libri
GEROLDBUCH, WIEN	Gerold & Co.
GILBURG, WIEN	Gilhofers Buch und Kunst Antiquariat

GILHAG, LUZERN	..	Giohofer & Ranschburg, GmbH.
GSELLIUS, BERLIN	..	Gsellius'sche Buchhandlung
GUMPERTS, GÖTEBORG	..	Gumperts Bokhandel
HACHTER, PARIS	..	Hachette
HAFNIABOOKS, KØBENHAVN	..	Grønholt Pedersens Boghus
HECKBOOKS, WIEN	..	V. A. Heck
HEITZEDITION, STRASBOURG	..	Paul H. Heitz
HERBERTBOOK, BERN	..	Herbert Lang & Cie.
HYCBOOKS, AMSTERDAM	..	Halcyon Antiquariaat
IFFCASS, LONDON-WC2	..	Sheppard Press
INGOBOOKS, WIEN	..	Ingo Nebehay
ISRAELBOOK, AMSTERDAM		B. M. Israel
KLEMANTIK, STOCKHOLM		H. Klemmings Antikvariat
KREBSERCO, THUN	..	W. Krebser & Co.
LAURIARTH, PARIS	..	Arthur Lauria
LIBLAGET, PARIS	..	Léonce Laget
LIBHANKARD, BRUXELLES	..	Hankard Librairie, S.P.R.L.
LIBORIENT, PARIS	..	Paul Geuthner
LIBRANNICA, KØBENHAVN	..	Branners Bibliofile Antikvariat
LIBRATUL, BRUXELLES	..	Fl. Tulkens
LIBREMON, NEUCHATEL	..	Mme. Eugene Reymond
LIBRI, NAPOLI	..	Libreria di lo Schiavo
LIBRIKA, ATHENS	..	Libraire Kauffmann
LIBRIRE, MILANO	..	Renzo Rizzi
LIBRISACK, GENÈVE	..	H. Sack

LIBRISANTIK, STOCKHOLM	..	Libris Antikvariatet
LIBRORUM, BUREN	.. ..	Frits A. M. Knuf
LIBROSC, FIRENZE ..	.. ..	Leo Olschki
LIVRANCIEN, LAUSANNE ..	..	Maurice Bridel
LUBARDON, MADRID	.. ..	Louis Bardon
LUDROS, HILVERSUM	.. ..	Ludwig Rosenthals Antiquariaat
MADLIGERSCHWAB, ZÜRICH	..	Hilde & Rud. Madligerschwab
MEDIAEVIST, BONN	.. ..	Emil Semmel
MEDIZINBUCH, FREIBURG	..	Hans Ferdinand Schulz
MILLBOOKS, SOEST		Antiquariaat van Coevorden
MOBIN, AMSTERDAM	.. ..	C. P. J. van der Peet
MOLINSUR, MADRID	..	Gabriel Molina
MUSIKANTIQUAR, TUTZING	..	Hans Schneider
MUSIKDOB, WIEN ..	.. ..	Ludwig, Doblinger
NATURA, BERLIN ..	.. ..	R. Friendländer & Sohn
NORDANTIQUARIAT, ROSTOCK	..	Norddeutsches Antiquariat
NUMISMATIQUE, AMSTERDAM	..	Jacques Schuman
OFLIBRI, BRUXELLES	.. ..	Office International de Librairie, S.P.R.L.
PIBY, PARIS ..	.. .. ..	Pierre Berès
PINCBOOKS, TEL-AVIV	.. ..	F. Pinczower
POLIFILO, MILANO ..	.. ..	Il Polifilo
PRELIBER, TORINO ..	.. ..	Arturo Pregliasco

ROENNELLBOK, STOCKHOLM	..	G. Rönnell
ROOSBOOKS, PARIS	.. ..	Jean Rousseau-Girard
ROTHACBUCH, BERLIN	.. ..	Oscar Rothacker
SANBABILA, MILANO	..	Peppi Battaglini
SANDIQUAR, WIESBADEN	.. ..	Dr. Martin Sändig
SCHUMANNBUCH, ZÜRICH	..	Helmut Schumann
STATLIVRE, GENÈVE	.. ..	M. Slatkine & Fils
SWEZEIT, AMSTERDAM	.. ..	Swets & Zeitlinger
THOMLIB, PARIS	.. ..	Lucien Scheler
THULANTIK, STOCKHOLM	..	Thulin's Antikvariat
THULIMAGO, LINDINGO	.. ..	P. Thulin
UPSALABOK, UPSALA	.. ..	A. Cederbergs Eftr., A.B.
VIRIDITAS, AMSTERDAM	.. ..	B. R. Grüner
VITRUV, BERLIN	.. .. ..	Bruno Hessling
WALEDIT, PARIS	.. .. ..	Editart
WEGA, LUGARNO	.. .. ..	Fuchs & Reposo
WIDAWAKE, PARIS	.. .. ..	Dawson-France, S.A.
WUENDISCH, HEIDELBERG	..	Hans Wündisch

REFERENCE BOOKS

BIBLIOGRAPHIE   NACHSCHLAGEBÜCHER

THE AFRICAN BOOK WORLD AND PRESS: A DIRECTORY. Third revised edition at £46.50. Published by Hans Zell Publishers. An imprint of K. G. Saur Verlag, 14 Saint Giles, P.O. Box 56, Oxford OX1 3EL.

AFRICAN BOOKS IN PRINT, 1984. 2 vols. 1402pp. An index by author, title and subject of over 18,750 works in English, French and African languages. £85.00 the set. Edited Hans Zell. Published by Mansell, 6 All Saints Street, London N1 9RL.

AMERICAN BOOK PRICES CURRENT. 35,000 entries for books, autographs and manuscripts sold at auction, U.S.A., Canada, Europe, S. Africa and Australia. 1984, Vol. 90, 1,000pp. American Book Prices Current, P.O. Box 236, Washington CT 06793, U.S.A.

AMERICAN BOOK TRADE DIRECTORY. Lists every kind of book outlet, over 20,000 in 5,000 American and Canadian cities, also book wholesalers, clubs, libraries, publishers etc. 28th edition. Postpaid £92.50. Bowker Publishing Company, Erasmus House, 58-62 High Street, Epping, Essex CM16 4BU.

AMERICAN LIBRARY DIRECTORY, Lists 35,000 American and Canadian Libraries. Revised annually. £102.50. 35th edition. Bowker Publishing Company, Erasmus House, 58-62 High Street, Epping, Essex CM16 4BU.

AMERICAN PUBLISHER'S DIRECTORY. 1st edition 1978, 390pp. K. G. Saur, Shropshire House, 2-10 Capper Street, London WC1E 6JA.

BOOK-AUCTION RECORDS. A priced and annotated record of books sold at auction in England, Europe and North America. Vol. 8 (1982-83). £50.00. Published annually by Wm. Dawson and Sons, Cannon House, Park Farm Road, Folkstone, Kent CT19 5EE, England.

BOOKDEALERS' AND COLLECTORS' YEAR-BOOK AND DIARY. Annual reference book and desk diary showing book-fairs, anniversaries etc. Published every November for the following year: Sheppard Press Limited, P.O. Box 42, Russell Chambers, London WC2E 8AX.

BOOKDEALERS IN INDIA, PAKISTAN, SRI LANKA etc. A directory of dealers in secondhand and antiquarian books in the Southwest Asian sub-continent. First edition 1977. £3.50. Published by Sheppard Press Limited, P.O. Box 42, Russell Chambers, Covent Garden, London WC2E 8AX.

BOOKDEALERS IN NORTH AMERICA. A directory of dealers in secondhand and antiquarian books in Canada and the United States of America. Ninth edition. £10.50. Published by Sheppard Press Limited, P.O. Box 42, Russell Chambers, Covent Garden, London WC2E 8AX.

THE BOOKMAN'S GLOSSARY edited by Jean Peters, 6th edition. £20.25. Published by Bowker Publishing Co., P.O. Box 5, Epping CM16 4BU.

BOOKMAN'S GUIDE TO AMERICANA. Eighth Edition. By Norman Heard. £17.50. Published by The Scarecrow Press, Inc., Metuchen, New Jersey, U.S.A. Distributors: Bailey Bros. & Swinfen Ltd., Warner House, Folkstone, Kent.

BOOKMAN'S PRICE INDEX. Volume 1 through 28 in print. Edited by Daniel F. McGrath. Published by Gale Research Company, Book Tower Detroit, Michigan 48226, U.S.A. £110.00 per volume.

BOOKS IN PRINT. 1982-83. Lists 600,000 books in print from American publishers and distributors: Annually in October. Postpaid price in U.S.A. £172.00 for 6-volume set. Bowker Publishing Company, Erasmus House, 58-62 High Street, Epping, Essex CM16 4BU.

A BOOK WORLD DIRECTORY OF THE ARAB COUNTRIES, TURKEY AND IRAN. Compiled by Anthony Rudkin and Irene Butcher. Lists Newspapers, Periodicals, Libraries and Booksellers. £27.50. Published by Mansell, 6 All Saints' Street, London N1 9RL.

BRITISH BOOKS AND LIBRARIES. A series of eight tape/slide programmes. £42.50 each. The British Council, 65 Davies Street, London W1Y 2AA. Distributed by Sweet and Maxwell.

BRITISH BOOKS IN PRINT. Lists books in print of British publishers. Annually in November. Post paid price in Britain £78.00. Overseas £90.00. Published by J. Whitaker and Sons Limited, 12 Dyott Street, London WC1A 1DF.

BRITISH NATIONAL BIBLIOGRAPHY. Records each week new British books with cumulations in last issue of month, two interim cumulations and annual volume. Published by the British Library Bibliographic Services Division, 2 Sheraton Street, London W1V 4BH.

CATALOGUE BIBLIOGRAPHIQUE DES VENTES PUBLIQUES. Compiled by O. Matterlin. An illustrated record of 14,000 books sold at auction 1980-1982 in France, Belgium, Monaco, Britain and America. 10th edition £60.00. Published biennially by Éditions Mayer, 224 Avenue du Maine, 75014 Paris.

CUMULATIVE BOOK INDEX. A world list of books in the English language. Eleven issues a year and permanent bound annual cumulation. Bound four, five, or six year cumulations through 1956; two years cumulations 1957 through 1968. Published by the H. W. Wilson Company, 950 University Avenue, Bronx, New York 10452, U.S.A.

DIRECTORY OF AMERICAN BOOK SPECIALISTS, 4th edition 1981. Published by Continental Publishing Co., 1261 Broadway, New York, NY 10001. U.S.A.

DIRECTORY OF AMERICAN BOOK WORKERS. Compiled by Renée Roff. $20.95 including postage. Published by Nicholas T. Smith, P.O. Box 66, Bronxille, NY 10708, U.S.A.

A DIRECTORY OF DEALERS IN SECONDHAND AND ANTIQUA-RIAN BOOKS IN THE BRITISH ISLES. 11th edition, (1984-86) £12.00. (N. America $25). Published by Sheppard Press, P.O. Box 42 Russell Chambers, Covent Garden, London WC2E 8AX.

DIRECTORY OF SPECIALIZED AMERICAN BOOKDEALERS. 350pp. £10.25. Published by The Moretus Press, 274 Madison Avenue, New York, N.Y. 10016, U.S.A.

EIGHTEENTH CENTURY BRITISH BOOKS, an author union cata-logue extracted from the British Museum, Bodleian Library and Univer-sity Library Cambridge Catalogues, by F. J. G. Robinson, G. Averley, D. R. Esslemont and P. J. Wallis. Published by Wm. Dawson & Sons, Cannon House, Folkestone, Kent. 1981. 5 vols. £1,250.00

FIRST PRINTINGS OF AMERICAN AUTHORS: Contributions Towards Descriptive Checklists. Four volumes. Matthew J. Bruccoli, Series Editor. C. E. Frazer Clark, Jr., Managing Editor. Richard Layman, Project Editor. Benjamin Franklin V, Associate Editor. 1,648 pages. Annotations; Author portraits; Reproductions of 3,000 title pages, dust jackets, and bindings; Cumulative index to volumes 1-4 in Vol. 4. £280.00 set. Published by Gale Research Co., Detroit, MI 48226.

GUIDE DES LIBRAIRES D'ANCIEN ET D'OCCASION par Denis Basane, donne l'adresse de 273. librairies Editions Hubschmid et Bouvet, 11 rue de Sèvres F-75006 Paris.

INTERNATIONAL BIBLIOGRAPHY OF REPRINTS/ INTERNATIONALE BIBLIOGRAPHIE DER PRINTS. Band I, Books and Serials; Band II, Annuals and Periodicals. DM. 240,-. Published by K. G. Saur Verlag, München, Germany.

INTERNATIONAL BIBLIOGRAPHY OF THE BOOK TRADE AND LIBRARIANSHIP. 1981. DM. 148,-. K. G. Saur Verlag, München, Germany.

INTERNATIONAL BOOK COLLECTORS DIRECTORY, $35.00. Pegasus Press, P.O. Box 1350, Vashon WA 98070, U.S.A.

INTERNATIONAL BOOKS IN PRINT. 3rd edition. 1983. English language title published outside the U.S.A. and U.K. 2 vols, 1,500pp, DM398,-. K.G. Saur, Verlag, München, Germany.

INTERNATIONAL DIRECTORY OF ANTIQUARIAN BOOKSEL-LERS. Published by I.L.A.B. A world list of members of organisations belonging to the International League of Antiquarian Booksellers. 8th edition. 1984.

INTERNATIONAL DIRECTORY OF ARTS. Art Address Verlag, Bowker Publishing Company, 58-62 High Street, Epping, Essex CM16 4BU.

INTERNATIONAL DIRECTORY OF BOOK COLLECTORS. 4th edition, £18.50. Published by the Trigon Press, 117 Kent House Road, Beckenham, Kent BR3 1JJ, England.

INTERNATIONAL MAPS AND ATLASES IN PRINT. ed. Kenneth Winch. £17.50. Bowker Publishing Company, Erasmus House, 58-62 High Street, Epping, Essex CM16 4BU.

JAHRBUCH DER AUKTIONSPREISE für Bücher, Handschriften und Autographen. Veröffentl. bei Dr. Ernst Hauswedell & Co., Rosenberg-strasse 113, D-7000 Stuttgart 1, Deutschland. Bericht über Bücher, Handschriften und Manuskripte, die auf Auktionen in Deutschland,

Holland, Österreich und der Schweiz im Laufe eines Jahres gehandelt werden. Im Anhang eine Liste wichtiger Händler und ihrer Spezialitäten.

LIBRARIES IN THE UNITED KINGDOM AND THE REPUBLIC OF IRELAND. 10th edition, £9.95. Library Association Publishing, 7 Ridgemont Street, London WC1E 7AE.

LES LIVRES DISPONIBLES. Index of French books in print. 6,210pp. listing 261,289 French language books. Cercle de la Librairie, 35 rue Grégorie de Tours, F-75279, Paris. Cedex 06.

MEDICAL BOOKS AND SERIALS IN PRINT 1982. 1,800pp. £71.75. Published by R. R. Bowker Company, New York.

BRITISH PAPERBACKS IN PRINT. A guide to over 50,000 paperback books, in print in Great Britain. Published by J. Whitaker & Sons Limited, 12 Dyott Street, London WC1A 1DF, at £25.00 U.K., £30.00 Export.

PUBLISHERS IN THE UNITED KINGDOM AND THEIR ADDRESSES. A list of over 2,000 publishers. U.K. £2.80, outside Europe £4.00. Published by J. Whitaker & Sons Limited, 12 Dyott Street, London WC1A 1DF.

PUBLISHERS WEEKLY YEARBOOK. 252pp. £46.50. 1984 edition. Publishing Co., P.O. Box 5, Epping, Essex CM16 4BU.

A SHORT-TITLE CATALOGUE OF BOOKS PRINTED IN ENGLAND, SCOTLAND & IRELAND AND OF ENGLISH BOOKS PRINTED ABROAD. 1475-1640. Second revised and enlarged. Vol. 2: I-Z. By W. A. Jackson. F. S. Ferguson and Katherine F. Pantzer. Published by The Bibliographical Society, British Library, Great Russell Street, London WC1B 3DG, at £70.00

SUBJECT GUIDE TO BOOKS IN PRINT 1982-83. Classifies more than 50,000 non-fiction titles in-print of almost every American publisher under 62,500 subject headings. Issued annually, £116.00 for 3 volume set. Bowker Publishing Company, Erasmus House, 58-62 High Street, Epping, Essex CM16 4BU.

TASCHENBUCH DER AUKTIONSPREISE ALTER BÜCHER. Annual record of auction prices of old books in Germany, Austria and Switzerland. Volume 7 (Season 1983). £34.50. Published by S. Radtke. Aachen. Germany.

TITLES OF ENGLISH BOOKS AND OF FOREIGN BOOKS PRINTED IN ENGLAND. By A. F. Allison and V. F. Goldsmith. Published by Wm. Dawson & Sons Ltd., Cannon House, Folkestone, Kent. Vol. 1: 1475-1640. £10.00. Vol. 2: 1641-1700. £20.00.

ULRICH'S INTERNATIONAL PERIODICALS DIRECTORY 1982. (23rd edition). A guide to over 67,000 world periodicals under 385 subject headings. Each entry tells where magazine is published, price frequency of issue, where indexed or abstracted, whether it carries advertisements, books reviews, or any of twenty descriptive characteristics. 2 vols. £116.50. Bowker Publishing Company, Erasmus House, 58-62 High Street, Epping, Essex CM16 4BU.

USED BOOK PRICE GUIDE. Standard reference work for pricing rare, scarce and used books. 5-year edition hard cover, $79.00. Price Guide Publishers, 525 Kenmore Station, Kenmore, WA 98028, U.S.A.

VERZEICHNIS LIEFERBARER BÜCHER (German Books in Print) 1983, 13th edition. K. G. Saur, Shropshire House, 2-10 Capper Street, London WC1E 6JA.

WHITAKER'S CUMULATIVE BOOK LIST. A complete record of British book production. Annual volume. £18.00. Published by J. Whitaker & Sons Limited, 12 Dyott Street, London WC1A 1DF.

WORLD GUIDE TO SPECIAL LIBRARIES, 1983. DM240,-, edited by Helga Lengenfelder. Published by K. G. Saur Verlag, München, Germany.

PERIODICALS

JOUNAUX   ZEITSCHRIFTEN

THE AMERICAN BOOK COLLECTOR. Six times a year. Annual subscription $18.50 (individual), $23.25 (institution). Editor: Anthony Fair. Published by Moretus Press, 274 Madison Avenue, New York, NY 10016.

ABMR (ANTIQUARIAN BOOK MONTHLY REVIEW). Monthly magazine containing articles, book reviews, auction reports and catalogue news. Editor: Jennifer Hainsworth. ABMR Publications Ltd., 52 St. Clement's, Oxford OX4 1AG. TN: (0865) 721615.

AB BOOKMANS WEEKLY: ANTIQUARIAN BOOKMAN. Founded 1948. Weekly and AB Bookmans Yearbooks (two parts). Editor and published: Jacob L. Chernofsky, AB Weekly, P.O. Box AB, Clifton, NJ 07015, U.S.A. Telephone (021) 772-0020.

AUS DEM ANTIQUARIAT. Published from Römerstrasse 7. D-8000 München 40. TN: (089) 34 13 31. Monthly. Editor: Dr. Karl H. Pressler.

L'ARGUS DU LIVRE ANCIEN & MODERNE. Tous les trois mois. Description et prix des ouvrages passés en ventes publiques en France et à l'Etranger. Rédaction, 18 rue Dauphine, 76006 Paris, France.

THE BIBLIOTHECK, edited from Saint Andrews University Library. Bibliographical articles, notes and reviews of Scottish interest. Annual supplement lists books, reviews, essays and articles on Scottish literature published in the preceding year. Published by a Scottish Group of the Library Association from the National Library of Scotland, Edinburgh EH1 1EW.

THE BOOK COLLECTOR, 90 Great Russell Street, London WC1B 3PS. Telephone: 01-637 3029. Established 1952, Quarterley Subscription £15.00 ($35), plus post and packing £1.50 ($2.50).

THE BOOKDEALER. Trade weekly for secondhand and antiquarian books for sale and wanted. Published by Werner Shaw Limited, Suite 34, 26 Charing Cross Road, London WC2H 0DH. Telephone: (01) 240 5890.

THE BOOKSELLER. Weekly journal of the new book trade in Britain. Subscription £40.00 per annum. Published by J. Whitaker and Sons Limited, 12 Dyott Street, London WC1A 1DF. Telephone 01-836 8911.

BOOKS FROM FINLAND, quarterly English-language journal of writing from and about Finland. Subscription Fmk.100 per annum. Published by Helsinki University Library, P.O. Box 312, SF-00171, Helsinki 17.

BOOKS OF THE MONTH AND BOOKS TO COME. Monthly list of all books published in U.K. during the month and forthcoming publications for next two months. J. Whitaker & Sons, 12 Dyott Street, London WC1A 1DF.

BÖRSENBLATT FÜR DEN DEUTSCHEN BUCHHANDEL (Angebotene und Gesuchte Bücher). Buchhändler-Vereinigung G.m.b.H., D-6000 Frankfurt am Main. Postfach 2404.

BRITISH LIBRARY JOURNAL, Established 1975, a scholarly journal devoted to the study of the library's collections and to the historical archives preserved in the Department of Manuscripts. Oxford University Press, Journals Department, Walton Street, Oxford OX2 6DP. TN: (0865) 56767.

BULLETIN DU BIBLIOPHILE, 18 rue Dauphine, F-75006 Paris, France.

THE CLIQUE. The antiquarian booksellers weekly. Established 1890. By subscription to booksellers only. Contains advertisements and lists of books wanted and for sale in Britain and elsewhere. Published by The Clique, c/o Stoate & Bishop (Printers), Saint James Square, Cheltenham, Glos. GL50 3PU. TN: (0242) 36741.

L'ESOPO, Revista trimestrale di bibliofilia. Mario Scognamizlio, via Rovello 1,20121 Milano, Italy.

FINE PRINT. A Review for the Arts of the Book. Quarterly, January, April, July and October. Published by Fine Print, P.O. Box 3394, San Francisco, CA 94119, U.S.A.

GAZZETTINO LIBRARIO. Richieste ed offerte di libri antichi e moderni. Pubblicazione bimestrale. Gazzettino Librario, Via J. Nardi 6, 50132 Firenze, Italy.

THE LIBRARY. Transactions of the Bibliographical Society, quarterly, £24 per annum. Oxford University Press, Journals Department, Walton Street, Oxford OX2 6DP.

LIBRARY ASSOCIATION RARE BOOKS GROUP NEWSLETTER, Editor: Dr. Brian Hillyard, National Library of Scotland, George IV Bridge, Edinburgh EH1 1EW. Correspondence about subscriptions to Miss J. Archibald, English Antiquarian Section, British Library Reference Division, Great Russell Street, London WC1B 3DG.

THE LITERARY REVIEW, 51 Beak Street, London W1R 3DH. TN: (01) 437 9392. Telex: 919034. Editor: Gillian Greenwood.

LONDON REVIEW OF BOOKS, Tavistock House South, Tavistock Square, London WC1H 9JZ, TN: (01) 388 6751.

NEW YORK REVIEW OF BOOKS, 250 West 57th Street, New York, NY 10107, U.S.A.

PUBLISHER'S WEEKLY. Weekly reports of new books published; promotion, market and foreign book news, etc. Enlarged Spring and Falls numbers, containing information and announcements on publishing programmes. Subscriptions: 1 year $107.00, 2 years $214.00; 3 years $321.00. Published by R. R. Bowker Co., P.O. Box 1428, Riverton, NJ 08077, U.S.A.

QUILL AND QUIRE, Journal of the Canadian Book Trade, 56 The Esplanade, (Suite 213), Toronto, Ontario M5E 1A7. TN: (416) 364 3333.

TAAB WEEKLY, THE LIBRARY BOOKSELLER, P.O. Box 239, W.O.B. West Orange, NJ 07052, U.S.A. Founded 1944. Provides the antiquarian bookseller with a direct link to libraries and private buyers. Publisher: Albert Saifer.

THE TIMES LITERARY SUPPLEMENT. Published by Times Newspapers Ltd., Priory House, Saint John's Lane, London EC1M 4BX. TN: (01) 253 3000. Telex: 264971.

WHITAKER'S CLASSIFIED MONTHLY BOOK LIST. Classified under 53 subject headings, books published during the month and forth coming titles for the following two months. J. Whitaker and Sons Ltd., 12 Dyott Street, London WC1A 1DF.

THE WORLD OF BOOKS. Monthly. Poacher Publications, P.O. Box 10, Lincoln LN5 7JA.

LIST OF COUNTRIES
LISTE DES PAYS
VERZEICHNIS DER LÄNDER

	English	*Français*	*Deutsch*
BELGIE/BELGIQUE	BELGIUM	BELGIQUE	BELGIEN
BULGARIYA	BULGARIA	BULGARIE	BULGARIEN
CESKOSLOVENSKO	CZECHO-SLOVAKIA	TCHECO-SLOVAQUIE	TSCHECHO-SLOWAKEI
DANMARK	DENMARK	DANEMARK	DANEMARK
DEUTSCHLAND	GERMANY	ALLEMAGNE	DEUTSCHLAND
ELLAS	GREECE	GRÈCE	GRIECHENLAND
ESPAÑA	SPAIN	ESPAGNE	SPANIEN
FRANCE	FRANCE	FRANCE	FRANKREICH
ISLAND	ICELAND	ISLANDE	ISLAND
ISRAEL	ISRAEL	ISRAEL	ISRAEL
ITALIA	ITALY	ITALIE	ITALIEN
JUGOSLAVIJA	YUGOSLAVIA	YOUGOSLAVIE	JUGOSLAWIEN
KYPRIAKI DIMOKRATIA KIBRIS CUMHURIYETI	CYPRUS	CHYPRE	ZYPERN
LIECHTENSTEIN	LIECHTENSTEIN	LIECHTENSTEIN	LIECHTENSTEIN
LUXEMBOURG	LUXEMBOURG	LUXEMBOURG	LUXEMBURG
MAGYARORSZAG	HUNGARY	HONGRIE	UNGARN
MALTA	MALTA	MALTE	MALTA
NEDERLAND	NETHERLANDS/HOLLAND	PAYS-BAS	NIEDERLANDE
NORGE	NORWAY	NORVÈGE	NORWEGEN
ÖSTERREICH	AUSTRIA	AUTRICHE	ÖSTERREICH
POLSKA	POLAND	POLOGNE	POLEN
PORTUGAL	PORTUGAL	PORTUGAL	PORTUGAL
ROMINA	ROUMANIA	ROUMANIE	RUMÄNIEN
SCHWEIZ/SUISSE/SVIZZERA	SWITZERLAND	SUISSE	SCHWEIZ
SOYUZ SOVYETSKIKH SOTSIALISTICHESKIKH RESPUBLIK (C.C.C.P.)	U.S.S.R.	U.R.S.S.	U.D.S.S.R.
SUOMI	FINLAND	FINLANDE	FINNLAND
SVERIGE	SWEDEN	SUÈDE	SCHWEDEN

EXPLANATORY NOTE

The information given, if available, for each entry is:

Name and address of business.

Name of proprietor if different from business name. [Prop:]

Telephone number and telegraphic address. [TN: and TA:]

Date of establishment. [Est:]

Type of premises occupied. If they are described as a shop or store they are, unless otherwise stated, open to the public and members of the trade without appointment during normal business hours. If described as a storeroom or private premises, information as to whether an appointment is necessary or not is added.

Type and size of the business. Whether the firm deals in new books also and the size of the normal stock of secondhand and antiquarian books.

Under 2,000 volumes = very small stock.

2,000–5,000 volumes = small stock.

5,000–10,000 volumes = medium stock.

10,000–20,000 volumes = large stock.

20,000+ volumes = very large stock.

In what subjects, if any, [Spec:] the business specialises and if catalogues are issued. [Cata:]

Language in which correspondence can be conducted in addition to the local language. [Corresp:]

Bank and account number. [B:]

Membership of any trade associations. [M:]

EXPLICATIONS

Dans chaque cas les détails suivant ont, si possible, été fournis:

Nom et adresse de la maison.

Nom du propriétaire s'il diffère du nom de la maison. [Prop:]

Numéro de téléphone et adresse télégraphique. [TN et TA:]

Date de la fondation. [Fondé:]

Genre de local occupé. S'il est décrit comme boutique il est ouvert au public et aux commerçants négociants pendant les heures normales d'ouverture sans qu'il soit nécessaire de prendre préablement un rendezvous. Si, par contre, il est décrit comme dépôt ou domicile il est indiqué si un rendez-vous est nécessaire ou non.

Type et grandeur de la maison. Si elle fait aussi le commerce de livres neufs et l'étendue du stock en livres anciens et d'occasion.

Moins que 2,000 volumes = assez restreint stock.

2,000–5,000 volumes = restreint stock.

5,000–10,000 volumes = moyen stock.

10,000–20,000 volumes = important stock.

20,000+ volumes = très important stock.

Si la maison se spécialise dans un certain domaine, si oui, lequel, [Spec:] et si des catalogues sont issus. [Cata.]

Langues, autres que celle du pays, dans lesquelles une correspondence est possible. [Corresp:]

La Banque et le numéro du compte. [B:]

Si le marchand est membre d'une association de négociants. [M:]

ERLÄUTERUNGEN

Jede Eintragung enthält wo möglich folgende Angaben:

Name und Adresse der Firma.

Names des Besitzers, falls anders als der Firmenname. [Prop:]

Telefon- und Telegrammadresse. [TN: und TA:]

Datum der Gründung. [Gegründet:]

Art des Lokals. Wo es als Laden beschrieben ist, ist es, wenn nicht speziell erwähnt, für das Publikum und Branchen-mitglieder während der normalen Geschäftszeit ohne vorherige Anmeldung geöffnet. Wo es als Lagerraum oder Wohnung bezeichnet ist, wird angegeben, ob vorherige Anmeldung erwünscht wird oder nicht.

Art und Grösse des Geschäfts. Ob die Firma auch mit neuen Büchern handelt, und die Grösse des Vorrat an antiquarischen Büchern.

Weniger als 2,000 Bände = sehr kleiner Vorrat.

2,000–5,000 Bände = kleiner Vorrat.

5,000–10,000 Bände = mittelgrosser Vorrat.

10,000–20,000 Bände = grosser Vorrat.

20,000+ Bände = sehr grosser Vorrat.

Auf welchem Gebiet die Firma spezialisiert, wenn überhaupt, [Spez:] und ob Kataloge enthältlich sind. [Kata:]

In welcher Sprache, abgesehen von der Landesprache, korrespondiert werden kann. [Korresp:]

Bank und Kontonummer. [B:]

Mitgliedschaft von Geschäftsverbänden. [M:]

TRANSLATION

TRADUCTION   ÜBERSETZUNG

	English	*Français*	*Deutsch*
	P. O. Box	Boîte Postale	Postfach
Prop.:	Proprietor	Propriétaire	Inhaber
T.N.:	Telephone	Téléphone	Telefon
T.A.:	Telegraphic Address	Adresse Télégraphique	Telegramm-Adresse
	Established	Fondé	Gegründet
	Premises	Locaux	Geschäftsräume
	Shop	Boutique	Laden
	Storeroom	Dépôt	Lagerräume
	Private House	Domicile	Wohnung
	By Appointment	Sur Rendez-Vous	Nach Vereinbarung
	Closed	Fermé	Geschlossen
	Monday	Lundi	Montag
	Tuesday	Mardi	Dienstag
	Wednesday	Mercredi	Mitwoch
	Thursday	Jeudi	Donnerstag
	Friday	Vendredi	Freitag
	Saturday	Samedi	Samstag
	Morning	Matin	Morgen
	Afternoon	Aprésmidi	Nachmittag
	Very Small Stock	Assez Restreint Stock	Sehr Kleiner Vorrat
	Small Stock	Restreint Stock	Kleiner Vorrat
	Medium Stock	Moyen Stock	Mittelgrosser Vorrat
	Large Stock	Important Stock	Grosser Vorrat
	Very Large Stock	Très Important Stock	Sehr Grosser Vorrat
Spec.:	Specialities	Specialités	Specialgebiete
Cata.:	Catalogues on Request	Catalogues Sur Demande	Kataloge auf Wunsch
Corresp.:	Correspondence	Correspondance	Korrespondenz
B:	Bank	Banque	Bank
C.P.:	Post Cheque Accounts	Comptes de Chèques Postaux	Postsheck-Konten
M:	Member	Membre	Mitglied

English SPECIALITIES	*Français* SPÉCIALITÉS	*Deutsch* SPEZIALGEBIETE
Agriculture	Agriculture	Landwirtschaft
Auctioneers	Ventes aux enchères	Auktionen
Autographs and Manuscripts	Autographes et manuscrits	Autographen und Handschriften
Bibliography	Bibliographie	Buchwesen
Biography	Biographies	Biographie
Collecting	Livres pour collectionneurs	Bücher für Sammler
Crafts and useful arts, food and drink	Arts et métiers, gastronomie	Kunstgewerbe Speise und Getränk
Entertainments	Théatre et cinéma	Theater und Kino
Eroticism and curious	Curiosités	Erotik
Fiction	Fiction, romans	Prosadichtung
Fine and rare editions	Beaux livres	Schöne und seltene Bücher
Foreign	Livres etrangères	Ausländisch
History	Histoire	Geschichte
Juvenile	Livres d'Enfants	Kinderbücher
Law and criminology	Droit et criminologie	Recht
Medicine	Médecine	Medizin
Music	Musique	Musik und Noten
Natural history	Sciences naturelles	Naturwissenschaften
Pictorial art	Beaux arts	Kunst und Graphik
Poetry	Poésie	Dichtkunst
Religion and philosophy	Religions et philosophie	Theologie und Philosophie
Periodicals	Périodiques	Zeitschriften
Remainders and overstocks	Soldes	Restauflage
Science	Sciences exactes	Wissenschaften
Sociology	Sociologie	Soziologie
Sport and games	Sports et jeux	Sport und Spiele
Technical and educational	Technique et érudition	Technik
Topography and travel	**Régionalisme** et voyages	Topographie und Reisen

GEOGRAPHICAL SECTION
SECTION GÉOGRAPHIQUE
GEOGRAPHISCHER ABSCHNITT

BOOKWORMS: INSECT PESTS OF BOOKS
by Norman Hickin, Ph.D., F.I.Biol., F.Z.S., F.R.E.S. etc.

A detailed study of the insect pests that infest and attack books, methods of prevention and treatment. 16 plates, 50 line drawings in text. A5 format, bound cloth boards, laminated jacket. ISBN: 0 900661 38 0 £15.00. ($24.00). Ready winter 1985.

Every librarian and collector must have one.

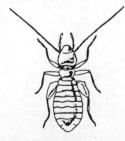

SHEPPARD PRESS LIMITED

BELGIE   BELGIQUE
BELGIUM   BELGIEN

Associations: Verbände

S.B.L.A.M. =Syndicat Belge de la Librairie Ancienne et Moderne, rue de Chêne 21, B-1000 Bruxelles TN: (02) 513 0525.

C.B.L. =Cercle Belge de la Librairie.

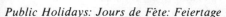

Public Holidays: Jours de Fête: Feiertage

Jan. 1: Easter Monday: May 1: Ascension Day: Whitmonday: July 21: Aug. 15: Nov. 1 and 11: Dec. 25.

Jan. 1: Lundi de Pâques: May 1: Ascension: Lundi de Pentecôte: Juillet 21: Août 15: Nov. 1 et 11: Dec. 25.

Jan. 1: Ostermontag: Mai 1: Himmelfahrt: Pfingstmontag: Juli 21: Aug. 15: Nov. 1 und 11: Weihnachstag.

ANVERS / ANTWERPEN (Antwerp):
AUBEL
BRUXELLES / BRUSSEL (Brussels):
BRUGGE / BRUGES:
COURTRAS / KORTRIJK
GENT / GAND (Ghent):
HASSELT
LIÈGE / LUIK (Lütich):
LOUVAIN / LEUVEN
MALINES / MECHELEN
MONS
NAMUR
OOSTENDE
REDU
VERVIERS

ABELARD, 7 RUE F. DONS, 1050 BRUXELLES. TN: 649 75 84.

P. ADAEN, 210 TORHOUTSTR, OOSTENDE. TN: (059) 70 62 82.

ADAM, 42 RUE MELLERY, 1020 BRUXELLES. TN: 478 79 02.

NOËL ANSELOT, HAMAIDE 102, 6914 REDU. TN: (061) 65 54 02. Spec: Histoire, Belgicana, éditions suisses anciennes, sciences spaciales, Economie politique, Beaux livres rares et anciens. B: 063–0236497–46.

APOLLO GALERIES, 23–24 PLACE ST. GUDULE, 1000 BRUXELLES. TN: 217 14 66.

ARCHIVES S.A. 76 RUE DE LA MONTAGNE, 1000 BRUXELLES. TN: 511 52 67.

ARS GRAPHICA, 14 WINKELGALERIJ, BOTERMARKT, 2800 MECHELEN, TN: (015) 20 95 90.

LE BATEAU-LIVRE, 14 RUE DES EPERONNIERS, 1000 BRUXELLES.

LE BIBLIOPHAGE, 17 RUE DE L'ETUVE, 4000 LIEGE. TN: (041) 22 06 03. Cata.

BOOK MARKET, RUE DE LA MADELEINE 47, B-1000 BRUXELLES. Prop: Gilbert A. Toussaint. TN: (02) 512 92 53. Fondée en 1963. Boutique. Important stock. Spec: histoire; beaux-arts; religions; romans, science-fiction anciens et modernes en francais, anglais, neerlandais et allemand; jeux et jouets anciens. Corresp: English, Deutsch, Dutch. B: Banque Bruxelles Lambert, Compte 310 1301208 39.

LA BORGNE AGASSE, 18 RUE DE L'ATHENEE, 1050 BRUXELLES. TN: 511 84 42.

LE CADRE D'ART, RUE ST. PAUL 33, 4000 LIEGE. TN: (041) 22 38 17. Spec: Gravures anciennes, Topographie, Encadrements, Objets de vitrines. B: Banque Nagelmaekers 634–4582501–02. S.B.L.A.M.

LA BOUQUINERIE DES CARMES, RUE ST. PAUL 35, 4000 LIEGE. Prop: D. Higny. TN: (041) 23 16 76. Spec: Beaux-Arts, Beaux livres illustrés, Editions originales, Curiosités bibliophiliques et littéraires, Varia. S.B.L.A.M.

M. CHABANNE, 26B RUE DU FORT, BRUXELLES. TN: 537 73 32.

LIBRAIRIE DES CHERCHEURS, GALERIE DU COMMERCE 66-68, 1000 BRUXELLES, Prop: Ch. Bekart. TN: (02) 217 26 49. Spec: Beaux-Arts. CCP: 000–0062421–50. S.B.L.A.M.

LIBRAIRIE CHEVALIER, 176A RUE BLAES, 1000 BRUXELLES. TN: (02) 5131677. Fondée 1952. Boutique; fermé samedi et lundi. Très restreint stock. Spec: histoire. Corresp: Français. S.B.L.A.M.

LIBRAIRIE DES CIMES, Square Steurs 15, 1030 Bruxelles. Prop: Fr. Depadt. TN: (02) 217 91 09. Spec: Alpinisme, Exploration, Spéléogie, Voyages, Bibliographie. B: 001–0311380–86. S.B.L.A.M.

GERARD CRUCIS, rue St. Jean 33, 1000 Bruxelles. TN: (02) 512 12 00. Spec: Beaux-Arts, Beaux livres illustrés, Littérature générale, Critique littéraire, Histoire. C.P: 000–0346088–02. S.B.L.A.M.

W. DEGHELDERE, 2 Smedenstr, Brugge 1. TN: (050) 33 88 58.

GEORGES A. DENY, rue du Chêne 5, 1000 Bruxelles. TN: (02) 511 71 45 Established 1943. Shop, closed Saturday afternoon. Small stock. Spec: early science and technology, old and rare books. Cata. Corresp: English, Français. B: Banque de Bruxelles, No. 310–0768525–80. CP: Bruxelles 000 0753951–67. S.B.L.A.M., S.L.A.M.

ANTIQUARIAAT JOHAN DEVROE, L. Vanderkelenstraat 43, 3000 Leuven. TN: (016) 23 97 16. Spec: Livres anciens, Manuscrits, Topographie, Atlas et Cartes anciennes. B: 230-0390041–24. S.B.L.A.M.

LIBRAIRIE DES ELEPHANTS, Place Van Meenen 19, 1000 Bruxelles. Prop: Antoine Jacobs. TN: (02) 539 06 01. Sur rendez vous. Spec: Librairie générale, Editions originales, Livres Illustrés, Organisation de Ventes publiques, catalogue sur demande. C.P. 000–1167633–44. S.B.L.A.M.

LE LIBRAIRE ALAIN FERRATON, Rue Ernest Allard 39, B-1000 Bruxelles. TN: (02) 512.73.54. Fondée en 1975. Boutique. Moyen stock. Spec: Moyen age; erudition; histoire; beaux-arts; musique; litterature française. Cata: 10 par an. Corresp: English, Dutch. CPP: 000-088 1856 29. S.B.L.A.M., L.I.L.A.

LIBRAIRIE DES GALERIES, Galerie du Roi, 2, 1000 Bruxelles. Prop: J. Bouloukhère. TN: (02) 511 24 12. Established 1941. Shop. Small stock, also new books. Spec: art, architecture, antiquarian. Corresp: Français. B: Soc. Gén. Banque, 210–0281 186–35. CP: Bruxelles 000-0064515-10 70. C.B.L.

PIERRE-M. GASON, 8 Place de la Victoire, 4580 Aubel. TN: 087/68 63 42. Spec: Belgicana, Siècle des lumières et Révolution française. C.P: 000–0831566-82. S.B.L.A.M.

YVES GEVAERT, rue du Pinson 160, 1170 Bruxelles. TN: (02) 660 23 72. Sur rendez-vous. Spec: Arts plastiques XIX et XXme siecle. C.P: 000 0182023-51. S.B.L.A.M.

3

PAUL GOOSSENS, Greenhillstraat 45, 8320 Brugge. TN: 050 361057. Established 1984. House premises. Stock can be seen without appointment afternoons except Monday. Medium stock. Spec: religion, history, humanism. Cata: monthly. Corresp: English, français, Deutsch. B: ASLK 001 1464974 59.

FERNAND GOTHIER, LIBRAIRIE UNIVERSITAIRE, place du 20 Août 11, 4000 Liège. TN: (041) 232 776 and 230 594. Established 1828. Shop. Medium stock of second-hand and antiquarian books, also new books. Spec: history, documentation. Cata: 4 a year. Corresp: English, Français, Deutsch. B: Banque Nagelmackers, No. 634 8243803 39. CP: 000–0117340–67.S.B.L.A.M., C.B.L.

LIBRAIRIE ANCIENNE ET MODERNE PAUL GOTHIER, rue Bonne Fortune 3 et 5, Liège. TN: (041) 32 24 19. Established 1828. Two Shops. Very large stock, also new books. Spec: Belgicana, erudition, XV and XVI centuries, old and rare. Cata: 6 a year. Corresp: Français. B: Nagelmackers, 4000 Liège. CP: Liège 51604–97. S.B.L.A.M. Cercle Belge de la Librarie. I.L.A.B.

LE GRENIER DU COLLECTIONNEUR, avenue Orban 238, 1150 Bruxelles. Prop: Jean-Léo. Established 1967. Postal business only. Spec: toys, children's books, performing arts, tobacco, food and drink, Napoléon, books for collectors, curiosities, printed ephemera. Cata: On request. Corresp: English, Français. B: Société Générale de Banque, No. 210 0155242 94. CP: Bruxelles 0075057 76. S.B.L.A.M., L.I.L.A.

JEAN-JACQUES HANKARD, 25 rue de la Paix, 1050 Bruxelles. TN: (02) 512 36 42. Established 1910. Shop. Very large stock. Spec: philosophy, history, arts, fine editions; occult (also new books). Corresp: English, Français. B: Société Générale de Banque, No. 837007. CP: Bruxelles 000–0031602 77. S.B.L.A.M.*

FRÉDÉRIC VAN HOETER, 61 Rue Saint-Quentin, Bruxelles 1040. Prop: Dr. and Mrs. Peter Braune. TN: (02) 230 95 63. Established 1958. Private premises, appointment necessary. Small stock. science, topography, technology, old and rare. Corresp: English, Deutsch.

IN DEN EENHOORN, Ezelstraat 84, Bruges. Prop: Titia Vandevelde. TN: (050) 34246. Established 1954. Shop, open every day 9–12; 14–19 hours. Medium stock. Corresp: English, Deutsch, Français, Italiano, Español, Russian. B: Gemeentekredet 063 0197289–26. CP: Brussel 000–1074713–50.

A. VAN LOOCK, RUE SAINT JEAN 51, 1000 BRUXELLES. TN: (02) 512 74 65. Established 1945. Shop and storeroom. Very large stock. Spec: old and rare, science travel, old engravings. B: Banque de Bruxelles, No. 310 0076328 75. CP: Bruxelles 0098837 91. S.B.L.A.M., S.L.A.M., L.I.L.A.

BOEKHANDEL JOS. MARÉCHAL, MARIASTRAAT 10, 8000 BRUGGE. TN: (050) 33 13 05 and (050) 33 00 23. Est: 1902. Shop. Very small stock sec. and antiq. and very large stock new books. Corresp: English, Français, Deutsch, Dutch. B: Gen. Bank 280–0220 362–15. CP: 000–00 415 18–02. V.B.V.B., C.B.L., S.B.L.A.M.

LIBRAIRIE DU MIROIR, RUE DU MIROIR 9–11, 7000 MONS. Prop: Chanoine. TN: (065) 34 69 02. Spec: Librairie générale, Livres anciens du XVIme au XVIIIme siecle, Histoire locale, Topographie. Ouverture du mardi au samedi de 10.00 à 18.00 heures. B: 270–0486723–30. S.B.L.A.M.

LIBRAIRIE LOUIS MOORTHAMERS, RUE LESBROUSSART 124, 1050 BRUXELLES. TN: (02) 6 47 85 48. TA: Curiobook Bruxelles. Shop. Very large stock: also Public Auctions. Spec: Documentation, catalogues, Cata: regularly. Corresp: English, Français, Deutsch. B: Banque de Bruxelles, A/310–0380002–42. S.B.L.A.M., C.B.L.

M. MOORTHAMERS, 5 WAPPER, ANTWERPEN. TN: 233 15 65.

ALAIN MOREL DE WESTGAVER, RUE SAINT-JEAN, 1000 BRUXELLES. TN: 640 22 53.

MUSSEJONG, 201 PROVINCIESTR, ANTWERPEN. TN: 231 52 05.

PARADIS DES CHERCHEURS, 245 CHAUSSÉE DE CHARLEROI, B-1060 BRUXELLES. Prop: Charles Losson. TN: (02) 538 52 35. Fondée en 1969. Boutique ouvert l'aprés-midi, Fermé samedi et Lundi. Important stock. Spec: Bandes Dessinées; publications, documents, révues, pamphlets 1930–1950; vieux jouets; cartes postales anciennes. Corresp: English, Deutsch, Dutch.

FRANCINE VAN DER PERRE, RUE DE LA MADELEINE 23, 1000 BRUXELLES. TN: (02) 511 75 59. Established 1954. Shop. Medium stock, also new books. Spec: genealogy, heraldry, topography. Corresp: English, Français. B: Société Générale de Banque, Agence Agora, 210 0280 304 26. CP: Bruxelles 000-0205771 34. S.B.L.A.M., I.L.A.B.

PIQUE-PUCES, 204 CHAUSEE DE WAVRE, 1050 BRUXELLES. TN: 673 57 16.

5

✓ **JEAN-MARIE VAN DE PLAS,** 10 RUE DES EPERONNIERS, 1000 BRUXELLES. TN: (02) 5 122 296. B: Société Générale de Banque, 210–0280342–64.

✓ **POSADA ART BOOKS S.P.R.L.,** RUE DE LA MADELEINE 27, 1000 BRUXELLES. Prop: M.C. Oleff. TN: (02) 511 08 34. Spec: Visual Art, Occult sciences. S.B.L.A.M.

LA PROUE, 6 RUE DES EPERONNIERS, 1000 BRUXELLES. Prop: H. Mercier. TN: 513 03 09. Established 1945. Magasin. Large stock, also new books. Spec: modern art, Belgian literature, poetry, surrealism. Cata: 4–5 a year. Corresp: English, Deutsch, Flemish. B: Banque de Bruxelles, 310–0675–121. CP: Bruxelles 000–0770913–54. S.B.L.A.M.

DE RENAISSANCE VAN HET BOEK, WALPOORTSTRAAT 7, 9000 GENT. Prop: Mme. Derryx dit Derks. TN: (91) 254808. Established 1970. Shop. Medium stock. Spec: gravures et cartes anciennes; livres Épuisés, livres anciens, médecine, litterature. Corresp: English, Français, Niederlandse. B: Crédit Lyonnais, Koophandelplein 11, Gent, No. 694 45 10475 48. S.B.L.A.M.

LIBRAIRIE A. ROMBAUT, LIEVESTRAAT 14, 9000 GENT. Prop: Charles Lammens. TN: (091) 235646. Established 1923. Shop. Medium stock, also new books. Spec: fine arts, music; genealogy; topography. Corresp: English, Français, Deutsch, Dutch. B: Gemeentekrediet van Belgie, No. 062 1154650 18. CP: 000–0156937 88. S.B.L.A.M.

ANTIQUARIAAT SANDERUS, BRUGSESTRAAT 88, 8510 KORTRIJK. Prop: Philippe Devroe. TN: (056) 35 25 41. Spec: Zeldzame en waardevolle oude boeken, Topografie van de XVde tot XIXe eeuw, Plaatselijke geschiedenis, Curiosa, Varia. B: 285–0549521–45. S.B.L.A.M.

TRISTAN SCHWILDEN, Galerie Bortier 5, 1000 Bruxelles. TN: (02) 512 21 81. Spec: Livres anciens et modernes, Gravures, Photographies anciennes. B: 310–0702520–35. S.B.L.A.M.

LIBRAIRIE SIMONSON, Chaussée de Charleroi 227, 1060 Bruxelles. (succ. R. Degreef). TN: (02) 538 31 58. Spec: Beaux livres illustrés anciens et modernes, Editions originales, Reliures de maitres, Livres de la période romantique, Autographes de toutes les époques. C.P: 000–0027226–66. S.B.L.A.M.

M. SION, 15 Steendam, Gent. TN: 25 43 99.

DE SNUFFELAAR, Ketelpoort, 9000 Gent. TN: 25 95 56.

E. SPEECKAERT, 53 Boulevard Saint-Michel, B-1040 Bruxelles. TN: (02) 736.43.29. TA: Speebooks. Fondée en 1978. Boutique, fermé samedi, dimanche, lundi. Restreint stock. Spec: Beaux livres anciens; reliures; manucrits et autographes; architecture; bibliographie. Cata: 1 ou 2 par an. Corresp: Vlaamse, Français, English. B: Kredietbank, Compte 437 6158581 89. CCP: 000-1122952 80. M: Association belge des experts. I.L.A.B.

LEON STERNBERG, Lange Leemstraat 27, 2018 Antwerpen. TN: (03) 233 56 81. Sur rendez-vous. Spec: Livres anciens et modernes, Autographes. B: 220–0546239–68. S.B.L.A.M.

LIBRAIRIE-EDITIONS THANH-LONG, 34 rue Dekens, 1040 Bruxelles. Prop: Jacques Baruch. TN: (02) 733 16 18. Established 1963. Shop, open Monday, Wednesday and Saturday 14 to 21.30 hours. Large stock, also new books. Spec: Far East, books in Vietnamese language. Cata: 3 a year. Corresp: English, Français. B: National Westminster, External Account, London, No. 25677098. CP: Bruxelles 006867091. S.B.L.A.M., L.I.L.A.

TREFPUNT, 98 Boterlaarbn, 2100 Deurne-Zuid. TN: 322 46 45.

FL. TULKENS, 21 rue du Chêne, Bruxelles 1. TN: (02) 513 05 25. TA: Libratul Bruxelles. Spec: old and rare, old bindings, fine arts. B: Banque Bruxelles-Lambert. Compte 310–0073998–73. CP: Bruxelles 000–0077268–56. S.B.L.A.M.

ÉMILE VAN BALBERGHE, Rue Vautier 4, B-1040 Bruxelles. TN: (02) 649 46 08. Fondée en 1976. Domicile; sur rendez-vous seulement. Assez restreint stock. Spec: manuscrits; livres anciens, rares et précieux. Cata: 4 par an. CPP: 000 7751830 29. M: S.B.L.A.M., L.I.L.A.

7

A.W. VANDEVELDE, Dweersstraat 6, 8000 Bruges. Established 1967. Shop and storeroom. Medium stock, also new books. Spec: Dutch literature, Flandrica, the Far East. Corresp: English, Français, Deutsch. B: Banque Bruxelles Lambert, Bruges, No. 380 0009456 21. CP: Bruxelles: 000–1012181–83.

MIREILLE VANLAECKEN, Bloemendalestraat 73, 8030 Beernem (bij Brugge). S.B.L.A.M.

VARIA LIBRAIRIE, rue Soeurs de Hasque 15, 4000 Liege. Prop: D. Higny. TN: (041) 22 40 12. Spec: Beaux-Arts, Beaux livres illustrés, Editions originales, Curiosités bibliophiliques et littéraires, Varia. S.B.L.A.M.

HENDRIK VAN VELDEKE, 50 B.10, Guffenslaan, 3500 Hasselt. Prop: Elisabeth Hermans. TN: 011.22.74.45. Est. 1983. Shop, by appointment. Small stock. Spec: topography, belgicana. Corresp: English.

CHRISTIAN F. VERBEKE, Bloemendalestraat 73, 8030 Beernem (bij Brugge). TN: 050/78 13 79. Spec: Livres anciens, Topographie, Gravures, Littérature anglaise. B: BBL 310–046413879–002. S.B.L.A.M.

LIBRAIRIE AU VIEUX QUARTIER, Rue des Fripiers 11, B-5000 Namur. Prop: Adrienne Goffin. TN: (081) 71 19 89. Fondée en 1976. Boutique fermé mardi. Moyen stock. Spec: Régionalisme belge; gravures topographiques belge. Cata: un par an. Corresp: English, Niederlandse. CCP: 000 1033675-43. S.B.L.S.M., L.I.L.A.

M. VILAIN, 287 Ten Eekhovelei, 2100 Deurne. TN: 324 21 28.

WAHLE ET COMPAGNIE S.P.R.L., rue du Méry 14a, 4000 Liege. Prop: Eugène Wahle. TN: (041) 32 21 13. Spec: Littérature générale, Histoire de Belgique, Régionalisme, Estampes. C.C.P. 000–0021557–23. S.B.L.A.M.

MARC VAN DE WIELE, St. Salvatorkoorstraat 3, 8000 Brugge. TN: (050) 3363 17. B: 550–3816500–28. S.B.L.A.M.

CH. DE WYNGAERT, 129A rue R. Vandevelde, B-1030 Bruxelles. TN: (02) 242 8076. Fondée en 1949. Boutique et Dépôt. Important stock. Spec: histoire naturelle (surtout separata). Cata: 2 par mois. Corresp: English. B: Banque Bruxelles Lambert, Compte 310.0059471.96. CCP: 00-1158202-22.

BULGARIYA

BULGARIA   BULGARIE   BULGARIEN

SOFIA.

"HEMUS", 6 ROUSKI BOULEVARD, SOFIA. State Export-Import Enterprise for all books.*

ANTIKVARNI KNIGI, 19 ULITSA GRAF IGNATIEV, SOFIA. Shop, open 9–13 and 14–18 hours, Saturdays 8–14 hours. Large stock Bulgarian and foreign, also new books. Corresp: Deutsch, Français.*

ČESKOSLOVENSKO

CZECHOSLOVAKIA
TCHEKOSLOVAKIE
DIE TSCHECHOSLOWAKEI

BRATISLAVA: BRNO (Brünn): ČESKÉ BUDĚJOVICE (Budweis): DVUR KRĹOVÉ: GOTTWALDOV: HRADEC KRĹOVÉ: HODONÍN: JABLONEC (Gablonz): JIHLAVA (Iglau): KARLOVY VARY (Karlsbad): KOLÍN: KOŠICE: KROMĚŘIŽ: LIBEREC (Reichenberg): LOUNY: MOST: NÁCHOD: NITRA: OLOMOUC: OPAVA: OSTRAVA: PARDUBICE: PLZEŇ (Pilsen): PRAHA (Prag, Prague): TABOR: TEPLICE LAZNE V. CECHACH: TRNAVA: ÚSTÍ: ZILINA: ZNOJMO.

KNIHA, MALÉ NÁMĚSTI NO. 11, PRAHA 1. SHOP. TN: 23 39 18. Large stock. Spec: foreign literature (English, French, German); topography.

KNIHA, ULICE RADNICE, PRAHA 1. Shop. Small stock. Spec: fine and rare; also some prints, etc.

KNIHA, KARLOVA ULICE 16. PRAHA 1. TN: 240275. Shop. Large stock of prints, drawings, manuscripts, and autographs.

KNIHA n.p., ULICE 28, ŘÍJNA 13, PRAHA 1. TN: 23 72 57/8. Shop. Very large stock of Czech and foreign literature. Spec: poetry and drama. Corresp: English, Deutsch, Français, Russian.

KNIHA n.p., 2 SKOŘEPKA, PRAHA 1. TN: 24 77 08.

KNIHA n.p., KARLOVA ULICE, 2 PRAHA 1. TN: 23 42 82. Shop. Medium stock, also prints and drawings. Corresp: English, Deutsch, Français, Russian.

KNIHA n.p., 36 JEČNÁ, PRAHA 2. TN: 22 22 26.

KNIHA n.p., 5 DLAŽDENÁ, PRAHA 2. TN: 22 18 61.

KNIHA n.p., MYSLÍKOVA, PRAHA 2. TN: 23 44 02. Secondhand musical literature. Medium stock. Corresp: Deutsch.

KNIHA n.p., 42 NÁMĚSTÍ REPUBLIKY, PLZEŇ. TN: 354 93.

KNIHA n.p., 12. Cs. Armady, Karlovy Vary. TN: 34 13.

KNIHA n.p., 12 Pařížska, Ustí n/L. TN: 28 70.

KNIHA n.p., 4 Pražská, Liberec. TN: 42 04.

KNIHA n.p., 169 V. Kopečky, Hradec Králové. TN: 53 25.

KNIHA n.p., 2 Namesti Osvobození, Pardubice. TN: 20270.

KNIHA n.p., 28 Česká Ul., Brno. TN: 22501.

KNIHA n.p., 9 Ostruznická, Olomouc. TN: 55 79.

KNIHA n.p., 15 Leninova 212, Gottwaldov. TN: 27 12.

KNIHA n.p., 4 Zámeck Ul., Ostrava. TN: 218 71.

KNIHA n.p., 2 Komenskémo Jablonec n/Nis. TN: 43 70.

KNIHA n.p., Riegrovo Náměstí 10, Kroměříž. TN: 30 00.

KNIHA n.p., 13 Kollarova, Znojmo. TN: 32 07.

KNIHA n.p., 109 Leninova, Louny. TN: 263.

KNIHA n.p., Náměstí 9 Května 30, Prostějov. TN: 3812.

KNIHA n.p., 1 Bezručova, Most. TN: 21 26.

KNIHA n.p., Lenninova Ul. 15, Teplice Lázně v Čechách. TN: 48 13.

KNIHA n.p., 6 Palackého, Tábor. TN: 4219. Est. 1953. Shop. Large Stock. Corresp: German.

KNIHA n.p., 4 Stalingradská, Hodonín. TN: 2195.

KNIHA n.p., Ulice 9 Května 1, Brno. TN: 24863.

KNIHA n.p., 32 Kirovova, Praha 5-Smíchov. TN: 53 35 60.

KNIHA n.p., 25 OSTRONZNÁ, OPAVA. TN: 26 35.

KNIHA n.p., ŽIŽKOVO N. 31, Č. BUDEJOVICE. TN: 27 91.

KNIHA n.p., 37 GOTTWALDOVO NÁMĚSTÍ, DVUR KRÁLOVÉ N/L. TN: 2513.

KNIHA n.p., 58 NÁMĚSTÍ ŘÍJNOVÉ REVOLUCE, NÁCHOD. TN: 34 43.

KNIHA n.p., 20 VINOHRADSKÁ, PRAHA 2—VINOHRADY. TN: 24 42 26.

KNIHA n.p., 29 PALACKÉHO, JIHLAVA. TN: 22003.

KNIŽNÍ VELKOOBCHOD n.p., ÚSTŘEDNÍ NÁKUP ANTIKVARIÁTU, 55 SPÁLENA, PRAHA 2. TN: 23 23 23.

KNIŽNÍ VELKOOBCHOD n.p., EXPORTNÍ STREDISKO ANTIKVARIÁTU, 65 STEPÁNSKÁ, PRAHA 2. TN: 24 65 61.

SLOVENSKÁ KNIHA n.p., SEDLIÁRSKÁ 9, BRATISLAVA. TN: 30117.

SLOVENSKÁ KNIHA n.p., 10 MICKIEWICZOVA, BRATISLAVA. TN: 501 64. Very large stock. Corresp. Deutsch.

SLOVENSKÁ KNIHA n.p., 45 LENINOVA, NITRA. TN: 22 04.

SLOVENSKÁ KNIHA n.p., 2 HVIEZDOSLAVOVA, TRNAVA. TN: 24 23.

SLOVENSKÁ KNIHA n.p., 4 MARX ENGELSA, ZILINÁ. TN: 20067. Est: 1918. Corresp: English, Deutch, Français, Italian.

SLOVENSKÁ KNIHA n.p., 29 LENINOVA, KOŠICE. TN: 24 27.

SLOVENSKÝ KNIŽNÝ VELKOOBCHOD n.p., (odor antikvariát), 21 DUNAJSKÁ, BRATISLAVA. TN: 512 64.

DANMARK

DENMARK   DANEMARK
DÄNEMARK

Associations: Verbände

A.B.F.   = Den danske Antikvarboghandlerforening.
          Silkegade 11, DK-1113 København,
          TN: (01) 135335.

D.B.F.   = Den danske Boghandlerforening.

D.F.F.   = Den danske Forlaeggerforening.

K.D.F.   = Københavns Detailhandlerforening.

Public Holidays: Jours de Fête: Feiertage

Jan. 1: Easter: Whitmonday: Ascension Day: Day of Prayer: Jun. 5: Dec.
25 and 26.

Jan. 1: Pâques: Lundi de Pentecôte: Ascension: Jour de Prière: Juin 5:
Dec. 25 et 26.

Jan. 1: Ostermontag: Pfingstmontag: Himmelfahrt: Busstag: Juni 5: Dez.
25 und 26.

AALBORG: AARHUS: HILLDERØD: HOLTE: KØBENHAVN
(Copenhagen): LYNGBY: NAESTVED: NYKOBING FALSTER:
ROSKILDE: SKØRPING SORØ.

ANTIKVARIATET ALDUS, S. Boulevarden 38, København. TN: 01 22
84 22.*

AMAGER BØGER & BILLEDER, Amagerboulevarden 118,
København. Prop: J. Birland. TN: 01 57 31 84.

A.M.O. ANTIKVARIAT & FORLAG, Ordr. Jagtory 91, København.
TN: 01 63 99 10.

CARL ANDERSEN, Å-Boulevarden 60, 2200 København-n. Prop:
Peter Andersen. TN: 01 39 62 71. CP: København 509 44 61. A.B.F.

S.C. ANDERSENS ANTIKVARIAT, ALHAMBRAVEJ 22, 1826, KØBENHAVN-V. TN: 01 24 8833. Established 1944. Shop, early closing Saturday. Large stock. Spec: science-fiction, detective fiction, pocket-books, also stamps for collectors. Cata: 1 a year. Corresp: English, Français, Deutsch. B: Daurmandsbanken, G1. Kongevej 107, København-V. CP: København 58248. A.B.F.

ANTIKVARBODEN, GAMMEL JERNBANEVEJ 4, KØBENHAVN. Prop: Aage Mortensen. TN: 01 17 48 32.

ANTIKVARIAT, ISTEDVEJ 49, KØBENHAVN. TN: 01 31 77 71 Shop. Small stock sec. and antiq. also prints.*

ANTIKVARIAT 70, ORDRUPVEJ 70A, KØBENHAVN. TN: 01 63 03 61.*

ANTIKVARIATET, ELMEGADE 24, KØBENHAVN. TN: 01 39 11 51.

ARCADE PRINTS, CITY ARKADEN, ØSTERGADE 32, KØBENHAVN. Prop: Boghallens Antikvariat. TN: 01 15 48 28. Spec: old prints and maps.

ART & PRINT, KOMPAGNISTRAEDE 25, KØBENHAVN. Prop: Frode Andersen. TN: 01 12 97 62.

AXELSEN BOOKSELLERS ApS., ØSTERGADE 44, KØBENHAVN. TN: 01 11 61 00. Old and rare maps and prints; also new books.

BJØRKLUNDS ANTIVARIAT, AMAGERBROGADE 12, KØBENHAVN. TN 01 57 41 72.

BJØRNVIG, HOLM & MØLLER ApS, ODDEN HOVEDGÅRD, MYGDAL DK-9800 HJØRRING. Prop: Peter Holm Rasmussen. TN: (08) 97 5. 57. Open afternoons June to September. Otherwise by appointmen only. Spec: curiosities, first editions, general literature, illustrate books, old and rare books. A.B.F.

BLAAGAARDSPLADS ANTIKVARIAT, BLAAGAARDSGADE 25 KØBENHAVN. Prop: Ole Kjaer. TN: 01 39 69 24.

BLUMES ANTIKVARIAT, VAERNEDAMSVEJ 9, KØBENHAVN. TN: 01 3 04 53.

BØCKMANN'S ANTIKVARIAT, ROSENSGADE 11, DK-8000 AARHUS-C Prop: H. Aabenhus. TN: 06–120278. Established 1942. Shop, earl closing Saturday. Very large stock. Spec: art, first editions, old print Cata: occasionally. Corresp: English, Deutsch. B: Sparekassen SDS 980-01-02092. CP: 4 18 74 23.
Also at AABOULEVARDEN 39. DK-8000 AARHUS-C. Shop.

BOGANTIKVAREN, Ø FARIMAGSGADE 59, KØBENHAVN. Prop: F.H. Brasch. TN: 01 26 38 94.

BOG-BORSEN, STUDIESTRAEDE 10, 1455 KØBENHAVN-K. Prop: Kristian Andersen. TN: 01 13 2580. Established 1935. Shop. Very large stock, also new books. CP: København 10 56 379.

BOGHALLENS ANTIKVARIAT, RAADHUSPLADSEN 37, DK 1585 KØBENHAVN-V. Prop: Ole Dam. TN: 01 118511, extension 397. Spec: fine and old, manuscripts, finely bound English sets, art books, freemasonry. A.B.F., A.B.A.

ANTIKVARIATET BOGHYTTEN, ABSALONSGADE 28, KØBENHAVN. Prop: H. Jørgensen. TN: 01 22 61 62. Shop. Large stock sec. and antiq.

BRANNERS BIBLIOFILE ANTIKVARIAT ApS, BREDGADE 10, 1260 KØBENHAVN-K. Prop: Mrs. Maria Bloch. TN: 01 15 91 87. TA: Librannica, København. Shop, closed Saturday afternoons. Small stock sec. and antiq., also old maps. Cata: occasionally. Spec: fine and rare; old maps. Corresp: English, Deutsch, Français, Italiano. B: Københavns Handelsbank, St. Kongensgade afd. København. Account 168297. CP: 648 9559. S.L.A.C.E.S. (Switzerland); I.I.L.A

BRØNDUM ANTIKVARIAT, ST. BRONDUM GL. SKOLE, DK-9520 SKØRPING. Prop: Birgit Møller Sørensen. TN: (08) 33 95 59. Open Friday afternoons or by appointment. Catalogues occasionally. A.B.F.

BRØNSHØJ ANTIKVARIAT, FREDERIKSSUNDSVEJ 128H, KØBENHAVN. Prop: N. Jensen. TN: 01 60 09 92.

ARNOLD BUSCK, FIOLSTRAEDE 24, 1171 KØBENHAVN-K. Manager: C.F. Simonsen. TN: 01 12 24 53. TA: Bookbusck København. Spec: art, architecture, bibliography topography. CP: København 3457. A.B.F.

BYENS ANTIKVARIAT, SMEDEBAKKEN 7, 1455 KØBENHAVN-K. Prop: Richard Sørensen. TN: 02 24 16 60. Established 1930. Shop, early closing Saturday. Medium stock. Cata. Corresp: Deutsch. B: Københavns Handelsbank, account 117633. CP: København 88099. A.B.F.

DANSK BOGSERVICE, AMAGERFAELLEDVEJ 9, DK-2300, KØBENHAVN.

ENGHAVE PLADS ANTIKVARIAT, ENGHAVEPLADS 3, KØBENHAVN. TN: 01 24 92 04. Shop. Large sec. and antiq. stock; also prints

FREDE ENGHOLST, STUDIESSTRAEDE 35, 1455 KØBENHAVN-K. TN: 01 13 48 51. Spec: Topography, history. CP: 9 12 66 94. A.B.F.

FANTASK ApS., Sankt Pedersstraede 18, DK-1453 København-K.
Prop: Soren Pedersen & Rolf Bülow. TN: 01 11 85 38. Est: 1971.
Shop. Small stock sec. and antiq. also new books. Spec: science
fiction*, comics. Corresp: English, Deutsch. B: Handelsbanken
Account 4180–853669. CP: 4 07 44 59.

DAN FOG, Graabrødretorv 7, 1154 København-K. TN: 01 11 40 60.
TA: Musicentre, København. Est: 1906. Shop, closed Saturdays and
Mondays. Medium stock sec. and antiq. Spec: sheet music and books
on music. Cata: monthly. Corresp: Deutsch, English, Français. B:
Københavns Handelsbank, Account No. 4001–169 165. CP:
København 900 41 49; Hamburg 4000 02–207; Arnhem 65 26 45; Bern
30 195 50; Stockholm 7 43 88–0. A.B.F.

FREDERIKSBERG ANTIKVARIAT, Gammel Kongevej 120, 1850
København-V. Prop: Leif Nørballe. TN: 01 24 9708. Spec: arts and
crafts, Scandinavian literature, periodicals. CP: København 84635.
A.B.F.

FREDERIKSBORG ANTIKVARIAT, blehaven 10, DK-3400 Hillerød.
Prop: Aage Arendrup. TN: (02) 26 07 58. Est: 1973. Private premises;
appointment necessary. Very large stock sec. and antiq. Spec: First
editions, documents, manuscripts, Royal papers. Cata: 1 a year.
Corresp: English, Deutsch. CCP: 8 22 51 84.

ANTIKVARIATET FREDERIKSDAL, Kongevejen 43, DK-2840 Holte.
Prop: J.I. Hamre. TN: (02) 42 21 47. Shop, closed Wednesdays. Large
stock sec. and antiq. Spec: biography; history. Corresp: English.

FRIMANNS ANTIKVARIAT, Strandboulevarden 166, København.
TN: 01 29 40 77.*

GLADSAXE ANTIKVARIAT, Søborg Hovedgade 195, København.
Prop: Erik Hansen. TN: 01 67 16 46.*

J. GRUBB'S ANTIKVARIAT, Nørregade 47, Dk-1165 København-K.
TN: 01 15 9402. Shop. Very large stock. Spec: theology, philosophy,
philology, history, fiction. Corresp: English, Deutsch. CP: Københavr
700 1398. A.B.F.

J. GUSTAFSSON, VOLDEN 12, 8000 AARHUS-C. TN: 061 26806. Established 1926. Shop, early closing Saturday. Large stock. Corresp: English, Deutsch. B: Aarhus Privatbank. CP: Aarhus 35156. A.B.F.

HARCKS ANTIKVARIAT, FIOLSTRAEDE 34, 1171 KØBENHAVN-K. TN: 01 1213 44. A.B.F.

NILS HARTMUND, GAMMEL KONGEVEJ 163, DK-1850 KØBENHAVN. TN: 01 31 63 56.*

HEDENBORG'S ANTIKVARIAT, DRONNING MARGARETHESVEJ 4, ROSKILDE. TN: Roskilde 03 35 89 13. A.B.F.*

HILLERØD ANTIKVARIAT, SLOTSGADE 57, DK-3400 HILLERØD. Prop: Hanne Omø. TN: (02) 26 14 98. Closed Saturday afternoon. A.B.F.

HOLTE ANTIKVARIAT, KONGEVEJ 43, DK-2840 HOLTE, Prop: Jens Hamre. TN: (02) 42 21 47. Wednesday by appointment only, closed Saturday afternoon. Spec: children's books. A.B.F.

HELGE JENSEN, BOGENSEVEJ 485, 5270 ODENSE N. Prop: Helge Jensen. TN: (09) 97 84 07. By appointment only. Spec: occultism. A.B.F.

SOLV. JENSEN, BORGBJERVEJ 11, KØBENHAVN. TN. 01 21 01 77.

KAABERS ANTIKVARIAT, SKINDERGADE 34, 1159 KØBENHAVN-K. TN: 01 154177. Spec: fine arts; maps and prints. A.B.F., L.I.L.A.

KNAGSTEDS ANTIKVARIAT, KOMPAGNISTRAEDE 8, 1208 KØBENHAVN-K. TN: 01 13 37 70. A.B.F.

KOBBERSTIKHUSET, KRONPRINSENSGADE 4, KØBENHAVN. Prop: V. Severin Petersen. TN: 01 14 91 72.*

KJELD LARSEN, ENGHAVEVEJ 5, KØBENHAVN. TN: 01 24 06 00. Shop, closed Saturday afternoons. Medium stock sec. and antiq.

LYNGBY ANTIKVARIAT, JERNBANEV 1A, 2800 LYNGBY. Prop: Mary Slot. TN: 02 87 20 70.

LYNGE & SON, SILKEGADE 11, 1113 KØBENHAVN. TN: 01 15 53 35. Spec: Arctic (Greenland); linguistics; natural science; rare books; periodicals. A.B.F.

MARTINS ANTIKVARIAT, FALKONERALLÉ 65, KØBENHAVN. Prop: Oda Andersen. TN: 01 60 72 72.*

ANTIKVARIAT MØRK, TEGLGÅRDSSTRAEDE 6, KØBENHAVN. Prop: G. Vestergarrd. TN: 01 13 81 25.

17

MUSICA ANTIQUA, ALLEEN 54, KØBENHAVN. TN: 01 50 19 68. Spec: music scores and books on music.

NAESTVED ANTIKVARIAT, VINHUSGADE 13, KØBENHAVN. TN: 03 73 17 17.

NANSENSGADE ANTIKVARIAT, NANSENSGADE 70, 1366 KØBENHAVN-K. Prop: Jess T. Jessen. TN: (01) 142426. Closed Saturday afternoon. Spec: modern Scandinavian firsts, radical literature, history, politics, psychology. A.B.F.

HANS ARNE NIELSEN, NØRRE FARIMAGSGADE 31, KØBENHAVN. TN: 01 15 01 89.*

OVE NIELSEN, VALDEMARSGADE 30, KØBENHAVN. TN: 01 22 23 83.*

H.C. NØRGART, FIOLSTRAEDE 15, 1171 KØBENHAVN-K. TN: 01 15 48 52. Est: 1922. Shop. Large stock sec. and antiq; also prints. Spec: art; prints. CP: 8024790. A.B.F.

NØRREBRO ANTIKVARIAT, GRIFFENFELDSGADE 45, DK-2200 KØBENHAVN. Prop: Ole Bjørklund Petersen. TN: 01 39 30 16.

NOTABENE, ØSTERBROGADE 96, KØBENHAVN. TN: 26 12 03.

Dr. OCTOPUS, AAHUSGADE 2, KØBENHAVN. TN: 01 26 28 48.

OLE HOS ANTIKVARIAT, JAGTVEJ 51, KØBENHAVN. TN: 01 85 20 45.

MARINUS OLSEN, STUDIESTRAEDE 41, 1455 KØBENHAVN-K. Prop: Hans Olsen. TN: 01 13 66 24. A.B.F.

ONKEL BUTTES EFTF, FREDRIKSBORGVEJ 29, KØBENHAVN. TN: 01 10 67 55.

ERIK PALUDAN—INTERNATIONAL BOOKSELLER, FIOLSTRAEDE 10, 1171 KØBENHAVN-K. TN: 01 15 06 75. Established 1947. Shop, early closing Saturday. Very large stock, also new books. Spec: humanities. Cata: 5–6 a year. Corresp: English, Deutsch. B: Københavns Handelsbank. CP: København 1921.

PEGASUS, BLAAGAARDSGADE 3, KØBENHAVN. TN: 01 35 98 28.

GUNNAR PILEGAARD, ALGADE 65, AALBORG. TN: (08) 13 90 00 and 13 92 20. Est: 1963. Shop. Very large stock sec. and antiq. Corresp: English, Deutsch, Français. Cata: about 2 a year. B: Norresundby Bank, Aalborg, Account No. 20 00 37–1. CP: 5 10 85 19. A.B.F.

ANTIKVARIAT PINKERTON, NANSENSGADE 68, 1366 KØBENHAVN-K.
Prop: Bjarne Nielsen. TN: (01) 139540. Closed Saturday afternoon.
Spec: Crime and detective fiction A.B.F.

ANTIKVARIAT PIXI, ENGHAVSVEJ 28B, KØBENHAVN. TN: 01 23 36 40.

ROSENKILDE OG BAGGER, 3 KRON-PRINSENS-GADE, P.O. BOX 2184,
DK-1017 KØBENHAVN. Managing Director Hans Bagger. TN: (01) 15
70 44. TA: Bogkunst København. Est: 1941. Shop Closed Saturdays.
Very large stock sec. and antiq. also New Books. Spec: Voyages &
Travels; maps & views; Scandivavica and Arctica; Bibliography. Cata:
10 to 12 a year. Corresp: English, Deutsch. B: Den danske Bank,
Nytorv afdeling, København, Account No. 14089–1. CP: København
700 1146. A.B.F., Den danske Boghandlerforening.

R. SALFELT, GAMMEL KONGEVEJ 146, KØBENHAVN. TN: 01 24 05 11.*

SEIDENFADENS ANTIKVARIAT, VAERNDAMSVEJ 5, KØBENHAVN. TN:
01 24 17 69.

K.E. SKAFTE, DK-4800 NYKOBING FALSTER. TN: 3-85 15 06. Est: 1962.
Appointment necessary. Spec: arms and armour from east and west;
horology; portrait miniatures. Cata: occasionally; on each speciality.

SKAKHUSET [THE CHESS HOUSE], 24 STUDIESSTRAEDE, 1455
KØBENHAVN K. Prop: Stellan Persson. TN: 01 14 62 91. Est: 1947.
Shop. Small stock, also new books. Spec: chess books. Cata: every 18
months. Corresp: English, Deutsch, Svenska. B: Den Danske Bank,
Vesterbro afd. København. Account 12075–6. CP: 20 58 715.

SKANDINAVISK ANTIQUARIAT, GAMMEL STRAND 48, KØBENHAVN.
TN: 01 12 60 60.*

TEFAN SKOVLE, NØRREBROGADE 8, KØBENHAVN. TN: 01 37 09 05.

ANTIKVARIAT SKOVLE & SKOVLE, DAG HAMMERSKJOLDALLEE 42,
KØBENHAVN. TN: 01 26 00 03. Shop. Small stock sec. and antiq. also
records and tapes.

SORØ ANTIKVARIAT, FREDERIKSBERGVEJ 8, 4180, SORØ. Prop: Bjarne
Zukunft. TN: 03 63 35 85. Est: 1900. Storeroom; by appointment only.
Very large stock. Cata: 15 a year. Corresp: English, Deutsch. B:
Sjallandske Bank.

SUNDBY ANTIKVARIAT, MIDDELGRUNDSVEJ 5, KØBENHAVN. TN: 01 59
57 01.*

19

DANMARK   DENMARK

THUESENS ANTIKVARIAT, Fiolstraede 23, 1171 København-K. Prop: Hans. Chr. Thuesen. TN: 01 119962. Established 1933. Shop. Medium stock. Corresp: English, Deutsch. B: Bikuben, No. 825–800188. CP: København 20 31566. A.B.F., I.L.A.B.

BUNDESREPUBLIK
DEUTSCHLAND
FEDERAL GERMANY
ALLEMAGNE FÉDERALE

Associations: Verbände

V.D.A. = Verband Deutscher Antiquare, E.V.,
Die Vereingung von Buchanti-
quaren, Autographen- und Gra-
phikhandlern, Zum Talblick 2
D-6246 Glashütten im Taunus
TN: (06194) 6947.

B.V.D.B. = Borsenverein des Deutscher
Büchhandels.

Public Holidays: Jours de Fète: Feiertage

Jan. 1; Good Friday: Easter Monday: May 1: Ascension Day:
Whitmonday: Jun. 17: Nov. 17: Dec. 25 and 26.

Jan. 1: Vendredi-Saint: lundi de Pâques: Mai 1: Ascension: Lundi de
Pentecôte: Jun. 17: Nov. 17: Déc. 25 et 26.

Jan. 1: Karfreitag: Ostermontag: Mai 1: Himmelfahrt: Pfingstmontag:
Jun. 17: Nov. 17: Dez. 25 und 26.

Section Teil	Postcode Postleitzahl	
I	1000	BERLIN (WEST)
II	2000–3999	NORDDEUTSCHLAND, ALLEMAGNE (NORD), NORTHERN GERMANY
III	4000–5999	NORDRHEIN & RUHR
IV	6000+	MAIN, TAUNUS & PFALZ
V	7000+	SUDWESTDEUTSCHLAND, ALLEMAGNE (SUDOUEST), SOUTHWEST GERMANY
VI	8000+	BAYERN, BAVIERE, BAVARIA

I

BERLIN   Postcode: Postleitzahl 1000

HARVEY ABRAMS-BOOKS, AN DEN HUBERTSHAUSERN 21, 1000 BERLIN 38. TN: 801 2900. Gegrüdet 1980. Wohnung; Besuch nicht möglich. Kleiner Vorrat. Spec: Olympische Spiele; Sportgeschichte. Cata: in unregelmässiger Folge. Corresp: English, Français. B: Barclays Bank 11015387.

ANTIQUARIAT AN DEN CECILIENGÄRTEN, RUBENSSTR. 14, D-1000 BERLIN-FRIEDENAU 41. Prop: Volker Kunze. TN: 852 10 25. Samstag geschlossen.

TORSTEN BALAND, SPIELHAGENSTR. 13, D-1000 BERLIN-CHARLOTTENBURG 10. TN: 3 41 10 14. Samstag Nachmittag geschlossen. Spec: Illustr. Büchers Sexualwissenschaft.

RÜDIGER BARASCH, HÄHNELSTR. 5, D-1000 BERLIN-FRIEDENAU 41. TN: 852 62 14. Laden Samstag Nachmittag geschlossen. Spec: Bibliophilie; Deutsche Literatur; Welt-Literatur; Philosophie; Psychologie; Pädagogik.

GALERIE GERDA BASSENGE, ERDENERSTRASSE 5 A, D-1000 BERLIN 33. TN: (030) 892 90 13. Galerie. Spec: Autographen, Graphik. V.D.A.

ARTHUR BAUER, NESTORSTRASSE 1, 1000 BERLIN 31. TN: 3 23 47 58.

ANTIQUARIAT BEHRENS, LEIBNIZSTRASSE 47, D-1000 BERLIN 12. Prop: Stefan Behrens. TN: (0 30) 3 23 62 95. Samstag Nachmittag geschlossen. Spec: Literatur in Erst- und Gesamtausgaben, Pressendrucke, Illustrierte Bücher, Preussica, Kunstwissenschaft. Kat. 3 jährlich. V.D.A.

BERLINER ANTIQUARIAT, RHEINSTRASSE 6, D-1000 BERLIN-FRIEDENAU 41. Prop: Wolfgang Heinze. TN: 851 10 24. Laden Samstag Nachmittag geschlossen. Spec: Geographie; Geschichte; Orts- u. Landeskunde; Kunst; Literatur; Illustrierte Bücher; Berolinensien.

BERLINER MUSIKANTIQUARIAT, PESTALOZZISTR. 23. D-1000 BERLIN-CHARLOTTENBURG 12. Prop: Robert Hartwig. TN: 8 51 10 24. Samstag Nachmittag und Mittwoch geschlossen. Spec: Musik, Noten, Theater, Film, illustr. Bücher, Kinderbücher, Orts-und Landeskunde, Postkarten. 106

BICKHARDT'SCHE BUCHHANDLUNG, KARL-MARX-STRASSE 168, 1000 BERLIN-NEUKÖLLN 44. Prop: Peter Severin. TN: (080) 687 40 78. Gegründet 1879. Laden, Samstag Nachmittag und Mittwoch Nachmittag Geschlossen. Spec: Berolinensia: Geistes- und Naturwissenschaften: Graphik. Cata. B: Berliner Bank, Konto Nr. 7 050 600 000. CP: Berlin-West 3924–104. V.D.A.

THOMAS BLÖCKER, NÜRNBERGER STRASSE 50–56, D-1000-BERLIN-CHARLOTTENBURG 30. TN: 24 31 45 Samstag Nachmittag geschlossen. Spec: deutsche Literatur d. 20 Jahrh. in Erstausg.

BUCH-DIENST G.m.b.H., APOSTEL-PAULUS-STRASSE 18, 1000 BERLIN. TN: 7 82 40. 08

DAS BÜCHERFASS I, PFALZBURGER STRASSE 12, BERLIN-WILMERSDORF 15. Prop: Edgar A. Ruff. TN: 883 66 89. Morgens und Samstag Nachmittag geschlossen. Spec: dekorative Graphik, Stadtansichten, Bücher zu Geschenkzwecken.

DAS BÜCHERFASS II, HERTELSTR. 5, POSTFACH 209, D-1000 BERLIN-FRIEDENAU 41. Prop: Edgar A. Ruff. TN: 821 00 33. Spec: Bibliophiles und Wissenschaftliches Antiquariat; Graphik. Kataloge auf Anforderung.
Auch am Lagen: RHEINSTRASSE 45, HOF 1, AUFGANG 2. 4½ Treppen; nach Vereinbarung. Abteilungen zu Goethe, Theologie, Jura, Zeitschriften.

BÜCHERKELLER, HAUPTSTRASSE 103, D-1000 BERLIN-SCHÖNEBERG 62. TN: 7 81 56 69. Samstag Nachmittag geschlossen. Spec: Taschenbücher, Bildbände.

DIE   BÜCHERLAUBE,   Weimarer   Str.   29,   D-1000
Berlin-Charlottenburg 12. Prop: Klaus D. Pudlich. TN: 312 44
83. Laden, Montag bis Freitag Nachmittags und Samstag morgen
offen. Spec: Literatur; Geschichte; Kunst.

ECKARD DÜWAL, Schlüterstr. 17, D-1000 Berlin-Charlottenburg
12. TN: 313 30 30. Samstag Nachmittag geschlossen. Spec:
Autographen; Graphik.

R. FRIEDLÄNDER & SOHN G.m.b.H., Dessauer Strasse 28–29, 1000
Berlin 61. Geschäftsführer: Hans-Werner Kyrieleis. TN: (030)
2622328. Est: 1828. Lagerräume, Besuch nach Vereinbarung, Lager
nicht zugänglich. Sehr grosser Vorrat. Spec: Naturwissenschaften
(Botanik, Zoologie, Geologie U.S.W.). Cata: 4 pro Jahr. Corresp:
English. CP: Berlin West 91 12–100. V.D.A.

GSELLIUS'SCHE BUCH-, ANTIQUAR- UND GLOBENHANDLUNG
G.m.b.H., Hertastrasse 16, 1000 Berlin 37. Prop: R. Scheringer und
U. Stöhr TN: 030 813 3027. Gegründet 1737. Lagerräume und Büro.
Spec: Bücher des 15. bis 20. Jahrhunderts; Bibliophilie;
Geisteswissenschaften und alte Naturwissenschaften; Geschichte;
Philosophie; Berlin; Goetheana; Literatur und Kunst; alte
Stadtansichten und Landkarten. Cata: circa 5–10 pro Jahr. Corresp:
English, Français. B: Berliner Commerzbank, Konto 12 399 20 00. CP:
Berlin-west 5049–109. V.D.A.,

MAX GÜNTHER, Charlottenbrunnerstrasse 5a, 1000 Berlin 33.
Prop: Gertrud Knapps. TN: 823 29 50. Gegründet 1894. Wohnung,
nur nach Vereinbarung. Grosser Vorrat. Spec: Seltenheiten;
Sammlerstücke, Luxusdrucke, Moderne Bibliophilie, Deutsche
Literatur, Gesamtausgaben, Kulturgeschichte; Baedeker. Cata: in
unregelmässiger Folge. Corresp: English, Français. B: Deutsche Bank.
CP: Berlin-West 713 68–104. B.V.D.B., V.D.A.

ROBERT   HARTWIG,   Pestalozzistr.   23,   D-1000
Berlin-Charlottenburg 12. TN: 312 91 24 und 891 19 72. Samstag
Nachmittag und Mittwoch geschlossen. Spec: Musik; Noten; Theater;
Film; Illustrierte Bücher; Kunst; Literatur; Kinderbücher.

MANFRED HENKE, Motzstr. 59, D-1000 Berlin-Schöneberg 30. TN:
24 74 68. Laden: Montag bis Freitag Nachmittags und Samstag
morgen offen. Spec: Altertumsüwissenüschaften; Geschichte.

THEODOR HENNIG, Motzstr. 25, D-1000 Berlin-Schöneberg 30.
TN: 211 54 56. Samstag Nachmittag geschlossen. Spec: Berlin;
Geschichte; Kunst; Literatur; Philosophie.

ANTIQUARIAT HENNWACK, LANGENSCHEIDTSTRASSE 4, D-1000 BERLIN-SCHÖNEBERG 62. TN: 782 86 86. Samstag Nachmittag geschlossen. Spec: Kunst, Politik, Geisteswissensch., grosse Auswahl antiquarischer Taschenbücher.

HANS-ERICH HERO, WIELANDSTRASSE 13, 1000 BERLIN 12. TN: 3 23 25 85.

HANS-JOACHIM JESCHKE, WINTERFELDSTRASSE 51, D-1000 BERLIN-SCHÖNEBERG 30. TN: 784 16 33. Besuch nach Vereinbarung. Spec: Literatur; Bibliophilie; Geographie; Orts-und Landeskunde; Kulturgeschichte; Kataloge auf Anforderung.

KIEPERT G.m.b.H. HARDENBERGSTRASSE 4–5, 1000 BERLIN 12. Prop: Robert Kiepert. TN: (030) 31 07 11. Gegründet 1897. Spec: Naturwissenschaften; Technik; Geowissenschaften Landkarten. Corresp. English. B. Berliner Diskonto Bank, Konto 460 4120; First National City Bank, London, Konto 013 37 4; First National City Bank, New York, Konto 0275 9109. CP: Berlinwest 1800–100. B.V.D.B., L.I.A., S.B.L.A.M. (Belgien). Berliner Verleger- und Buchhändlervereinigung

ANTIQUARIAT KLETTE & KÖLSCH, MARKELSTRASSE 58, D-1000 BERLIN-STEGLITZ 41. TN: 792 73 59/855 67 81. Mo-Fr nachmittags und Samstag morgen offen.

HANS HORST KOCH, KURFÜRSTENDAMM 216, 1000 BERLIN 15. TN: (030) 882 63 60. TA: Buchkoch Berlin-West. Gegründet 1950. Lagerrüme, Montag-Freitag 11–18 Uhr. Sehr grosser Vorrat. Spec: Alte und Schöne Bücher; Bibliographie. Corresp: English, Français. B: Berliner Bank, Konto-Nr. 2407890 500. CP: Berlin-West 7199–107. V.D.A.

KREUZBERGER ANTIQUARIAT, YORCKSTR. 75, D-1000 BERLIN-KREUZBERG 61. Prop: Bernd Gärtner. TN: 786 81 03. Samstag geschlossen. Spec: Philosophie; Theologie; Psychologie; Geschichte; Politik; Kataloge.

BUCHHANDLUNG KUBIAK, MARTIN-LUTHER-STR. 125, D-1000 BERLIN-SCHÖNEBERG 62. Prop: Elke Hermes. TN: 782 28 49. Samstag nachmittag und Donnerstag nachmittag geschlossen.

ANTIQUARIAT IM KUDAMM-KARREE, KURFÜRSTENDAMM 206-208, D-1000 BERLIN-CHARLOTTENBURG 15. Prop: Klaus Hollmann. TN: 881 45 81. Mi-Fr 15–22 Uhr, Sa und So 12–22 Uhr. Spec: dekorative Graphik.

LANGE UND SPRINGER G.m.b.H. & CO., ANTIQUARIAT, OTTO-SUHR-ALLEE 26–28, D-1000 BERLIN 10. TN: (030) 3422011. TA: Langebuch Berlin. Gegründet 1980. Laden und Lagerräume, Samstag geschlossen. Sehr Grosser Vorrat. Spec: Medizin (Besonders alte); Mathematik; Physik, Chemie, Technik; Naturwissenschaften; Zeitschriften. Cata: 8–10 pro Jahr. Corresp: English. B: Deutsche Bank Berlin AG, Berlin 10. Konto Nr. 030 1150 716. CP: Berlin West 456 20–108 V.D.A.

MARIA LIST, EISENACHER STR. 111, D-1000 BERLIN-SCHÖNEBERG 30. TN: 216 75 65. Samstag Nachmittag geschlossen.

CHRISTA LUMMERT, SKALITZER STR. 75, D-1000 BERLIN-KREUZBERG 36. TN: 618 20 77. Nur Postversand. Spec: Literatur; Geschichte; Kunst.

MACKENSEN & NIEMANN, UTRECHTER STRASSE 42, D-1000 BERLIN-WEDDING 65. TN: 465 33 39. Mo-Fr nachmittags, Samstag morgen offen.

MAGISTER TINIUS, HACKERSTR. 4, D-1000 BERLIN-FRIEDENAU 41. Prop: Peter H. Ober u. Hansjörg Viesel. TN: 851 80 54. Montag und Samstag Nachmittag geschlossen.

HERBERT MEINKE, STUBENRAUCHSTRASSE 70, D-1000 BERLIN-FRIEDENAU 41. TN: 852 9390. Mo-Fr nachmittags, Samstag morgen offen, und nach Vereinbarung. Spec: Geographie, frühe Abenteuerlit.

DIE FUNDGRUBE DER BUCHHANDLUNG A. MENGER, ALBRECHTSTRASSE 122, D-1000 BERLIN-TEMPELHOF 42. TN: 752 50 44/45. Samstag Nachmittag und Dienstag geschlossen.

GALERIE NIERENDORF, HARDENBERGSTRASSE 19, 1000 BERLIN 12. Prop: Florian Karsch. TN: 785 60 60. Spec: Kunst; Gemälde; Skulptur; Graphik, Deutsche Expressionisten. V.D.A.

Dr. MARGARETHE NOELLE GEMÄLDE, MEINEKESTRASSE 11, 1000 BERLIN 15. TN: (030) 8 81 71 66. Gegründet 1942. Nach telefonischer Vereinbarung. Spec: Zeichnungen und Graphik des 18–20. Jahrhunderts. B: Deutsche Bank 1 300 813. CP: Berlin-West 1766 19–100. V.D.A.

HANS PELS-LEUSDEN, KURFÜRSTENDAMM 59–60, D-1000 BERLIN-CHARLOTTENBURG 15. TN: 323 20 44. Samstag Nachmittag geschlossen. Spec: Pressendrucke; Illustrierte Bücher; Literatur; Kunstwissenschaft; Kataloge.

GISELA PLÄHN, INNSBRUCKER STR. 4, D-1000 BERLIN-SCHONEBERG. TN: 854 29 72. Samstag Nachmittag geschlossen. Spec: Rossica; Slavica.

PRO LIBRO, PARISER STR. 14, D-1000 BERLIN-WILMERSDORF 15. Prop: Waltraud Materne. TN: 883 54 30. Samstag Nachmittag geschlossen. Spec: Literatur u. Literaturwissenschaft; Philosophie; Geschichte; Politik; Kulturgeschichte; Theater.

GÜNTER RICHTER, BREITE STRASSE 29, 1000 BERLIN 33. TN: (030) 823 81 79. Gegründet 1945. Laden, Samstag Nachmittag geschlossen. Spec: Militaria; Geschichte; Politik; alte Landkarten und Staüdteansichten (Merian). Auch neue Bücher. Cata. B: Bank für Handel und Industrie, Depka 12, 1 Berlin 45, Baselerstrasse, Konto 127786. V.D.A., B.V.D.B.

ROTKÄPPCHEN, BRUSSELER STRASSE 14, D-1000 BERLIN-WEDDING 65. Prop: Klaus Franken. TN: 453 57 25. Mo-Fr nachmittags, Samstag morgen. Spec: Kinderbücher.

CHRISTIANE SAWHNEY, WINTERFELDTSTRASSE 44, D-1000 BERLIN-SCHÖNEBERG 30. TN: 216 45 28. Samstag Nachmittag geschlossen.

LUTZ SCHÄFER, JOHANN-SIGISMUND STR. 15, D-1000 BERLIN-WILMERSDORF 31. TN: 892 89 44. Samstag geschlossen, tel. Anmeldung erwünscht.

WOLFGANG SCHEBELLA, ZELTINGER PL. 9/13, D-1000 BERLIN-FROHNAU 28. TN: 401 22 97/401 68 61. Mittwoch geschlossen.

27

RICHARD   SCHIKOWSKI, MOTZSTRASSE   30,   D-1000
BERLIN-SCHÖNEBERG 30. TN: 24 54 95. Samstag Nachmittag
geschlossen. Spec: Astrologie; Okkultismus; Yoga; Westöstliche
Weisheit.

SCHOMAKER & NIEDERSTRASSER, BUNDESALLEE 221, D-1000
BERLIN-WILMERSDORF 15. TN: 24 98 34. Samstag Nachmittag
geschlossen. Spec: Kunst; Literatur; Archaeologie; Alte Berliner
Ansichten und Pläne.

ERIKA SCHROEDER, WINTERFELDSTR. 46, D-1000 BERLIN-SCHÖNEBERG
30. TN: 215 48 19. Samstag Nachmittag geschlossen.

PETER SCHWARZ, EISENACHER STR. 43, D-1000 BERLIN-SCHOÜNEBERG
62. Samstag geschlossen. Spec: Esoterik; Kunst; Philosophie;
Erstausgaben.

GERHARD   SENZEL, KNESEBECKSTRASSE   13/14,   D-1000
BERLIN-CHARLOTTENBURG 12. TN: 312 58 87.

WALTER SEUFFER, STEGLITZER DAMM 57, 1000 BERLIN 41. TN: (030)
796 3848. Wohnung, Besuche nur nach Vereinbarung. Mittelgrosser
Vorrat auch neue Bücher. Spec: Naturwissenschafen. Cata: 1 order 2
jährlich. V.D.A.

MATTHIAS   SEVERIN, MERANER   STRASSE   6,   D-1000
BERLIN-SCHONEBERG 62. TN: 8 54 65 45. Mo-Fr nachmittags,
Samstag morgen, und nach Vereinbarung.

MANFRED SIEG, FASANENSTR. 45, D-1000 BERLIN-WILMERSDORF 15.
TN: 881 89 54. Samstag Nachmittag geschlossen. Spec; Kunst: Musik,
Theologie.

THOMAS   SONNENTHAL, CAUERSTRASSE   20/21,
BERLIN-CHARLOTTENBURG 10. TN: 342 56 38. Mo, Di, Do, Fr 14-18
Uhr, Sa 12-14, langer Sa 12-17 Uhr. Spec: Philosophie, Psychologie,
Esoterik, Astrologie, Kunst, Geschichte, Politik, Taschenbücher.

RUDOLF J. SPRINGER, FASENENSTRASSE 13, 1000 BERLIN 12. TN: (030)
313 9088. Spec: 20 Jahrhundert (Luxusdrucke–Mappenwerke).
V.D.A.

ANTIQUARIAT B.F. STADELMANN, DIESELSTRASSE 5, 6070 LANGEN.
TN: (0 61 03) 7 98 36. Nach Vereinbarung. Spec: Kulturgeschichte,
Technik, Kriminologie, Zigeuner. Kat. selten. B: Dresdner Bank 1918
631. V.D.A.

WOLFGANG STASCHEN, POTSDAMER STR. 138, 1000 BERLIN 30. TN: 2622075. Gegründet 1958. Laden, Mittwoch Morgen geschlossen. Mittelgrosser Vorrat. Spec: Stahlstich Ansichten. Corresp: English, Français. B: Deutsche Bank Berlin 6217707. CP: Berlin-West 11 27 27.

HUGO STREISAND, EISLEBENER STRASSE 4, 1000 BERLIN 30. TN: 24 23 14. Spec: Politik und Staatswissenschaften; Soziologie; Pädagogik. B: Berliner Bank, Konto 417296. CP: Berlin-West 7518. V.D.A.

STRUPPE UND WINCKLER, POTSDAMERSTRASSE 103, 1000 BERLIN 30. Prop: Helmut Hildebrandt. TN: (030) 261 10 88. Gegründet 1890. Spec: Recht, Wirtschaft. Cata. B: Berliner Bank, Konto 32 07689 400. CP: Berlin-West 207–101. V.D.A.

RIEWERT Q. TODE, DUDENSTR. 22, D-1000 BERLIN-KREUZBERG 61. TN: 786 51 86. Samstag Nachmittag geschlossen. Spec: Polit. Literatur; Schöne Literatur D. 20. Jh.; Soziologie; Theologie; Erstausgaben; Kinderbücher; Kleine Galerie.

WEDDINGER ANTIQUARIAT, WILLDENOWSTR. 5B/E. BURGSDORFSTR., D-1000 BERLIN-WEDDING 65. Prop: Wolfgang Jeske. TN: 461 20 75. Samstag Nachmittag geschlossen. Spec: Sozialismus; DDR; Literatur.

WASMUTH   BUCHHANDLUNG   &   ANTIQUARIAT   KG., HARDENBERGSTRASSE 9A, 1000 BERLIN 12. TN: 31 69 20 und 313 82 93. TA: Buchwasmuth Berlin. Gegründet 1872. Laden, Samstag Nachmittag geschlossen. Mittelgrosser Vorrat, auch neue Bücher. Spec: Kunst; Architektur; Archäologie. Cata: 4 pro Jahr. Corresp: English, Français. B: Bank für Handel und Industrie, Uhlandstrasse 9–11, 1 Berlin 12, Konto 694 390. CP: Berlin-West 100 39. V.D.A., B.V.D.B.

CARL WEGNER, MARTIN-LUTHER-STRASSE 113, 1000 BERLIN 62. Prop: Carlos Kühn. TN: 782 2491. Gegründet 1953. Laden. Grosser Vorrat. Spec: Literatur; Philosophie, Sozialwissenschaften- Berlinensia; Theater; Städteansichten und Landkarten. Cata: 1 oder 2 pro Jahr. Corresp: English. B: Berliner Disconto Bank Konto 391–1302. B.V.D.B.

BUCHHANDLUNG ZIEGAN OHG, POTSDAMER STR. 180, D-1000 BERLIN-SCHÖNEBERG 30. TN: 216 20 68 nach Vereinbarung. Spec: Biologische Naturwissenschaften.

II

NORTHERN GERMANY: NORDDEUTSCHLAND: ALLEMAGNE (NORD)

Postcodes: Postleitzahlen 2000+ & 3000+

2202 BARMSTEDT	3522 KARLSHAFEN
3300 BRAUNSCHWEIG	3500 KASSEL
2800 BREMEN	2300 KIEL
	2400 LÜBECK
	3140 LÜNEBURG
3011 GEHRDEN	3550 MARBURG
3400 GÖTTINGEN	
	2900 OLDENBURG
	3360 OSTERODE
2000 HAMBURG	3017 PATTENSEN
3000 HANNOVER	3120 WITTINGEN

ARNO ADLER, HÜXSTRASSE 55, 2400 LÜBECK. (POSTFACH 2048). Prop: Kurt Adler. TN: (0451) 74466. Gegründet 1932. Laden und Lagerräume, Samstag Nachmittag geschlossen. Sehr grosser Vorrat, auch neue Bücher. Spec: Geschichte; Kulturgeschichte; Hansische Geschichte; Wirstschafts- und Sozialwissenschaften; Lübeck. Cata: 2 pro Jahr. Corresp: English. B: Handelsbank in Lübeck. CP: Hamburg 32683-207. V.D.A., B.V.D.B.

ANTIQUARIAT AMELANG, CRANACHSTRASSE 45, 2000 HAMBURG 52. Prop: Hans Benecke, KG. TN: (040) 897 484. TA: Buchamelang, Hamburg. Gegründet 1806. Wohnung, nur nach Vereinbarung. Kleiner Vorrat. Spec: Pressendrucke und illustrierte Bücher: Erstausgaben seit 1800; alte Kinderbücher; Exilliteratur. Cata: 6 oder 7 pro Jahr. Corresp: English. B: Dresdner Bank Konto 5 220 440. CP: 365 566 Hamburg. V.D.A.

WALTER ANDRAEAS, WISCHHOFSTIEG 5, 2000 HAMBURG 65. TN: 6 01 92 83.

ALTONAER ANTIQUARIAT, AM FELDE 91, 2000 HAMBURG 50. Prop H.-H. Tiedmann. TN: (040) 39 69 70.

ANTIQUARIAT IM HINTERHAUS, KÖNIGSWORTHERSTRASSE 19 D-3000 HANNOVER.

ARMARIUM BUCHHANDLUNG UND ANTIQUARIAT, Zum See 10, 2313 Raisdorf Über Kiel. Prop: Hermann Kullmann. TN: (0 43 07) 54 22. Mo–Fr offen, Sa nach Vereinbarung. Spec: Geschichte, Historische Hilfswissenschaften, Kirchengeschichte, Slawistik. V.D.A.

PETER BABENDERERDE, Grosse Burgstrasse 35, 2400 Lübeck. TN: (0451) 70776. Gegründet 1840. Laden und Lagerräume. Sehr grosser Vorrat an dekorativer Graphik, Städteansichten und Landkarten. Cata. Corresp: English, Français. B: Handelsbank, Lübeck, Konto 21075. CP: Hamburg 617-208. V.D.A., B.V.D.B.

ANTIQUARIAT BARME, Krumdal 24, 2000 Hamburg 55. TN: 86 29 41.

ANTIQUARIAT BARTKOWIAK, Körnerstrasse 24, 2000 Hamburg 60. TN: 2 79 36 74.

BRIGITTE BAUER, Ofenerstrasse 17, 2900 Oldenburg. TN: (0441) 7 43 50. Private promioos; appointment necessary.

BÄRENREITER ANTIQUARIAT, Heinrich-Schutz-Allee 35, 3500 Kassel-Wilhelmshöhe. Prop: Dr. Karl Vötterle. Gegründet 1946. B: Deutsche Bank, Kassel. CP: Frankfurt-am-Main 531 12. V.D.A.

GALERIE J.-H. BAUER, Burgstrasse 25, 3000 Hannover. V.D.A.

I. BECKER, Lister Meile 49, D-3000 Hannover.

W. BRANDES, Postfach 1660, Wolfenbüttlerstrasse 12, 3300 Braunschweig. Prop: Ulrich Schneider. TN: (0531) 75003. TA: Buchbrandes. Gegründet 1949. Auktionen zweimal Jährlich. Corresp: English, Français. B: Deutsche Bank, Braunschweig, Kontonummer 1976190. CP: 1403–300. V.D.A., Bundesverband Deutscher Kunstevcrsteigerer.

R. BRAATZ, Knooper Weg 28, 2300 Kiel.

ANTIQUARIAT BREMER UND SCHLAK, Kornmarkt 4–5, 3340 Wolfenbüttel, Prop: Günter Bremer. TN: (053 31) 15 15. Samstag Nachmittag geschlossen. Spec: Braunschweig/Harz, Dekorative Graphik, Exlibris, Büchersuchdienst. B: Deutsche Bank 1 913 672. CP: Hannover 1037 11–309.

DAS BÜCHERHAUS, Wiesenstrasse 21, 3012 Langenhagen. Prop: Hermann Wiedenroth. TN: (05 11) 73 97 70. Nach Vereinbarung. Spec: Weltliteratur in Erst- und Gesamtausgaben, Illustrierte Bücher, Geistes- und Naturwissenschaften, Kunst- und Kulturgeschichte. Kat. 6 jährlich. CP: Postscheck Hannover 827 30–305. V.D.A.

31

DAS BÜCHERKABINETT, POSTSTRASSE 14–16, 2000 HAMBURG 36. Prop: Carlota Simon, Dr. Maria Conradt. TN: (040) 34 32 36. TA: Buecherkabinett Hamburg. Gegründet 1931. Spec: Wertvolle alte Bücher; Alte dekorative Graphik. Corresp: English, Français, Italiano. B: Vereins- und Westbank Hamburg 1/33975 (BLZ 200 300 00). CP: Hamburg 73566–203 (BLZ 200 100 20).

DER BÜCHERWURM, OTTENSER HAUPTSTRASSE 60, 2000 HAMBURG 50. TN: 3 90 02. 50.

CABINET DER GESCHICHTE, ESPLANADE 17, 2000 HAMBURG 36. Prop: J. Knudsen. TN: 34 56 21.

COMMERZCABINETT, HUMBOLDTSTRASSE 125, 2000 HAMBURG 76. Prop: Dr. Paul C. Martin. TN: (040) 2 20 24 33. Nach Vereinbarung. Spec: Wirtschafts-, Sozial- und Finanzgeschichte, Börsen, Autographen, Historische Wertpapiere, Ökonomie-Ephemera. Kat. 2 bis 6 jährlich. V.D.A.

F. VON DAAKE, LOTHRINGER 32, D-3000 HANNOVER.

JÜRGEN DINTER, ANTIQUARIAT FÜR PHILOSOPHIE, BUCHHOLZSTRASSE 8–10, KÖLN. TN: (0)221 626401. Gegründet 1982. Wohnung, nur nach Vereinbarung. Kleiner Vorrat. Spec: Philosophie, Inkunabeln, Alte Drucke. Cata: 2–3 pro Jahr. Corresp: English, Francais, Italiano.

F. DÖRLING, NEUER WALL 40, 2000 HAMBURG 36. Prop: W. Goerigk. TN: 36 46 70. TA: Doerlingant, Hamburg. Gegrundet 1797. Laden und Galerie, Samstag geschlossen. Sehr grosser Vorrat. Spec: alte und seltene Bücher; Autographen, Manuskripte, Briefe, Dokumente; alte Landkarten. Cata: 2 pro Jahr. Corresp: English, Français, Italiano. B: Deutsche Bank Hamburg, Konto 02–02127. CP: Hamburg 1825–203. B.D.K.

ALICE ELCHLEPP, Schillerstrasse 14, 3360 Osterode a. Harz. Spec: Alte Graphik, Militaria, Geschichte. Cata. B: Volksbank Konto 9506 402. V.D.A.

N.G. ELWERT UNIVERSITÄTSBUCHHANDLUNG, Reitgasse 7–9, 3550 Marburg (Lahn). Prop: Dr. Wilhelm Braun-Elwert. TN: (06421) 25024. TA: Elwert, Marburg, Gegründet 1726, priviligiert 1783. Laden und Lagerräume, Samstag Nachmittag geschlossen. Sehr grosser Vorrat, auch neue Bücher. Spec: Deutsche Orts- und Landeskunde; Geschichte; Germanistik; Hippologie; Geographie; Theologie. Cata: 2 oder 3 pro Jahr. Corresp: English, Français. B: Stadtsparkasse Marburg, Konto 4000 0169. CP: Frankfurt am Main 3899–605. B.V.D.B., V.D.A., Hessiche Verleger- und Buchhandlerverband, Arbeitsgemeinschaft wissenschaftlicher Sortimenter.

K-Th. ENGELBRECHT, Laves 76, D-3000 Hannover.

EPPENDORFER ANTIQUARIAT, Gärtnerstrasse 31, 2000 Hamburg 20, Prop: Wolfgang Pruss. TN: 47 27 29.

FUNDGRUBER FÜR BÜCHERFREUNDE, Dammtordamm 4, 2000 Hamburg 36. TN: 34 50 16.

HEINZ GÄRTNER, Marienstrasse 105, D-300 Hannover.

DIETER GÄTJENS, Antiquariat, Brahmsallee 28, D-2000 Hamburg 13.

ROLF-PETER GERLING, Fedelhören 89. 2800 Bremen. TN: 32 58 62.

GÖTTINGER ANTIQUARIAT, Mauerstrasse 16/17, 3400 Göttingen. Prop: Erich Gross. TN: (0551) 57503. Gegründet 1946. Laden, Samstag Nachmittag geschlossen. Sehr grosser Vorrat. Spec: Geisteswissen schaften, Geschichte der Naturwissenschaft, Alte Bucher. Cata: Monatlich 2. Corresp: English, Français. B: Kreissparkasse, Göttingen, Konto 81702. CP: Hannover 126290. V.D.A., B.V.D.B.

ANTIQUARIAT GÖTZ, Nernstrasse 16, 2800 Bremen 33. TN: (0421) 25 62 42. Nach Vereinbarung. Spec: Illustrierte Bücher des 16–19. Jahrhunderts, Dekorative Graphik. B: Bremer Landesbank 496 400. CP: Hamburg 206 69 206. V.D.A.

ANTIQUARIAT AM HAFEN, Bernhardt-Nacht-Strasse 95, 2000 Hamburg 4. Prop: H. Rosenberg. TN: 3 19 52 90.

HAMBURGENSIEN-MEYER, POSTSTRASSE 2–4, 2000 HAMBURG 36. Prop: Franz H. Meyer. TN: 35 25 96. Spec: Graphik; Landkarten; Topographie. V.D.A.

HORST HAMECHER, GOETHESTRASSE 74, 3500 KASSEL. TN: (0561) 131 79. Gegründet 1947. Lagerräume, Besuche nach Vereinbarung. Sehr Grosser Vorrat. Spec: Geisteswissenschaften. Cata: 10 pro Jahr. Corresp: English. B: Stadtsparkasse Kassel (BLZ 520 501 51) Konto 016 295. CP: Frankfurt am Main 31013–602. B.V.D.B.

GEBRÜDER HARTMANN, SCHWARZER BÄR 7, D-3000 HANNOVER. TN: 44 18 93.

W. HASCHTMANN, ANTIQUARIAT FUR RECHTSWISSENSCHAFT, KNÜLL 15, 2306 SCHONBERG.

HAUSWEDELL UND NOLTE, PÖSELDORFERWEG 1, 2000 HAMBURG 13. Prop: Ernst Nolte. TN: (040) 448366 und 4103622. TA: Hausnolte Hamburg. Gegründet 1927. Lagerräume. Spec: Autographen und Handschriften, alte Graphik; Auktionen. Cata: 4–6 pro Jahr. Corresp: English, Français. B: Vereins- und Westbank, Hamburg Konto Nr. 43/00125 (BLZ 20030000). CP: Hamburg 137 207–204. V.D.A. Bundesverband deutscher Kunstversteigerer, V.E.B.U.K.U (Schweiz), S.L.A.M. (France).

P. HEINEN, DEHNHAIDE 1, 2000 HAMBURG 76. TN: (040) 2 99 58 07.

WALTER HEINZE, BISMARCKSTRASSE 23, 2900 OLDENBURG. TN: 7 75 21.

HENNIES UND ZINKELSEN, MARIENSTRASSE 14 UND 18, D-3000 HANNOVER. TN: (0511) 85 10 98.

ANTIQUARIAT PAUL HENNINGS, ALTSTÄDTER STRASSE 15, 2000 HAMBURG 1. Prop: Rüdiger Fritsche. TN: (040) 32 60 74. Gegründet 1931. Laden. Samstag Nachmittag geschlossen. Sehr grosser Vorrat, auch neue Bücher. Cata: 4 pro Jahr. Corresp: English, Français. B: Bank für Gemeinwirtschaft, Hamburg. (BLZ 200 101 11) Konto: 1 166 481 2. CP: Hamburg 518 48–207.

"HESPERUS", JAKOBSTRASSE 20, D-3000 HANNOVER. Prop: Wigbert Schulze. TN: 62 87 42.

ANTIQUARIAT A.M. HOFWEG, HOFWEG 57, 2000 HAMBURG 76. Prop: Annette Blattermann. TN: 22 28 67.

ANTIQUARIAT RUTHILD JÄGER, STEINWEG 17, 2120 LÜNEBURG-OEDEME. TN: (0 41 31) 4 27 97. nach Vereinbarung. Spec: Alte Stadtansichten und Landkarten aus aller Welt, Geographie, Landeskunde. Kat. 1 jährlich. CP: Hamburg 1709 53–207, V.D.A.

J.E. JÜRDENS HILLMANNPLATZ, 2800 BREMEN. TN: 31 18 41.

ANTIQUARIAT KAAK, OLE HOOP 9, 2000 HAMBURG 55. TN: 86 77 26.

ANTIQUARIAT KEMMER, EPPENDORFERWEG 248, 2000 HAMBURG 20. TN: 48 39 61.

ANTIQUARIAT A. KLITTICH-PFANKUCH, KLEINE BURG 12, 3300 BRAUNSCHWEIG. TN: (05 31) 4 67 61. Gegründet 1919. Nach Vereinbarung. Spec: Landeskunde, Geschichte, Militaria, Dekorative Graphik. 6 bis 8 Lagerkataloge, 1 Auktionskatalog jährlich. B: Volksbank Braunschweig. V.D.A.

C. KOECHERT, DACHSTRIFT 14, 3000 HANNOVER, TN: (0511) 65 08 13.

H. KULLMANN, ZUM SEE 10, 2313 RAISDORF.

KARL-HEINZ KÜSTERS, GUSTAV-ADOLF-STRASSE 12, 3000 HANNOVER. TN: 32 35 11.

HERMANN LAATZEN, WARBURGSTRASSE 18, 2000 HAMBURG 36. TN: 44 41 60.

ANTIQUARIAT LEUNER, BISHOFSNADEL 15, 2800 BREMEN. TN: 32 32 05.

FRANZ LEUWER, AM WALL 171, 2800 BREMEN. Prop: Werner Siebert. TN: (0421) 321828. Gegründet 1905. Mittelgrosser Vorrat. Spec: Deutsche Literatur- und Geistesgeschichte des 18. und 19. Jahrhunderts; Geographie; Landeskunde Norddeutschland; Kunstwissenschaft, Dekorative Graphik. CP: Hamburg 6480. V.D.A., B.V.D.B.

LIBRESSO, ANTIQUARIAT AN DER UNIVERSITÄT, BINDERSTRASSE 24, 2000 HAMBURG 13. Prop: Hartmut Lerner. TN: (040) 451663. Gegründet 1967. Laden, Samstag geschlossen. Sehr grosser Vorrat. Spec: Geisteswissenschaften. Cata: 2 oder 3 pro Jahr. Corresp: English. B: Dresdner Bank Hamburg, Konto Nr. 407 1219. CP: Hamburg 82688–201.

AXEL LÜDERS, HEUSSWEG 33, 2000 HAMBURG 19, TN: 40 57 27.

ACHIM MAKROCKI, QUELLENSTRASSE 14, 3500 KASSEL. TN: (0561) 45609. Gegründet 1966. Sieben Lagerräume: vorzugsweise nach Vereinbarung. Sehr grosser Vorrat. Spec: Zeitschriften, Literature (Englische und Amerikanische). Werkausgaben. Corresp: English. B: B.H.F. Bank A.G. Konto 20–10628–2. CP: Frankfurt am Main 2598 33–609.

W. MAUKE SÖHNE, KARL-MUCK-PLATZ 12, 2000 HAMBURG 36. Prop: Ernst und Jochen D. Harms. TN: (040) 34 53 41. Gegründet 1796. Laden. Kleiner Vorrat, auch neue Bücher. Spec: Recht, Steuern; Periodica. Corresp: English. B: Hamburger Sparkasse, Kontonummer 1280/119999. CP: 9180–209. B.V.D.B., Nordeutscher Verleger und Buchhändler Verband, Arbeitsgemeinschaft wissenschaftlicher Sortimenter.

M. MIELKE, SCHLÄGERSTRASSE 33, D-3000 HANNOVER. TN: 88 49 60.

ANTIQUARIAT REINHOLD PABEL, KRAYENKAMP 10B, D-2000 HAMBURG 11.
Auch ENGLISCHE PLANKE 6, HAMBURG 11.

TRAUTE PLÖGER, OSTFEUERBERGSTRASSE 35, 2800 BREMEN. TN: 38 52 49.

H. PREIDEL, ANTIQUARIAT FÜR MEDIZIN, POSTFACH 1128, BISMARCKSTRASSE 20, 3007 GEHRDEN/HANNOVER. TN: (05108) 4766. TA: Preidelbuch Gehrden. Gegründet 1959. Lagerräume; Besuche nach Vereinbarung. Mittelgrosser Vorrat. Spec: alte Medizin. Corresp: English. B: Stadtsparkasse Hannover Konto Nr. 155 446. CP: 117879–306. V.D.A., I.L.A.B.

ANTIQUARIAT ST. GERTRUDE, GERTRUDEN KIRCHHOF 2, 2000 HAMBURG 1. TN: 33 60 50

BERNHARD SCHÄFER, CONRADISTRASSE 2, 3522 KARLSHAFEN. TN: 05672–503. Gegründet 1957. Laden. Mittelgrosser Vorrat. Spec: Graphik (Ex-libris Bookplates). Corresp: English, Français. B: Stadtsparkasse Karlshafen. CP: Frankfurt am Main 188 643 601. V.D.A.

SIGISMUND SCHMIDT. EPPENDORFER MARKTPLATZ 15, 2000 HAMBURG 20. TN: 47 41 55.

BERND SCHRAMM, DÄNISCHE STRASSE 26, 2300 KIEL. Spec: Dekorative Graphik; Wertvolle Bücher, Auktionen, Ostseeländer. B: Deutsche Bank, Kiel, Konto Nr. 5/50459. V.D.A.

ANTIQUARIAT SCHROEDER UND WEISE, LEHRTERSTRASSE, 3000 HANNOVER-ANDERTEN. TN: (0511) 51 34 20.

J.A. STARGARDT, RADESTRASSE 10, 3550 MARBURG. Prop: Günther und Klaus Mecklenburg. TN: 22040. Gegründet 1830. Laden und Lagerräume, Samstag Nachmittag geschlossen. Mittelgrosser Vorrat. Spec: Autographen; Auktionen; Genealogie und Heraldik. Cata: 2–3 pro Jahr. Corresp: English, Français. B: Commerzbank, Marburg. CP: Frankfurt-am-Main 11601–604. V.D.A., B.V.D.B.

ANTIQUARIAT BEIM STEINERNEN KREUZ, 2800 BREMEN 1. TN: (0421) 70 15 1 5.

ANTIQUARIAT STORM, HAKENSTRASSE 2A, 2800 BREMEN. TN: 32 59 09.

Dr. S. THEIMANN, VIOLENSTRASSE 33–35, 2800 BREMEN, TN: 32 59 03.

ANTIQUARIAT HANS WÄGER, LAVESSTRASSE 6, 3000 HANNOVER. TN: 32 17 25.

KARL DIETER WAGNER, ROTHENBAUMCHAUSSEE 1, 2000 HAMBURG 13. TN: (040) 410 43 74. Gegründet 1967. Laden, Samstag geschlossen. Grösse Vorrat; nur Musikliteratur und Musiknoten. Corresp: English. B: Vereins- und Westbank Hamburg, Konto Nr. 43–03012. CP: Hamburg 3097 92–205. B.V.D.B., Gesamtverband Deutscher Musikfachgeschäfte e.V.

HORST WELLM, BENNIGSERWEG 1, D-3017 PATTENSEN 1. TN: (05101) 13361. Gegründet; 1967. Wohnung; nur nach Vereinbarung Mittelgrosser Vorrat. Spez: Bibliographie; Orts- und Landesgeschichte; Wissenschaften. Cata: 2 pro Jahr. Corresp: English B: Volksbank Pattensen/Hann. (BLZ 251 933 31) Kontonummer 14011. CP: Hannover Kontonummer 141248–302,

MAX WIEDEBUSCH, DAMMTORSTRASSE 20, 2000 HAMBURG 36. TN: (040) 35 31 27. Laden. Mittelgrosser Vorrat; auch neue Bücher.

ANTIQUARIAT IRENE WIEHE, HILDERSHEIMERSTRASSE 46, 3000 HANNOVER. TN: 88 84 34.

WISSENSCHAFTLICHES ANTIQUARIAT, HUMBOLDTSTRASSE 6, 2800 BREMEN. TN: 70 31 51.

Dr. ROBERT WOHLERS & CO., LANGE REIHE 68, 2000 HAMBURG 1. TN: 24 77 15.

GUNTER ZIMMERLING. JOHANNISWALL 3, 2000 HAMBURG 1. TN: 33 63 03

III

RHEIN & RUHR

Postcodes: Postleitzahlen 4000+ & 5000+

5100 AACHEN	4400 MÜNSTER
5483 BAD NEUNAHR-	4054 NETTETAL
AHRWEILER	4040 NEUSS
4800 BIELEFELD	5450 NEUWIED
4630 BOCHUM	5960 OLPE
5300 BONN	4500 OSNABRUCK
4100 DUISBERG	5449 PFALZFELD
4000 DÜSSELDORF	4905 SPENGE
4300 ESSEN	4542 TECKLENBURG
4830 GÜTERSLOH	5500 TRIER
5000 KÖLN (Cologne)	5620 VELBERT
4150 KREFELD	5600 WUPPERTAL

ANTIQUARIAT AIX LA CHAPPELLE, PONTSTRASSE 10, D-5100 AACHEN. Prop: Eberhard B. Talke.

"ARMARIUM" BUCHHANDLUNG UND ANTIQUARIAT, JAHNSTRASSE 116, 4000 DÜSSELDORF 1. Prop: Hermann Kullmann. TN: 346378. Gegründet 1961. Laden und Lagerräume, Samstag Nachmittag geschlossen. Mittelgrosser Vorrat. Spec: Geschichte; bes. historische Hilfswissenschaften. Cata. Corresp: English, Français. B: Stadt-Sparkasse Düsseldorf, Konto 1009 2914. CP: Köln 12 2098. V.D.A., B.V.D.B.

C.G. BOERNER, KASERNENSTRASSE 14, 4000 DÜSSELDORF. Prop: Ruth-Maria Muthmann. TN: 13 18 05. TA: Boernerkunst Düsseldorf. Gegründet 1826. Laden, Samstag nach Vereinbarung. 9 bis 13 Uhr. Spec: Alte und Neuere Graphik; Alte Handzeichnungen. Cata: 2 pro Jahr. Corresp: English, Français. B: Bankhaus C. G. Trinkaus & Burkhardt, Düsseldorf. (BLZ 300 30880) Konto 739–014. CP: Essen 21446–437.

BOUVIER UNIVERSITÄTSBUCHHANDLUNG G.m.b.H., AM HOF 32, 5300 BONN. Prop: Herbert Grundmann K.G. TN: 65 44 45. Gegründet 1828. Laden und Lagerräume. Grosser Vorrat, auch neue Bücher. Spec: Geisteswissenschaft; Bibliophilie. Cata: periodische. Corresp: English, Français. B: Stadt Sparkasse Bonn. CP: Köln 16 667. B.V.D.B.

FRIEDRICH   BURCHARD, SONNBORNERSTRASSE   144,   5600 WUPPERTAL-SONNBORN. TN: 740337 und 742696. TA: Burchard Wuppertal. Gegründet 1907. Laden und Lagerräume, Samstag Nachmittag und Mittwoch Nachmittag geschlossen. Sehr Grosser Vorrat, auch neue Bücher. Spec: Alte Dekorative Graphik. Corresp: English, Français. B: Stadtsparkasse 640 607. CP: Köln 23935–502. V.D.A.

CARL F. CHRISPEELS, COMBAHNSTRASSE 15, 5300 BONN 3. (POSTFACH 30 02 60). TN: (0228) 471815. Gegründet 1964. Lagerräume, Samstag geschlossen. Mittelgrosser Vorrat. Spec: Kunst und Geschichte bis zum 15. Jahrhundert. Cata: 4 pro Jahr. Corresp: English, Français, Español, Italiano. B: Deutsche Bank, Bonn 3, Konto 095 4917. CP: Köln 1720 89. V.D.A.

ARIBERT   D.   CLAASSEN, BUCH-   UND   KUNSTANTIQUARIAT, HARDTSTRASSE 8, 5483 BAD NEUENAHR-AW 1. TN: (0 26 41) 2 82 05. Nach telefonischer Vereinbarung. Spec: Alte Städteansichten, Landkarten, Dekorative Graphik, Wertvolle Bücher des 15.–19. Jahrhunderts. B: Commerzbank Bad Neuenahr. CP: Postscheck Köln 2317 31–507. V.D.A.

URSULA DEMPWOLF, DAMASCHKEWEG 19A, D-4830 GÜTERSLOH.

HARTMUT ERLEMANN, MÜNSTERSTRASSE 71, 4700 HAMM 1. TN: 02381-6731 35.

ANTIQUARIAT M. UND R. FRICKE, POSTSTRASSE 3, 4000 DÜSSELDORF 1, POSTSTRASSE 3, 4000 DÜSSELDORF 1. TN: (02 11) 32 32 34. Spec: Architektur, Fotografie, Kunst, Literatur des 20. Jahrhunderts. Kat. 3 bis 4 jährlich. B: Dresdner Bank 419 196 100. V.D.A.

ANTIQUARIAT   GANSEFORTH,   HOHESTRASSE   47,   4000 DÜSSELDORF-ALTSTADT. TN: (0211) 13 16 76.

WINFRIED GEISENHEYNER, Postfach 480155, Roseneck 6, D-4400 Münster-Hiltrup. TN: (02501) 7884. Gegründet 1981. Wohnung; Besuch nur nach Vereinbarung. Kleiner Vorrat. Spez: Wissenschaften; Erdkunde. Drucke des 15. bis 16. Jahrhunderts; Naturwissenschaften Medizin, Technik. Cata: 4 pro Jahr. Corresp: English. B: Volksbank Münster, Kontonummer 1004445 300. CP: Stuttgart 86414–701.

ANTIQUARIAT GUNDEL GELBERT, St. Apern Strasse 4, 5000 Köln 1. TN: (02 21) 21 69 71. Samstag Nachmittag geschlossen. Spec: Literatur des 18.–20. Jahrhunderts in Erst- und Gesamtausgaben, Bibliophile und illustrierte Bücher, Kunst und Kulturgeschichte, Graphik. B: Sparkasse 9 472 051. CP: Köln 2937 96–508. V.D.A.

ANTIQUARIAT GRANIER G.M.B.H., Welle 9, 4800 Bielefeld 1. Prop: Jochen Granier. TN: (05 21) 6 71 48. Samstag Nachmittag und Montag geschlossen. Spec: Alte Drucke, Dekorative Graphik, Illustrierte Bücher, Literatur, Westfalen. Kat. 1 bis 2 jährlich. B: Bank für Gemeinwirtschaft 10 048 488. V.D.A.

JOCHEN GRANIER, Buch und Kunstauktionen, Gadderbaumer Strasse 22, 4800 Bielefeld 1. TN: (0521) 14 10 27. Samstag geschlossen. Spec: Wertvolle Bücher, Dekorative Graphik, Moderne Kunst. Kat. 4 bis 6 jährlich. B: Commerzbank 5 135 355. CP: Hannover 4009 01–304. V.D.A.

DAS GRAPHIK-KABINETT, Humboldtstrasse 80, 4000 Düsseldorf 1. Prop: Rainer Gerlinghaus. TN: (0211) 67 31 36. Gegründet 1911. Samstag und Mittwoch nachmittags geschlossen. Spec: Dekorative Graphik, Illustrierte Bücher, Städteansichten, Landkarten. B: Stadtsparkasse 11 029 253. V.D.A.

DIE GRAVÜRE, Rüttenschneider Strasse 56, 4300 Essen 1. Prop: Elisabeth Kellermann. TN: (0201) 79 31 82. Samstag Nachmittag geschlossen. Spec: Landkarten, Stadtansichten, Karikaturen, H. Daumier. B: Commerzbank 3 102 001. V.D.A.

ANTIQUARIAT GERO HABELT, Königsheimstrasse 12, 5300 Bonn 1. TN: (02 28) 23 20 15 T Buchhabelt Bonn Nach telefonischer Vereinbarung. Spec: Landeskunde, Rheinland, Volkskunde, Kulturgeschichte, Kunst. Kat. monatlich. V.D.A.

Dr. RUDOLF HABELT, G.m.b.H., AM BUCHENHANG 1, 5300 BONN.
(Postfach 150104). TN: 23 20 15. TA: Buchhabelt Bonn. Gegründet
1948. Lagerräume, nur nach Vereinbarung. Sehr Grosser Vorrat.
Spec: Archäologie; Altertums Wissenschaft. Cata: 4–6 pro Jahr.
Corresp: English, Français. B: Deutsche Bank, Bonn, Konto 0320481.
CP: Köln 526 76–501. V.D.A., B.V.D.B.

ANTIQUARIAT HARLINGHAUSEN, ARNDTSTRASSE 5, 4500
OSNABRÜCK. TN: (05 41) 43 39 29. Besuche nur nach Voranmeldung.
Kat. 1 jährlich. B: Stadtsparkasse 513 010. V.D.A.

EDMUND HERTLING, ZUM WINGERT 15, D-6200 AARBERGEN. TN:
(06120) 5179.

ANTIQUARIAT HEUBERGER, DÜPPELSTRASSE, KÖLN-DEUTZ 21. TN:
(02211) 88 49 14.

WERNER HEYBUTZKI, PFEILSTRASSE 8, 5000 KÖLN 1. TN: (0221)
216131. Gegründet 1948. Laden. Mittelgrosser Vorrat, auch neue
Bücher. Spec: Erstausgaben. Cata: 3 pro Jahr. Corresp: English. B:
Stadtsparkasse Köln 23782956. CP: Köln 90922–507. V.D.A.,
B.V.D.B., L.I.L.A.

THEO HILL, SCHILDERGASSE 107, 5000 KÖLN. TN: 21 29 72. Spec: Alte
und moderne Graphik. CP: Köln 56412. V.D.A.

JOHANNES HÖFS, GERTRUDENSTRASSE 33, KÖLN 1. TN: 23 28 77.

ANTIQUARIAT B. HÜNING, ROTHENBURG 52, 4400 MÜNSTER, TN:
(0251) 4 46 71.

ANTIQUARIAT GUNNAR KALDEWEY, POSTSTRASSE 3, 4000
DÜSSELDORF 1. TN: (02 11) 32 60 11. Nach Voranmeldung. Spec:
Einbände, Gastronomie, Illustrierte französische Bücher. Kat. V.D.A.

SIBYLLE KALDEWEY, Poststrasse 3, D-4000 Düsseldorf 1. TN: (0211) 32 70 34. Gegründet: 1975. Laden, Sonnabend geschlossen; Besuch vorzugweise nach Vereinbarung. Kleiner Vorrat. Spez: Literatur in Erstausgaben; illustrierte Bücher; Pressendrucke. Cata: 6 pro Jahr. Corresp: English. B: H. Aufhäuser, München, Kontonummer 1809202. CP: München 44787–807. M: V.D.A.

HANS-JÜRGEN KETZ, Scharnhorststrasse 92, D-4400 Münster. TN: (0251) 52 10 82. Gegründet: 1978. Besuch nur nach Vereinbarung Spez: Alte Uhren-Literatur und Graphik; Wissenschaft; Technik; Orts- und Landeskunde. Cata: alle 2–3 Jahre. Corresp: English, Français. B: Sparkasse Münster Kontonummer 306670. CP: Dortmund 762 19–462. M: V.D.A.

BUCH UND KUNSTANTIQUARIAT BRIGITTA KOWALLIK, Klarissenstrasse 5, 4040 Neuss. TN. (0 21 01) 2 48 32. Samstag Nachmittag geschlossen. Spec: Literatur, Geographie, Reisen, Naturwissenschaft, Dekorative Graphik. Kat. 1 jährlich. B: Dresdner Bank 111 381 100. CP: Essen 1080 52–433. V.D.A.

ANTIQUARIAT KRAEMER UND HANSEN, Arndstrasse 7, D-4500 Osnabrück.

REINHARD KUBALLE, Sutthauser Strasse 19, D-4500 Osnabrück. TN: (0541) 55287. Gegründet: 1971. Lagerräume, Samstag geschlossen; Besuch nur nach Vereinbarung. Sehr grosser Vorrat. Cata: 10 pro Jahr. Corresp: English. M: V.D.A.

WILHELM KUHRDT, Paulusstrasse 28, 4800 Bielefeld. Spec: Literatur; Geschichte; Erstausgaben. V.D.A.

WALTER KUTTNER, Lohmühler Berg 31, 5620 Velbert-:Neviges 15. TN: (002053) 3670. Gegründet 1949. Wohnung; nur Versand. Mittlerer Vorrat. Cata: 2 pro Jahr. Corresp: English, Français, B: Deutsche Bank 154 061 6. CP: Essen 244110 439.

GÜNTHER LEISTEN, St. Engelbertstrasse 24, D-5068 Odenthal-Voiswinkel. TN: (02202) 785 40. Gegründet 1951. Besuche nach Vereinbarung. Kleine Vorrat. Spec: Schöne und Seltene Bücher; Graphik. Corresp: English, Français. CP: 12 30 66–501. V.D.A., I.L.A.B.

Dr. KONRAD LIEBMANN, LORTZINGSTRASSE 1, 4500 OSNABRÜCK. TN: (0541) 23032. Gegründet 1972. Etagengeschäft. Dienstag–Samstag, 09.00–13.00 Kleines Lager. Spec: Erstausgaben Philosophie und Wissenschaft, Einbände, Graphik. Cata: 1 pro Jahr. Corresp: English, Français. B: Deutsche Bank Osnabrück, Konto Nr. 3883162. B.V.D.B., Landesverband der Niedersächsischen Buchhändler und Verleger.

CLAUS LINCKE, KÖNIGSALLEE 96, 4000 DÜSSELDORF. TN: 329257. Gegründet 1846. (als Deiters Buchhandlung). Spec: Alte und seltene Bücher; Erstausgaben; Topographie und Reisen; Alte und moderne Graphik; Illustrierte Bücher. CP: Köln 1977. V.D.A.

G. LOHMANN, TALSTRASSE 10, D-4802 HALLE (WESTFALEN). TN: (05201) 7483. Besuche nach Vereinbarung. V.D.A.

HANS MARCUS, RITTERSTRASSE 10, 4000 DÜSSELDORF. TN: 32 59 40 und 32 77 48. Gegründet 1936. Spec: Alte illustrierte, Bücher Graphik. B: Commerzbank, Düsseldorf. V.D.A.

HANS K. MATUSSEK, MARKTSTRASSE 13, 4054 NETTETAL. TN: (02153) 3057. V.D.A.

F. und A. MEHREN, TELGENWEG 8, 4400 MÜNSTER. TN: 26517. Spec.: Theologie, Philosophie. Cata: Monatlich. Corresp: English. B: Stadtsparkasse Kto. 95151742 (BLZ 40050150). CP: Dortmund 19163–463.

KONRAD MEUSCHEL, KAISERPLATZ 5, 5300 BONN. TN: 22 41 28. Gegründet 1969. Spec: Goetheana; autographen; alte und seltene Bücher. Corresp: English, Français. B: Dresdner Bank, Bonn, Konto 2 227 022. CP: Köln 2 389–500. V.D.A., VEBUKU (Schweiz), L.I.L.A.

CLEMENS MÜLLER, KAPELLENWEG 59, 5600 WUPPERTAL-BARMEN. TN: (0202) 59 89 11. Besuche nach Vereinbarung. Gegründet 1955. Spec: Topographie; Osteuropa. Südeuropa. Bankhaus V.D. Heydt, Wuppertal–Elberfeld. CP: Essen 85333. V.D.A.

OFFERMANN   UND   SCHMITZ,   ANTIQUARIAT, WITTELSBACHERSTRASSE 31, 5600 WUPPERTAL 2. Prop: Hans-Martin Schmitz. TN: (0202) 55 58 73. Nach Vereinbarung. Spec: Japanische und chinesische Graphik. Kat. V.D.A.

ORANGERIE-REINZ GALERIE, HELENENSTRASSE 2, 5000 KÖLN 1. Prop: Gerhard F. Reinz. TN: (0221) 234684. TA: Orangerie Köln. Gegründet 1959. Galerie, Sontag Montag und Samstag Nachmittag geschlossen. Spec: Graphik und Gemälde, 20. Jahrhundert. Cata. Ausstellungskataloge. Corresp: English, Français. B: Belgische Bank Köln, Kontonummer 2510–21 58. CP: Köln 166259–505. V.D.A., Rheinischer Kunsthändler Verband. Bundesverband deutscher Galerien.

ANTIQUARIAT PIERMONT, POSTFACH 21 02 32, 5300 BONN 2; ROLANDSTRASSE 13, 5480 REMAGEN-ROLANDSWERTH. TN: (022 28) 18 73. Nach Vereinbarung. Spec: Französische Bücher und Zeitschriften, Wirtschafts- und Sozialwissenschaften, Geschichte, Französische Revolution. Kat. B: Deutsche Bank Bonn 2 148 609. CP: Köln 2492 24–502. V.D.A.

ANTIQUARIAT CONSTANTIN POST, ZÜLPICHER STRASSE 16, 5000 KÖLN 1. TN: (02 21) 23 17 09. Samstag Nachmittag geschlossen. Spec: Illustrierte Bücher des 20. Jahrhunderts, Psychologie. Kat. 4 jährlich. B: Bankhaus I.II. Stein 10 008–001. CP: Köln 2524 88–508. V.D.A.

WALTER PRINZ UND SIEGFRIED UNVERZAGT, LIMBURGERSTRASSE 14–16, 5000 KÖLN 1. TN: (02211) 21 13 85.

ANTIQUARIAT J. REINHARDT, KIRCHPLATZ 10, D–802 HALLE (WESTF.). Prop: Paul E. Erdlen. TN: (05201) 2238. Gegründet 1949. Nach telefonischer Vereinbarung. Sehr grosser Vorrat. Spec: Judaica; Masonica; Occulta; Kulturgeschichte; Geschichte; Orts- und Landeskunde; Literatur; seltene Bücher. Corresp: English, Français. V.D.A., I.L.A.B., B.V.D.B.

FRANZ ROBERG, FRIEDRICHSTRASSE 45, 4000 DÜSSELDORF. TN: 38 31 48.

C. ROEMKE & CIE., APOSTELNSTRASSE 7, 5000 KÖLN. Prop: Friedrich Tacke und Ina Mennenöh. TN: (0221) 21 76 36. TA: Roemke Köln. Gegründet 1865. Laden. Sehr kleiner Vorrat, auch neue Bücher. Spec: Evangelische Theologie; Coloniensiae. B: Kölner Bank, Köln. CP: Köln 3440–503. B.V.D.B.

LUDWIG RÖHRSCHEID G.m.b.H., AM HOF 28, 5300 BONN. TN: 631281.
Telex: 08869523. Gegründet 1818. Seltene Bücher aller Gebiete,
Literatur, Geschichte, Landeskunde, Dekorative Graphik. Ankauf und
Verkauf ganzer Bibliotheken und wertvoller Einzelwerke. Kataloge auf
Wunsch. Corresp: English. B: Dresdner Bank, Bonn, Konto 2 077 681.
CP: Köln 34118–507.

HERMANN SACK, BAHNSTRASSE 61, 4000 DÜSSELDORF. TN: 36 99 55.

SCHARIOTH'SCHE ANTIQUARIAT, HUYSSENALLEE 58, D–4300 ESSEN
1. TN: (0201) 22 49 06.

KUNSTANTIQUARIAT   Dr.   GERHARD   SCHNEIDER,
RHODE-GOLDSIEPEN 12, 5960 OLPE. TN: (027 61) 6 12 15. Nach
telefonischer Vereinbarung. Spec: Alte Stadtansichten und
Landkarten, Dekorative Graphik, Ansichtenwerke. Kat
unregelmässig. B: Sparkasse Olpe–Drolshagen–Wenden 1 446. CP
Dortmund 1193 72 460. V.D.A.

FERDINAND SCHÖNINGH, DOMHOF 4C, 4500 OSNABRÜCK. (Postfach
4060). TN: 285 24. Gegründet 1888. Laden und Lagerräume, Montag
bis Freitag 15.00–18.00 und nach Vereinbarung. Sehr grosser Vorrat
Spec: Geschichte; Literatur; Kunst. Cata: 6 pro Jahr. Corresp: English
Français. B: Deutsche Bank, Osnabrück, Konto 6–02342 und
Commerzbank, Osnabrück, Konto 53–415 32. CP: Hannover 946 46
V.D.A.

HANNO SCHREYER, EUSKIRCHENERSTRASSE 57–59, 5300 BONN 1. TN
621059. TA: Buchschreyer Bonn. Gegründet 1953. Laden und
Lagerräume, Samstag Nachmittag geschlossen. Grosser Vorrat. Spec
Alte Landkarten, alte dekorative Graphik, illustrierte Bücher 15. bi
20. Jahrhundert. Corresp: English, Français. B: Sparkasse Bonn
Konto 9035. CP: Köln 121364–503. V.D.A., L.L.A.B.

A. SINDERN, JUNGBRUNNENWEG 15, 4800 BIELEFELD. TN: 7 17 67.

D. SKUTTA, HUMBOLDTSTRASSE 80, 4000 DÜSSELDORF 1. TN: 67 31 36.

Th. STENDERHOFF & CO., ALTER FISCHMARKT 21, 4400 MÜNSTER
Prop: Theo. Hobbeling. TN: 44749. Gegründet 1912. Laden, Samsta
Nachmittag Geschlossen. Sehr grosser Vorrat. Spec: Alte Bücher
Theologie, Philosophie, Geschichte, Literatur, dekorative Graphik
Städteansichten, Landkarten. Cata: 8 pro Jahr. Corresp: English
Français. B: Deutsche Bank, Münster, Konto 104 901. CP: Dortmun
858 20–461. V.D.A.

STERN-VERLAG JANSSEN & CO., Postfach 7820, Friedrichstrasse 26, 4000 Düsseldorf. Prop: H. und K. Janssen. TN: (0211) 373033. Gegründet 1900. Laden, Samstag Nachmittag geschlossen. Sehr grosser Vorrat, auch Neue Bücher. Spec: Geisteswissenschaften; Modernes Antiquariat. Cata: 3 pro Jahr. Corresp: English, Français. B: Stadtsparkasse Düsseldorf. Konto 47 00 00 13. CP: Köln 13976. B.V.D.B.

ANTIQUARIAT NIKOLAUS STRUCK, Wilhelmstrasse 5, 5449 Pfalzfeld. TN: (067 46) 2 18. Mo–Fr. morgens offen. Spec: Alte Stadtansichten, Landkarten, Dekorative Graphik, Atlanten, Ansichtenwerke, Landes-und Ortsgeschichte. Kat. ca. 6 jährlich. B: Kreissparkasse Rhein-Hunsrück 12/116 190. CP: Ludwigshafen 635 67–672. V.D.A.

WOLFGANG SYMANCZYK, Hubertusweg 32, 4040 Neuss. TN: 46 43 23. Gegründet 1958. Wohnung und Lagerräume, Samstag Nachmittag geschlossen. Grosser Vorrat, auch neue Bücher. Spec: Klassische Philologie; Geschichte der Wissenschaften. Cata: 12 pro Jahr. Corresp: English. B: Stadtsparkasse Neuss, Konto 23 46 09. CP: Köln 220 954–505.

HANS TROJANSKI, Blumenstrasse 11, 4000 Düsseldorf. TN. 13 24 34. Gegründet 1924. B: Bankhaus Simon, Düsseldorf. CP: Essen 3895–436.

UKIYO-E GALERIE, Citadellstrasse 14, 4000 Düsseldorf 1. Prop: Herbert Egenolf. TN: (02 11) 32 05 50. Nach telefonischer Vereinbarung. Spec: Japanische Farbholzschnitte und japanische illustrierte Bücher des 18.–20. Jahrhunderts. Kat. 1 jährlich. B: Commerzbank 1 714 120. V.D.A.

URBS & ORBIS, Göddertzgarten 42. 5309 Meckenheim-Merl. Prop: Klaus Semmel TN: (022 25) 35 88. Gegründet 1954.

KUNSTANTIQUARIAT VALENTIEN, Niederwall 14, 4800 Bielefeld. Prop: H. Valentien. TN: (0521) 64420. Gegründet 1954. Laden. Montags nur nach Vereinbarung Mittelgrosser Vorrat, auch neue Bücher. Spec: alte Städteansichten und Landkarten. B: Sparkasse Bielefeld 20156. B.L.Z. 48050161. V.D.A.

VENATOR, KG., CÄCILIENSTRASSE 48 (IM KUNSTHAUS LEMPERTZ) 5000 KÖLN. Prop: Rolf Venator. TN: 23 29 62. Gegründet 1946. Laden, Samstag Nachmittag geschlossen. Sehr kleiner Vorrat. Spec: Alte und moderne Bibliophilie; Dekorative Graphik; Auktionen. Cata. Corresp: English, Français. B: Bankhaus J.H. Stein, Köln, Konto 34002. CP: Köln 12010. V.D.A.

Dr. HELMUT VESTER, FRIEDRICHSTRASSE 7, 4000 DÜSSELDORF. TN: 382843. Gegründet 1954. Spec: Medizin, Naturwissenschaften. B: Kreissparkasse, Düsseldorf. CP: Köln 21149. V.D.A.

GALERIE VÖMEL, KÖNIGSALLEE 30, 4000 DÜSSELDORF. Prop: Alex. und Edwin Vömel. TN: (0211) 32 74 22. TA: Galerievoemel Düsseldorf. Spec: Gemälde, Handzeichnungen, Skulpturen, Graphik. CP: Köln 68204–502. V.D.A.*

WERNER   WEICK,   BUCH-   UND   KUNSTANTIQUARIAT, STERNSTRASSE 2, AM MARKT, 5300 BONN 1. TN: 0228/657822 Gegründet 1975. Laden. Kleiner Vorrat. Spec: Alte und Seltene Bücher: Illustrierte Bücher, Alte Stadtansichten; Landkarten, Dekorative und Alte Graphik, Topographie. Corresp: English. B: Dresdner Bank Bonn, Kontonummer 2313 285. CP: Köln 187063–504.

H. Th. WENNER, POSTFACH 4307, HEGERSTRASSE 2–3, 4500 OSNABRÜCK. TN: (0541) 25516. Telex: 94955. Gegründet 1945. Laden und Lagerraum, Samstag Nachmittag geschlossen. Sehr grosser Vorrat. Cata: 5–6 pro Jahr. Corresp: English. B: Deutsche Bank, Kontonummer 6/07010. CP: Hannover 17182–300. V.D.A.

ECKHARD WÜNNENBERG, HOLLESTRASSE 1, HAUS D. TECHNIK, D-4300 ESSEN.

AUVERMANN UND REISS KG, ZUM TALBLICK 2, 6246 GLASHÜTTEN. Prop: Detlev Auvermann. TN: (0 61 74) 69 47/69 48. Besuche nur nach Voranmeldung. TA: Interbook Königstein. Spec: Frühsozialismus, Romanistik, Hispanistik, Geisteswissenschaftliche Zeitschriften und Monographien. B: Bethmann Bank Frankfurt 27 097 500. CP: Frankfurt 2603 87 601. V.D.A.

"BIBLIOGRAPHICUM", HAUPTSTRASSE 194, 6900 HEIDELBERG. Prop:
Erna Tenner. V.D.A.

GALERIE BRUMME FRANKFURT, BRAUBACHSTR. 34, 6000
FRANKFURT-AM-MAIN. Prop: Siegfried, Dörte and Edmund Brumme.
TN: (0611) 28 72 63. Gegründet 1950. Laden, Montag Morgen und
Samstag nachmittag geschlossen. Spec: Landkarten, Alte Graphik,
Topographie. Cata: 1 pro Jahr. Corresp: English, Französisch. B:
ADCA, Frankfurt, Konto Nr. 600 31 332. CP: Frankfurt 5263–602.
V.D.A., Verband Hessischer Antiquitätenhändler.
Auch: KIRSCHGARTEN 11, 6500 MAINZ. TN: (061 31) 22 80 74.
Montag Morgen und Samstag Nachmittag geschlossen. B: Hypo-Bank
4 430 130 302; Volksbank 186 832 010.
Und: TAUNUSSTRASSE 40, 6200 WIESBADEN.TN: (061 21) 52 66 63.
Montag Morgen und Samstag Nachmittag geschlossen. B: Dresdner
Bank 100 419 000. CP: Frankfurt 900 77–609. Spec: Atlanten,
Geographie, Stadteansichten, Landkarten, Illustrierte Bücher des
15.–19. Jahrhunderts. Kataloge 1 jährlich. V.D.A.

SIEGFRIED BRUMME, BUCH UND KUNSTANTIQUARIAT,
KIRSCHGARTEN 11, 6500 MAINZ. TN: (0 61 31) 22 80 74. Nach
Vereinbarung. Spec: Atlanten, Geographie, Städteansichten,
Landkarten, Illustrierte Bücher des 15.–19. Jahrhunderts. B: Dresdner
Bank 237 033 500. CP: Frankfurt 361 63–609. V.D.A.

IV

MAIN, TAUNUS & PFALZ

Postcodes: Postleitzahlen
6000+

100 DARMSTADT	6700 LUDWIGSHAFEN
252 DIEZ	6500 MAINZ
072 DREIEICH	6082 MÖRFELDEN
000 FRANKFURT-AM-MAIN	6370 OBERURSEL
300 GIESSEN	6050 OFFENBACH
246 GLASHÜTTEN	6600 SAARBRÜCKEN
900 HEIDELBERG	6226 WALLUF
238 HOFHEIM	6731 WEIDENTHAL
750 KAISERSLAUTERN	6200 WIESBADEN
240 KÖNIGSTEIN	

ANTIQUARIAT COBET, EYSSENECKSTRASSE 40, D-6000 FRANKFURT AM
MAIN 1. TN: 591505.

ANTIQUARIAT "CHRISTO", ALTE GASSE 67, FRANKFURT M. Prop: Sattler Missirloglou. TN: 069 283579. Gegründet 1956. Laden. Grosser Vorrat. Spec: Geschichte, Kunst, bis 1920. Corresp: English.

HARRI DEUTSCH, NATURWISSENUSCHAFTLICHE FACHBUCH-HANDLUNG, GRÄFSTRASSE 47, 6000 FRANKFURT AM MAIN TN: (8611) 777338. Laden. Sehr kleiner Vorrat, auch neue Bücher. Spec: Naturwissenschaften. Corresp: English. CP: Frankfurt/M. 112722–607. B.V.D.B.

DRESDNER   ANTIQUARIAT   PAUL   ALICKE, KURT-SCHUMACHER-STRASSE 33–35, D-6000 FRANKFURT AM MAIN. TN: (0611) 281027. TA: Paulbooks, FrankUfurtmain. Laden. Sehr grosser Vorrat. Spec: Kochbücher; Automobilen; Eisenbahnen; Literatur. Corresp: English, Français, Español, Italiano. B: Gross Gerauer Volksbank, Kontonummer: 60 29 604. CP: Frankfurt 41 429–606. M: Akademie für Welthandel.

ANTIQUARIAT GEORG EWALD, GROSSE BOCKENHEIMER STRASSE 29 6000 FRANKFURT 1.TN: 069 287413. Gegründet 1982. Laden, morgens und Samstag Nachmittag geschlossen. Grosser Vorrat. Spec: Deutsche Literatur 20. Jahrhundert; Exil-Literatur 1933–1948. Corresp English, Francais. B: Frankfurter Sparkasse v. 1822, Konto 24947: BLZ 500 50201. CP: 139727–603, PS Frankfurt. B.V.D.B. Hessische Buchhändlerverband.

JOSEPH FACH, FAHRGASSE 8, 6000 FRANKFURT-AM-MAIN. 1. Prop Werner und Rolf Fach. TN: (069) 287761. Gegründet 1928. Grosse Vorrat. Spec: Graphik; Handzeichnungen; Illustrierte Bücher Corresp: English, Français. CP: Frankfurt-am-Main 115607–603 V.D.A.

FRANKFURTER BÜCHERSTUBE, BÖRSENSTRASSE 2–4, 6000 FRANKFURT-AM-MAIN. Prop: Richard Schumann. TN: 28 14 94 Gegründet 1920. Spec: Kunstgeschichte; Illustrierte Bücher; Alte Kinderbücher. B: Georg Hauck & Sohn, Frankfurt-am-Main. CP Frankfurt-am-Main 47420. V.D.A.

FRANKFURTER KUNSTKABINETT, HANNA BEKKER VOM RATH G.m.b.H., BÖRSENPLATZ 13-15, 6000 FRANKFURT-AM-MAIN. Prop Joachim Cuppers and Mongüt Wegner. TN: (0611) 281085 Gegründet 1947. Laden und Lagerräuume Samstag Nachmitta geschlossen. Spec: Kunst des 20. Jahrhunderts. Cata. Corresp: English Français. B: Dresdner Bank AG, Frankfurt-am-Main, Konto 1 61 599–00.

GALERIE OLAF GREISER, Schröderstrasse 14, 6900 Heidelberg. TN: (062 21) 40 15 87. nach Vereinbarung. Spec: Gemälde und Handzeichnungen, Künstlergraphik 15.–20 Jahrhundert, Stadtansichten, Landkarten, Heidelbergensien. Kat. 1 bis 2 jährlich. B: Vereinsbank 27–10 770. V.D.A.

JOHANNES GUTENBERG BUCHHANDLUNG, Grosse Bleiche 29, 6500 Mainz. (Auch In der Universität). Prop: Josef A. Kohl. TN: 24890. Gegründet 1946. B: Mainzer Volksbank, Mainz. CP: Ludwigshafen 27790. V.D.A.

OTTO HARRASSOWITZ, Taunusstrasse 5, 6200 Wiesbaden. Prop: Felix Oswald Weigel. TN: 52 10 46. Gegründet 1872. Lagerräume. Grosser Vorrat, auch neue Bücher. Spec: Deutsche Literatur; Orientalistik. Cata. Corresp: English, Français. B: Deutsche Bank, Wiesbaden. CP: Frankfurt-am-Main, 654 27. V.D.A.

AUGUST HASE, im Trutz 2, 6000 Frankfurt-am-Main. Prop: Anna-Maria Hase. TN: (0611) 55 37 77. Gegründet 1932. Samstag Nachmittag geschlossen. Spec: Autographen; Graphik; Kunst; Postgeschichte. Cata: 3. pro Jahr. B: Stadtsparkasse, Frankfurt am Main. CP: Frankfurt-am-Main 524 89. V.D.A.

D. HOBUCHER Alt Rödellgeun 13, 6000 Frankfurt am Main 90. TN: 7 89 46 61.

ERNST HOFFMANN, Weissadlergasse 3, 6000 Frankfurt-am-Main. Prop: Klaus Peter Hoffmann. TN: 28 37 81. TA: Buchhoffmann Frankfurt-am-Main. Gegründet 1929. Laden, Samstag Nachmittag geschlossen. Grosser Vorrat. Spec: Inkunabeln; Holzschnittbücher; Humanismus; Reformation; Alte Drucke; Deutsche Literatur; Dekorative Graphik. Cata: 2 pro Jahr. Corresp: English, Italiano. B: Bankhaus Gebrüder Bethmann, Konto 15404–5–00. CP: Frankfurt-am-Main 22760. V.D.A., I.L.A.B.

WILHELM HOFMANN G.m.b.H., Bismarckstrasse 98, 6700 Ludwigshafen. TN: 0621/516001. Gegründet 1889. Laden. Spec: Landkarten und Literatur, Pfalz und Rhein. CP: Ludwigshafen 4663. V.D.A.

KARL MARX BUCHHANDLUNG, G.m.b.H., JORDANSTRASSE 11, 6000
FRANKFURT 90. TN: 069 778803 & 778807. Gegründet 1970. 2 Läden
und Lagerraum, Samstag Nachmittag geschlossen. Nur nach
Vereinbarung. Grosser Vorrat, auch neue Bücher. Spec:
Arbeiterbewegung; Geschichte (bes. 20. Jahrhundert); Literatur (bes.
20. Jahrhundert); Philosophie. Cata: 3 oder 4 pro Jahr. Corresp:
English, Français, Italiano, Español. B: Dresdner Bank,
Frankfurt/Main BLZ 50080000 Konto 220630400. CP:
Frankfurt/Main BLZ 50010060 Konto 328050.609. B.V.D.B.
Hessischer Landesverband.

KEIP, KG WISSENSCHAFTLICHES ANTIQUARIAT HAINERWEG
46–48, 6000 FRANKFURT-AM-MAIN 70. TN: 614011. Gegründet 1959.
Sehr Grosser Vorrat. Spec: Recht; Wirtschaft Geschichte und
Gesellschaft; zeitschriften; Altedrucke. Corresp: English. B:
Dresdner Bank AG, 3500068, (BLZ 500 800 00) Frankfurt-am-Main.
CP: Frankfurt-am-Main 213810–603. V.D.A.

ANTIQUARIAT JÜRGEN KOCH, 1 MITTELWEG 9, FRANKFURT AM
MAIN. TN: 59 20 09. Spec: Einzelwerken und Sammlungen,
Graphiken und Postkarten.

KUNSTANTIQUARIAT PETER H. KÖHL, DUDWEILER STRASSE 10,
6600 SAARBRÜCKEN 3. TN: (06 81) 3 32 42. Samstag Nachmittag
geschlossen. Spec: Alte Stadtansichten und Landkarten, Saarländische
Orts- und Landesgeschichte, Alte und dekorative Graphik, Illustrierte
Bücher. Kat. 1 oder 2 jährlich. B: Deutsche Bank 0 409 904. V.D.A.

V. KÖRNER, KETTENHOFWEG 57, FRANKFURT AM MAIN 1. TN: 72 35 73.

MEICHSNER UND DENNERLEIN, DREIEICHSTRASSE 52, FRANKFURT
AM MAIN 70. TN: 61 69 65.

GÜNTER NOBIS, FORSTSTRASSE 12, 6200 WIESBADEN. TN: (06121)
541106. Gegründet 1962. Spec: Illustrierte Bücher; Literatur; Buch-
und Schriftwesen; Kulturgeschichte; alte Drucke. Cata:
Unregelmässig. Corresp: English, Français. B: Dresdner Bank
Frankfurt am Main, Konto Nr. 2 031 188. CP: Frankfurt 688 36–607
V.D.A.

W. OTT, FRANKFURTER STRASSE 56, 6050 OFFENBACH (MAIN). TN: 81 6:
79.

RUDOLF PATZER, Mainzer Berg 23, 6739 Weidenthal. TN: 06329
362. TA: Patzer, Weidenthal (Pfalz). Gegründet 1698. Wohnung, nur
nach Vereinbarung. Grosser Vorrat. Spec: Bibliographie und
Buchwesen; Zeitschriften. Cata: 4, und 3–6 Listen pro Jahr. Corresp:
English. B: Kreissparkasse. Bad Dürkheim. Konto 02503365.

RAINER PÖLCK, Antiquariat-Grafikum, Alt Rödelheim 15,
Frankfurt am Main 90. TN: 7 89 39 45.

REISS UND AUVERMANN, Buch- und Kunstantiquariat, Zum
Talblick 2, 6246 Glashütten im Taunus. Prop: Godebert M. Reiss
and Manfred Samtleben. TN: (061 74) 69 47 und 6948. Besuche nur
nach Voranmeldung. Spec: Alte Drucke, Naturwissenschaften,
Illustrierte Bucher, Topographie, Dekorative Graphik. Cat.
(Auktionen). B: Bethmann Bank Frankfurt 27 363 700. CP: Frankfurt
3195 95–607. V.D.A.

KUNSTHANDLUNG HELMUT H. RUMBLER, Braubachstrasse 36,
6000 Frankfurt-am-Main. TN: (069) 29 11 42. Gegründet 1970.
Galerie. Nur alte Meistergraphik. Grossen Lager. Cata: 1 oder 2 pro
Jahr. Corresp: English, Français, Italiano. B: Frankfurter Volksbank
E.G. 14410–0; CP: Frankfurt/M 32297–605. V.D.A.

Dr. MARTIN SÄNDIG G.m.b.H., Kaiser-Friedrich-Ring 70, 6200
Wiesbaden. Prop: Kraus-Thomson-Organization Limited. Gegründet
1923. Lagerräume, Mittelgrosser Vorrat. Spec: Geschichte der
Naturwissenschaften; Mathematik; Technik. Cata: 6 pro Jahr.
Corresp: English; Français.. B.V.D.B., V.D.A.

ANTIQUARIAT UND VERLAG GEORG SAUER, Gerichtsstrasse 7,
6240 Königstein im Taunus. TN: (0 61 74) 36 50. Nach
Vereinbarung. Spec: Rechts- Wirtschafts-und Sozialwissenschaften,
Geschichte, Literatur, Francofurtensien. Kat. 4 jahrlich. B:
Bethmann-Bank, Frankfurt 29 805 700. CP: Frankfurt 228 92–601.
V.D.A.

GESCHWISTER SCHMIDT, Karl-Marx-Strasse 15, 6750
Kaiserslautern. Prop: Fritz Schmidt. TN: (0631) 9 20 25. V.D.A.

I. SCHMIDT UND C. GÜNTHER, Ubierstrasse 20, 6238 Hofheim.
TN: (061 92) 53 86. Spec: Kunstbucher, Pressendrucke, Bücher mit
orig. Graphik, Bibliophilie, Französische Bucher des 18. Jahrhunderts.
Kat. 2 bis 3 jahrlich. B: Hypo-Bank Mainz 4 430 300 607.
Kreissparkasse 2 089 940. CP: Frankfurt 740 95 603. V.D.A.

KARL FRIEDRICH SCHNEIDER, SELTERSWEG 38, 6300 GIESSEN. TN: (0641) 743 52. Wissenschaftlicher Literatur; Hessiaca; Dekorative Graphik. V.D.A.

ANTIQUARIAT SCHRAGE, SCHAUMBURGERSTRASSE 20, D-6252 DIEZ.

H. SCHUTT, ARNSBURGER STRASSE 76, FRANKFURT AM MAIN 60. TN: 43 95 43.

S. SEIFFERT, HÖHENSTRASSE 43, FRANKFURT AM MAIN 60. TN: 49 61 30.

BURKHARD F. STADELMANN, DIESELSTRASSE 5, 6070 LANGEN TN: (061 03) 7 98 36. Besuche nach Vereinbarung. V.D.A.

KURT G. STOLZENBERG, GR. SEESTRASSE 63, FRANKFURT AM MAIN 90. TN: 70 13 79.

TECHNISCHES ANTIQUARIAT, LAUTESCHLAGERSTRASSE 4, 6100 DARMSTADT. Prop: Dipl.-Wirtsch.-Ing. Rudolf Wellnitz. TN: 76548. Gegründet 1948. Laden und Lagerräume, Samstag Nachmittag geschlossen. Sehr grosser Vorrat, auch neue Bücher. Spec: Mathematik; Naturwissenschaft; Technik. Cata. Corresp: English, Français. B: Sparkasse, Darmstadt, Konto 557269. CP: Frankfurt-am-Main 77213. V.D.A.

Dr. HELMUT TENNER K.G., SOFIENSTRASSE 5, 6900 HEIDELBURG. TN: (062 21) 2 42 37. TA: Buchtenner Heidelburg. Gegründet 1864 Buroräume im 1. Stock: Samstag geschlossen. Kleiner Vorrat. Spec Erstausgaben; Deutsche Literatur; Naturwissenschaften Auktionen. Corresp: English, Français. B: Deutsche Bank Heidelburg Konto Nr. 04/63240. CP: Karlsruhe 18302–755. V.D.A.

BIBLIOGRAPHICUM E. TENNER, HAUPTSTRASSE 194, 6900 HEIDELBURG. TN: (062 21) 2 62 52. Samstag Nachmittag geschlossen Spec: Städteansichten, Landkarten, Dekorative Graphik. V.D.A.

TRESOR AM RÖMER, GALERIE, BUCH UND KUNST ANTIQUARIAT BRAUBACHSTRASSE 15, PASSAGE TECHN. RATHAUS, FRANKFURT 1. TN 28 12 48.

KARL VONDERBANK, KG., GOETHESTRASSE 11, 6000 FRANKFURT-AM-MAIN. TN: 28 24 90. Gegründet 1866. Laden Samstag Nachmittag geschlossen. Spec: Alte und Moderne Graphik Kunst. Corresp: English, Français. CP: Frankfurt-am-Main 9758 V.D.A.

ELISABETH WELLNITZ, Sachsenstrasse 35, 6100 Darmstadt. TN: (06151) 54716. Gegründet 1959. Wohnung, nur nach Vereinbarung. Sehr kleiner Vorrat. Spec: Geschichte; Politik; Wehrwesen. Cata: 2 pro Jahr. Corresp: English. B: Sparkasse Darmstadt, BLZ 508 501 50 Konto 54 56 51. CP: Frankfurt-am-Main (BLZ 500 100 60) 6409–606.

WIENER BÜCHERSTUBE, Eschersheimer Landstrasse 18, 6000 Frankfurt-am-Main. Prop: Dr. Maria Sieber. TN: 55 60 43. Spec: Deutsche Literatur; Wissenschaften; Dekorative Graphik. V.D.A.

ARNO WINTERBERG, Buch und Kunstantiquariat, Blumenstrasse 15, 6900 Heidelberg. TN: (0 62 21) 2 26 31. Samstag nachmittag geschlossen. Spec: Alte und moderne Graphik, Zeichnungen und Gemälde, Illustrierte Bücher. B: Volksbank Heidelberg 29 354 006. V.D.A.

WISSENSCHAFTLICHES ANTIQUARIAT UND BUCHVERTRIEBS GMBH, Sandweg 115, Frankfurt am Main 1. TN: 44 50 22.

ZEIL-ANTIQUARIAT, Zeil 24, 6000 Frankfurt-am-Main. Prop: Mady Henle. TN: 284914. Gegründet 1975. Laden. Mittelgrosser Vorrat, auch wenig neue Bücher. Corresp: English, Français. B: Deutsche Bank Frankfurt, Konto Nr. 2630861. CP: Frankfurt 29885–608.

V

SOUTH WESTERN GERMANY: SUDWEST- DEUTSCHLAND: ALLEMAGNE (SUDOUEST)

Postcode: Postleitzahl 7000+

7080 AALEN	7750 KONSTANZ
7470 ALBSTADT	7947 MENGEN
7936 ALLMENDINGEN	
7570 BADEN-BADEN	7537 REMCHINGEN
7847 BADENWEILER	7410 REUTLINGEN
7180 CRAILSHEIM	7407 ROTTENBURG
7300 ESSLINGEN	7811 ST. PETER
7505 ETTLINGEN	7000 STUTTGART
7800 FREIBURG in BR.	7400 TÜBINGEN
7340 GEISLINGEN	
7824 HINTERZARTEN	7900 ULM
7100 HEILBRONN	7987 WEINGARTEN

B.M.C.F. ANTIQUARIAT, Am Rain 23, 7936 Almendingen. Prop: Rainer Feucht. TN: (07391) 1276. Gegründet 1975. Wohnung, nur nach Vereinbarung. Grosser Vorrat. Spec: Curiosa, Folklore Karikatur, Erotica, Hexenwesen, Utopisch-Phantastische-Literatur. Homosexualität. Cata: Regelmässig. Corresp: English, Français Español. B: Postscheck Stuttgart 66367–706.

ANTIQUARIAT ERIKA BARTSCH, Gottfried-Keller-Strasse 10 7505 Ettlingen. TN: (0 72 43) 34 26. Nach Vereinbarung. Spec Kinderbücher, Illustrierte Bücher. Kat. ca 2 jährlich. V.D.A.

HERBERT BLANK, Melonenstrasse 54, 7000 Stuttgart 75. TN: (0′ 11) 47 21 30. Nach Vereinbarung. Spec: Philosophie, Deutsch Literatur in Erst- und Gesamtausgaben, Illustrierte Bücher un Pressendrucke, Germanistik. B: Landesgirokasse 2 892 515. CP Stuttgart 770 44-704. V.D.A.

BROCKHAUS ANTIQUARIUM, Am Wallgraben 127, 700 Stuttgart 80. (Postfach 800 205). TN: (0711) 29 55 51. Telex 7255705 (brod.) TA: Fab, Stuttgart. Spec: Geographie, Ethnologie Africana, Americana, Asiatica, Arctica, Alte Reisen in Ferne Länder Cata. Corresp: English. B: Deutsche Bank, Stuttgart, Konto 11–2 818. CP: Stuttgart 24 35–708. V.D.A., B.V.D.B.

BUCH UND KUNST, Münzgasse 16, 7750 Konstanz. Prop: Georg Scheringer. TN: (0 75 31) 2 41 71. Samstag Nachmittag geschlossen Spec: Bücher 15.–20 Jahrhundert, Kunst, Landeskunde, Geistes- un Naturwissenschaften. B: Sparkasse 063 073. CP: Karlsruhe 115′ 01–758. V.D.A.

BÜCHERSTUBE AM SEE, Kreuzlingerstrasse 11, 775 Konstanz-Bodensee. Prop: Peter Neser. TN: (075 31) 2 21 76. Spec Geisteswissenschaften, Geschichte, Badensia. Kat. 5 jährlich. E Volksbank 542 903. CP: Karlsruhe 394 43–758. V.D.A.

H. FRANZ, Jakobstrasse 8, 7000 Stuttgart 1. TN: 24 52 08

R. GAITANIDES, Wagenburgstrasse 111, 7000 Stuttgart A. TN: 4 11 65.
auch Senefelderstrasse 74a, 7000 Stuttgart. TN: 62 80 80.

KARL GESS, KANZLEISTRASSE 5, 7750 KONSTANZ. (Postfach 190). Prop: Eberhard Gess. TN: (07531) 22320. TA: Buch Gess Konstanz. Gegründet 1842. Laden. Mittelgrosser Vorrat. Spec: Geschichte; Philosophie; Literaturwissenschaft. Cata: 4 oder 5 pro Jahr. Corresp: English, Français. B: Deutsche Bank, Kontonummer 124 800, Komstanz; Midland Bank Account 557 619, London. CP: Karlsruhe 305. V.D.A.

J.J. HECKENHAUER, HOLZMARKT 5, 7400 TÜBINGEN. (Postfach 1728). Prop: Herbert Friedrich Sonnewald. tn: (07071) 23018. Gegründet 1823. Laden. Sehr grosser Vorrat. Spec: Theologie, Geschichte; Slavis tik, Länder. Cata: 2 pro Jahr. Corresp: English, Français, Español, Russisch. B: Landesgirokasse, Tübingen, Konto 4700 337. CP: Stuttgart 929–704.V.D.A.

HEINZELMANN UND HERRMANN, ALEXANDERSTRASSE 157, 7000 STUTTGART 1. TN: 6 40 65 31.

ADOLF KAPP, BAHNHOFSTRASSE 17, 7407 ROTTENBURG. (Postfach 46). Prop: Alfons Unteregger. TN: 1760. Gegründet 1923. Laden und Lagerräume, Samstag Nachmittag geschlossen. Mittelgrosser Vorrat. Spec: Katholische Theologie. Cata: periodische. Corresp: English, Français. B: Volksbank Rottenburg, Konto 10974008. CP: Stuttgart 40776. B.V.D.B.

HEINRICH KERLER, PLATZGASSE 26, 7900 ULM. (Postfach 2668). Prop: Winfried Bader. TN: (0731) 63978. Gegründet 1877. Laden, Samstag Nachmittag geschlossen. Mittelgrosser Vorrat. Spec: Landeskunde Baden-Württemberg. Cata: 4 oder 5 pro Jahr. Corresp: English, Français. B: Sparkasse Ulm, Konto 113 674. Ulmer Volksbank, Konto 185 0008. CP: Stuttgart 12143–700. B.V.D.B.

ANTIQUARIAT PETER KIEFER, KIRCHSTRASSE 4, D-7537 REMCHINGEN-WILFERDINGEN. Spec: Afrika.

KARL KNÖDLER, KATHERINENSTRASSE 8–10, 7410 REUTLINGEN. TN: 35004. Gegründet 1936. Laden und Lagerräume, Mittwoch Nachmittag geschlossen. Grosser Vorrat, auch neue Bücher. Cata: Listen für Spezialgebiete. Corresp: English. B: Dresdner Bank, Reutlingen. CP: Stuttgart 180 09. V.D.A., B.V.D.B.

VALENTIN KOERNER G.m.b.H., H.-SIELCKENSTRASSE 36, 7570 BADEN-BADEN. (POSTFACH 304). TN: (07221) 22 423. Gegründet 1954. Wohnung, nur nach Vereinbarung. Mittelgrosser Vorrat. Spec: Bibliographie 16. Jahrhunderts. Corresp: English, Français. B: Dresdner Bank, Konto 622 39 77. CP: 92121–757. V.D.A., B.V.D.B.

MARGOT LÖRCHER O.H.G., HEUBERGSTRASSE 42, 7000 STUTTGART 1.
Prop: Dorrit Lörcher und Dr. Heide Bücklein. TN: (0711) 461248.
Gegründet 1971. Wohnung; Besuche nur nach Vereinbarung. Kleiner
Vorrat. Spec: Japanische Farbholzschnitte. Cata: 4 pro Jahr. Corresp:
English. B: Bayer. Vereinsbank München (BLZ 700 202 70) Konto
Nr. 604223. CP: 1296 89-708 Stuttgart. V.D.A., Landesverband d.
Kunst und Antiquitatenhändler Baden-Württembergs e.V. (auch in
München).

RENATE MEHRDORF, KARL-JÄGER-STRASSE 6, D-7100 HEILBRONN.
TN: (07131) 53805.

OTTO MOSER, TÖLZERSTRASSE 24, 8022 GRÜNWALD. TN: (089) 6 41 12
65. Dekorative Graphik. V.D.A.

MÜLLER & GRÄFF, CALWERSTRASSE 54, 7000 STUTTGART-1. TN:
(0711) 294174 Gegründet 1802. Spec: Kunst; Geschichte; Literatur:
Graphik; Baden-Württembergische Landeskunde; Theologie. B:
Dresdner Bank, Stuttgart. CP: Stuttgart. 1618 179. V.D.A.

FRITZ NEIDHARDT, RELENBERGSTRASSE 20, 7000 STUTTGART. TN: 22
33 20. Gegründet 1952. Lageräume Besuche nach Vereinbarung,
Samstag geschlossen. Kleiner Vorrat. Spec: Schöne illustrierte Bücher
und Graphik. Corresp: English. B: Girokasse Stuttgart Konto 2035626.
V.D.A.

PETER NESER [BÜCHERSTUBE AM SEE], KREUZLINGERSTRASSE 11,
7750 KONSTANZ-BODENSEE. TN: (07531) 2 21 76. TA: Bücherstube
Konstanz. Gegründet 1925. Laden, Mittwoch Nachmittag geschlossen.
Mittelgrosser Vorrat, auch neue Bücher. Spec: Gechichte; Deutsche
Literatur; Politik; alte Drucke. Cata: 8 pro Jahr. Corresp: English. B
Volksbank, Konstanz. V.D.A.

L. G. RÖTH, PFARRSTRASSE 21, 7000 STUTTGART 1. TN: 24 18 52.

ANTIQUARIAT GERH. RENNER, AN D. UNTEREN BERG (FUCHSFARM)
POSTFACH 1648, 7470 ALBSTADT 2. TN: (07432) 5114. Gegründer
1957. Laden, Besuche Nach Vereinbarung. Sehr grosser Vorrat, auch
neue Bücher. Spec: alte Wissenschaften, Mathematik. Cata: 2 pro
Jahr. Corresp: English, Français. B: Kreissparkasse Albstadt, Konto
809 108. CP: Stuttgart 104 328. B.V.D.B.

LUDWIG HELMUT SCHILLER, AM BIRKENRAIN 28, 7811 ST. PETER. TN: (07660) 308. TA: Schillerbuch. Gegründet 1961. Wohnung; Besuche nur nach Vereinbarung. Mittelgrosser Vorrat. Spec: Philosophie, Theologie, Geschichte. Cata: 3 pro Jahr. Corresp: English, Français. B: Sparkasse Hochschwarzwald, Kontonummer 50 3351 9. CP: Karlsruhe 11 81 38. V.D.A., B.V.D.B.

SCIENTIA VERLAG UND ANTIQUARIAT, ADLERSTRASSE 65, 7080 AALEN (WÜRTTEMBERG). Prop: Kurt Schilling. TN: (07361) 6 13 38. TA: Scientia Aalenwuertt. Spec: Recht, Philosophie. B: Deutsche Bank, Aalen, Konto Nr. 15–22150, V.D.A.

SONNEWALD-HECKENHAUER, WALDHOF 1, 7947 MENGEN. Prop: Herbert Friedrich Sonnewald. TN: (07572) 8231. Gegründet 1823. Nur nach Korrespondenz. Spec: Theologie; Geschichte; Slavische Länder. Corresp: English, Français, Español, Russisch. B: Landesgirokasse, Tubingen, Konto 4700337, 011337. CP: Stuttgart 929–704. V.D.A.

J.F. STEINKOPF, POSTFACH 1116, MARIENSTRASSE 3, 7000 STUTTGART. Prop: Frieder Weitbrecht. TN: (0711) 22 40 21. TA: Steinkopf Stuttgart. Gegründet 1792. Laden und Lagerräume. Sehr grosser Vorrat, auch neue Bücher. Spec: Kunst; Theologie; Topographie. Cata. 3 pro Jahr. Corresp: English, Français, Dansk. B: Landesgirokasse Stuttgart 1 290 761. (BLZ 600 510 01). CP: Stuttgart 849–707. V.D.A.

STUTTGARTER ANTIQUARIAT, RATHENAUSTRASSE 21, 7000 STUTTGART 1. Prop: Dr. F. Kocher-Benzing. TN: (0711) 25 44 02. Gegründet 1959. Wohnung, nur nach Vereinbarung. Mittelgrosser Vorrat. Spec: 16. Jahhunderts; deutsche Literatur; Erstausgaben. Cata: 5 pro Jahr. Corresp: English, Français. B: Baden-Württembergische Bank, Stuttgart, Konto 2371. CP: Stuttgart 9641–707. V.D.A., I.L.A.B.

GERTRUD THELEN, ANTIQUARIAT, HAARWEG 1, D-7570 BADEN-BADEN. TN: (07221) 54116.

INGE UTZT, TAUBENHEIMERSTRASSE 30, 7000 STUTTGART-BAD CANSTATT 30. TN: 55 19 99.

GALERIE VALENTIEN, KÖNIGSBAU, 7000 STUTTGART. Prop: Dr. Fritz C. Valentien. TN: 29 27 09. Gegründet 1933. Laden und Lagerräume, Samstag Nachmittag geschlossen. Mittelgrosser Vorrat, auch neue Bücher. Spec: Kunstgeschichte; christlich Archäologie; angewandt Kunst. Cata: 2 pro Jahr. Corresp: English, Français. B: Städt. Girokasse, Stuttgart, Konto 1693. CP: Stuttgart 10125. V.D.A.

J. VOERSTER, RELENBERG STRASSE 20, 7000 STUTTGART. TN: 29 71 86. Gegründet 1966. Laden, Samstag geschlossen. Mittelgrosser Vorrat. Spec: Musik; Theater; Deutsche Literatur. Corresp: English. B: Deutsche Bank, Stuttgart, Kontonummer 14/56888. CP: Stuttgart 77955 701. V.D.A.

PETER WEBER, KUNSTANTIQUARIAT, EICHSTRASSE 12, 7570 BADEN-BADEN. TN: (0 72 21) 2 55 71. Mittwoch nachmittag und Samstag geschlossen. Spec: Dekorative Graphik, Gemälde, V.D.A.

BUCH UND KUNSTANTIQUARIAT FRIEDRICH WEISSERT, CHARLOTTENSTRASSE 21C, 7000 STUTTGART 1. TN: (07 11) 24 22 56. Samstag geschlossen. Spec: Städteansichten, Landkarten, Dekorative Graphik, Illustrierte Bücher. B: Dresdner Bank. V.D.A.

GALERIE ELFRIEDE WIRNITZER, LILIENMATTSTRASSE 6, HAUS LAUSCHAN, 7570 BADEN-BADEN. TN: (07221) 26725. Gegründet 1955. Wohnung, Besuche nur nach Voranmeldung. Spec: Graphik. Cata: unregelmässig. Corresp: English, Français. B: Dresdner Bank, Baden-Baden, Kontonummer 6 233 284. CP: Karlsruhe 120/194 755. V.D.A.

VI

BAYERN: BAVIÈRE: BAVARIA

Postcode: Postleitzahl
8000+

8581 ALLADORF	8070 INGOLSTADT
8800 ANSBACH	8084 INNING
8900 AUGSBURG	8059 MOOSINNING
8201 BAD FEILNBACH	8000 MÜNCHEN (Munich)
8600 BAMBURG	8110 MURNAU
8201 DETTENDORF	8500 NÜRNBERG
8501 ECHING	8201 OBING
8011 EGLHARTING	8012 OTTOBRUNN
8520 ERLANGEN	8390 PASSAU
8805 FEUCHTWANGEN	8134 PÖCKING
8228 FREILASSING	8183 ROTTACH EGERN
8510 FÜRTH	8399 ROTTHALMÜNSTER
8210 GIEBINGPOSTPRIEN	8656 THURNAU
8002 GRÄFELFING	8132 TUTZING
8022 GRÜNWALD	8212 ÜBERSEE/CHIEMSEE
8048 HAIMHAUSEN	8213 WILHELMING
8670 HOF	8592 WUNSIEDEL
8021 HOHENSCHAEFTLARN	8700 WÜRZBURG

THEODOR ACKERMANN, LUDWIGSTRASSE 7, 8000 MÜNCHEN. TN: 28 47 87. Gegründet 1865. Laden, Samstag Nachmittag geschlossen. Sehr grosser Vorrat. Spec: Geisteswissenschaften; Alte Drucke; Autographen. Cata: 6–8 pro Jahr. Corresp: English, Français, Dutch. B: Merck, Finck & Co., München. CP: München 116 25–806. V.D.A., B.V.D.B.

M. ASANIN, SCHELLINGSTRASSE 58, MÜNCHEN 40. TN: 2 72 3379.

SUSANNE BACH, JAKOB-KLAR-STRASSE 10, 8000 MUNCHEN 40.

R. BARTH, FÜRTHER STRASSE 89, NÜRNBERG 80. TN: 0911 28 99 66.

HERMANN BEISLER, OSKAR-V. MILLER RING 33, 8000 MÜNCHEN 2. TN: (089) 28 34 52. Samstags und August geschlossen. Spec: Alte Städteansichten und Landkarten, Bavarica. Kat. 1–2 jährlich. V.D.A.

HEINRICH BÖHRINGER, Marktplatz 2, 8592 Wunsiedel. TN: (09232) 2117. Gegründet 1867. Laden, Samstag Nachmittag geschlossen. Sehr kleiner Vorrat, Auch neue Bücher. Spec: Böhmen, Bayern. Corresp: English, Español. CP: 68 533–854 Nürnberg. B.V.D.B.

KLAUS VON BRINCKEN, Theresienstrasse 58 und Pacellistrasse 2, 8000 München 2. TN: (089) 28 25 53 und 29 88 15. Samstag Nachmittag geschlossen. Spec: Städteansichten, Landkarten, Dekorative Graphik. B: Bayerische Hypotheken- und Wechselbank 6 890 107 018. V.D.A.

HERMANN BUB, Postfach 5328, Kürschnerhof 7, 8700 Würzburg 1. TN: (0931) 9 36 75 und 1 28 76. Samstag Nachmittag geschlossen. Spec: Africana, Dekorative Graphik, Alte Bücher, Süddeutsche Landeskunde. Kat: 1 jährlich. CP: Nürnberg 1670 63–852.

BÜCHERKABINETT, Türkenstrasse 21 (Innenhof), 8000 München 40. Prop: Eva Michalek. TN: (089) 28 24 47. Spec: Musik, Tanz, Theater, Film, Zirkus. Kat. jährlich. B: Bayerische Vereinsbank 903 986. CP: München 2554 69–808. V.D.A.

DE PROFUNDIS ANTIQUARIAT, Postfach 21H, D-8012 Ottobrunn. Gegründet: 1981. Lagerräume; Besuch nicht möglich. Mittlegrosser Vorrat. Spez: Einzelbände von Büchern und Zeitschriften. Cata: 4 pro Jahr. Corresp: English, Français, Hollandsche.

HELMUTH DOMIZLAFF, Hocherlach 35, 8212-Übersee (Chiemsee). TN: (0 86 42) 441. Gegründet 1933. Wohnung, nur nach Vereinbarung. Drucke des 15 und 16 Jahrhunderts. B: Merck, Finck & Co., 217921. CP: München 18633. V.D.A.

BUCH- UND KUNSTANTIQUARIAT AM DOMPLATZ, Domplatz-Luragogasse. 8390 Passau. Prop: Heiner Henke. TN: (0851) 2141. Gegründet 1972. Laden. Kleiner Vorrat. Corresp: English. B: Sparkasse Passau: Konto Nr. 360560. CP: 295576–850 Nürnberg.

F. DÖSSINGER, Hohenzollernstrasse 156, München 40. TN: 3 08 6L 36.

M. EDELMANN, Postfach 9360, Breitegasse 52 und 54, 8500 Nürnberg–11. Prop: Heiko Kistner. TN: 20 32 94. Gegründet 1886. Laden. Grosser Vorrat, auch neue Bücher. Spec: Literatur des Ausgehenden, 19. und 20. Jahrhunderts. Corresp: English. B: Bayerische Vereinsbank, Nürnberg, Kontonummer 6331440. CP: Nürnberg 160 19-850. B.V.D.B.

B. ENDRES, Utzschneiderstrasse 10, München 5. TN: 2 60 87 63.

GEORGE J. ERDLEN, Obermarkt 5, Postfach 1109, 8110 Murnau am Staffelsee. TN: (0 88 41) 51 09. Spec: Botanik, Zoologie, Geographie, Anthropologie, Ethnologie, Gewissenschaften. Kat. 2 jährlich.

KUNSTGALERIE ESSLINGEN, Possartstrasse 12, D-8000 München 80. Prop: Ralph D.I. Jentsch. TN: (089) 470 4265. Gegründet 1968. Spec: Kunst des 20. Jahrhunderts. Graphik des deutschen Expressionismus. Grosser Bestand. Cata: 3 pro Jahr. Corresp: English. B: Deutsche Bank München 6578520. CP: München 19889-800. Verband Deutscher Antiquare. Landesverband der Kunst- und Antiquitätenhändler Bayern. Bundesverband Deutscher Galerien.

Dr. RETO FEURER, WANNINGERSTRASSE 7, D-8201 OBING/OBERBAYERN. TN: (08624) 1604. Gegründet 1980. Versandantiquariat (Wohnung), Besuche nach Vereinbarung. Kleiner Vorrat. Spec: Literatur und Kunst des 20. Jahrhunderts (Erstausgaben, Widmungsexemplare, illustrierte Bücher, Film und Fotografie). Cata: 2-3 pro Jahr. Corresp: English, Français, Italiano. B: Raiffeisenbank Obing, Konto 45179. CP: München 2414 62–807.

GERARD GOLDAU, GASTEIG 4, 8022 GRÜNWALD. TN: (089) 641 30 23. Gegründet 1957. Lagerräume, nur nach Vereinbarung. Mittelgrosser Vorrat. Spec: Militaria, Geschichte. Cata: 3 oder 4 pro Jahr. Corresp: English, Italiano. B: Raiffeisenbank, Grünwald, Konto 226 513. CP: München 123 201–801.

E. HAGENSTEIN, SCHLEISHEIMERSTRASSE 9, MÜNCHEN 2. TN: 5 23 36 7 2.

H. HAMMERSTEIN, TÜRKENSTRASSE 37, MÜNCHEN 40. TN: 28 51 83.

ANTIQUARIAT HANNAK, SCHLOSSBERGSTRASSE 4 D-8110 MURNAU.

HARTUNG UND KARL, KAROLINENPLATZ 5A, 8000 MÜNCHEN 2. TN: (089) 284034. TA: Buchauktion München. Gegründet 1972. Büro; Samstag geschlossen. Auktionen, 2 pro Jahr. Spec: Bücher; Autographen; Graphik. Corresp: English, Français. B: H. Aufhaüser München, Kontonummer 195545. CP: München 66953–808. V.D.A., B.D.K., I.L.A.B.

ELSA HAUSER, SCHELLINGSTRASSE 17, 8000 MÜNCHEN 13. Prop: Elsa Kern. TN: (089) 28 11 59. Gegründet 1911. Samstag Nachmittag geschlossen. Spec: Alte und Moderne Graphik; Alte Drucke; Bibliophile Bücher des 15–20. Jahrhunderts. V.D.A.

E. HILLENBRAND, RINDERMARKT 10, MÜNCHEN 2. TN: 26 62 59. *Auch* BARERSTRASSE 3, MUNCHEN 2. TN: 59 45 95.

HANS HÖCHTBERGER. MAUERKIRCHERSTR. 28, 8000 MÜNCHEN 80. TN: 983686. Gegründet 1969. Lagerräume und Wohnung, nur nach Vereinbarung. Mittelgrosser Vorrat. Spec: Erstausgaben Deutscher Literatur; Illustrierte Bücher; Kunstwissenschaft Buchwesen; Literatur- und Kunstzeitschriften. Cata: 2–3 pro Jahr. Corresp: English, Français. B: Bayerische Hypotheken; und Wechselbank, München, Konto 4410123954. CP: München 226945–807.

GERHARD HOFNER, KLEINWEIDENMÜHLE 10, NÜRNBERG 90. TN: 26 01 11.

JÜRGEN HOLSTEIN ANTIQUARIAT G.m.b.H., POSTFACH 68, FELDAFINGERSTRASSE 37, 8134 PÖCKING. TN: (08157) 2675. Gegründet 1966. Besuche nach Telefonischer Vereinbarung. Grosser Vorrat. Spec: Kunst und Kunstdokumentation 20. Jahrhundert. Cata: 4 pro Jahr. Corresp: English. B: HypoBank München Konto Schwabing Nr. 318 016–6008. CP: München 238 87–806.

A. HÜFNER, THERESIENPL 1, NÜRNBERG 1. TN: 20 43 17.

H. HUGENDUBEL, SALVATORPLATZ 2, 8000 MÜNCHEN 2. TN: 2389 330. TA: Hugendubel München. Telex 529 651. Gegründet 1880. Laden und Lagerräume. Grosser Vorrat, auch neue Bücher. Spec: Bavarica; Bibliophilie; Alte Drucke; Militaria. Spezialkataloge. Corresp: English, Français. B: Bayerische Hypotheken- und Wechsel-Bank, München, Konto 685 000 1454, CP: München 15500–809. V.D.A., B.V.D.B.

ALTE GRAPHIK JULIA F. ILIU, BARER STRASSE 46, 8000 MÜNCHEN 40. TN: (0 89) 2 00 06 00. Samstag geschlossen. Spec: Stadtansichten, Landkarten, Dekorative Graphik, Genre. CP: 1015 21809.V.D.A.

ANTIQUARIAT KÖNIG, UNTERE SCHMIEDGASSE 8, NÜRNBERG 70. TN: 0911 22 51 69.

"JOURNALFRANZ" ARNULF LIEBING G.m.b.H. & CO.. POSTFACH 5840, WERNER-VON-SIEMMENS-STRASSE 5, 8700 WÜRZBURG. TN: (0931) 21120. Telex 68472 (Liewued). TA: Journalfranz. Gegründet 1923. Lagerraum, Samstag geschlossen. Grosser Vorrat. Spec: Zeitschriften; Geisteswissenschaften. Cata: 3 pro Jahr; Listen monatlich. Corresp: English. B: Dresdner Bank; Staudtische Sparkasse, Würzburg; National Citybank, New York. CP: Nürnberg 922–855.

KARL & FABER, KAROLINENPLATZ 5A, 8000 MÜNCHEN 2. Prop: George und Louis Karl & Karl Hartung. TN: 28 30 24. TA: Karlanti München. Spec: Alte Bücher: Kunst; Graphik. B. H. Aufhäuser, München. CP: München 7268. V.D.A.

Dr. EMIL KATZBICHLER, WILHELM-RING 7. 8201 FRASDORF. TN: (08051) 25 95. Gegründet 1962. Büro und Lagerräume; Besuche nur nach Vereinbarung. Grosser Vorrat. Nur Musikliteratur, Musikdrucke und Musikautographen. Cata: 3 oder 4 pro Jahr. Corresp: English, Français. B: Sparkasse Prien, Konto Nr. 252 411. CP: München 18 5254. V.D.A., Gesamtverband deutscher Musikfachgeschäfte.

GALERIE WOLFGANG KETTERER, BRIENNERSTRASSE 25, 8000 MÜNCHEN 2. TN: (089) 59 11 81. V.D.A.

E. und R. KISTNER, WEINMARKT 6, 8500 NÜRNBERG. Prop: Rolf Kistner. TN: 203482. Gegründet 1886. Laden und Lagerräume. Sehr grosser Vorrat. Spec: alte Bücher und Graphiken. Corresp: English. B: B.V. Bank Nürnberg Kontonummer 6311857. CP: Nürnberg 12881–857. V.D.A.

J. KITZINGER, SCHELLINGSTRASSE 25, 8000 MÜNCHEN. TN: (089) 28 35 37. Gegründet 1890. Laden. Grosser Vorrat. Spec: Wissenschaften; Kunst; Geschichte. Cata: Jahrlich. Corresp: English, Français. B: Bayerische Hypotheken und Wechselbank, München. CP: München 10841–804. B.V.D.B., V.D.A.

ANTIQUARIAT KLAUSSNER, PROFESSOR-KURT-HUBER-STRASSE 19, 8032 GRÄFELFING (MÜNCHEN). Prop: Inge Klaussner. TN: (089) 852602. Spec: Deutsche Literatur; Erstausgaben; Kulturgeschichte; Reisen, Expeditionen; Bavarica. V.D.A.

RUDOLF KLEINERT, ALLADORF NO. 66, D-8656 THURNAU. TN: (09271) 666. Gegründet: 1961. Wohnung: nur nach Vereinbarung. Mittelgrosser Vorrat. Spec: Medizin. V.D.A. Cata: 3–5 pro Jahr. M: V.D.A.

RAINER KÖBELIN. SCHELLINGSTRASSE 99, 8000 MÜNCHEN 40. TN: 285 640. Laden. Spec: Militaria; Alte Naturwissenschaft; Literatur; Dekorative Graphik. B: Bayerische Vereinsbank, München, Ko

CARL-ERNST KOHLHAUER, GRASER WEG 2, 8805 FEUCHTWANGEN. TN: (09852) 9292. Gegründet 1957. Wohnung, nur nach Vereinbarung. Mittelgrosser Vorrat. Spec: alte Medizin und Naturwissenschaften (Graphik, Bücher und Autographen). Cata: Unregelmässig. Corresp: English. B: Sparkasse Feuchtwangen Konto 42. CP: Frankfurt-am-Main 185 256–609. V.D.A.

OTTO KOLB, VON-MANN-STRASSE 2, 8670 HOF. TN: (09281) 85200. Gegründet 1949. Lagerraum. Sehr kleiner Vorrat, auch neue Bücher. Spec: Stahlstiche. Cata: 2 pro Jahr. B: Sparkasse Rehau, Kontonummer 205 344. CP: Nürnberg 723 96–859. B.V.D.B., V.D.A.

KUHN, BREITSCHEIDSTRASSE 49, NÜRNBERG 40. TN: 44 71 60.

PETER LEISSLE, DAISERSTRASSE 40, MÜNCHEN 70. TN: 7755 78.

KUNSTANTIQUARIAT STEPHAN LIST, BARER STRASSE 39, 8000 MÜNCHEN 40. TN: (089) 28 19 60.

MARGOT LÖRCHER o.H.G., MEYERBEERSTRASSE 53, 8000 MÜNCHEN, 60. Prop: Dorrit Lörcher und Dr. Heide Bücklein. TN: (089) 8888407. Gegründet 1971. Wohnung; Besuche nur nach Vereinbarung. Kleiner Vorrat. Spec: Japanische Farbholzschnitte. Cata: 4 pro Jahr. Corresp: English. B: Bayer. Vereinsbank München, (BLZ 700 202 70) Konto Nr. 604 223. CP: 1296 89–708 Stuttgart. V.D.A., Landesverband d. Kunst und Antiquitatenhändler Baden-Württembergs e.V. (auch in Stuttgart).

ANTIQUARIAT WALTER MERGENTHALER, TEXTORSTRASSE 22, 8700 WÜRZBURG. TN: (0931) 5 23 79. Samstag Nachmittag geschlossen. Kat. 4 jährlich. B: Castell-Bank 467. CP: Nürnberg 1170 63-853. V.D.A.

KUNSTANTIQUARIAT OTTO MOSER, TÖLZER STRASSE 24, 8022 GRÜNWALD. TN: (089) 6 41 12 65. Gegründet 1951. Nach Vereinbarung. Spec: Dekorative Graphik. B: Bayerische Vereinsbank, München 484 056. CP: München 1233 08-801. V.D.A.

GALERIE ZUR MÜHLE, BILLESBERGER HOF, 8059 MOOSINNING. Prop: Siegfried Billesberger. TN: (0 81 23). Täglich ab 14.00 Uhr. Spec: Handzeichnungen und Graphik des 16.-19. Jahrhunderts. Kat. 2 bis 3 jährlich. B: Bankhaus Aufhäuser, München 180 262. CP: Munchen 1750 72-800. V.D.A.

ANTIQUARIAT KARLHEINZ MURR, KAROLINENSTRASSE 4, 8600 BAMBERG. (Postfach 4037). TN: (0951) 277 28. Gegründet 1954. Zwei Läden. (telefonisch immer zu sprechen). Grosser Vorrat. Spec: alte Graphik, Städte-Ansichten und Landkarten. Bestand ca. 30,000 Originalstiche, auch neue Bücher. Cata: 3 bis 5 pro Jahr. Corresp: English. B: Bayerische Vereinsbank Bamberg, Konto 372 84 98. CP: Nürnberg 215 88–851. B.V.D.B., V.D.A., Bayerischer Buchhändler- und Verlegerverband.

NICKEL-ZADOW, PLOBENHOFSTRASSE 4, HAUPTMARKT, NÜRNBERG. TN: (0911) 20 97 52.

PHILOGRAPHICON, GALERIE FÜR ALTE GRAPHIK IM ANTIC-HAUS, NEUTURMSTRASSE 1, 8000 MÜNCHEN 2. Prop: Rainer Rauhut. TN: (0 89) 22 50 82. Samstag Nachmittag geschlossen. Spec: Stadtansichten, Landkarten, Dekorative Graphik aus fünf Jahrhunderten. Kat. 1 jährlich. B: Deutsche Bank 4 509 253. CP: 27 12-803. V.D.A.

Dr. KARL H. PRESSLER, RÖMERSTRASSE 7, 8000 MÜNCHEN 40. TN: (089) 34 13 31. Gegründet 1954. Büro und Lagerräume; nur nach Vereinbarung, Sehr grosser Vorrat. Spec: Literatur, Geschichte, Bibliographie, Schöne und seltene Bücher. Corresp: English. B: Dresdner Bank, Mainz, Konto 2 343 952. CP: München 351734-802. B.V.D.B., V.D.A., A.B.A., Editor of *Aus dem Antiquariat*.

KLAUS RENNER, 8021 HOHENSCHAEFTLARN. TN: 08178 3796 Gegründet 1957. Büro, Mitte August-Mitte Sept. geschlossen Besuche nur nach Vereinbarung. Kleiner Vorrat, auch neue Bücher. Spec: Ethnologie; Archäologie, Anthropologie. Cata: 4 pro Jahr. Corresp: English. B: Raiffeisenbank Schaeftlarn 8761. CP: München 962 17. B.V.D.B.

GERHARD SCHEPPLER, GISELASTRASSE 25, 8000 MÜNCHEN 40. TN: (089) 348174. Gegründet 1966. Lagerräume; Samstag geschlossen. Besuche 9.00–13.00 Uhr und 15.00–17.30 Uhr: Samstags nur nach Vereinbarung. Mittelgrosser Vorrat. Spec: Kunst; Geographie; Geschichte; Okkulta; Philosophie; Theologie. Cata: 2 pro Jahr. B: Bayerische Hypotheken Bank, München, Kontonummer 6060391422 (BLZ 70020040). CP: München 67163–809. M: V.D.A., B.V.D.B.

ANTIQUARIAT PAUL SCHINDEGGER, HEIDENPOINT 26, 8228 FREILASSING. TN: (0 86 54) 6 41 85. Nach Voranmeldung. Spec: Geschichte, Politik, Moderne Architektur, Buchkunst. Kat. 4 jährlich. CP: Frankfurt 3299 77–604. V.D.A.

KUNSTANTIQUARIAT MONIKA SCHMIDT, TÜRKENSTRASSE 48, 8000 MÜNCHEN 40, UND SCHLOSS HAIMHAUSEN, 8048 HAIMHAUSEN. TN: (089) 28 42 23 und (081 33) 64 13. Samstag Nachmittag geschlossen. Spec: Dekorative und alte Graphik, Alte Stadtansichten und Landkarten, Japanische Farbholzschnitte, Illustrierte Bücher. B: Hypo-Bank 6 890 201 200. CP: München 2649 20–800. V.D.A.

SCHMIDT PERIODICALS G.m.b.H., DETTENDORF, 8201 BAD FEILNBACH 2. TN: (08064) 221. TA: Periodica-Bad Feilnbach Oberbayern. Gegründet 1963. Lagerräume; nur nach Vereinbarung. Grosser Vorrat. Spec: Zeitschriften. Cata: Häufig. Corresp: English, Français, Español, Italiano. B: Kreissparkasse Bad Aibling, Konto Nr. 70300. CP: Deutsche Bank, Rosenheim Konto Nr. 8313355.

HANS SCHNEIDER, MOZARTSTRASSE 6, 8132 TUTZING ÜBER MÜNCHEN. TN: (08158) 3050 TA: Musikantiquar Tutzing. Gegründet 1949. Lageräume, nur nach Vereinbarung. Musik (ausschliessl.) sehr grosser Vorrat. Cata. Corresp: English, Français. B: Raiffeisenbank, Tutzing, Konto 808970. CP: München 14602. V.D.A., B.V.D.B. Gesellschaft für Musikforschung.

R. SCHREPF, NÜRNBERGER STRASSE 31, 8510 FÜRTH. TN: 0911 77 31 88.

HARTMUT R. SCHREYER, AUF DEM KREUZ 9, D-8900 AUGSBURG. TN: (0821) 3 64 68. Gegründet: 1976. Laden, Montag bis Freitag 14–18 Uhr; Samstag 9–13 Mn. Grosser Vorrat. Spec: Literatur: Kunst; Geschichte; Bavarica. Cata: 2 pro Jahr. Corresp: English. B: Stadtsparkasse Augsburg. Kontonummer 0248799. CP: München 239917–806.

GALERIE STANGL, BRIENNERSTRASSE 11, 8000 MÜNCHEN. Prop: Otto Stangl. TN: 29 99 11. Gegründet 1947. Galerie, Samstag Nachmittag geschlossen. Kleiner Vorrat, auch neue Bücher. Spec: Kunst. Corresp: English, Français. CP: München 13512. V.D.A., B.V.D.B.

ANTIQUARIAT MICHAEL STEINBACH, DEMOLLSTRASSE 1/I 8000 MÜNCHEN 19. TN: (089) 1 57 16 91. Nach Vereinbarung. Spec: Illustrierte Bücher, Literatur in Erst-ausgaben, Bibliophilie, Bücher über Kunst und Kunstgewerbe. Kat. 1 bis 2 jährlich. B: H. Aufhäser 357 774. CP: München 2565 56–802. V.D.A.

INGELORE STRENG, LANDWEHRSTRASSE 2, 8000 MÜNCHEN 2.

THELEM ANTIQUARIAT, MÖLKEREISTRASSE 19, POSTFACH 50, 8399 ROTTHALMÜNSTER. TN: (0 85 33) 71 56 und 73 50. Nach Vereinbarung. Spec: Bibliophilie, Illustrierte Bücher des XV. bis XX. Jahrhunderts, Einbände, Pressendrucke, Welt-literatur in Erstausgaben. Kat. 2 bis 3 jährlich. CP: München 2535 88–804. V.D.A.

E. VON DEN VELDEN, NEUREUTHER STRASSE 1. 8000 MÜNCHEN 40. TN: 37 70 91. Spec: Zeitschriften. B: Bayerische Hypotheken- und Wechselbank, München, Konto 5803538630. CP: München 482 78–802. V.D.A.

RAINER GERD VOIGT, LANGERSTRASSE 2/IV, D-8000 MÜNCHEN 80. TN: (089) 4703066. Wohnung; Besuch nur nach Vereinbarung. Sehr kleiner Vorrat. Spec. Alte Medizin; Kunst-Wissenschaften; Reise-beschreibungen. Cata: 2 pro Jahr. Corresp: English, Français, P.B.F.A.

ED. WALZ, LERCHENFELDSTRASSE 4, 8000 MÜNCHEN 22. Prop: Anneliese Jamin. Spec: Graphik und Zeichnungen des 15–20 Jahrhunderts; Städteansichten und Landkarten. CP: München 15921. V.D.A.

BERNHARD   WENDT,   HAUPTSTRASSE   29,   8084 INNING-BUCH/AMMERSEE, ÜBER MÜNCHEN. TN: Inning (Ammersee) (08143) 342. Gegründet 1953. Wohnung, Besuch nur nach Vereinbarung. Mittelgrosser Vorrat. Spec: Inkunabeln; alte Drucke; Humanismus; Reformation und Gegenreformation; Theologie vor 1850; Geisteswissenschaften. Corresp: English, Française. B: H. Aufhäuser, München, Konto 379 077. V.D.A., B.V.D.B.

ROBERT WÖLFLE OHG., AMALIENSTRASSE 65, 8000 MÜNCHEN 40. Prop: Gertrud Wölfle; Dr. Lotte Roth-Wölfle: Dr. Christine Pressler. TN: 28 36 26. Laden, Samstag Nachmittag geschlossen. Spec: Alte Drucke; Alte Naturwissenschaften; Geisteswissenschaften; Kunst; Graphik des 15–20 Jahrhunderts; Bavarica. CP: München 31781. V.D.A.

HEINZ WÜNSCHMANN, WASSERTURMSTRASSE 14, 8520 ERLANGEN. Spec: Kunst, Philosophie. V.D.A.

BUCH UND KUNSTAUKTIONSHAUS F. ZISSKA & R. KISTNER, UNTERER ANGER 15, 8000 MÜNCHEN 2. TN: (089) 26 38 55. Samstag geschlossen. Spec: Alte Drucke, Naturwissenschaften, Illustrierte Bucher, Topographie, Dekorative Graphik. Versteigerungskat. 2 bis 3 jährlich. B: Bankhaus Max Flessa & Co. 770 505. CP: München 70 98–807. V.D.A.

DEUTSCHE DEMOKRATISCHE REPUBLIK

GERMAN DEMOCRATIC REPUBLIC
RÉPUBLIQUE ALLEMAGNE
DEMOCRATIQUE

BERLIN: DRESDEN: JENA: HALLE: KARL-MARX-STADT: LEIPZIG: MAGDEBURG: POTSDAM: ROSTOCK: WEIMAR

ANTIQUARIAT UNTER DEN LINDEN, UNTER DEN LINDEN 37/45, 1080 BERLIN. TN: 22 919 39. Laden. Mittelgrosser Vorrat.

DRESDENER ANTIQUARIAT, BAUTZNER STRASSE 27, 806 DRESDEN. TN: 53368. Gegründet 1953. Laden, Sonnabend geschlossen. Besuche nur nach Vereinbarung. Sehr grosser Vorrat. Spec: Bibliophile; Kunstwissenschaft. Cata: 2 pro Jahr. B: I.H.B. Dresden, Konto 5151–13–31. CP: Dresden 14043. Börsenverein Dt. Buchhändler zu Leipzig.

EVANGELISCHE BUCHHANDLUNG MAX MÜLLER, ERNST-THÄLMANN-STRASSE 23, POSTFACH 229, 9010 KARL-MARX-STADT. TN: 62416. Laden. Grosser Vorrat, auch neue Bücher. Spec: Geistes-und Kunstwissenschaften. B: GB Mitte, Karl-Marx-Stadt Kontonummer 6214–34–90500. CP: Leipzig 7499–57–39810. M: BörsenUverein der Deutschen Buchhändler zu Leipzig.

GRAFIK-GALERIE, RITTERSTRASSE 4 (THEATERPASSAGE), DDR-7010 LEIPZIG. Laden.

HALLESCHES ANTIQUARIAT, GROSSE-STEIN-STRASSE 77–78, DDR-4010 HALLE, Laden und Versand.

ANTIQUARIAT JENA, WAGNERGASSE 22, DDR-6900 JENA, Laden.

LEIPZIGER ANTIQUARIAT, ANTIQUARIAT GESELLSCHAFTSWIS-SENSCHAFTEN, GRIMMAISCHE STRASSE 25, DDR-7010 LEIPZIG. Laden.

LEIPZIGER ANTIQUARIAT, ANTIQUARIAT NATURWISSENSCH-AFTEN, Nicolaistrasse 3–9, DDR-7010 Leipzig. Laden.

MAGDEBURGER ANTIQUARIAT, Hassebachplatz 4, DDR-3010 Magdeburg. Laden.

MUSIKALIEN ANTIQUARIAT, Thomaskirchhof 15, DDR-7010. Leipzig. Laden.

NORDDEUTSCHES ANTIQUARIAT, Kröpeliner Strasse 14, DDR-25 Rostock. (Postfach 30). TN: 34052. TA: Nordantiquariat Rostock. Gegründet 1955. Laden und Lagerräume. Besuche nur nach Vereinbarung. Sehr grosser Vorrat. Cata: 10 pro Jahr. Corresp: English, Russisch. Börsenverein der Deutschen Buchhändler zu Leipzig.

ANTIQUARIAT DES VOLKSBUCHHANDELS, Rosenhof 6, DDR-9010 Karl-Marx-Stadt. Laden.

WEIMAR ANTIQUARIAT, Schillerstrasse 10, DDR-5300 Weimar. Laden.

POTSDAMER ANTIQUARIAT, Friedrich-Ebert-Strasse 27–28 DDR, 1500 Potsdam. Laden.

ZENTRALANTIQUARIAT DER DDR. Talstrasse 29, 701 Leipzig. (Postfach 1080). TN: 293641 3. TA: Zentralanti Leipzig. Gegründet 1949. Laden und Lagerräume. Sehr grosser Vorrat. Spec: Wissenschaften; Kunst; Graphik. Cata: English, Français, Russian. B: I.H.B., Leipzig, Kontonummer 5611–18–55. CP: Leipzig 56226.

ZENTRALES ANTIQUARIAT BERLIN, Rungerstrasse 20, DDR-1026 Berlin. TN: 27 92 195. Lagerräume, nur nach Vereinbarung. Sehr grosser Vorrat. Corresp: English.

ELLAS

GREECE GRÈCE GRIECHENLAND

ATHINE (Athènes, Athens)

ACADEMIC BOOKSTORE, HIPPOCRATUS STREET 33, ATHENS. Prop: Efthimiou D. Triantafyllou. TN: 25996. Established 1927. Shop. Also new books.

LES AMIS DU LIVRE, 9 VALAORITOU STREET, ATHENS 134. Prop: Julia & Augusto Spandonaro. TN: 3615 562. Established 1960. Shop. Very large stock. Spec: travel books about Greece. engravings; maps; views and landscapes. Corresp: English, Français, Deutsch, Italiano.

PANAYIOTIS GEORGIOU & COMPANY, P.O. 622, ATHENS. TN: 632 891. Spec: encyclopedias and dictionaries; books on Greece; old maps. Also publishers' representatives. Corresp: English, Français.

B.N. GREGORIADES, RUE PHIDIAS 2. ATHÈNES 142. TN: 620 205 et 602 327. Spec: livres anciens.

DION P. KARAVIAS, 67 ASCLIPIOU STREET, 10680 ATHENS. TN: 3620465. Shop. Medium stock, also new books. Spec: Greece.

CHRISTOS KATSICALIS, ZAMBAKIS BOOKSHOP, 14 MASSALIAS STREET, ATHENS 144TN. TN: 3614 531. Est: 1932. Shop. Very large stock sec and antiq. also new books. Spec: maps and prints; old and rare books; scientific periodicals. Cata: 2 a year. Corresp: English, Français. B: National Bank of Greece, Account No. 742 299.

LIBRARIE KAUFFMANN, 28 STADIUM STREET, ATHENS-132. Spec: Greece, Turkey, maps, engravings.

TAVROS STAVRIDIS, PANAGHITSAS 18, KIFISIA, 14562 ATHENS. TN: 8017079. Est. 1973. Shop. Small stock sec. and antiq. books. Spec: books, prints and maps on Greece, Cyprus, Turkey. Cata: 3 a year. Corresp: English, Français. B: Credit Bank, Kifisia Branch, No. 211008651. Association of Greek Antique Dealers.

ANGELOS ZAMBAKIS, LE BIBLIOPHILE, 14 MASSALIS, ATHENS 144. TN: 614 531. Shop. Spec: maps; prints; old and rare books. Also new books. Corresp: English, Français.

ESPAÑA

SPAIN   ESPAGNE   SPANIEN

ALMERIA: BARCELONA: MADRID:
PALMA DE MALLORCA: SAN SEBASTIAN: ZARAGOZA
(Saragossa)

LIBRERIA ANTIGUA Y MODERNA, CALLE DE LOS LIBREROS 2, MADRID 13. Prop: Antonio de Guzman. Spec: history; art. Corresp: English. Shop.

LIBRERIA ANTICUARIA ARISTEUCOS, PASEO DE LA BONANOVA 14, G. BARCELONA 080 22. TN: 2478255. Prop: Mariano Castells-Plandiura. Est. 1967. Private premises: Appointment necessary. Spec: Hispánica old and rare; Spanish, Castellano, Catalan and Latin language books 15th to 19th; Gastronomy; Medicine Cartography of Catalonia. Cata: occasionally. Corresp: English, French, German and Catalan. B: Banco Comercial. Transatlantico, Avenida Diagonal 446, Barcelona.

BENEIT J. BARBAZAN, CALLE DE LOS LIBREROS 4, MADRID. TN: 247 04 33.

BLAZQEZ BARBERO, CALL MOYANO 5, MADRID. TN: 239 97 26.

LIBRERIA PARA BIBLIOFILOS LUIS BARDON, PLAZA DE SAN MARTIN 3, MADRID. (Apartado Postal 7092). TN: 21 55 14. TA: Lubardon Madrid. Established 1946. Shop. Very large stock, also new books. Cata. Corresp: English. B: Banco de Santander, Sucursal, Calle de Galdo 1, Madrid, Account No. 815. A.B.A.

LIBRERIA ANGEL BATLLE Y TEJEDOR, CALLE DE LA PAJA 23, BARCELONA (2). TN: 3015884. Established 1900. Shop. Very large stock. Spec: engravings; ex-libris; antiquarian; popular art. Cata.

LIBRERIA JOSE A. FERNANDEZ BERCHI, CLAUDIO MOYANO 26, MADRID. Sec. and antiq. Shop.

LIBRERIA SAN BERNARDO, CALLE SAN BERNARDO 63, MADRID 8. Prop: Antonio Chiverto. Shop. Large stock sec. and antiq. Spec: fine and rare.

LIBRERIA BOSCH. CARLOS ARNICHES 15, MADRID. Sec. and antiq. stock Shop.

LIBRERIA EL CALLEJON, Calle Preciados 2, Madrid. TN: 221 71 67.

LIBRERIA ANTICUARIA ANGEL CARACEDO, Pelayo 76, Madrid. TN: 419 53 36.

LA CASE DE LA TROYA, Luna 21 (portada roja), Madrid. TN: 2219478. Cata.

FIOL, LLIBRES, OMS 45–A, Palma de Mallorca, 07003. Prop: Miguel Fiol Roig. TN: 221428. Established 1950. Shop, early closing Saturday. Large stock. Spec: rare ,books on the Western Mediterranean; Spanish and English XX century. Corresp: English, Français. B: Banco Central, No.

LIBRERIA ANGEL GOMIS, Luna 17 Y Estrella 6, Madrid 13. Sec. and antiq. stock. Shop.

LIBRERIA FRANCISCO GOMIS, Claudio Moyano 27, Madrid 7. Sec. and antiq. stock. Shop.

LIBRERIA GRANATA, Reyes Carolicos 8, Almeria. Manager: Antonio Moreno. A.B.A.

ADOLF M. HAKKERT, Calle Alfambra 26, Las Palmas TN: 277350.
Est: 1952. Very small stock sec. and antiq. Spec. Classical Philology;
ancient history, Byzantium. Corresp. English, Deutsch

LIBRERIA HESPERIA, Plaza de Los Sitios 10, Zaragoza. (Apartado
Postal 272). Prop: Luis Marquina y Marin. TN: (34–76) 235367.
Established 1953. Shop and storeroom, open evenings Monday to
Friday. Very large stock, also new books. Spec: Hispanica old and rare;
Americana. Cata: 2 a year. Corresp: English, Français, Italiano. B:
Banco Central, Oficina Principal, Zaragoza. Account No. 0892280.
M: ABA.

LIBRERIA MANTEROLA, Manterola 8, San Sebastian. TN: 42 50 72.
Sec. and antiq. stock. Spec: rare and curious, especially *del pais vasco*.

LIBRERIA MIRTO, Ruiz de Alarcon 27, Madrid 14. Prop: Señora
Herminia Allanegui. TN: 239 83 31. Established 1950. Shop. Large
stock. Spec: Spanish literature and fine arts. Cata: occasionally.
Corresp: English. B: Banco Español de Crédito. A.B.A.

GABRIEL MOLINA—SUCESORA, Travesia del Arenal 1, Madrid.
Prop: Señora Antonia Molina Rico. TN: 266 44 43. Established 1870.
Shop. Spec: old and rare; curious; also new books. Cata. Corresp
Français. B: Banco Hispano Americano. A.B.A.

PAUL ORSSICH, Apartado 177, Mahon, Menorca. Spec: Spain and
Balearic Islands pre 1900.

PARA BIBLIOFILOS, Pl. San Martin 3, Madrid.

PORTER-LIBROS, Avenida Puerta del Angel 9, Barcelona. A.B.A.

LIBRERIA DE ESTANISLAO RODRIGUEZ POSSE, San Bernardo 27
Madrid 8. Sec. and antiq.

EL RENACIMIENTO, Huertes 49, Madrid. TN: 429 26 17.

LIBRERIA RIPOLL, San Miguel 12, (Apartado 338), Palma de
Mallorca. TN: 22 13 55. Medium stock sec. and antiq. Spec
autographs, fine and rare.

LA LIBRERIA DEL SOL I DE LA LLUNA, Carrer de la Çanuda 24
Barcelona 2.

SANTO VANASIA, Calle Victor Hugo 1, Madrid 4. TN: 22 23 076.

LIBERIA ANTICUARIA EL VIADUCTO, Plaza Cruz Verde 1
Madrid. TN: 241 30 30.

FRANCE

FRANKREICH

Association: Verband

S.L.A.M. =Syndicat du Livre Ancien et des Metiers Annexes, 117 Boulevard Saint-Germain, 75006 Paris, TN: 329 2101 et 633 8000.

Public Holidays: Jour de Fête: Feiertage

Jan. 1: Easter Monday: May 1: Ascension: Whitmonday: Jul. 14: Aug. 15: Nov. 1 and 11: Christmas Day.

Jan. 1: lundi de Pâques: Mai 1: Ascension: lundi de Pentecôte: Jul. 14: Août 15: Nov. 1 et 11: Déc. 25.

Jan. 1: Ostermontag: Mai 1: Himmelfahrt. Pfingstmontag: Jul. 14: Aug. 15: Nov. 1 und 11: Dez. 25.

Banks: Banques: Banken

B.F.   =Banque de France

B.I.C.S.   =Banque Industrielle et Commerciale

B.N.C.I.   =Banque National de Commerce et Industrie

C.C.F.   =Crédit Commerciale de France

C.F.C.B.   =Compagnie Française de Crédit et de Banque

C.I.C.   =Crédit Industriel et Commercial

C.L.   =Crédit Lyonnais

C.N.   =Crédit du Nord

C.N.E.P.   =Comptoire National d'Escompte de Paris

S.G.   =Société Génfale

77

FRANCE

I   PARIS: Arrondissements 1er—4e; 5e; 6e; 7e; 8e; 9e; 10e—20e
    Districts

II FRANCE (NORD): NORDFRANKREICH: NORTHERN
    FRANCE
    Postcodes: Postleitzahlen: 14; 50; 59; 76; 78; 91; 92; 95

III FRANCE (OUEST): WESTFRANKREICH: WESTERN
    FRANCE
    Postcodes: Postleitzahlen: 17; 24; 28; 29; 33; 35; 37; 41; 44
    45; 49; 72.

IV FRANCE (EST: OSTFRANKREICH: EASTERN FRANCE
    Postcodes: Postleitzahlen: 21; 25; 38; 42; 54; 57; 67; 68; 69
    71; 73; 89.

V   FRANCE (SUD): SUDFRANKREICH: SOUTHERN FRANCE
    Postcodes: Postleitzahlen: 06; 11; 13; 30; 31; 34; 64; 81; 82
    83; 84.

VI MONACO

I
PARIS Arrondissements 1er-4e

LIBRAIRIE 'LES ARCADES', 8 RUE DE CASTIGLIONE, F-75001 PARIS.

LES CHEVAUX LÉGERS, 34 RUE VIVIENNE, 75002 PARIS. TN: 2362311
S.L.A.M. Prop: Pierre de Kerangué et Malo Pollès. Boutique ferm
Samedi Apres Midi et Adût. Spec: Bretagne, Provence; Droi
beaux-arts.

YVES CURT, 119 RUE SAINT-DENIS, 75001.

LIBRAIRIE DELAMAIN, 155 RUE SAINT-HONORÉ, 75001 PARIS. Géran
Roger Scelles. Directeur: Philippe Baldassari. TN: 261 48 78. Fondé
en 1710. Boutique. Important stock. Spec: Livres Armorié:
Litterature 17, 18, 19e siècles. Cata: 1 par an. B: Banque Parisienne d
Crédit, 40 blvd. du Montparnasse, 75015 Paris Compte: 210 0567 :
Littérature Française 1910–1950. S.L.A.M.

LIBRAIRIE-GALERIE JEAN FOURNIER, 44 RUE QUINCAMPOIX, 7500
PARIS. TN: (1) 277.32.31. Fermée lundi. Spec: Beaux-arts; estampe
périodiques (beaux-arts); livres illustrés. Cata. S.L.A.M.

78

LIBRAIRIE FRANÇAISE ET ÉTRANGÈRE GALIGNANI, 224 RUE DE RIVOLI, 75001 PARIS. TN: 260 76 07. Spec: littérature anglaise; beaux-arts. S.L.A.M.

ANTOINE GRANDMAISON, LIBRAIRIE "LES ARCADES", 8 RUE DE CASTIGLIONE, 75001 PARIS. Prop: Daniel Founès. TN: 260 62 96. Fondée en 1884. Boutique. Moyen stock, aussi les livres neufs. Spec: belles reliures; histoire; beaux-arts. Corresp: English. B: Morgan Guaranty Trust Company. Compte No 410 156 009. CP: Paris 1203–75. S.L.A.M., S.B.L.A.M.

RAPHAËL KATZ, 157 Rue Saint-Martin, 75003 Paris. TN: 887 52 76.

KERANGUÉ ET POLLÈS, 34 RUE VIVIENNE, 75002 PARIS. TN: 236 23 11.

GERARD LEQUELTEL, 6 RUE D'AMBOISE, 75002 PARIS. TN: (1) 296.56.47. Fermé samedi et août. Ventes publiques. S.L.A.M.

LIBRAIRIE DES VICTOIRES, 4 BIS PLACE DES PETITS PÈRES, 75002 PARIS. Prop: Isabelle Maurel. TN: 260 98 13. Fondée en 1974. Boutique, Fermée samedi. Très restreint stock. Spec: livres d'enfants; livres illustrés; modes 1900–1925. Corresp: English. S.L.A.M, L.I.L.A.

GALERIE FRANCOIS MIRON, 62 RUE FRANCOIS MIRON, 75004 PARIS. TN: 277 76 xx.

ALBERT PETIT-SIROUX, 45, 46, 47 GALERIE VIVIENNE, 75002 PARIS. TN: (1) 296.06.24. Fermée juillet et août. Spec: vieux papiers; cartes postales; varia; régionalisme; livres illustrés du XXe siècle; biographie; histoire. S.L.A.M.

LIBRAIRIE POURSIN, CITE NOËL, 22 RUE RAMBUTEAU, 75003 PARIS. TN: (1) 887 13.73. Ouvert les après-midi ou sur rendez-vous. Spec: régionalisme; histoire; memoires; Catalogues sur demande. S.L.A.M.

PAUL ROULLEAU, 108 RUE SAINT-HONORÉ, 75001 PARIS. TN: 233 49 52. Spec: militaria; estampes. S.L.A.M.

SOCIÉTÉ HÉBRAICA JUDAICA, 12 RUE DES HOSPITALIÈRES ST.-GERVAIS, 75004 PARIS. Gérant: B. Liebermann. TN: 887 32 20. Fondée en 1920. Boutique, fermé Samedi. Moyen stock. Spec: Judaica et Hebraica; en toutes langues. Corresp: English, Deutsch, Español. B: Société Génerale, 32 Rue des Archives, 75004 Paris. Agence F., Marais, Compte No. 2003384-4. S.L.A.M.

LIBRAIRIE SYLVIE, 26 PLACE VOSGES, 75003 PARIS. TN: 887 94 34.

JOSIANE VEDRINES, 38 RUE DE RICHELIEU, 75001 PARIS. TN: (1) 296.10.12. Fermé samedi et août. Spec: numismatique; histoire; archéologie; biographie; bibliographie. S.L.A.M.

PARIS Arrondissement 5e

JACQUES BENELLI, 244 RUE SAINT-JACQUES, 75005 PARIS. TN: 633 73 51.

MARCEL BOISGERAULT, 31 FOSSÉS SAINT-MARCEL, 75005 PARIS. TN: 535 98 40.

MICHEL BON, 4 RUE FREDERIC-SAUTON, 75005 PARIS. TN: 633.91.94. Spec: archéologie, ethnographie, glyptique, hermétisme. numismatique, orientalisme. Cata. S.L.A.M.

LIBRAIRIE DU CAMÉE, 75005 PARIS. Prop: Michel Trochon. TN: 707 62 31. Fondée en 1950. Boutique, fermé samedi aprés midi. Moyen stock. Spec: ouvrages documentaires. Cata: 5 par an. Corresp: English. B B.I.C.-R.N.P. Saint Denis, 14 21 04577 1. CP: Paris 2931 11 S.L.A.M., L.I.L.A.

DIDIER CART-TANNEUR, 11 BIS RUE VAUQUELIN, 75005 PARIS. TN: (1) 336.02.85. Fermé mardi matin et août. Spec: agriculture; botanique art et archtecture des jardins; eaux et forêts. S.L.A.M.

FLORENCE DE CHASTENAY, 76 RUE GAY-LUSSAC, 75005 PARIS. TN: 033 05 78. Boutique. Spec: demonologie; fantastique. S.L.A.M.

LIBRAIRIE DUCHEMIN, 18 RUE SOUFFLOT, 75005 PARIS. Prop: A. Chauny et P. Quinsac. TN: (33–1) 354 79 16. Fondée en 1868. Boutique fermée samedi. Très important stock, nous faisons aussi des livres neufs. Spec: droit. B: B.N.P., Agence Sorbonne, compte 259005. CP: Paris 586 80. S.L.A.M.

EX-LIBRIS, 11 RUE VICTOR COUSIN, 75005 PARIS. Prop: Charles Blackburn. (Une division d'Europeriodiques S.A.) TN: (1) 325 50 16. Fondée en 1964. Fermé Samedi. Spec: Voyages; Extrême-Orient; Maghreb; Islam; Cartes; Exotica. Corresp: English, Japonaise. B: Lloyds Bank International (France) Ltd., 43 Boulevard Capucines, 75002 Paris, Compte 121 646547. CCP: Paris 1987834. S.L.A.M., A.B.A., L.I.L.A.

LIBRAIRIE DE LA FACULTÉ DES SCIENCES, RUE DES URSULINES. 75005 PARIS. TN: 033 23 04. Fondée en 1961. Boutique. Spec: ouvrages tirés a part, périodiques de sciences naturalles. Cata. Corresp: English, Español. B: B.I.C.S., 64 rue Monge, 75005 Paris, Compte 4014–017249. S.L.A.M.

JACQUES GABAY, 151 BIS. RUE SAINT-JACQUES, 75005 PARIS. TN: (1) 354.64.64. Spec: Sciences exactes; sciences naturelles; médecine ancienne; philosophie; voyages; langues anciennes. S.L.A.M.

GIBERT JEUNE, 23 QUAI SAINT-MICHEL, 75005 PARIS. TN: 354 5732. Fondée en 1886. Très important stock. Spec: beaux-arts; luxe. Aussi les livres neufs. Cata: 2 par an. Corresp: English, Deutsch, Italiano. B: B.N.P. CP: Paris 5837–11. S.L.A.M.

L'INVITATION AU VOYAGE, 15 QUAI SAINT-MICHEL, 75005 PARIS. Prop: Claude Menetret. TN: 354 94 74. Fondée en 1952. Boutique. Assez restreint stock. Spec: voyages. B: C.I.C. CP: Paris 7922–31. S.L.A.M.

LIBRAIRIE J. JOLY, 6 RUE VICTOR-COUSIN, 75005 PARIS. TN: 326 58 15. Fondée en 1937. Sur rendezvous dépot. Très important stock. Spec: droit ancien et moderne; periodiques juridiques. Cata. B: Crédit Lyonnais, Agence U, 22 boulevard St-Michel, Paris. CP: Paris 1409–14.

ALFRED MADER, 67 RUE SAINT-JACQUES, 75005 PARIS. TN: 326 3323. Boutique. Fermée lundi et août. Moyen stock, aussi les livres neufs. Spec: philosophie; occultisme. Cata. B: Crédit Lyonnais, Agence U., Paris. CP: Paris 74995. S.L.A.M.

BERNARD MAILLE, 3 RUE DANTE, 75005 PARIS. TN: 325 51 73. Spec: sciences et médicine.

R.-G. MICHEL, 17 QUAI SAINT-MICHEL, 75005 PARIS. TN: 354 77 75. Spec: éstampes; dessins. B: Crédit Lyonnais, Agence U, Compte 6057–W. CP: Paris 569–24. S.L.A.M.

LIBRAIRIE A.-G. NIZET, 3 bis PLACE DE LA SORBONNE, 75005 PARIS. TN: (354) 79 76. Fondée en 1922. Boutique. Très important stock. Spec: érudition; belles-lettres. Cata: 1 par an. Corresp: English. B: C.I.C. Agence M, Paris. Compte 14 677/51. CP: Paris 473 88.

AU PLAISIR DU TEXTE, 8 RUE DES FOSSÉS ST.-JACQUES, 75005 PARIS. Succursale de A.G. Nizet. TN: 354 82 92. Stock moyen. Spec: littérature ancienne et moderne; linguistique; livres illustrés.

SARTONI-CERVEAU, 13 QUAI SAINT-MICHEL, 75005 PARIS. TN: (1) 354 75 73. Spec: anciennes estampes; gravures; images; voyages géographie; marine. S.L.A.M.

LIBRAIRIE PHILOSOPHIQUE J. VRIN, 6 Place de la Sorbonne, 75005 Paris. Prop: Andrée Vrin. TN: 354 03 47. Fondée en 1843. Boutique, fermé Samedi. Très important stock, édite aussi livres d'érudition. Spec: philosophie, littérature; médecine; histoire; économie politique. Cata: 10 par an. B: B.N.P., Agence Sorbonne, Compte 270 061. CP: Paris 196 30 30 T. S.L.A.M.

PARIS Arrondissement 6e

LIBRAIRIE DE L'ABBAYE, 27 rue Bonaparte, 75006 Paris. TN: 354 89 99. Fondée en 1904. Boutique. Très important stock. Spec: autographes. Cata: 8 par an. B: Barclays, Agence 175. C.L.E.F.

MARCEL ADLER, 3 Quai Malaquais, 75006 Paris. TN: (021) 27 80 00. Spec: livres illustrés; beaux-arts. (*aussi* 5 Boulevard de Grancy, 1006 Lausanne, Suisse)

LIBRAIRIE DES ALPES, 6 rue de Seine, 75006 Paris. Prop: Mme. Elise Vibert-Guigue. TN: (1) 326 90 11. Boutique, fermée lundi. Moyen stock. Spec: alpinisme, pyreneisme: Jules Verne. Cata: 1 par an. Corresp: English. B: Crédit Commercial de France. Compte 070 228 6210. CP: 250 4336 K. Paris. S.L.A.M.

L'AMATEUR D'ART, 38 rue de Vaugirard, 75006 Paris. Prop: Michel Screpel. TN: (1) 354 00 85. Spec: Editions originales; voyages; livres romantiques illustrés; histoire. Cata. S.L.A.M.

LIBRAIRIE-GALERIE ARENTHON, 3 Quai Malaquais, 75006 Paris. Prop: L. Desalmand. TN: (1) 326 86 06. Fermée dimanche et août. Spec: beaux-arts, estampes, livres illustrés modernes, affiches. Cata. S.L.A.M.

LIBRAIRIE D'ARGENCES, 38 rue Saint-Sulpice, 75006 Paris. TN: 354 05 60. Spec: histoire; religion; philologie. Cata. B.N.P. CP: Paris 8114–70. S.L.A.M.

LES ARGONAUTES, 74 rue Seine, 75006 Paris. TN: 3266 70 69.

FABRICE BAYARRE, 21 rue de Tournon, 75006 Paris. TN: (1) 354 91 99. Spec: voyages; sciences; medicine; marine; manuscrits; livres illustrés modernes. S.L.A.M.

BERCHE ET PAGIS, 60 rue Mazarine, 75006 Paris. TN: 354 27 67. Boutique, fermé lundi. Spec: histoire; voyages; beaux-arts.

A. BLANCHARD, 9 RUE DE MÈDICIS, 75006 PARIS. TN: 326 90 34. Fondé
en 1922. Boutique. Restreint stock. Spec: mathematique, physique,
Chimie, sciences naturelles. Corresp: English, Deutsch. B: Crédit
Lyonnais, Agence U, 421 Compte 7173 Y, boulevard St.-Michel,
Paris. S.L.A.M.

LIBRAIRIE BONAPARTE, S.A.R.L., 31 RUE BONAPARTE, 75006 PARIS
Prop: Madame J. Buisson. TN: 326 9756. Fondèe en 1937. Boutique.
Restreint stock, aussi les livres neufs. Spec: Spectacles; thèâtre; danse,
marionnettes, etc. Cata. Corresp: English. B: C.I.C., Succursale F
Compte 18.012.73. CP: Paris 925 80. S.L.A.M.

BOUQUINERIE DE L'INSTITUT S.A., 12 RUE DE SEINE, 75006 PARIS.
Gérant: Alain Mazo. TN: 326 beaux-arts; estampes. S.L.A.M.

ALAIN BRIEUX, 48 RUE JACOB, 75006 PARIS. TN: 260 2198. TA: Alibri
Paris. Fondée en 1960. Boutique. Fermée samedi et août.Stock
specialisé et livres neufs de documentation sur l'histoire des sciences et
de la medécine. Spec: médecine; sciences. Cata. Corresp: Deutsch
English. B: Banque Worms, Compte 401 35 390 A. CP: Paris 16 528
04. S.L.A.M.

CLAUDE BUFFET, 7 RUE SAINT-SULPICE, 75006 PARIS. TN: 326 61 79
Fondée en 1923. Boutique. Fermée Lundi. Moyen stock. Spec
littérature Française et traductions XIXe et XXe siecles. Corresp
English, Deutsch. B: B.N.P., Agence Boulevard Saint-Germain, No
213743 15. CP: La Source 3378740. J. S.L.A.M., L.I.L.A.

LIBRAIRIE DU CAMEE, 34 RUE SERPENTE, 75006 PARIS. Prop: Miche
Trochon. TN: (1) 326 21 70. Ouvert de 14 h. à 19 h., fermé samedi e
août. Spec: métiers; artisanat; écologie; techniques anciennes
S.L.A.M.

ROBERT CAYLA, 28 RUE SAINT-SULPICE, 75006 PARIS. TN: 326 4887
Boutique. Spec: éditions originales modernes; romantiques; manuscrit
autographes. S.L.A.M.

PHILIPPE CHABANEIX, 33 RUE MAZARINE, 75006 PARIS. TN: 32
8483. Boutique, fermé Lundi. Spec: éditions originales moderne
littérature générale; poésie. S.L.A.M.

MAISON CHARAVAY, 3 RUE DE FURSTENBERG, 75006 PARIS. Pro
Michel Castaing. TN: 354 59 89. TA: Charautographe Paris. Fondé
en 1830. Boutique. Fermée samedi. Très important stock. Spe
autographs et documents historiques. Cata: 4 par an. B: Créd
Lyonnais. CP: Paris 54 04 22. S.L.A.M.

GEORGES CHAUVIN, 78 RUE MAZARINE, 75006 PARIS. TN: 326 1066. Boutique. Spec: histoire; géographie; philosophie; religions. CP: Paris 11019–67. S.L.A.M.

LIBRAIRIE I. CHMELJUK, 1 RUE DE FLEURUS, 75006 PARIS. TN: 548 36 68. Fondée en 1930. Magasin. Moyen stock. Spec: Slavisme, Europe de l'Est. Cata: 4 par an. Corresp: anglais. B: Credit du Nord, 21 rue de Vaugirard, 75006 Paris. CP: Paris 1290 91. M: S.L.A.M.

CLAVREUIL, 37 RUE SAINT-ANDRÉ-DES-ARTS 75006 PARIS. TN: 326 7117. Boutique. Spec: histoire. CP: Paris 11 196 27. S.L.A.M.

RENÉ CLUZEL, 61 RUE DE VAUGIRARD, 75006 PARIS. TN: 222 38 71. Fondée en 1973. Boutique. Stock moyen. Fermée lundi. Spec: beaux livres anciens et rares du 16ème au 19ème; littérature éditions originales; reliures; livres illustrés; occultismes; curiosa anciens; livres d'enfants. Cata: sur demande. Corresp:

GASTON COLAS, 84 BOULEVARD RASPAIL, 75006 PARIS. TN: 548 1958. Boutique fermée samedi. Spec: beaux-arts; architecture;archéologie; costumes. CP: Paris 19401. S.L.A.M.

PIERRE COLAS, 38 RUE DE VAUGIRARD, 75006 PARIS. TN: 033 0085. Fermé Août. Spec: beaux-arts; voyages. CP: Paris 12258–82. S.L.A.M.

C. COULET & A. FAURE, 5 RUE DROUOT, 75006 PARIS. TN: 770 84 87 et 770 86 38. Fondée 1883. Boutique. Important stock. Spec: editions originales; livres illustrés. Cata: 10 par an. B: B.F.C.E., 21 boulevard Haussman, Paris 9e. CP: Paris 9401-86. S.L.A.M.

JEAN COULET, 1 RUE DAUPHINE, 75006, PARIS. TN: 326 42 40.

FRANCIS DASTÉ, 16 RUE DE TOURNON, 75006 PARIS. TN: 326 52 89. Fondée en 1942. Boutique fermé samedi.Moyen stock. Spec: Histoire et topographie de Paris; bibliophilie. Cata: 1 par an. Corresp: English. CP: Paris 5222–31. S.L.A.M.

JEAN DESCHAMPS, 22 RUE VISCONTI, 75006 PARIS. TN: 326 9797. Ouvert de 15.30 à 18.00; fermée août. Spec: 19ème siecle. CP: Paris 97543. S.L.A.M.

MICHELE DHENNEQUIN, 76 RUE DU CHERCHE-MIDI, 75006 PARIS. TN: (1) 222 18 53. Fermé samedi après-midi. Spec: voyages (anciennes colonies francaises); ethnographie; ethnologie, orientalisme. S.L.A.M.

GALERIE DOCUMENTS, RUE DE SEINE 53, 75006 PARIS. Prop: Michel Romand. TN: 354 50 68. Fondée en 1954. Boutique, fermé lundi matin et août. Moyen stock. Spec: affiches originales. "Fin de Siecle". Corresp: English. B: Union de Banques a Paris, Compte 88 107 520 00 8. CP: Paris 11 629 48. S.L.A.M., Chambre Syndicate de l'Estampe et du Dessin.

JEAN-PIERRE DUTEL, 17 RUE MAZARINE, 75006 PARIS. TN: 354 17 77.

L'ENVERS DU MIROIR, 19 RUE DE SEINE, 75006 PARIS. Prop: Ivan Bonnefoy. TN: 354 45 13. Spec: poesie.

ESPAGNON ET LEBRET, 1 RUE DE FLEURUS, 75006 PARIS. TN: (1) 549 06 96. Fermé lundi matin. Spec: Editions originales; livres illustrés; économie politique, histoire sociale. Cata: S.L.A.M.

LIBRAIRIE FLAMMARION, 4 RUE CASIMIR DELAVIGNE, 75006 PARIS. TN: 033 3014. Spec: éditions originales; beaux-arts. CP: Paris 81424. S.L.A.M.

LIBRAIRIE LE FRANÇOIS, 91 BOULEVARD SAINT-GERMAIN, 75006 PARIS. TN: 325 30 49. Spec: médecine. S.L.A.M.

CHRISTIAN GALANTARIS, 15 RUE DES SAINTS-PÈRES, 75006 PARIS. TN: 703 49 65. Fondée en 1974. Boutique. Spec: éditions originales; livres illustrés; reliures, autographes. Ventes aux enchères. Corresp: English, Español. B: B.N.P., 1 rue de Médicis, 75006 Paris. Compte 210 010 16. S.L.A.M. Fondée en 1974. Boutique. Spec: beaux livres anciens et modernes; livres illustrés; reliures, autographes.

LIBRAIRIE DU SPECTACLE GARNIER ARNOUL, 39 RUE DE SEINE, 75006 PARIS. TN: 033 8005. Prop. et Dir.: Francis Garnier Arnoul et Bengt Svensson. Fondée en 1951. Boutique. Stock important, aussi livres neufs. Spec: théâtre; musique; ballet; cirque; mime; marionnettes; cinéma; affiches; gravures; photos; autographs seulement sur les Spectacles. Cata. Corresp: English, Sveg. B: B.I.C.S., 226 Boul. Saint-Germain, 75007 Paris, Compte 4019–001954. CP: Paris 8124–40. S.L.A.M., L.I.L.A.

LIBRAIRIE ORIENTALISTE PAUL GEUTHNER S.A. 12 RUE VAVIN, 75006 PARIS. TN: 634 71 30 TA: Liborient Paris. Fondée en 1902. Boutique Fermé samedi. Spec: Afrique; archéologie; Assyriologie; Egypte; Islam; Extrême Orient; voyages; linguistique; religion; périodiques. Corresp: English, Deutsch. B: Banque Crédit Commercial de France, Agence Odéon, 75006 Paris. Compte 070/2076080. CP: Paris 1524–50 (France) et 9897–97 (Etranger). S.L.A.M.

FRANÇOIS GIRAND, 76 RUE DE SEINE, 75006 PARIS. TN: 325 1033. Boutique. Spec: géographie; régionalisme livres á gravures. CP: Paris 15279–95. S.L.A.M.

LIBRAIRIE GIRAUD-BADIN, 22 RUE GUYNEMER, 75006 PARIS. TN: (1) 548 30 58. Boutique, Fermé samedi et août. Spec: ventes aux encheáres; manuscrits livres illustrés: bibliographie. Cata. B: B.N.P. CP: Paris 50247. S.L.A.M.
Aussi 2 RUE DE FLEURUS, 75006 PARIS.

LIBRAIRIE GUÉNÉGAUD, S.A.R.L., 10 RUE DE L'ODÉON, 75006 PARIS. TN: 326 07 91. Prop: Jean-Etienne Huret. Fondé en 1947. Boutique. Important stock. Spec: Régionalisme. Cata: 2 par an. Corresp: English. B: Banque B.N.P., 5 rue de la Pompe, 75116 Paris Compte 271265-39. CP: Paris 6027 86. C.L.E.F., Cercle de la Libraire.

J. HUETZ DE LEMPS, 70 RUE DU CHERCHE-MIDI, 75006 PARIS. TN: 222 61 31. Boutique, fermé lundi. Moyen stock. Corresp: English, Español. B: Banque de France, compte 317221. CP: Paris 827716. S.L.A.M.

JEAN HUGUES. 1 RUE DE FURSTENBERG, 75006 PARIS. TN: 326 7476. Spec: manuscrits; reliures; beaux livres anciens. S.L.A.M.

L'INTERMÉDIAIRE DU LIVRE, 88 RUE BONAPARTE, 75006 PARIS. Prop: Bernard Hiard. TN: 633 00 50. Fondée en 1952. Boutique fermée août. Important Stock. Spec: Réligion, Philosophie, Histoire. Cata: 2 par an. B: C.L. 5363 D. CP: 814021. S.L.A.M.

PAUL JAMMES, 3 RUE GOZLIN, 75006 PARIS. TN: 326 47 71. Fondée en 1925. Sur rendezvous. Important stock. Spec: littérature; livres anciens; typographie; bibliographie estampes. Corresp: English, Deutsch, Italiano, Español. B: Banque de France, Paris-Raspail, Compte 323 612. CP: Paris 1361 80. S.L.A.M.

LIBRAIRIE RENÉ KIEFFER, 46 RUE SAINT-ANDRÉ DES ARTS, 75006 PARIS. Prop: Michel Kieffer. TN: 326 47 11. Fondée en 1903. Boutique. Important stock. Spec: illustrés modernes; éditions originales. Cata: 4 par an. B: B.N.P. 200 048/60. CP: Paris 370 147. S.L.A.M.

HENRI LAFFITTE LIBRAIRE, 13 RUE DE BUCI, 75006 PARIS. Prop: Henri Lafitte. TN: 326 6828. Fondé en 1936. Boutique. Important stock. Spec: Littèrature, histoire contemporaine, revues, bibliophilie. Cata: 3 par an. B: B.N.P. Saint-Germain, Paris. Compte 214 364 92. CP: Paris 600–90. S.L.A.M., L.I.L.A.

LIBRAIRIE LEONCE LAGET, 75 RUE DE RENNES, 75006 PARIS. TN: 548 90 18. TA: Liblaget Paris 110. Fondée en 1955. Boutique, fermé samedi. Moyen stock, aussi les livres neufs. Spec: beaux-arts architecture. Cata. Corresp: English. B: Union de Banques á Paris, and Westminster Foreign Bank, Paris. CP: La Source 3154500. S.L.A.M. L.I.L.A.

DIDIER LECOINTRE ET DENIS OZANNE, 9 RUE DE TOURNON, 75006 PARIS. TN: (1) 326 02 92. Fermé lundi. Spec: photographie architecture; génie civil; livres d'enfants. Cat: sur demande. S.L.A.M.

MARCEL LECOMTE, 17 RUE DE SEINE, 75006 PARIS. TN: 326 8547. Fondée en 1928. Magasin, fermé lundi. Très important stock. Spec: livres illustrés; beaux-arts; estampes originales. B: C.I.C., 57 rue de Rennes, Paris. CP: Paris 341 652. S.L.A.M.

LIBRAIRIE DU PONT NEUF R.G., 1 RUE DAUPHINE, 75006 PARIS. TN: 326 4240. Boutique. Spec: livres illustrés, litterature, voyages, reliures.

ALEXANDRE LOEWY, 85 RUE DE SEINE, 75006 PARIS. TN: 354 1195.
Boutique. Fermé Lundi. Moyen stock, gravures, dessins. Spec: livres
illustrés modernes: reliures. Corresp: English, Deutsch. Cata. B:
C.C.F., 2 Carrefour de L'Odéon, Paris 6e. Compte 070 218 4640. CP:
Paris 1518–91. S.L.A.M.

BERNARD LOLIÉE, 72 RUE DE SEINE, 75006 PARIS. TN: 326 5382.
Boutique. Spec: Surrealisme; éditions originales; livres illustrés;
autographes. B: C.C.F., 2 Carrefour de l'Odéon, Paris 6e. CP: Paris
6697–19. S.L.A.M.

LIBRAIRIE C. MAFART, 9 RUE MAÎTRE ALBERT, 75006 PARIS. TN: 329
39 20

JEAN-JACQUES MAGIS, 47 RUE SAINT ANDRÉ-DES-ARTS, 76006 PARIS.
TN: 326 50 57. TA: Magislibri. Telex: JJM 202351 F. Fondée en
1925. Boutique, fermé samedi et août. Très important stock. Spec:
livres anciens en sciences économiques, politiques et juridiques. Cata: 2
par an. Corresp. English, Español, Deutsch, Italiano. B: C.I.C. Agence
M. Compte 11 050 47. CP: Paris 7929 26. S.L.A.M., Compagnie des
experts specialisés.

LIBRAIRIE D'AMERIQUE ET D'ORIENT ADRIEN MAISONNEUVE,
11 RUE ST. SULPICE, 75006 PARIS. Prop: Jean Maisonneuve. TN: 326
86 35. Fondée en 1926. Boutique, fermée samedi et août. Très
important stock, aussi les livres neufs. Spec: l'Orient et l'Orientales.
Cata: sans périodicité. Corresp: English, Español, Deutsch. B: Crédit
Lyonnais, Agence V Paris, Compte 6534 J et 6535 K. CP: Paris
849–13.C. S.L.A.M., Syndicat des Editeurs, Cercle de la Librairie.

YVES MARGOTAT, 8 RUE DE L'ODÉON, 75006 PARIS. TN: 326 9818.
Fondée en 1963 (ancien Librairie René Colas 1913). Boutique. Moyen
stock. Spec: bibliographie, typographie; livres rares; littérature
Française; histoire. Cata: 1 par an. Corresp: English. B: Banque de
France, W 350 006. CP: Paris 1492. S.L.A.M.

FERNAND MARTINEZ, 97 RUE DE SEINE, 75006 PARIS. TN: (1) 633 08
12. Spec: cartes géographiques anciennes; décoration; régionalisme.
S.L.A.M.

JEAN-CLAUDE MARTINEZ, 21 RUE SAINT-SULPICE, 75006 PARIS. TN:
326 3453. Spec: beaux-arts; Orientalism, Religiòns.

ALAIN MAZO, 15 RUE GUÉNÉGAUD, 75006 PARIS. TN: 326 3984. Spec:
beaux-arts; livres illustrés; gravures modernes. CP: Paris 5721–88.
S.L.A.M.

LES MEILLEURS LIVRES, 18 boulevard Saint-Michel, 75006 Paris. Boutique. Stock important. Spec: érudition.

LIBRAIRIE MONGE, 5 rue de L'Echaudé, 75006 Paris. Prop: G. Zyssman. TN: 633 1984. Fondée en 1952. Boutique. Spec: histoire des sciences et de la médecine (seulement). Cata. CP: Paris 7019–40. S.L.A.M.

CHARLES MORIN, 102 rue de Cherche-Midi, 75006 Paris. TN: 548 0391. Fondée 1939. Boutique, Ouverte de 13h à 18h30; fermée le lundi. l'après-midi. Restreint stock. Cata: par an et listes thèmatiques.

LES NEUF MUSES, 41 Quai des Grands-Augustins, 75006 Paris. TN: (1) 326 38 71. Fermé lundi. Ouvert les après-midi et sur rendez-vous. Spec: autographes; manuscrits; éditions originales dedicacées et livres illustrés romantiques et modernes. S.L.A.M.

LIBRAIRIE NICAISE S.A., 145 boulevard Saint Germain, 75006 Paris. TN: 326 62 38. Fondée en 1943. Boutique. Important stock aussi livres neufs. Spec: éditions originales et illustrés; surrealisme et livres-objets; gravures modernes. Corresp: English. B: B.I.C.S., 226 b Saint Germain, 75007 Paris. CCP: Paris 892494. L.I.L.A., Compagnie des Libraires Experts de France (CLEF).

F. DE NOBELE, RUE BONAPARTE 35, 75006 PARIS. TN: (1) 326 0862. TA: Denobelef, Paris. Fondée en 1920. Boutique, Fermé samedi. Important stock, aussi les livres neufs. Cata: parfois. Corresp: English. B: B.N.P. 133 Bd St Germain, 75006 Paris, Compte 210 791. CP: Paris 394–22. Cercle de Librairie. S.L.A.M., Syndicat librairie ancienne Suisse, Belgique.

LIBRAIRIE PALLADIO, 66 RUE DU CHERCHE-MIDI, 75006 PARIS. TN: (1) 544 24 54. Fermée lundi et août. Spec: beaux-arts; architecture; critique littéraire; histoire; art militaire; littérature; livres d'enfants; régionalisme Paris. S.L.A.M.

J.-P. PARROT, 59 RUE DE RENNES, 75006 PARIS. TN: 548 5638. Fondée en 1905. Boutique, fermé lundi matin. Restreint stock. Spec: littérature; histoire; beaux-arts. Cata. Corresp: English, Deutsch. B: U.B.P. 62 rue Bonaparte, Paris 6e. CP: Paris 11221–80. S.L.A.M.

PARSIFAL [S.A.R.L.], 80 BOULEVARD RASPAIL, 75006 PARIS. Prop: M. Clavey. TN: (1) 548 89 11. Fermé lundi et août. Spec: beaux-arts; archéologie; architecture; cartes géographiques anciennes; estampes; généalogie; héraldique; histoire; emagerie; régionalisme. S.L.A.M.

EDITIONS A. & J. PICARD, 82 RUE BONAPARTE, 75006 PARIS. Prop: Chantal Pasini-Picard. TN: 326 96 73. Fondée en 1869. Boutique. Important stock. Spec: archéologie; histoire; religions; architecture; beaux arts. régionalisme. Cata: 6 par an. Corresp: English. B: C.I.C. Agence F, 57 rue de Rennes, Paris, Compte 16 691–37. CP: Paris 19164. Syndicat des Editeurs, Cercle de la Librairie.

J.-H. PINAULT, 36 RUE BONAPARTE, 75006 PARIS. TN: 633 0424. Fondée en 1917. Boutique. Moyen stock. Spec: littérature française; marine; medecine; minuscules; livres en petit format. Cata. B: U.B.P., Compte 88–131070–001. CP: Paris 2.854.86.5.

JEAN POLAK, 8 RUE DE L'ÉCHAUDÉ, 75006 PARIS. TN: 326 05 91. Fondée en 1938. Boutique. Très important stock. Spec: marine et voyages dans les cinq continents. Corresp: English, Deutsch, Español. B: Crédit Lyonnais, Agence U, 22 Boulevard St-Michel, 75006 Paris. CP: Paris 6282–10. S.L.A.M., L.I.L.A.

PONT TRAVERSÉ, 8 RUE DE VAUGIRARD, 75006 PARIS. Prop: M.-J. Lacaze. TN: (1) 548 06 48. Fermé lundi. Ouvert l'après-midi. Spec: poésie; éditions originales modernes; fantastique; surréalisme; littérature traduite; beaux-arts. S.L.A.M.

LA PORTE ETROITE, 10 rue Bonaparte, 75006 Paris. Gérant: Claude Schualberg. TN: (1) 354 26 03. Fondée en 1921. Boutique. Moyen stock. Livres neufs et anciens. Spec: beaux-arts. Cata: 1 par an. Corresp: English, Español, Deutsch, Italiano. CP: Paris 7725 59 U. S.L.A.M., L.I.L.A.

PAUL PROUTÉ S.A., 74 rue de Seine, 75006 Paris. TN: 326 89 80. Fondée en 1876 (1920). Boutique. Restreint stock, aussi gravures. Cata: 3 par an. Corresp: English, Deutsch. B: C.C.F. 070 21332920. CP: Paris 508 79. S.L.A.M. Syndicat des antiquaires; Chambre Syndicale de l'estampe.

ROBERT PROUTÉ, 12 rue de Seine, 75006 Paris. TN: 326 9322. Fondée en 1894. Boutique, fermé Lundi. Spec: gravures. CP: Paris 77057. S.L.A.M.

LIBRAIRIE PUGNO, 19 Quai des Grandes-Augustins, 75006 Paris. TN: 326 1480. Boutique. Spec: musique et littérature musicale. CP: Paris 12148–84.

LIBRAIRIE RIEFFEL, 15 rue de l'Odéon, 75006 Paris. Prop: Alain Delbès. TN: 033 92 93. S.L.A.M.

EMILE ROSSIGNOL, 8 rue Bonaparte, 75006 Paris. TN: 326 7431. Boutique. Spec: editions anciennes; incunables; manuscrits. Cata: 1 par an. B: U.B.P. rue Bonaparte 75006 Paris, Compte 88 135 070 003. CP: Paris 12884–21. S.L.A.M.

LIBRAIRIE EUGÉNE ROSSIGNOL, 4 rue de l'Odéon, 75006 Paris. TN: 354 68 20. Fondée en 1880. Ouverte Mardi, Mercredi, Jeudi. Très important stock. Spec: 16, 17, 18 siecles; et tous livres rares. CP: Paris 204138. S.L.A.M.

MAURICE ROUAM, 29 rue Mazarine, 75006 Paris. TN: 326 1271. Boutique, fermé Lundi. Spec: éditions originales; bibliographie; livres illustrés. CP: Paris 1899–41. S.L.A.M.

JEAN-PAUL ROUILLON, Galerie J.P.R., 27 rue de Seine, 75006 Paris. TN: 326 73 00. Spec: estampes; topographie. S.L.A.M.

LIBRAIRIE ROUSSEAU-GIRARD, 2 ter rue Dupin, 75006 Paris. TN 548 31 37. TA: Rousbooks. Fondée en 1939. Boutique. Fermée samedi. Stock important livres d'occasion. Spec: Littérature française; sciences naturelles et exactes. Cata. Corresp: English. S.L.A.M.

OLIVIER ROUX-DEVILLAS, 12 RUE BONAPARTE, 75006 PARIS. TN: 354 6932. Boutique. Spec: sciences anciennes; autographes; americana. CP: Paris 14473–12. S.L.A.M.

SAFFROY, 3 QUAI MALAQUAIS, 75006 PARIS. Prop: Mme Janine Naert. TN: 326 09 19. Fondée en 1880. Fermée samedi et août. Spec: autographes; documents historiques. Cata: autographes; 6 par an. Corresp: English. S.L.A.M.

GASTON SAFFROY, 4 RUE CLÉMENT, 75006 PARIS. TN: 326 25 92. Fondée en 1880. Boutique. Fermée août. Moyen stock. Spec: Généalogie; documentation; héraldique; histoire régionale. Cata: 2 par an. CP: Paris 883 09. S.L.A.M.

SAGOT LE GARREC & CIE, 24 RUE DU FOUR, 75006 PARIS. Prop: Jean-Claude Romand. TN: 326 4338. Boutique, fermé lundi matin et août. Spec: beaux-arts. S.L.A.M.

LIBRAIRIE ORIENTALE H. SAMUELIAN, 51 RUE MONSIEUR-LE-PRINCE, 75006 PARIS. TN: 326 88 65. Fondée en 1930. Boutique. Moyen stock, aussi les livres neufs. Spec: Orientalisme; Arabie; Arménie; Extr. Orient; etc. Corresp: English, Deutsch. B: B.N.P., Siège Sorbonne. Cte Dépôt 270.589, Cte Export 270.593. CP: Paris 1278–35. S.L.A.M., L.I.L.A.

LIBRAIRIE STENDHAL, 41 RUE MAZARINE, 75006 PARIS. Prop: Dominique Baudoin. Spec: histoire; littérature; livres illustrés romantiques ou modernes; régionalisme; reliures; vieux papiers. Cata. S.L.A.M.

THÉODORE TAUSKY, 33 RUE DAUPHINE, 75006 PARIS. TN: 734 4065. Spec: autographes; manuscrits; documents historiques. S.L.A.M.

LIBRAIRIE THOMAS-SCHELER, 19 RUE DE TOURNON, 75006 PARIS. Prop: Lucien Scheler et Bernard Clavreuil. TN: 326 9769. TA: Thomlib, Paris. Fondée en 1932. Boutique, fermé lundi. Moyen stock. Spec: Médicine, sciences, voyages, litteraturé incunables, gothiques. Cata. Corresp: English. CP: Paris 271–41. S.L.A.M., L.I.L.A., Cercle de la Librairie.

LIBRAIRIE ROBERT D. VALETTE, 11 RUE DE VAUGIRARD, 75006 PARIS. TN: (1) 326.45.64. Fermé lundi et du 1.8. au 10.9. Spec: autographes; éditions originales; gothiques; incunables; livres illustrés romantiques ou modernes; manuscrits; reliures. S.L.A.M.

JEAN VIARDOT, 15 RUE DE L'ECHAUDÉ, 75006 PARIS. TN: 633 60 07. Fondée en 1957. Boutique, fermé Samedi. Important stock. Spec: éditions originales; livres illustrés; sciences; voyages. Cata: 2–3 par an. Corresp: English. B: Crédit du Nord, Bd. Raspail 28, 75007 Paris. Compte 102.067.2. CP: 16 663 63. S.L.A.M., L.I.L.A.

RENÉ VIGNERON, LES ARGONAUTES, 74 RUE DE SEINE, 75006 PARIS. TN: 326 7069. Spec: autographes; manuscrits; éditions originales, livres illustrés. CP: Paris 7965–83. S.L.A.M.

D. WEIL, 1 RUE DU DRAGON, 75006 PARIS. TN: 222 19 14. Fondée en 1949. Par correspondance et sur rendez-vous. Stock important. Spec: Périodiques anciens et modernes, littéraires. Cata: sans pèriodicité. Corresp: English. B: B.I.C.S., Compte 313/1 Agence St.-Germain. 226 Boulevard Saint-Germain, 75007 Paris. CP: Paris 10 384 69. S.L.A.M., L.I.L.A.

GALERIE LUCIE WEIL. AU PONT DES ARTS. 6 RUE BONAPARTE, 75006 PARIS. TN: (1) 354.71.95.Fermée lundi et aout. Spec: estampes: gravures: livres illustrés ou modernes. S.L.A.M.

MADAME S. ZLATIN, 46 RUE MADAME, 75006 PARIS. TN: 222 06 47. Fondée en 1950. Domicile; 3 ème étage droite; ouvert de 14 á 18 heure, et sur rendez-vous. Fermé de 15 août au 15 septembre. Spec: liveres sur le Theátre, danse, cirque, marionnettes, musique et architecture théâtrale. Cata. CP: Paris 93–7473. S.L.A.M.

PARIS Arrondissement 7e

L'ARGUS DU LIVRE. 17 AVENUE DE LA BOURDONNAIS, 75007 PARIS. Prop: Maurice Dambournet. TN: (1) 602.90.75. sur rendez-vous. Spec: livres luxe, editions originales, livres epuises en tous genres. S.L.A.M.

AZATHOTH ET CIE, 107 RUE SAINT-DOMINIQUE, 75007 PARIS. TN: 5555 06 49.

GILBERTE COURNAND, 14 RUE DE BEAUNE, 75007 PARIS. TN: 261 24 42. Fondée en 1951. Boutique. Spec: livres, éstampes et sculptures sur la danse et les ballets. CP: Paris 11726–78. S.L.A.M.

LIBRAIRIE ELBÉ. 213BIS, BOULEVARD SAINT GERMAIN, 75007 PARIS. Prop: Jean-Louis Bonvallet. TN: 548 77 97. Boutique. Moyen stock, aussi livres neufs. Spécialités: Chasse, Equitation, Gastronomie, Beau-Arts, Voyages. Topographie: Cartes, Gravures. Catalogues. Corresp: English, Deutsch, Español, Italiano. Paris) C.C.P. Paris 16 885 84 Y

LIBRAIRIE GALLIMARD, 15 BOULEVARD RASPAIL, 75007 PARIS. TN: 548 2484. Boutique. Spec: éditions originales; beaux-arts; livres illustrés. CP: Paris 408–80. S.L.A.M.

EDMOND LASSARE, 1 bis RUE DE LA CHAISE, 75007 PARIS. TN: 551 66 12. S.L.A.M.

LIBRAIRIE MARC LOLIÉE, 40 RUE DES SAINTS-PÈRES, 75007 PARIS. TN: 548 40 19. Fondée en 1920. Boutique. Moyen stock. Spec: livres illustrés; éditions originales; livres anciens; autographes. Cata. Corresp: English. B: B.N.P., 133 boulevard Saint Germain, 75006 Paris. Compte. 210 419. CP: Paris 1002 80. S.L.A.M.

PIERRE PETITOT, 234 BOULEVARD SAINT-GERMAIN, 75007 PARIS. TN: 548 0527. Fondée en 1877. Boutique. Moyen stock, aussi les livres neufs. Spec: art militaire. Cata. Corresp: English. B: Crédit Lyonnais, Agence X-424, Compte 5840A. S.L.A.M.

PIERRE SIEUR, 3 RUE DE LA UNIVERSITÉE, 75007 PARIS. TN: 260 75 94. Fondée en 1945. Boutique. Moyen stock. Spec: jouets anciens et cartes á jouer anciennes et modernes; numismatique; autographes; documents historiques; curiosités. CP: Paris 6 803 26. S.L.A.M.

EDGAR SOETE, LIBRAIRIE SALET, 5 QUAI VOLTAIRE, 75007 PARIS. TN: 548 72 41. Fondée en 1930. Boutique, fermé Lundi. Important stock. Spec: XVe au XIX siecle; bibliophilie; documentation; reliures; gastronomic. Cata: 2 par an. Corresp: English. B: B.N.P. CP: Paris 2108 87. S.L.A.M.

PARIS Arrondissement 8e

ART DE VOIR, 166 BOULEVARD HAUSSMANN, 75008 PARIS. Prop: R. Crozemarie. TN: (1) 562.50.07. Spec: livres illustrés modernes; belles reliures; héraldique, régionalisme. S.L.A.M.

PIERRE BERÈS, 14 AVENUE DE FRIEDLAND, 75008 PARIS. TN: 227 0099. TA: Piby Paris. Spec: manuscrits, beaux livres; reliures. Cata. CP: Paris 1593 68. S.L.A.M.

LIBRAIRIE AUGUSTE BLAIZOT S.A., 164 FAUBOURG SAINT-HONORÉ, 75008 PARIS. Président: Claude Blaizot. TN: 359 36 58. Fondée en 1840. Boutique. Spec: littérature française; éditions originales, livres illustrés; manuscrits et autographes. Cata: 3 ou 4 par an. B: B.N.P., CP: Paris 517–97. S.L.A.M.

PIERRE CHRÉTIEN, 178 Faubourg Saint-Honoré, 75008 Paris. TN: 359 5266. Boutique, fermé Samedi. Spec: manuscrits; reliures; éditions originales; livres illustrés. CP: Paris 28546. S.L.A.M.

JULLIEN CORNIC ART BOOKSHOP, 118 rue du Faubourg Saint Honore, 75008 Paris. TN: (1) 359 10 90. Fondé 1945. 2 Boutiques. Fermées lundi et août. Important stock. Spec: beaux-arts; arts décoratifs; mode. Cata: un par an. Corresp: English. S.L.A.M. et I.L.A.B.

MADAME COUTURIER, 7 rue de Duras, 75008 Paris. TN: 265 4480. Fondé en 1940. Fermé Samedi. Spec: livres anciens et modernes. Cata: 4–5 par an. Corresp: English. B: Credit Lyonnais. CP: Paris 2639–84. S.L.A.M.

LIBRAIRIE DAVIS, 12 avenue Franklin-Roosevelt, 75008 Paris. Prop: Maurice Chalvert. TN: 359 1943. Spec: éditions originales; autographes. Cata. CP: Paris 38310. S.L.A.M.

GÉRARD FLEURY, Librairie François, 1er, 34 Avenue Montaigne, 75008 Paris. TN: 359 7077. Spec: voyages; livres illustrés; reliures. S.L.A.M.

RENÉ GONOT, Librairie Saint-Augustin, 99 boulevard Haussmann, 75008 Paris. TN: 265 27 31. Fondée en 1926. Boutique; fermé Samedi et Lundi matin; ouvert 12.00–19.00 hrs. Spec: literature et histoire en langues anglaise et française. Corresp: English. B: Societé Générale A.M. 200 218 06. M: A.B.A., S.L.A.M.

JACQUES HERBINET, 39 rue de Constantinople, 75008 Paris. TN: 522 61 15. Domicile. Important stock. Spec: ancien; modernes illustrés. Cata: Periodiques. Crédit Lyonnais. CP: Paris 17 337 72. S.L.A.M.

JADIS ET NAGUÈRE, 166 Faubourg Saint-Honoré, 75008 Paris. TN: 359 40, 52.

LIBRAIRIE LARDANCHET, 100 rue de Faubourg Saint-Honoré, 75008 Paris. TN: 266 68 32. B: Louis Dreyfus, rue Rabelais, Paris 8.

GALERIE MAEGHT, 13 rue de Téhéran, 75008 Paris. TN: 387 6149. S.L.A.M.

LIBRAIRIE DE MONTBEL ET CIE, 1 rue Paul Cézanne, 75008 Paris. Prop: Jacqueline Frachon. TN: 359 06 47. Fondé en 1947. Boutique, fermé Samedi. Restreint stock, aussi les livres neufs. Spec: chasse, équitation, vénerie, Pêche. Corresp: English. B: C.C.F. Agence St Augustin, Compte 50 218 5020. CP: Paris 16742–38. S.L.A.M.

HENRI PICARD FILS, 126 Faubourg Saint-Honoré, 75008 Paris. TN: 359 2811. Spec: beaux livres anciens; reliures. CP: Paris 28200. S.L.A.M.

PIERRE PICARD, 60 boulevard Malesherbes, 75008 Paris. TN: 387 3882. Fondée en 1937. Boutique. Spec: lavage, restauration de livres et gravures. CP: Paris 2154 83. S.L.A.M.

LIBRAIRIE GEORGES PRIVAT, 162 boulevard Haussmann, 75008 Paris. Prop: Bernard et Daniel Privat. TN: 562 25 64. Fondée en 1902. Boutique. Moyen stock. Cata. B: Crédit Lyonnais, Agence W. CP: Paris 557–78J. S.L.A.M.

V.R.I.L.L.E. EDITIONS PRO-FRANCIA, 3 rue Saint-Philippe du Roule, 75008 Paris. TN: 225 4354. Fondée en 1955. Boutique. Moyen stock, aussi les livres neufs. Spec: beaux-arts; archéologie; littérature française. Corresp: English. B: Crédit Lyonnais. CP: Paris 16365–88.

RIBOT VULIN, 8 rue de Rome, 75008 Paris. TN: (1) 387.39.46. Fermée lundi matin. S.L.A.M.

PARIS Arrondissement 9e

ARIOSO S.A.R.L., 6 rue Lamartine, 75009 Paris. Gérant: Bernard Peyrotte. TN: 526 71 22. Fondeé en 1936. Boutique. Moyen stock. Spec: musique. Corresp: Deutsch, English, Italiano. B: B.R.E.D. Compte No. 310 72 0632. CCP: 21.356 91. S.L.A.M.

LE BIBLIOPHILE RUSSE, 12 rue Lamartine, 75009 Paris. Prop: André Savine. TN: (1) 878.91.02. Sur rendez-vous. Spec: livres et documents en langue russe. S.L.A.M.

LIBRAIRIE BOURGUIGNAT, 10 bis Rue de Chateaudun, 75009 Paris. Prop: Pierre Bourguignat. TN: 874 76 80. Boutique, ouvere tous les aprés-midi sauf Samedi. Moyen stock. Spec: histoire de la locomotion (aviation, sciences, aerostation, chemins de fer, automobile, cycle, moto). Cata: 2 par an. Corresp: English. B: Crédit Commercial de France, 2 Carrefour de l'Odéon, 75006 Paris. Compte No. 070 229 4070. CCP: La Source 35 524 83 K.

JEAN-MARIE CAUSE, 36 rue Provence, 75009 Paris. TN: 874 68 30.

FRANÇOIS ET RODOLPHE CHAMONAL, 40 rue le Peletier, 75009 Paris. TN: 878 14 41. Spec: Beaux livres anciens, medecine et sciences; voyages; géographie; marine; Cata. S.L.A.M.

PAUL EPPE, 49 RUE DE PROVENCE, 75009 PARIS. TN: 874 6668. Spec: éditions originales; livres illustrés. CP: Paris 17764–49. S.L.A.M.

ANDRÉ GAUTHIER, 68 RUE FAUBOURG MONTMARTRE, 75009 PARIS. TN: 526 89 47.

GRENIER À LIVRES, 50 PASSAGE JOUFFROY, 75009 PARIS. TN: 824 98 89.

LIBRAIRIE HENNER, 9 RUE HENNER, 75009 PARIS. Prop: Alain Sinibaldi. TN: (1) 874 60 38 Fondée 1976. Boutique. Fermée lundi et samedi. Assez restreint stock. Spec: Beaux et rares livres; éditions originales; reliures.

CLAUDE JAVELLE, 32 RUE DE PROVENCE, 75009 PARIS. TN: 828 2174. Boutique. Moyen stock. S.L.A.M.

LOUIS LOEB-LAROCQUE, 36 RUE LE PELETIER, 75009 PARIS. TN: 878 11 18. Boutique fermé Samedi. Important stock. Spec: atlas: topographie; voyages; estampes. Coresp: English, Deutsch. B: Crédit Lyonnais, Agence F, Paris, Compte 6803 A. S.L.A.M.

PABIAN, 4 RUE DE CLICHY, 75009 PARIS. TN: 526 61 30. Prop: Stéphane Pabian. Boutique, fermée Lundi matin, et du 15 aout au 10 Septembre S.L.A.M.

SOCIÉTÉ LIVRES & MUSIQUE, 6 RUE LAMARTINE, 75009 PARIS. TN 744 71 22. Fondée en 1936. Boutique. Restreint stock. Spec: Partitions P. & Ch. Orchestre—Classique et Lyriques. B: Crédit Lyonnais Agence F.406, 50 rue Lafayette, Paris 9e., Compte 5468–Q. CP: Paris 21 356 91.

DIDIER TERROY, 39 RUE DE DOUAI, PARIS 75009. TN: 874 1893. Fondée en 1981. Domicile. Sur rendez-vous seulement. Stock assez restreint Spec: Spectacles; modes; graphisme; affiches anciennes. Cata: annuel Coresp: English, Espagñol. B: Crédit Lyonnais Paris Agence FB 828 Compte 5218 K.

PARIS Arrondissements 10e-20e

JO CHARLES ABELA, 11 RUE PIERRE-DÉMOURS, 75017 PARIS. Spec Cartes géogr. anciennes, estampes, orientalisme, voyages, livres illustr modernes. S.L.A.M.

AUX AMATEURS DE LIVRES, 62 Avenue de Suffren, 75015 Paris. Président: Marcel Blancheteau. TN: 567 1838 et 566 6091. Fondée en 1926. Boutique, fermé Samedi. Important stock, aussi les livres neufs. Spec: aéronautique; littérature française; beaux-arts; érudition. Cata: 1 par an. Corresp: English, Deutsch, Español. B: Société Nancéienne de Crédit, 11 rue d'Aguesseau 75008 Paris. C.C.P. 969–35 V. S.L.A.M.

SIMONE ANDRÉ, 111 Avenue Victor Hugo, 75016 Paris. TN: 727 86 91

ALEXANDRE BAER [J. BAER & CO.], 2–6 rue Livingstone, 75018 Paris. TN: 255 0144 aussi 606 1466. Fondée en 1785 à Francfort, la plus ancienne maison toujours entre les mains d'une même famille et pendant de longues années la plus importante librairie ancienne du monde). Bureau, fermée les lundis: sur rendez vous seulement. Spec: Livres trés rares concernant les Ameriques. Corresp: English, Deutsch. B: B.N.P., et Chase Manhattan Bank. CP: Paris 7040 74. S.L.A.M.

ALAIN BAUDRY, 60 Avenue de Suffren, 75015 Paris. TN: (1) 567.18.38. S.L.A.M.

FERNAND BEAUFILS, 169 avenue Victor-Hugo, 75016 Paris. TN: 727 9370. Spec: beaux-arts; éditions originales. CP: Paris 16233.29. S.L.A.M.

ANDRÉ BESSIÈRES, 12 rue Delambre, 75014 Paris. TN: 633 07 61. Fondée en 1962. Boutique, fermé Lundi. Moyen stock. Spec: littérature, beaux-arts, Histoire (Revolution et 19e siécle). Corresp:

ETIENNE BLOT, 42 rue Sortier, 75020 Paris. TN: 366 19 80.

HENRI BONNEFOY, 36 Avenue Villemain, 75014 Paris. TN: 543 17 17.

DANIEL BRUN, ÉDITION ET DIFFUSION M.P., 6 rue Clodion, 75015 Paris. TN: 579 25 49. Fondée en 1954. Domicile; par correspondance seulement. Moyen stock, aussi livres neufs. Spec: érudition; histoire, philosophie. Cata: 5 par an. Corresp: English. CCP: Paris 21 165-73 D. S.L.A.M.

GILBERT CAREL, 45 Avenue Saint-Mandé, 75012 Paris. TN: 343 19 28.

FRANCISCO CARRILLO, 86 Faubourg Saint-Antoine, 75012 Paris. TN: 344 79 76. Boutique, fermé l'après-midi. Spec: voyages; marine; Espagne. S.L.A.M.

MAX-PHILIPPE DELATTE, 15 RUE GUSTAVE COURBET, 75116 PARIS. TN: 553 70 93. Fondée en 1939. Boutique. Moyen stock, aussi les livres neufs. Spec: éditions originales, (Cata.), beaux-arts; littérature; érudition. B: B.N.P. Agence Victor Hugo, Compte 210 397. CP: 5286–51. A.L.A.M., Association culturelle des libraires de litterature générale, Cercle de la Librairie.

LIBRAIRIE DES DEUX GARES. 76 BOULEVARD DE MAGENTA, 75010 PARIS. Prop: Roger et Gerard Hirlam. TN: (1) 607 37.85. Fermé août. Spec: histoire: mémoires, Alsace; Lorraine: documentation, érudition. Cata. S.L.A.M.

LIBRAIRIE DUDRAGNE, 86 RUE MAUBEUGE 75010 PARIS. TN: 878 50 95.

LOUIS FERRARI, 140 RUE BELLEVILLE, 75020 PARIS. TN: 366 00 06.

ANDRE GAUTHIER S.A., B.P. 373–09, F 75424 PARIS CEDEX 09. TN: (1) 878.17.93. Est. 1963. Domicile, sur rendez-vous. Stock restreint. Spec: India. Cata: 4 par an. Corresp: English. B: 00082–69183–82–43–J. CP: Paris 1988504 M

ROBERTE GAUTRON, 10 RUE SOPHIE-GERMAIN, 75014 PARIS. TN: 327 21 92.

JEAN-PHILIPPE GELEY, 229 RUE DE TOLBIAC 75013, PARIS. TN: (1) 580.36.92. Uniquement sur rendez-vous ou par correspondance. Spec: orientalisme; voyages; sciences sociales; érudition. Cata. S.L.A.M.

RAYMOND GILQUIN, 34 RUE CHARONNE, 75011 PARIS. TN: 805 22 93.

EDOUARD HAMPARTZ, L'EPI DE BLÉ, 90 RUE DE LÉVIS, 75017 PARIS. TN: 622 1468. S.L.A.M.

LIBRAIRIE ANCIENNE HERVÉ, 62 RUE PIERRE LAROUSSE, 75014 PARIS. TN: 543 31 37.

ROGER LANGLAIS, 47 TER RUE ORSEL, 75018 PARIS. TN: 252 47 65.

JACQUES LEVY, 46 RUE D'ALÉSIA, 75014 PARIS. TN: 327 08 79. Fondée en 1940. Boutique, Ferméa Lundi. Important stock. Spec: littérature Générale; Judaica; Hebraica; histoire; curiosités. B: C.I.C., Succarsale B.O., 97 avenue du Général Leclerc, Paris 14e, Compte 14379 64. CP Paris 5634 31.

LIVRES, 105, RUE FAUBOURG SAINT DENIS, 75010 PARIS. TN: 523.07.24.

LIBRAIRIE MONTMARTROISE, 29 RUE DURANTIN, 75018 PARIS. Prop André Bugnard. TN: 076 4125. S.L.A.M.

BERNADETTE NANCON, 184 RUE SAINT-MAUR, 75010 PARIS. TN: 241 19 25.

JACQUELINE SOREL, 6 SQUARE JULES CHÉRET, 75020 PARIS. TN: 370 85 10.

LE TOUR DU MONDE, 9 RUE DE LA POMPE, 75116 PARIS. Prop: Jean-Étienne Huret. TN: 288 58 06. Fonddée en 1973. Boutique. Important stock. Spec: Voyages; livres d'enfants. Cata: 6 par an. Corresp: English. B: B.N.P. 5 rue de la Pompe, 75116 Paris. CCP: 3069217–la Source. S.L.A.M.

JEAN TOUZOT, 38 RUE SAINT-SULPICE, 75278 PARIS. TN: (1) 326.03.88. Spec: beaux-arts; critique littéraire; histoire; incunables; littérature; philosophie, régionalisme, reliures; sciences; voyages. S.L.A.M.

PATRICK VAISSON, 67 RUE SAINT-CHARLES, 75015 PARIS. TN: 578 03 19.

PATRICK VAISSON, 3 RUE MOINES, 75017 PARIS. TN: 229 49 19.

LIBRAIRIE VALLERIAUX, 98 BOULEVARD VOLTAIRE, 75011 PARIS. TN: (1) 700.50.43. Ouverte les après-midis. Fermée août. Spec: régionalisme province et Paris, histoire, érudition. Cata: S.L.A.M.

LIBRAIRIE VIOLET, 41 RUE VIOLET, 75015 PARIS. TN: 577 78 79.

II

FRANCE (NORD): NORDFRANKREICH: NORTHERN FRANCE

80000 AMIENS	95270 LUZARCHES
89200 AVALLON	78600 MESNIL LE ROI
27800 BRIONNE	28210 NOGENT LE ROI
14000 CAEN	93500 PANTIN
60200 COMPIEGNE	27340 PONT DE L'ARCHE
76200 DIEPPE	50580 PORT-BAIL
80730 DREUIL—LES-AMIENS	76000 ROUEN
91400 GOMETZ LE CHATEL	92210 SAINT CLOUD
29218 HUELGOAT	93400 SAINT-OUEN
91940 LES ULIS	78000 VERSAILLES
92130 ISSY LES MOULINEAUX	95450 VIGNY
59000 LILLE	91121 VILLEBON SUR
78430 LOUVECIENNES	YVETTE

MAURICE AMATTEIS, 12 Avenue Lys, Dammarie le Lys. TN: (6) 47 60 21.

L'ANE D'OR, Boite Postale 6, 95450 Vigny. Prop: Yves Lévy. TN: 039 20 66. Fondée en 1968. Domicile, sur rendez-vous seulement. Important stock. Spec: littérature, médicine, sciences humaines. Cata: 4 par an. Corresp: English, Deutsch, Español, Italiano. B: B.I.C.S., 1 rue Danté, 75005 Paris. Compte 404 1000 755. CP: 18 104–38 Paris. S.L.A.M., L.I.L.A.

LIBRAIRIE DES ARTS ET METIERS, 20 rue de Verdun, Lormaye, 28210 Nogent le Roi. Prop: Jacques Laget. TN: 37 43 44 29. Fondée: 1973. Domicile. Sur rendezvous seulement. Stock moyen livres d'occasion, livres neufs aussi. Spec: beaux-arts; histoire religieuse; érudition. Cata: 6 par an. Corresp: English. B: Crédit Lyonnais Dreux compte 63222 T.

ÉTIENNE BERTRAN, 110 rue Molière, 76000 Rouen. TN: (35) 70 79 96. Boutique.

LIBRAIRIE COLBERT, 11 bis rue Colbert (Place du Chateau), 78000 Versailles. TN: (3) 950.11.68. Spec: histoire; beaux-arts; varia. S.L.A.M.

G. et A. DARGENT, 11 rue Alain-Blanchard, 76000 Rouen. Boutique. Spec: Normandie, histoire litterature. CP: Rouen 167–01 G Rouen (Mlle A. Dargent).

DAWSON-FRANCE, S.A., zone Industrielle "La Prairie", 91121 Villebon-sur-Yvette. (B.P. 40). TN: (6) 909 01 22. Telex: 600394. Fondée en 1925. Bureaux et depôt, fermé samedi. Important stock. Spéc: périodiques. Cata: 2 par an. Corresp: English. B: Lloyds Bank Europe Ltd., 43 bd. des Capucines, 75002 Paris, Compte 121 643 017 CP: Paris 1071 62. S.L.A.M., L.I.L.A.

HENRI DUPONT, 141 boulevard de la Liberté, 59000 Lille. TN: 54 85 60. Fondée en 1949. Boutique, fermé lundi matin. Assez restreint stock, aussi les livres neufs. Spec: éditions originales, gravures estampes, tableaux. Corresp: English. B: Banque Worms, rue de Molinel, Lille. CP: 199–399. S.L.A.M.

LIBRAIRIE FAVEREAUX, 19ter rue de l'Hôpital-Militaire, 59000 Lille. Prop: Emile Favereaux. TN: (20) 54 40 31. Fondée en 1957 Boutique, fermé lundi matin. Restreint stock, aussi livres neufs. Spec régionalisme et varia. Cata: irregulier. B: Crédit du Nord a Lille Compte 100 87900200. S.L.A.M.

PATRICK FUENTES, 11 Pourtour des Halles, 8000 Amiens. TN: (22) 91 20 90.

LIBRAIRIE GALERIE 89, rue de Lyon 89, 89200 Avallon. Prop: Schrotter & Dhouailly. TN: 86 34 12 91. Fondée en 1972. Boutique. Stock moyen, livres neufs aussi. S.L.A.M. L.I.L.A.

MICHEL GUILLAUME & CIE., S.A.R.L., Librairie Generale du Calvados, 98 rue Saint-Pierre, 14000 Caen. TN: (31) 85 43 13. Fondée en 1900. Boutique. Moyen stock, aussi livres neufs. Spec: histoire; droit; sciences. B: B.N.P. Caen. CP: Paris 19007–28. S.L.A.M.

SERGE HELLUIN, 11 rue Leon-Blum, 80000 Amiens. TN: (22) 917257. Fermé lundi. Spec: critique littéraire; histoire; régionalisme. S.L.A.M.

XAVIER JEHANNO, 4 Place de l'Eglise, 78430 Louveciennes. TN: 969 8037. Fondée en 1945. Boutique. Ouverte: Samedi et Dimanche. Important stock. Spec: politique, histoire, voyages, régionalisme, beaux-arts, romans, cartes postales. Corresp: English. B: Société Générale.

LAGNEL-TASTEMAIN, 25 Boulevard Marechal-Leclerc, 14300 Caen. TN: 86 13 35. Boutique. Fermée lundi. Stock restreint. Spec: Normandie. Corresp: English. B: B.N.P. 223 130 04 C.P. Rouen 801 74Z. C.S.E.D.T.

LEFEBVRE, 38 rue de la Paroisse, 78000 Versailles. TN: (3) 950 44 84.

LESTRINGANT, 123 rue Général-Leclerc, 76000 Rouen. TN: 71 03 98. Fondée en 1702. Boutique, fermé Lundi. Livres rares par correspondance seulement. Assez restreint stock, aussi les livres neufs. Spec: histoire; Normandie. Corresp: English. CP: Rouen 269 W.

ARNOLD LEVILLIERS, 118 route de Chartres (RN 188), 91400 Gometz-le-Chatel (Essone). TN: 592 02 24 (Paris). Fondée en 1923. Domicile, par rendezvous seulement. Moyen stock. Spec: arts et métiers; gravures; dessins; beaux-arts. Corresp: English, Deutsch. B: Barclays Bank, Paris, Compte 02–41789–14. CP: Paris 30 38 87. S.L.A.M., S.L.A.C.E.S.

JULES LORIEUL, Normania, 3 Place du Castel, 50580 Port Bail. TN: 54 83 24. Boutique, fermé Lundi. Spec: Régionalisme; histoire; éditions originales. S.L.A.M.

LIBRAIRIE CHARLES LUCAS, 10 RUE ARMENGAUD, 92210 SAINT-CLOUD. TN: (Paris) 602 44 39. Fondée en 1947. Domicile, par rendezvous seulement. Restreint stock. Cata. Corresp: English, Deutsch. B: Banque de France, Bureau Central, 75001 Paris, Compte H 350 887. CP: 6913 38. S.L.A.M.

HENRI METAIS, 2 PLACE BARTHELEMY, 76000 ROUEN. TN: (35) 70 94 33. Fondée en 1961. Boutique. Restreint stock. Spec: regionalisme Normand. B: Credit Agricole. S.L.A.M., Syndicat National des Antiquaires.

GÉRARD MONFORT, ST.-PIERRE-DE-SALERNE, 27800 BRIONNE. TN: (32) 448741. Fondée en 1961. Dépôt; par rendezvous seulement. Important Stock. Spec: histoire, Litterature; droit. Cata. B: Banque de la Cité, Paris; B.R.E.D. Paris. CCP Rouen 187782 P.

DANIEL MORCRETTE, 4 AVENUE JOFFRE, 95270 LUZARCHES. (B.P. 26). TN: (3) 16 471 0158. Fondée en 1934. Domicile, sur rendezvous seulement. Très important stock. Spec: gastronomie; livres rares; autographes. Cata. Corresp: English. CP: Paris 795470.

JEAN MOREL, 33 RUE DU DR CARON, 76420 ROUEN. TN: (35) 60 00 06.

MORVRAN, BOITE POSTALE 22, BRIGNOU EN BERRIEN, 29218 HUELGOAT, BRETAGNE. Prop: Andre Jaugeon. TN: (98) 93 72 23. Dépôt et domicile; par rendezvous seulement. Moyen stock. Spec: Bretagne. Corresp: English. CCP: Rennes 485–07.

MICHAEL AND GWENOLA NEAL, BOOKSELLERS, 16 LE BOSQUET, 91940 LES ULIS, FRANCE. Fondée 1984. Private house. By appointment only, any time except August. Spec: Literary and scholarly periodicals; curious, unusual and scholarly works. Paris-American literature. Cata: un par an, listes quatre par an. Corresp: English, Français, Deutsch, Italiano, Español, Portuguese. B: Natwest, Castle Square, Brighton. A/c 53618629. Société Générale, 91940 Les Ulis 51620004.

OR DU TEMPS, 89 RUE OCTAVIE-DUCHELLIER, 80730 DREUIL-LES-AMIENS. TN: 16 (22) 447023.
Et MARCHE VERNAISON, ALLEE 5, STAND 91, Les Samedi, Dimanche et Lundi, 93400 Saint-Ouen.

GUY PROUTÉ, 15 RUE DU 18-JUIN, 92210 SAINT-CLOUD. TN: (602) 5115. Spec: estampes.

LIBRAIRIE PUZIN, 30 RUE DE LA PAROISSE, 78000 VERSAILLES. TN: 950 43 75. Fondée en 1900. Boutique, fermé Lundi matin. Important stock. Spec: histoire; livres anciens; gravures.

G. RAFFY, 85 RUE DES ROSIERS (STAND 83 MARCHÉ BIRON), 93400 SAINT-OUEN (SEINE-ST. DENIS). TN: 770 36 51. Boutique, ouvert Samedi, Dimanche, Lundi. Moyen stock. Spec: topographie, cartes geographiques. Cata. Corresp: Español. Cie. Nat. d'Experts.

LIBRAIRIE RAOUST, 11 RUE NEUVE, 59000 LILLE. Prop: Thérèse Raoust. TN: (20) 54 64 79. Fondée en 1822. Boutique, Fermé lundi matin et Août. Restreint stock, aussi les livres neufs. Spec: histoire; régionalisme, Flandre-Artois. B: S.G., Lille, Compte CCD 200 464 90 4649. CP: Lille 1729 16. S.L.A.M. Cercle de la Librairie.

ROGERS TURNER BOOKS LTD., 24 RUE DU BUISSON RICHARD, 78600 LE MESNIL-LE-ROI. TN: 3 912 11 91. Stockroom sur rendezvous seulement. Spec: horlogerie, histoire des sciences, histoire, études allemandes, linguistique. Cata: 8 par an.

LIBRAIRIE "SCIENCES NAT", 2 RUE ANDRE-MELLENNE, VENETTE, 60200 COMPIEGNE. TN: 16 (4) 4833110. Fermeé en août. Par correspondance. Spec: sciences naturelles. S.L.A.M.

SIMONE THOMAS, MARCHE VERNAISON, ALLEE 3/7, STAND 146, 136, AVENUE MICHELET, 93400 SAINT-OUEN. TN: (1) 2510885 et 8442758. Ouvert samedi, dimanche, lundi. S.L.A.M.

WLADIMIR TIRASPOLSKY, 69 AVENUE VICTOR-CRESSON, 92130 ISSY-LES-MOULINEAUX. SPEC: LANGUES ETRANGÈRES; SCIENCES NATURELLES.*

JEAN-BAPTISTE TRAINEAU, 33 RUE ROYALE, 78000 VERSAILLES. TN: 950 74 13. Fondée en 1961. Boutique, fermée lundi et Aout. Restreint stock. Spec: histoire, littérature. B: B.N.P. St. Louis, Verseilles. CCP: 476 389 J. Paris. S.L.A.M.

GALERIE VAUQUELIN, 4 RUE VAUQUELIN, 76200 DIEPPE. Prop: Michel Burollaud. TN: (35) 84 31 78. Boutique, ouvert tous les jours. Moyen stock. Spec: régionalisme; histoire; beaux-arts; littérature. B: Crédit Lyonnais, 76 Dieppe. Compte 8332 71298 P. CP: Rouen 226621 F.

III

FRANCE (OUEST): WESTFRANKREICH: WESTERN FRANCE

37400 AMBOISE	45000 ORLEANS
49000 ANGERS	
16000 ANGOULEME	24000 PERIGUEUX
33120 ARCACHON	86000 POITIERS
89200 AVALLON	29000 QUIMPER
41000 BLOIS	
33000 BORDEAUX	35000 RENNES
29200 BREST	37210 ROCHECORBON
28000 CHARTRES	VOUVRAY
33230 COUTRAS	45750 SAINT PRYVE
17000 LA ROCHELLE	SAINT MESMIN
72000 LE MANS	56370 SARZEAU
87000 LIMOGES	35510 THORIGNE-SUR-
44000 NANTES	VILAINE
79000 NIORT	37000 TOURS
89310 NOYERS-SUR-SEREIN	37250 VEIGNE

ARTS ET PHILATÉLIE, PLACE GUERIN, 26 RUE BUGEAUD, 29200 BREST Prop: Madame Fauché. TN: 98 80 40 38. Fondée 1973. Boutique Fermée lundi matin. Stock assez restreint.

PIERRE BACHELIER, 6 RUE NEUVE-DES-CAPUCINS, 44000 NANTES. TN (40) 89 39 62. Boutique. Très important stock. Cata. Corresp: English.

A. BELLANGER, 6 ET 8 PASSAGE POMMERAYE, 44000 NANTES. TN: (40) 48 67 93. Fondée en 1942. Dépôt, 4 étages, fermé lundi matin Important stock aussi les livres neufs. Spec: littérature, voyages Régionalisme, gravures. Cata: 4 ou 5 par an. B: B.N.P., et C.C.F. CP Nantes 10997–4. S.L.A.M.

MME. BIENVAULT, 31 RUE DE BORDEAUX, 37000 TOURS (INDRE-ET-LOIRE). Anciennement P. le Bods. TN: (47) 610071 Fondée en 1895. Boutique. Fermé Lundi. Important stock. Spec: livres anciens; gravures. S.L.A.M.

LE BOUQUINEUR, 10 RUE GAMBETTA, 37000 TOURS. Prop: Dorbon Ainé. TN: (47) 20 65 62. Sur rendez-vous. S.L.A.M.

LA BOUQUINERIE, 89 RUE DE LYON, 89200 AVALLON. Prop: Alain Schrotter. TN: (86) 34 12 91. Fondée en 1972. Boutique, fermé mercredi. Important stock, aussi livres neufs. Spec: histoire; régionalisme; livres illustrés. Cata: 1 par an. Corresp: English. B: B.N.P. Avallon, Compte No 201098. CCP Dijon 2 474 36 R. S.L.A.M., L.I.L.A.

LIBRAIRIE-GALERIE BRETONNE, 1 RUE DES FOSSÉS, 35000 RENNES. Prop: G. L. Thomas. TN: 30 98 80. Fondé en 1950. Boutique. Spec: Bretagne, folklore, gravures anciennes, Marine. Cata: 2 par an. Corresp: English. B: B.N.P. à Rennes. CP: Rennes 1702–15.

LE BOUQUINISTE, 162 GRAND-RUE, 86000 POITIERS. Prop: Daniele Brissaud. TN: (49) 88 01 81. Boutique, fermé lundi. Important stock. Spec: XVIe-XIXe siècle; documentation; sciences; voyages. Cata: 1 par an. B: Banque Nationale de Paris. Compte 260 079 96. CCP Limoges 2050 81 R. S.L.A.M.

BROCÉLIANDE, RUE DE LA REINE BÉRENGÈRE 21, 72000 LE MANS. Prop: Bernard Rebeyrol. TN: 16(43) 24 18 27. Fondée 1969. Boutique, fermé Dimanche a Mercredi inclus. Moyen stock. Spec: Caricature; livres illustrés et varia. Cata: trimestriel. Corresp: English. B: Credit Commercial de France, Le Mans. Compte 201 057. CP: 4 061 08 F, Nantes. S.L.A.M., L.I.L.A.

CANDIDE, 7 RUE MONTAULT, 49000 ANGERS. TN: 88 66 02. Fondée en 1969. Boutique, fermé Lundi. Important stock. Spec: régionalisme; beaux-arts; musicologie. Cata: 1 par an. Corresp: English. B: Crédit Lyonnais, Angers.

FRANÇOIS CHANUT, PLACE DE LA MADELEINE, 89310 NOYERS-SUR-SEREIN. TN: (86) 55 82 32. Fondée en 1974. Boutique, fermé mardi, et mercredi. Moyen stock. Spec: Bourgogne. S.L.A.M., L.I.L.A.

MME. FRANÇOISE COMELLAS, 7 RUE DU PETIT SAINT-PIERRE, 72000 LE MANS. TN: (43) 24 87 03. Vente par correspondence et sur rendezvous. Spec: livres anciens; histoire des sciences et de la médecine; voyages; livres d'enfants. B: Crédit Lyonnais. S.L.A.M.

HENRI DANIGO, 17 RUE MARC-SANGNIER, 29000 QUIMPER. Fondée en 1953. Domicile. Restreint stock. Spec: Bretagne et varia. Cata. B: C.L., Quimper. CP: Nantes 1549 15. S.L.A.M.

LIBRAIRIE DENIS, 50 RUE DE LA SCELLERIE, 37000 TOURS. Prop
Madame Denis. TN: (47) 05 02 79. Fondée 1926. Boutique, ouver
tous les apres-midi et le samedi toute la journée. Spec: livres anciens
histoire; estampes et lithographies. Cata: 2 par an. CP: 20 898 46 C
Paris. S.L.A.M.

GABRIEL DURANCE, 5 ALLÉE D'ORLÉANS, 44000 NANTES. TN: (40) 48
72 45. Fondée en 1815. Boutique, Fermée elundi matin. Trés importan
stock. Spec: régionalisme; histoire; voyages. Cata: 2 par an. Corresp
English, Deutsch, Italiano, Español. B: C.L. CP: Nantes 295–59
S.L.A.M.

YVES DURAND-NOEL, 38 RUE DE NORMANDIE, 3551(
THORIGNE-SUR-VILAINE. TN: (99) 620229. Sur rendezvous. S.L.A.M.

OLIVIER ENCRENAZ, 8 RUE DES DEUX-HAIES, 49000 ANGERS. TN: (41
880613. Fermé dimanche et lundi matin. Spec: Histoire; livre
illustraés; sciences et techniques anciennes, livres d'enfants
régionalisme (Anjou et ouest); varia; Cata. S.L.A.M.

JEAN MICHEL DE FLOESSER, 28 RUE DES REMPARTS, 3300(
BORDEAUX (GIRONDE). TN: (56) 48 77 71. Boutique. Fermée 15 em
juillet au 20 eme Août. Expert organisation vente publique. Spec
Érudition; médecine ancienne. Cata. CP: Bordeaux 23 23 05. S.L.A.M

LA GALCANTE, 2 RUE TEMPLE, 79000 NIORT. TN: (49) 28 19 89.

YVETTE HUILLET, MANOIR DE BEAUPRE, ROUTE DE MONTS, 3725(
VEIGNE. TN: 16 (47) 260240. Ouvert tous les jours et sur rendezvous
Spec: Littérature XIXe; édition originale; romantiques et modernes
reliures. S.L.A.M.

CAMILLE JOYAUX, 55 RUE DE LA SCELLERIE, 37000 TOURS. TN: (47
641786. Fermé 10-20 août environ. Spec: mémoires; littérature
reliures; voyages; sciences; S.L.A.M.

MME. JUHEL-DOUET, 3 RUE D'ANGLETERRE, 41000 BLOIS. TN: 79 1
84. Boutique. Moyen stock. Spec: régionalisme. Cata. Corresp
English. CP: Paris 5461–99. S.L.A.M.

GEORGES LAMONGIE, 2 RUE DE LA NATION, 24000 PERIGUEUX. TN
(53) 53 22 45. Fondée en 1924. Boutique. Moyen stock. Spec: roman
historie, sciences. Cata: 12 par en. CP: Limoges 2986. S.L.A.M.

MARCEL LAUCOURNET, 45 BOULEVARD CARNOT, 87000 LIMOGES. TN
(55) 77 43 39. Fondée en 1946. Boutique, fermé lundi. Restreint stoc
B: Banque Populaire. CCP: 734 92 J. S.L.A.M.

LIBRAIRIE LEFEBVRE, 1 RUE LUCIEN-PEAN, 45750 SAINT-PRYVÉ-SAINT-MESMIN. TN: (38) 66 63 24. Sur rendezvous de 14.30 à 19.30. Fermé août. Spec: Beaux-arts; édition originale; livres illustrés; équitation; chasse; régionalisme. S.L.A.M.

PIERRE LELANT, 18 RUE BERTIN, 49000 ANGERS. TN: (41) 43 89 70. Fondée en 1962. Très important stock. Spec: érudition, études litteraires. Cata: 3 par an. Corresp: English. B: Credit Agricole Angers Compte 02134918001. CP: Paris 18 791 98 M. S.L.A.M.

MAURICE LESTER, 13 bis RUE DU CYGNE (MARCHÉ AUX FLEURS), 28000 CHARTRES. TN: 667. Spec: éditions modernes; gravures; régionalisme. CP: Paris 87045. S.L.A.M.

LA MAISON DU LIVRE, 24 RUE DE LA CLOCHE VERTE, 16000 ANGOULÊME. Prop: Mme. Guillaume. TN: (45) 92 20 39. Fondée en 1947. Boutique, fermé Lundi; de préférence sur rendez-vous. Important stock, aussi quelques livres neufs de documentation, beaux-arts et régionalisme. Cata: parfois. Corresp: Deutsch, English. S.L.A.M., C.E.D.S.O.

MME. E. MARONNE, 37 RUE BOUFFARD, 33000 BORDEAUX. Fondée en 1930. Boutique, fermée lundi. Moyen stock. CCP: 416–07 u Bordeaux.

CHARLES MORIN, 9 RUE AUVRAY, 72000 LE MANS. TN: 24 35 81. Fondée en 1920. Boutique, fermé Lundi et Mardi. Moyen stock. Cata. B: B.N.P. Le Mans. CP: Rennes 11 74 72 J. S.L.A.M. Aussi 102 rue Cherche Midi, 75006 Paris.

LIBRAIRIE NANTAISE Y. VACHON. 3 PLACE DE LA MONNAIE, 44000 NANTES. Prop: Yves Vachon. TN: (40) 73 10 13. Fondée en 1972. Boutique, fermé lundi. Moyen stock. Spec: histoire (Guerre de Vendée); littérature; science; réligieuses. Cata: 4–5 par an. Corresp: English. B: B.P.B.A., 17 rue Racine, 44000 Nantes. Compte No. 36 021 14 817 6. CCP: Nantes 3771 66 X. S.L.A.M., L.I.L.A.

BERNARD PAPON, LES RIVAUX, B.P. 12, 24006 TRELISSAC-PERIGUEUX. TN: (53) 544090. Sur rendez-vous seulement. Cata. S.L.A.M.

QUARTIER LATIN, 21 RUE ALBERT-1ER, 17000 LA ROCHELLE. Prop: Franck-Noel Mornet. TN: (46) 41 28 05. Fondée en 1950. Magasin. Restreint stock, aussi les livres neufs. Spec: Régionalisme; enseignement. B: Credit du Nord, Agence de la Rochelle, Compte 267 877 002. CP: Bordeaux 119 036. S.L.A.M. Syndicat des libraires classiques de France.

"A LA RECHERCHE DU PASSE", Saint-Colombier, 56370 Sarzeau. Prop: Robert Chassaniol. Spec: Livres anciens, gravures. S.L.A.M.

ANNE-MARIE ROBICHON, 16 Quai de la Loire, 37210 Rochecorbon/Vouvray. TN: (47) 525535. Par correspondance et sur rendez-vous. Spec: Histoire; region; philosophie; religion; Cata. S.L.A.M.

LIBRAIRIE C. ET O. DE SEZE, 6 Place du General Leclerc, 24000 Perigueux. TN: (53) 53 40 73. S.L.A.M.

JACQUES STOVEN, 53 rue du Mail, 49000 Angers. TN: (41) 876593. Fermé lundi et du 14.7. au 20 août. Spec: beaux-arts; littérature; histoire; varia. Cata. S.L.A.M.

TRIAUD, Domaine de Choisy, ABZAC, 33230 Coutras, TN: (55) 49 26 22. Fondée en 1970. Domicile; sur rendezvous seulement. Très important stock. Cata.

"VIEILLE FRANCE", 65 boulevard Général-Leclerc, 33120 Arcachon. Prop: Georges Berthier. TN: (56) 83 19 14. Fondée en 1947. Boutique. Restreint stock. Spec: livres anciens-romantiques; médecine; varia; curiosités. Cata: 8–9 par an. Corresp: English, Español. B: B.F., 302142 Arcachon. CP: Bordeaux 31 02 20. S.L.A.M.

IV

FRANCE (EST): OSTFRANKREICH: CENTRAL AND EASTERN FRANCE

74000 ANNECY	74150 MARIGNY SAINT
71400 AUTUN	MARCEL
25000 BESANÇON	73550 MÉRIBEL-LES-ALLUE
58340 CERCY-LA-TOUR	57000 METZ
55140 CHALAINES	68100 MULHOUSE
73000 CHAMBERY	54000 NANCY
63000 CLERMONT FERRAND	69370 SAINT DIDIER
21000 DIJON	AU MONT D'OR
38000 GRENOBLE	42000 SAINT-ETIENNE
69000 LYON	67000 STRASBOURG
71000 MACON	54330 VEZELISE

LIBRAIRIE ABBE GIRARD, 6 rue de l'Abbe Girard, 63000 Clermont-Ferrand. Prop: M. Bayssat. TN: 16 (73) 924366. Spec régionalisme; voyages; orientalisme; estampes; varia. S.L.A.M.

JEAN-PIERRE ANDRÉ, A L'Homme de Fer 2 rue Jean-Baptiste Salle. Fondée en 1886 à Nancy. Boutique ouvert les Samedi, Dimanche et Fêtes.

MICHEL BARBIER, Bibliomax-Office, 7 rue de l'Enfer, 55140 Chalaines. TN: (29) 89 50 13. Fondée en 1969. Boutique, fermé mercredi. Moyen stock. Spec: spiritualité et museographie du papier. Cata: 2 par mois. B: Crédit Agricole Mutuel de la Meuse, Bureau de Vaucouleurs; Crédit Agricole Mutuel de l'Est à Nancy. CCP: 1887–50 R. S.L.A.M.

LIBRAIRIE DU BÂT D'ARGENT ET DU CHARIOT D'OR, 38 rue des Remparts d'Ainay, 69002 Lyon. Gérant: Pascal Chartier. TN: (7) 837 41 53. Fondée en 1936. Boutique ouvert tous les jours. Très important stock. Spec: livres anciens; histoire, littérature; régionalisme. Cata: et listes specialises. Corresp: Deutsch. B: B.E.C. Compte 20 203 924–3. CCP: 2004 47A.S.L.A.M.

PAUL BISEY, 35 Place de la Réunion, 68100 Mulhouse. TN: (89) 46 58 14. Fondée en 1906. Boutique, fermé lundi. Restreint stock. Spec: régionalisme. Cata. Corresp: English, Deutsch. B: C.M.D.P., St Paul. CP: Strasbourg 1977 J. S.L.A.M. Syndicat des librairies Alsace. Cercle de la Librairie. Paris.

LE BOUQUINISTE, 18 rue Lakanal, 38000 Grenoble. Prop: Andre Perrin. TN: (76) 870450. Spec: policiers; montagnes; disques. S.L.A.M.

BOUQUINS, rue de Boigne 13, 73000 Chambéry. Prop: Louis Fillet. TN: (79) 33 27 60. Fondée en 1975. Boutique fermé lundi. Restreint stock. Spec: Provinciana. B: Société Générale. CP: Lyon 5480 89 X. M: S.L.A.M.

LIBRAIRIE ANCIENNE CHAMBEFORT, 26 Place Bellecour, 69 Lyon. TN: (78) 37 32 15. Spec: beaux-arts, histoire, régionalisme. S.L.A.M.

JACQUES CHAMINADE, 8 rue de l'Isle, 74000 Annecy. TN: (50) 51 57 31. Fondée en 1972. Boutique. Moyen stock. Spec: régionalisme; livres anciens; histoire. Cata: 6 par an. B: B.N.P. Agence Annecy Compte 200 931/13. CCP Lyon 3 872 95 W.

CITÉ DES VIEUX LIVRES, 139 Grande Rue, 25000 Besançon. Prop: Albert George. TN: (81) 81 38 07. Fondée en 1950. Boutique, fermé lundi. Moyen stock. Spec: histoire locale, sciences religieuses. B: C.I.R.L., 54 Grande Rue Besançon, Compte 300/01 106306 CCP: Dijon 2.701.30H D.

BOUQUINERIE COMTOISE, S.A.R.L., 9 rue Morand, 25000 Besançon (Doubs). Prop: Jean-Paul Chenu. TN: (81) 81 02 93. Boutique, fermé Lundi. Grds stock, aussi les livres neufs. Spec: régionalisme (Franche-Comté); gravures. C.M.D.P. Besancon. S.L.A.M.

LIBRAIRIE JEAN-PAUL DELON, 74150 Marigny-Saint Marcel. TN: 01 29 14. Fondée en 1973. Domicile-sur Rendez-vous. Restreint stock. Spec: alpinisme; montagne; bibliographie, economie politique. Cata: 4 par an. B: Banque de Savoie, Agence de Rumilly, Compte 44 201 206. CCP: Lyon 6 898 16. S.L.A.M.

LIBRAIRIE DUBOUCHET, 2 rue Général Foy, 42000 Saint-Étienne (Loire). Prop: Yves Dubouchet. TN: (77) 32 36 59. Fondée en 1828. Boutique, fermé Lundi. Moyen stock. aussi les livres neufs. Spec: livres illustrés et anciens; erudition; régionalisme; varia. Cata: 6 par an. Corresp: English, Italiano. B: B.N.P., Compte 223 006, et Crédit Lyonnais, Compte 642840 R. CP: Lyon 5790. S.L.A.M.

LIBRAIRIE GANGLOFF, 13 Auguste Wicky, 68100 Mulhouse. Prop Pierre Gangloff. TN: (89) 46 52 25. Fondée en 1932. Boutique. Important stock. Spec: littérature; régionalisme (Alsace). Cata: 1 par an. Corresp: English, Deutsch. B: Banque Nationale de Paris, Compte 039 220. CCP: Strasbourg 21890. 35496430. S.L.A.M., L.I.L.A.

LOUIS GANGLOFF, 20 Place de la Cathédrale, 67000 Strasbourg TN: (88) 32 40 52. Fondée en 1927. Magasin, fermé lundi matin Important stock, aussi les livres neufs. Spec: régionalisme, Alsace Cata: 4 par an. Corresp: Deutsch, English. B: B.N.P., Strasbourg Compte 277 990–36. Strasbourg 1819–14T. S.L.A.M.

LIBRAIRIE LARDANCHET, 5 Route de Limonest, 69370 Saint-Didier au Mont d'Or. TN: 16 (7) 8358431. Spec: Editions originales anciennes et modernes; gothique; histoire; incunables; livres illustrés manuscrits; région (lyonnais reg. limit.) reliures. Cata. Vento publiques. S.L.A.M.

LIBRI, 20 RUE DU PONT, 71000 MACON. Prop: André Ruel. TN: (85) 38 15 09. (le matin jusqu'à 9.30). Fondée en 1961. Boutique, fermé dimanche, lundi et mardi. Assez restreint stock. Spec: régionalisme et varia. B: B.N.P. S.L.A.M., L.I.L.A.

S.A.R.L. LIBRAIRIE LE MEUR, 12 PLACE DU THEÂTRE, 21000 DIJON. TN: 67 13 03. Fondée en 1900. Boutique, fermé Lundi matin. Moyen stock. Cata. B: Société Générale, Dijon. CP: Dijon 410 655 C. S.L.A.M.

GUY METRA, 13 GRAND-RUE CHAUCHIEN, 71400 AUTUN. TN: (16 85) 52 02 81.

RENE MUNARI, 9 RUE BAYARD, 38000 GRENOBLE. TN: (76) 44 5784. Fermé lundi. Spec: franc-maçonnerie; atlas; périodiques; sciences et techniques; voyages; varia. Cata. S.L.A.M.

GERARD OBERLE, MANOIR DE PRON, MONTIGNY-S.-CANNE. 58340 CERCY-LA-TOUR. TN: (86) 50 51 17. Domicile: sur Rendez-vous. Moyen stock. Spec: Livres du xv-xx siecle manuscrits, colportage, gravures. Cata: 2 3 par an. Corresp. Deutsch, English. B: Scalbert Dupont, 40 rue de Clichy, 75009 Paris. Compte 072.71. C.C.P. Limoges 1261 81 E. S.L.A.M.

JEAN PEYSSON, 7 RUE DU PLAT, 69002 LYON. TN: 37 73 32. Boutique, fermé en Août. Spec: régionalisme; héraldique. CP: Lyon 4790–43. S.L.A.M.

LIBRAIRIE A. REMY, 25 RUE STANISLAS, 54000 NANCY. Fondée en 1912. Boutique, fermé lundi. Important stock. Spec: littérature; histoire; régionalisme. CP: 20 18 75 E. S.L.A.M.

LIBRAIRIE STENDHAL, 4 RUE DE SAULT, 38000 GRENOBLE. Prop: Jean Menagé. TN: (76) 46 41 69. Fondée en 1940. Boutique, fermé lundi. Moyen stock. Spec: Stendhal; littérature ancienne et moderne; alpinisme; voyages; éstampes. Corresp: English. B: C.L., Grenoble (Jean Menagé, 112 059 Y). CP: Grenoble 375 86 M. S.L.A.M., L.I.L.A.

JEAN ZALE, RUE MAZELLE 37, 5700 METZ. TN: (97) 740014. Fermée juillet. S.L.A.M.

V

FRANCE (SUD): SUDFRANKREICH: SOUTHERN FRANCE

81000 ALBI
83460 LES ARCS
13100 AIX EN PROVENCE
06600 ANTIBES
84000 AVIGNON

45190 BEAUGENCY
64200 BIARRITZ
83170 BRIGNOLES

06400 CANNES
83330 LE CASTELLET
81100 CASTRES

84200 GORDES

06800 HAUT DE CAGNES

13001 MARSEILLE
82200 MOISSAC
34000 MONTPELLIER

06000 NICE
30000 NÎMES

64000 PAU

13300 SALON-DE-
PROVENCE
64500 SAINT-JEAN-DE-LUZ
34200 SETE

83100 TOULON
31000 TOULOUSE

30400 VILLENEUVE-LES-
AVIGNON

ARTS ET LETTRES, "LE VIEUX CHATEAU", 83330 LE CASTELLET. Prop Mme A. Cadéo de Iturbide. TN: (94) 90 62 74. Fondée en 1950 Domicile, sur rendezvous seulement. Restreint stock. Spec: érudition livres anciens; travail et littérature générale. Cata: 6–8 par an. Corresp Deutsch, Italiano, Español. B: Caisse Régionale de Crédit Agricole Olliovles (83), Compte 66590.00.0.2. CP: Mme Cadéo de Iturbide Marseille 3982–68. S.L.A.M.

PAUL BATAILLE, "CALENDAL", 14 RUE CHÂTEAUREDON, 13 MARSEILLE TN: 54 07 68. Spec: beaux-arts; voyages; histoire; sciences. S.L.A.M.

114

LIBRAIRIE JEAN MICHEL BELLE, 16 Boulevard Jean Jaurès, 06300 Nice. TN: 93 88 42 44 et 93 85 60 02. Fondée 1979. Dépot. Stock moyen. Cata: 6 par an. Corresp: English. Seulement par correspondance. B: Credit Lyonnais 4 639 62 W Merseille. S.L.A.M.

LAURENT BORREANI, 11 Cours Saint-Louis, 13100 Aix-en-Provence. TN: (42) 62 40 28. Boutique. S.L.A.M.

JEAN CLAUDE BOTTIN, LIBRAIRIE NICOISE, 2 rue Défly, 06 Nice. TN: 85 36 69. Fondée en 1930. Boutique, fermé lundi; ouvert tous les jours de 14 h. á 18 h 30. Très important stock. Spec: érudition; critique littéraire; éditions originales; Provence. Corresp: English. B: Banque Sudameris. CP: Marseille 32652. S.L.A.M.

JEAN CAU, 22 rue Peyras et Bouquinerie Balaran, 52 rue du Taur, 31000 Toulouse. TN: (61) 21 93 50 et 23 34 94. Fermé lundi matin et juillet. Spec: régionalisme; histoire; montagne; midi-pyrénées. S.L.A.M.

BOUQUINERIE CEVENOLE, 10 rue Porte de France, Nîmes (Gard). Prop: Pierre Couetard. TN: 21 18 35. Fondée 1979. Boutique. Fermée Vendredi. Stock moyen. Spec: régionalisme. Cata: annuel. Corresp: English, Deutsch.

LIBRAIRIE CHAMPAVERT, 2 rue du Perigord, 31000 Toulouse. TN: 16 (61) 21 95 96. Fermé le mercredi. Spec: beaux-arts; livres illustrés romantiques et modernes, édition originale. S.L.A.M.

LIBRAIRIE XAVIER CHARMOY, 9 rue Guizot, F30000 Nîmes. TN: (66) 36 07 47.

GERARD CHWAT, 2 Place Saint-Pierre, 83170 Brignoles. TN: (94) 69 32 65.

LIBRAIRIE PIERRE CLERC, 13 rue Alexandre Cabanel, 34000 Montpellier. TN: (67) 66 05 97. Fondée en 1967. Boutique, ouvert du mardi au vendredi d 15 h à 19 h 30: autre jours sur rendezvous. Très important stock; aussi des livres neufs. Spec: littérature; histoire; régionalisme (Languedoc). B: C.C.F., Place Aristide Briant, Montpellier, Compte 305 203 939 0. CP: Montpellier 943 17. S.L.A.M., L.I.L.A., C.N.E.S.

ACQUES D'ASPECT, "LA LEGENDE", 58 rue d'Aubagne, 13001, Marseille. TN: (91) 54 36 34. Ouvert les après-midis. Spec: livres illustrés anciens et modernes en parfaite conditions; édition originale; livres d'enfants; livres illustrés romantiques et modernes; médecine, orientalisme; régionalisme; reliures. S.L.A.M.

VÉRONIQUE DARDOIZE, 30 RUE DE LA FERRAGE, F-30000 NÎMES.
Fermé lundi

LIBRAIRIE ANCIENNE ECHÉ, 19 RUE ANDRÉ DÉLIEUX, 31400
TOULOUSE. Prop: Patrice Eché. TN: 61 52 95 74. Fondée en 1973.
Domicile. Sur rendezvous seulement. Cata: 3 à 4 par an. Sur demande.
Corresp: English, Español, Deutsch. C.C.P. Toulouse 82267 M.

CECILE ELUARD-VALETTE, 43 RUE SOUS BARRI, OMM 06800 HAUT
DE CAGNES. TN: (93) 20 13 63. Spec: autographes. S.L.A.M.

LIBRAIRIE DE L'ESCURIAL, 29 RUE ALPHONSE KARR, 06000 NICE
Prop: Madame Michelle Benedetti. TN: (93) 88 42 44. Boutique
fermée samedi. Moyen stock. Spec: recherche de livres. Cata: 6 par an
Corresp: English. B: Credit Commercial de France. CP: 114 114
Marseille. S.L.A.M.

L'EX-LIBRIS, 57 RUE DES RECOLLETS, 30400 VILLENEUVE-LES-AVIGNON
TN: (90) 25 44 11. Sur rendez-vous. S.L.A.M.

GERALD GRUPPO, 13 RUE PUECH BERINGUIER, 81000 ALBI. TN: (63) 38
46 00.

HERVÉ HAFFNER, 6 RUE SERANE, 34000 MONTPELLIER. TN: (67) 92 56
32. Fondée en 1980. Boutique. Fermée samedi. Stock restreint. Spec
histoire; réligions; mémoires; littérature; varia. Cata: annuel. B: 244
54 F Montpellier.

JEANNE LAFFITTE, 25 COURS D'ESTIENNE-D'ORVES, 13001 MARSEILLE
TN: (91) 54 39 37. Fondée en 1972. Boutique, fermée lundi et août
neufs. Spec: Folklore français; histoire de France; livres illustrés
Corresp: English. CP: 58 98 47 C Marsellie. S.L.A.M.; Expert
spécialisés, S.N.E.S.

BOUQUINERIE DU LANGUEDOC, 12 RUE DE L'UNIVERSITÉ, 34000
MONTPELLIER. Prop: Gérard Collin. TN: (67) 60 67 57. Fondée en
1906. Shop, fermé Lundi. Très important stock. Spec: Régionalisme
érudition; livres universitaires; numismatique. Cata: 2 par an. Corresp
English, Español. B: B.F., Montpellier. CP: Paris 11 89 573. S.L.A.M
L.I.L.A., Expert C.N.E.S. et près de la Cour d'Appel.

LA LEGENDE, 58 RUE D'AUBAGNE, 13001 MARSEILLE. TN: (91) 54 36 34
C.C.P. Marseille 6 107 09.

LIBRAIRIE K, 17 RUE MAZARINE, 13100 AIX EN PROVENCE. Prop: Pierre Dedet. TN: 42 26 35 11. Anciennement Librairie Le Divan, Paris, fondée en 1920. Fermée le matin. Stock moyen. Spec: éditions originales; livres sur l'art; livres anciens. Cata: de temps en temps. Corresp: English. S.L.A.M.
Aussi 40 PLACE DU CAZDEUIL, 13100 AIX EN PROVENCE.

G. DE LUCENAY, 15 RUE PETITE-FUSTERIE, 84000 AVIGNON. TN: (90) 82 15 69. Fondée en 1970. Boutique, fermé lundi. Restreint stock. Spec: musique ancienne, XVIIIe et XIXe siècles. Corresp: English, Español. B: Crédit Agricole, Avignon. S.L.A.M., L.I.L.A.

HENRI MARTIN-BRÈS, 60 RUE GRIGNAN, 13001 MARSEILLE. TN: (91) 33 02 92. Fondée en 1940. Boutique fermée du 15 juillet au 15 août. Très restreint stock. Corresp: English. B: S.M.C. Marseille. CP 61346 Marseille. S.L.A.M., L.I.L.A.

LIBRAIRIE-GALERIE JACQUES MATARASSO, 2 RUE LONGCHAMP, 06000 NICE. TN: (93) 87 74 55. Fondée en 1950. Boutique, fermée lundi matin et octobre. Moyen stock. Spec: beaux-arts; livres illustrés; éditions originales. Corresp: English. B: Banque Populaire des Alpes Meridionales, Agence Nice-Buffa, 8 rue de la Buffa, 06000 Nice. CP: Marseille 15 35 01.N. S.L.A.M., Chambre Syndicale de l'Estampe.

LIBRAIRIE-GALERIE PAUL MAUREL, 27–29 BOULEVARD ALBERT 1ER, 06600 ANTIBES. TN. (93) 34 25 46. Fondée en 1967. Boutique (1er étage). Restreint stock. Spec: livres illustrés modernes; éditions originales; beaux-arts. Cata: 3 par an. Corresp: English. S.L.A.M.

S.A.R.L. BOUQUINERIE MONTBARBON, 1 RUE R. ANDRIEU, 83100 TOULON, TN: (1694). 93 49 39. Fondée en 1974. Boutique. Moyen stock. Cata: 5 par an. B: Banque Populaire, S.L.A.M.

LIBRAIRIE OCCITANIA, 46 RUE DU TAUR, 31000 TOULOUSE. Prop: Claude Thourel. TN: (61) 21 49 00. Fondée 1950. Boutique, fermé lundi matin. Restreint stock, aussi les livres neufs. Spec: régionalisme; estampes. Cata: 6 par an. CP: 48213 X Toulouse. S.L.A.M.

CLAUDE RICCARDI, 7 RUE MEYERBEER, 06000 NICE. TN: 31 68 27. Fondée 1940 (anciennement J. Rocca). Boutique. Moyen stock. Spec: érudition; sorciers; procès, XVIe au XXe s. Cata: 1 par an. Corresp: Italiano. B: B.P.A.M. Nice, Compte 12 021 06115 9.

LIBRAIRIE RIVARES, 3 RUE RIVARES, 64000 PAU. Prop: Bernard et Natasha Hauvette. TN: (59) 27 26 23. Fondée en 1954. Boutique. Important Stock. Spec: régionalisme; Pyreneisme; gravures; livres anciens. Cata: deux par an. Corresp: English.

LIBRAIRIE ROSSIGNOL, 1 RUE JEAN DAUMAS, 06400 CANNES. Prop: Louis Daniel Rossignol. TN: (93) 39 70 55. Fondée en 1928. Boutique. Fermé lundi. Moyen stock. Spec: varia; Africana; autographes. Cata: 4 par an. Corresp: English. B: Société Générale, Marseille, CCP: 36 39 92 H. S.L.A.M., C.N.E.S.

RENATA SAGGIORI. MAS DU PIN PERDU, LE COL DE GORDES, 84200 GORDES. TN: (90) 72 33 46. Spec: autographes et manuscrits; livres avec envoi; photographies. S.L.A.M.

LIBRAIRIE SAINT-JACQUES, 10 RUE SAINT-JACQUES, 64500 SAINT-JEAN-DE-LUZ. TN: (59) 261619. Boutique, fermée lundi et Octobre. Spec: histoire. S.L.A.M.

JEAN-LOUIS SAINTE-MARIE, B.P. 24. 6 RUE GUILERAN, 82200 MOISSAC. TN: 04 00 93. Fondée en 1929. Par Correspondance Seulement. Moyen stock. Spec: histoire; documentation; livres anciens. Cata: 6 par an. B: S.G., Compte 3915. CP: Toulouse 2105–04. S.L.A.M.

LE SALON DU LIVRE D'OCCASION, 26 RUE DU GRAND-FOUR, 13300 SALON-DE-PROVENCE. TN: (90) 56 45 15. Boutique, fermé lundi. S.L.A.M.

PHILIPPE SERIGNAN, 15 RUE JOSEPH-VERNET, 84000 AVIGNON. TN: (90) 86 57 40. Spec: sciences; voyages; Provence; économie politique. S.L.A.M.

THÉLÈME, RUE ST. SAVOURNIN NO. 29, MARSEILLE 13005. Prop: M. Carbonnel. TN: 16 91 48 08 25. Fondée 1978. Boutique. Stock important. Spec: Science-Fiction; fantastique; histoire. Corresp: English, Español, Italiano. B: Société Lyonnaise, compte 9498 41703 N.

ANDRÉ THÉROND, 40 RUE VICTOR HUGO, 81100 CASTRES. TN: (63) 59 31 43. Domicile, de preference sur rendez-vous. Important stock. Cata: 5 par an. Corresp: English. B: B.P.T.A. CP: Toulouse 1167 65 K.

LES' VIEUX ORDINAIRES, 8 RUE BAUDIN, 83000 TOULON. Prop: Etienne Francis. TN: (94) 89 59 24. Spec: livres anciens et modernes. gravures; affiches; cartes postales. S.L.A.M.

A.F. VOLTAIRE, 30 RUE ADOLPHE-THIERS, 13001 MARSEILLE. TN: (91) 48 60 58. Fondée en 1941. Magasin. Important stock. Cata. Corresp: English. CP: Marseille 286–81.

MONACO

LE CABINET DE L'ESTAMPE ET DU LIVRE ANCIEN, S.A.M. 51 RUE GRIMALDI, LE PANORAMA, MONACO, PRINCIPAUTE DE MONACO. Prop: M. F. Weissert. TN: (93) 30 46 79. S.L.A.M.

MONACO-GRAVURES, B.P.89, 32 BOULEVARD DES MOULINS, MONTE-CARLO, PRINCIPAUTE DE MONACO. Prop: Nicolas Vigna. TN: (93) 30 40 73. Fondée en 1973. Boutique ouvert 15.00–19.30 hrs. et sur Rendez-vous. Moyen stock livres et gravures. Spec: Regionalisme et Decoration. Cata: 1 par an. Corresp: English, Italiano. B: Lloyds Bank, 11 Boulevard des Moulins, Monte Carlo. Compte 306762. C.C.P. 6.116.89 U. S.L.A.M.

THE
BOOKDEALERS'
AND COLLECTORS'
YEAR-BOOK
AND DIARY

*Published each November
for the following year*

Contents include:

Review and Prospects – Current topics –
Societies and Associations – Services and Supplies –
Trade Periodicals, Recent Books for Bookmen –
Rules and Regulations affecting the book trade –
Register of Fine and Limited Editions – Alterations
and additions to the directories of dealers in
secondhand and antiquarian books and a
week-to-an-opening diary showing dates of
anniversaries, exhibitions, book fairs, etc.

Demy Octavo, sewn binding, card cover

SHEPPARD PRESS LIMITED
P.O. BOX 42 RUSSELL CHAMBERS
COVENT GARDEN, LONDON WC2E 8AX

ISLAND

ICELAND   ISLANDE

REYKJAVÍK

BOKAVARDEN, Hverfisgotu 52, Simi 29720, Reykjavik.

FORNBOKVERZLUNIN, Klapperstig 37, Reykjavík.

FORNBOKAVERZLUN KRISTJANSSONAR, Hverfisgotu 26, Reykjavík.

SIGURDUR GUSTAVSSON, Gardastraeti 40, 101 Reykjavík.

SNAEBJORN JONSSON & CO. H. F., Hafnarstraeti 4 Reykjavík. (P.O. Box 1131). TN: 13133 and 14281. TA: Books Reykjavik. Established 1927. Shop. Very small stock, also new books. Cata: 1 a year. Corresp: English. B: National Bank of Iceland, and Commercial Bank of Iccland.

BRAGI KRISTJONSSON, ANTIKVARIAT, P.O. Box 775, Skolavördustigur 20, Reykjavík. TN: 29720. TA: Unique Reykjavík. Est: 1959. Shop and storeroom. Large stock sec. and antiq. books. Spec: Icelandicana and norröna; Scandinavian books. Cata: 5 or 6 a year. Corresp: English, Deutsch, Dansk. B: Fisheries Bank of Iceland; Iceland Bank of Commerce.

ISRAEL

ISRAËL

JERUSALEM: TEL AVIV

ATIKA BOOKS, P.O. Box 1086, Yannai Street 3, Jerusalem. Prop: Mrs. H. Sapir (daughter of Dr. Meyer). TN: 224050. Est: 1935. Shop, but appointment necessary. Large stock. sec. and antiq. also a few new books. Spec: rare books on Palestine; old prints and maps of the Holy Land. Corresp: English, Deutsch, Hebrew.

LE CUISINIER, COOKBOOKS, P.O. Box 17221, Tel Aviv. Prop: Ephraim Gerry.

LOGOS BOOKSHOP, 38 Ben Yehuda Street, Tel Aviv. Prop: Walter Zadek. TN: 22 23 37. Established 1940. Shop, early closing Friday. Very large stock, also new books. Spec: anything about Palestine (old books, maps, engravings). Corresp: Ivrith, English, Deutsch, Français, Dutch. B: Bank Leumi Leisrael, Branch: Trumpeldor.

S. MATLOFSKY, Alfasi 7, Jerusalem 92302. TN: 02 633185. Est: 1977. Private premises. Closed Saturday. By appointment only. Medium stock. New books also. Spec: Judaica Hebraica. Cat: monthly. Corresp: Hebrew, English, Français. B: American Israel Bank—Rehavia 42386. CP: Bank Leumi—Rehavia 5473/87.

LUDWIG MAYER LIMITED, Shlomzion Hamalka 4, Jerusalem. (P.O. Box 1174). TN: 222628. Established 1908. Spec: Archaeology; Orientalia; mathematics; natural history. A.B.A.

F. PINCZOWER, 83 Sokolow Street, Tel Aviv. (P.O. Box 6008). TN: 443 448. TA: Pincbooks Tel-Aviv. Established 1939. House Premises, closed Friday 16.00 hours. Medium stock, also new books. Spec: military; contemporary history; Middle East. Cata: 3 a year. Corresp: English, Deutsch. B: Barclays Bank, Tel-Aviv, Account No. 13374. CP: Tel-Aviv 4128.

NISSEN PREMINGER, LTD., 9 Montefiore Street, Tel Aviv. (P.O. Box 29001). TN: 53027. TA: Promedice Tel Aviv. Spec: horology.

Z. WILUZANSKI, P.O. Box 3183, 58 Ben Jehuda Street, Tel Aviv 61031. TN: 297073, (Private 280369). Est. 1963, Shop, closed Saturdays. Small stock sec. and antiq. Spec: Judaica, Palestine, Maps. Corresp: Deutsch, English, Hebrew, Russian, Polish.

ZOHAR, 1 Nachlat-Benjamin, Tel Aviv. (P.O. Box 4814.) Prop: E. Sheftl. TN: 621106 (after hours 263045). Established 1940. Shop, open only Mondays and Thursdays, other times by appointment. Very large stock, also new books. Spec: Hebraica; Judaica; Orientalia. Cata: about 4 a year. Corresp: Hebrew, Yiddish, English, Français, Deutsch, Russian. B: Barclays Bank, Tel Aviv, Account No. 133571.

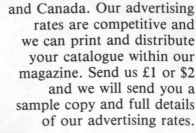

ITALIA

ITALY ITALIE ITALIEN

Association: Verband

A.L.A. =Associazione Librai Antiquari d'Italia, via
Jacopo Nardi 6, 50132 Firenze.

Public Holidays: Jours de Fête: Feiertage

Jan. 1 and 6: Mar. 19: Easter Monday: Apl. 25: May 1: Ascension:
Corpus Christi: Jun. 2 and 29: Aug. 15: Nov. 1 and 4: Dec. 8, 25 and
26.

Jan. 1 et 6: Mar. 19: lundi de Pâques: Avr. 25: Mai 1: Ascension: Fête-
Dieu: Jun. 2 et 29: Août 15: Nov. 1 et 4: Déc. 8, 25 et 26.

Jan. 1 und 6: Marz 19: Ostermontag: Apr. 25 Mai 1: Himmelfahrt:
Fronleichnam: Juni 2 und 29: Aug. 15: Nov. 1 und 4: Dez. 8, 25 und
26.

I

ROMA (ROM, ROME)

LIBRERIA ALESSANDRIA, Via Alessandria 216/a, Roma. Prop: Carlo
Misasi. TN: 858142. Established 1960. Shop. Small stock. Spec:
occult; science. Cata. Corresp: Français. CP: Roma 1/39793.

LIBRERIA ANTIQUARIA M. ARBICONE, Via Spalato 43, 00198
Roma.

LIBRERIA LA BANCARELLA, Via Cavour 119, Roma. Prop: Felice
Bertocchi. TN: (06) 462541. Established 1932. Shop, closed during
August. Small stock. Corresp: Français.

LIBRERIA ANTIQUARIA M.T. CICERONE, Via Cicerone 39–41,
00193 Roma. Prop: G. Brotrini. TN: (06) 312465. Cata.

LIBRERIA DOTTI, Via Della Scrofa 58, 00186 Roma. Prop: Sergio
Dotti. TN: (06) 6564755. Established 1951. Shop, closed Monday
morning. Large stock. Spec: sciences and literature. Cata: 6 a year.
Corresp: English, Français. B: Banca Nazionale Lavoro, Ag. 15. No.
828. CP: Roma 25182007. A.L.A.I., I.L.A.B.

LIBRERIA ANTIQUARIA DELL'IMPERO, Corso Rinascimento 6
00186 Roma. Cata.

LIBRERIA PASQUALE LOMBARDI, Via San Eufemia 11, 001
Roma. Established 1940. Shop. Large stock, also new books. Spe
religion; law. Cata: 1 a year. Corresp: English, Français, Deutsch.
Credito Italiano, Roma. CP: Roma 1/36606. A.L.A.I.

LIBRERIA ANTIQUARIA MONTENEGRO, Via Dei Gracchi 291/
00192 Roma. Spec: Art, architecture, literature, biography, fasci
history, local history, etc. Cata.

LIBRERIA GIA NARDECCHIA, S.R.L., Piazza Cavour 25, 0019
Roma. TN: (06) 352235. Established 1921. Shop, closed Saturda
Very large stock. Spec: Italian periodicals, old Italian books. Corres
English, Deutsch.

LIBRERIA ANTIQUARIA C.E. RAPPAPORT, Via Sistina 23, 0018
Roma. Prop: Elisabeth and James Seacombe. TN: 483826. Establishe
1906. Shop, closed Saturday. Medium stock. Spec: medicine; scienc
fine arts; literature. Cata: about 3 a year. Corresp: English, Françai
Deutsch. B: Banco di Sicilia, Agenzia 2 Roma, No. 41 00 98 450. C
Roma 35903004. A.L.A.I., L.I.L.A., A.B.A.(Int.). V.D.A.

LIBRERIA MARESCA RICCARDI, Via Banco S. Spirito 61, 0018
Roma. (06) 6 565 944. M: A.L.A.I.

LIBREIA ROMANA. Via del'Prefetti 16, 00186 Roma.

LIBRERIA S. AGOSTINO, Via S. Agostino 17/A, Roma. Prop: Michet
Chezubina. TN: (06) 655470. Established 1955. Shop. Medium stock
Spec: spectacle, music, art. Cata. Corresp: Français. CP: Rom
1/34465.

GUISEPPE SCARPIGNATO, Via Ripetta 156, 00186 Roma. TN: (06
655923.

LIBRERIA SFORZINI, Via Della Vite 43, 00187 Roma. Cata.

FIAMMETTA SOAVE, Via Guiseppe Cuboni 12, 00197 Roma. Cata.

FIAMMETTA SOAVE, Via Leccosa 4, Roma. TN: 06 6564285. Est
1974. Shop. Open daily 10.00 to 13.00, except Monday. Spec: Rome
Italian literature, old and rare books. Cata: occasionally. Corresp
French, English. A.L.A.I.

RENATO SPADUCCI—STUDIO BIBLIOGRAFICO, Piazza S. Giovanni in Laterano 18/B, 00184 Roma. P.O. Box 4097, 00182 Roma (APPIO). TN: (06) 7574114. Est: 1970. Storeroom. Business hours 16.00 to 19.00 hours, Monday, Wednesday and Friday. By appointment only. Medium stock. Cata: bi-monthly. C/C POST. 47653001.

II

ITALY

ASOLO	NAPOLI (Naples, Neapel)
BARI	PADOVA (Padua)
BOLOGNA	PARMA
BRESCIA	PERUGIA
CHIVARI	PISA
COMACCHIO	RAVENNA
COMO	REGGIO EMILIA
CUNEO	RIMINI
FIRENZE (Florence)	SIENA
GENOVA (Genoa, Genua)	TORINO (Turin)
LUCCA	TRIESTE
LUCIGNANO	UDINE
MILANO (Milan, Mailand)	VENEZIA (Venice, Venedig)
MODENA	VERONA

LIBRERIA "ACHILLE" DI A. MISAN, Piazza Vecchia 4, 34121 Trieste. TN: (040) 68525. A.L.A.I.

STUDIO BIBLIOGRAFICO AESSE, Via Castiglione, 30, 40124 Bologna. TN: (051) 277 779. A.L.I.A.

LIBRERIA ALBERTINA, Via Carlo Alberto 7, I-10123 Torino. TN: (011) 519 066.

A. DEGLI ALBIZI, Piazza Duomo 22r, Firenze. TN: (055) 211 237. Spec: fine arts; old prints; illustrated books. Cata. A.L.A.I.

DANILO ALLEGRETTI, 17 Viale Rosselli, 22100 Como. TN: 559801. Established 1950. Private premises, appointment necessary. Small stock. Cata. Corresp: English, Français. B: Banco di Roma, Account No. C.538. CP: Como 128 62223.

LIBRERIA ALPINA, Via C. Coronedi-Berti 4, 40137 Bologna. Prop: Gastone and Mario Mingardi. TN: (051) 345715. Established 1961. Storeroom, open normal business hours. Small stock, also new books. Spec: old and new books, prints and maps on mountaineering. Cata: 2–3 a year. Corresp: English. B: Banca Cooperativa di Bologna, Sede. No. 12833. CP: Bologna 19483403.

BOTTEGA AMBROSIANA, Via Vitruvio 47, 20124 Milano. TN: 227936. Spec: fine arts; religions; science. Cata. CP: Milano 3/51932.

AMERICAN BOOKSHOP, Largo Cairoli, Milano.

ANTIQUA LIBRI, Via Borgo Nuovo 27 2, I-20121 Milano. TN: (02) 704 457. Spec: books of 15th and 16th centuries. Cata. A.L.A.I.

LIBRERIA L'ARCHIVOLTO s.a.s., Via Marsala 2, 20121 Milano. TN: (02) 65 90 842.

LIBRERIA GIURIDICA ARDY, Piazza Sauli 4–2, 16123 Genova. TN: (010) 295508. Cata.

L'ARTE ANTICA, Via A. Volta 2, 10121 Torino. Prop: Teresa Salamon. TN: (011) 515834.

ANTIQUARIATO LIBRARIO BADO E MART, Via Dietro Duomo 14 Int 1, 35100 Padova. TN: (049) 23052.

LIBRERIA ANTIQUARIA LUIGI BANZI, Via Borgonuovo 10, 40125 Bologna. Prop: Dott. Mario Tamburello. TN: (051) 269088. Shop early closing Saturday. Very small stock. Spec: autographs. Corresp Français. B: Banco di Napoli-Filiale di Bologna. CP: Bologna 8/20182. A.L.A.I.

LIBRERIA S. BARDINI, Via XII Ottobre, 16121 Genova. TN: (010) 298956.

ANTIQUARIATO LIBRARIO Bado e Mart s.n.c.
Via Dietro Duomo, 14 Int. 1, 35100, Padova, Italy
Tel. 049 - 23052
Manuscripts – Incunabula
Illustrated books XVth-XIXth century
Geography – Fine Arts
Medicine – Old sciences
Old prints
Maps

LIBRERIA VINCENZO BERISIO, Via Port'Alba 28–29, 80134 Napoli. TN: (081) 328922. Cata.

LIBRERIA ANTIQUARIA BERRUTO, Via San Francesco da Paola 10 bis, 10123 Torino. Prop: Serafino Berruto. TN: (011) 839 6636. Established 1939. Shop, closed Monday mornings. Large stock. Spec: bibliography, Italian literature, topography (Italy, Piedmont). Cata. Corresp: English, Français. B: Credito Italiano. CP: Torino 20380101. A.L.A.I.

LIBRERIA BERTOCCHI, Strada Maggiore 70, 40125 Bologna. Prop: Piero Bertocchi. TN: (051) 23 37 57. Established 1967. Shop. Very large stock. Spec: old and modern medicine and periodicals. Cata: 3–4 a year. Corresp: English, Français. CP: 10752400.

BERTOLA & LOCATELLI MUSICA, Via Alba 53, 12100 Cuneo. Spec: Music, history, theatre, biography, monographs on individual musicians, dictionaries, reference works. Cata.

LIBRERIA ANTIQUARIA 'BIANCHINO DEL LEONE", Piazza Ansidei 4, 06100 Perugia. (C.P. 25). Prop: Silvestri Lodovico. TN: 66.323. Established 1946. Private premises, open normal business hours. Medium stock. Spec: libri; stampe; autografi. Corresp: English, Français, Deutsch. B: Banca Commerciale Italiana. CP: Perugia 12046–0.

IL BIBLIOFILO, Via Roma 45, I-53100 Siena. TN: (0577) 287 993.

LIBRERIA BONFANTI, Via Macedonio Melloni 19, 20129 Milano. TN: (02) 749 61 81. Spec: law; political science. CP: Milano 3/38504. A.L.A.I.

LE BOUQUINISTE, Via Principe Amedeo 29, 10123 Torino. Prop: Dott. Carla Viotto Maccono. TN: 876782. TA: Bouquiniste Torino. Spec: old and rare; old prints; Italian topography; history. CP: Torino 2/37491.

BOTTEGA APULJA DI MARIO SOMMA, Via Salvatore Cognetti 37, I-70121 Bari.

LICE BOURLOT, Piazza Castello 9, Torino, 10123. TN: (011) 53 48 65. TA: Bourlot Stampe Torino. Spec: prints—arts and crafts; costumes, sports and pastimes; atlases, maps and views. B: Credito Italiano. CP: Torino 2/22492. A.L.A.I.

LIBRERIA ANTIQUARIA BOURLOT, Piazza San Carlo 183, I–1012
Torino. Prop: Gian Vittorio Bourlot. TN: 53 74 05. Established 1848
Shop, closed Monday morning and during August. Large stock. Spec
old and rare; Italian literature and topography; old science; geography
old prints. Cata: 2 a year. Corresp: English, Français. B: Banco d
Roma, Torino. CP: Torino 2/18001. A.L.A.I., S.L.A.M.

LIBRERIA ANTIQUARIA BRIGHENTI, Via Malpertusoi 4012.
Bologna. (P.O. Box 506). Prop: Gino Brighenti. TN: (051) 584 070
Established 1952. Medium stock, also new books. Spec: early medicine
and science; economics; bibliography. Cata: 1 a year. Corresp: English
Français, Deutsch. B: Banca Commerciale Italiana, Bologna. CP
Bologna 8–9603. A.L.A.I., L.I.L.A.

GIAMPAOLO BUZZANCA, Piazzeta Pedrocchi 5, 35100 Padova. TN
(049) 651831. Shop, closed Mondays. Spec: prints, maps, drawings
illustrated books. A.L.A.I.

LIBRERIA INTERNAZIONALE C. CALDINI, Via Tornabuoni 89/91r
50123 Firenze. Prop: Giorgio Migliorini. TN: (055) 214474. Est
1971. Shop, closed Monday mornings. Medium stock sec. and antiq
also new books on art and local interest. Spec: art; manuscripts
incunabula. Cata: 2 a year. Corresp: French. B: Banca Toscana, ag
No. 8., Firenze, Account No. 9199/67. CP: 1795550. A.L.I.

LIBRERIA ANTIQUARIA CAPPELLINI, Corso Tintori 31r. I-5012
Firenze. TN: (055) 21 51 62.

LUIGI CARPANETO, Via Burlamacchi 31, 55100 Lucca.

CASALINI LIBRI, Via Benedetto Da Maiano 3, I-50114 Fiesol
(Firenze). TN: (055) 599 941.

LIBRERIA GASPARE CASELLA, Piazza Municipio 84, 80133 Napol
Prop: Dott. Guido Lo Schiavo. TN: (081) 324579. Storeroom, earl
closing Saturday. Medium stock. Cata: 1 a year. Corresp: English. F
Banca Commerciale Italiana. CP: Napoli 22869804.

GIOCONDO CASSINI, Via XXII Marco San Marco 2424, 3012
Venezia. TN: 31815. Spec: geography; old prints; Italian literature
Italian topography. A.L.A.I.

CAVALIERI D'ORO, Via Mazzini 84, 44022 Comacchio. Spe
autographs. B: Casa di Risparmio di Ferrara. CP: Comacchi
8/10879.

LIBRERIA ANTIQUARIA CAVRIOLO, Via Capriolo 16/D, 2510
Brescia. TN: (030) 295 732. A.L.A.I.

CARLO ALBERTO CHIESA, Via Bigli 11, 20121 Milano. TN: 79 86 78. Spec: old and rare; first editions and illustrated books 15th to 19th centuries; manuscripts; incunabula. L.I.L.A. A.L.A.I.

LIBRERIA CICERANO, Via G. Bausan 58, I-80121 Napoli.

LIBRERIA "IL COLLEZIONISTA", Via Madonnina 9, 20121 Milano. TN: (02) 866 665. A.L.A.I.

LIBRERIA COLONNESE, 33 Via S. Pietro A Majella, 80138 Napoli. P.O. Box 145. Prop: Gaetano Colonnese. TN: 081/459858. Est: 1965. Shop, closed Saturday afternoon. Medium stock. Spec: first editions, art; literature; prints; maps. Cata: 4

GALLERIA REGINA CORNARO, Via Regina Cornaro 214, I-31011 Asolo (Treviso). TN: (0423) 52 785. Spec: rare books and maps.

LIBRERIA ANTIQUARIA DALLAI, Piazza de Marini 11 rosso, 16123 Genova. Prop: Giovanna and Norina Dallai. TN. (010) 298338. Established 1939. Shop, closed Monday, and during August. Very small stock. Corresp: English, Français, Deutsch. B: Cassa di Risparmio, No. 7369/80.

LIBRERIA ANTIQUARIA 'IL DELFINO', Via Cesare Battisti 19A, 10123 Torino. Prop: Visani Meris. TN: (011) 83 96 775. Est: 1952. Boutique, closed Mondays. Very large stock. Spec: periodicals, Italian literature. Cata: occasionally. Corresp: Français. B: 11300 Credito Italiano CP: 2–13418. A.L.A.I.

DOCET', Via A. Righi 9/A, 40126 Bologna. Prop: D. Furgeri & C. TN: 23 07 57. Spec: old and rare books; prints. A.L.A.I.

LIBRERIA INT DRAGHI-RANDI Via Cavour 17–19 I-35122 Padova. TN: (049) 20425.

LIBRERIA ECLICTICA, Piazza Cavana, Trieste.

BOTTEGA D'ERASMO, Via Gaudenzio Ferrari 9, 10124 Torino. Prop: Dott. Angelo Barrera. TN: (011) 83 0331 and 831264. TA: Erasmus Torino. Spec: law; philology; philosophy; religion. CP: Torino 2/34095. A.L.A.I.

STUDIO BIBLIOGRAFICO "LA FENICE", Calle del Frutariol-S. Marco, 1850, 30124 Venezia. TN: (041) 38006 A.I. A I

LIBRERIA C. FIAMMENGHI, Via Malcontenti 11, 40126 Bologna. Cata.

LUIGI FINZI, Foro Buonaparte 12, 20121 Milano. TN: 86 25 79
Spec: fine arts; Italian literature and topography; theatre; old prints
Cata. B: Banca Vonwiller. CP: Milano 3/26748.

LIBRERIA FAUSTO FIORENTINO, Calata Trinita Maggiore 36
80134 Napoli. Cata.

LIBRERIA FLUMEN DANTIS di P. ZALI, Piazza Mazzini 12/1, 16043
Chivari (Genova). Cata.

A. FORNI EDITORE s.p.a., Via Gramsci 164, 40010 Sala Bolognesi
(Bologna). Spec: Folklore and dialects. Cata.

STUDIO BIBLIOGRAFICO FORTUNA, Via de' Pucci 4, I-50122
Firenze. TN: (055) 284 907. A.L.A.I.

IL GABINETTO DELLE STAMPE, Via Montenapoleone 3, 20121
Genova. TN: (02) 708082. Prop: Harry Salamon. A.L.A.I.

GALLINI, Via Del Conservatorio 17, 20122 Milano. TN: 70 98 20 and
70 28 58. Spec: music and music literature. B: Banco Ambrosiano
A.L.A.I.

GARISENDA LIBRI & STAMPE, S.A.S., Strada Maggiore 14/A
40125 Bologna. Prop: Maria Fiammenghi. TN: 231893. TA
Garisenda Bologna. Established 1959. Visits by appointment. Spec
geography; old prints; science; fine arts; illustrated books. Corresp
English, Français. B: Credito Romagnolo, Ag.13, N.437. CP: Bologna
8/25491.

LIBRERIA GIGLIO, Via Convenevole 37, 50047 Prato (Firenze)
Cata.

LUIGI GONNELLI & FIGLI, Via Ricasoli 14 rosso, Firenze. Prop: Aldo
Gonnelli. TN: 216835. Spec: autographs; old and rare books
manuscripts; old and modern prints; paintings. B: Monte dei Paschi d
Siena and Banca Steinhauslin. CP: Firenze 5/11376. A.L.A.I.

LIBRERIA ALBERTO GOVI, C.P. 321 Centro, I-41100 Modena. TN
office (059) 236 420; home (059) 218 170. A.L.A.I.

LIBRERIA ORESTE GOZZINI di PIETRO CHELLINI, Via Ricasoli 49
50122 Firenze. Prop: Pietro Chellini. TN: (055) 212433. Established
about 1870. Shop, closed Saturday afternoon. Very large stock. Spec
fine arts; history; jurisprudence; literature. Corresp. Français. Cata:
a year. B: Credito Italiano-Firenze, No. 38161. CP: Firenze 13087507
A.L.A.I.

G. C. GRIFONI, Via Emilia Levante 13, 40139 Bologna. TN: (051) 54 93 78. A.L.A.I.

LIBRERIA A. GUIDA, Via Port'Alba, 20/24, I-80134 Napoli. TN: (081) 459 894. A.L.A.I.

LIBRERIA FILOSOFICA KAIRÔS, Studio d'Arte, 11219 Milano-Isola, via Baldinucci 6, 20158 Milano. Prop: Dr. Edoardo Rozza. TN: (02) 60.30.66. TA: Kairos-Milano. Est: 1980. Storeroom, by appointment only. Medium stock. Spec: History of Italian towns; maps; views. Cata: two a year. Corresp: English, Français. B: C/C 6045 Ist. Banc. S. Paolo Torino Branch 5, Milano. Private Libraries Assn. London.

LEONARDO LAPICCIRELLA, 3 via Tornabuoni, 50123 Firenze. TN: 216 598. Spec: manuscripts; woodcut books; engravings. A.L.A.I.

LICOSA ANTIQUARIATO, Via Lamarmora 45, 50121 Firenze. TN: 579 751. Cata.

STUDIO BIBLIOGRAFICO LIDIS, Foro Bonaparte 12, 20121 Genova. Prop: Lea Boldi. TN: (02) 802073.

LIBRERIA LUIGI LOMBARDI, Via Constantinopoli 4 bis, 80138 Napoli. TN: (081) 211921. Est: 1935. Two Shops. Closed Saturday. Medium stock sec. and antiq., also new books. Spec: scientific; historical; curiosa; arts. Cata: 2 a year. Corresp: English. B: Banco di Napoli. Ag.14. CP: 18823807.

LIBRERIA ANTIQUARIA MANTUA, Via A. Doria 6, 10123 Torino. TN: (011) 538 744. A.L.I.A.

GAETANO MANUSÉ, Via Hoepli 3, Milano. TN: 80 72 46, 539 31 52. Established 1945. Storeroom, open normal business hours. Medium stock. Cata: 3 or 4 a year. Corresp: Deutsch, Français. B: Banca Popolaire di Bergamo, Milano. Account No. 10241. CP: Milano 450 53204. A.L.A.I.

LIBRERIA ANTIQUARIA MARTELLI, Via Santo Stefano 43, 40125 Bologna. Prop: Guiseppe Nociti. TN: (051) 227453. Established 1846. Studio appointment necessary, closed Monday morning. Medium stock. Spec: incunabula; first editions; Italian literature; folklore; art; history. Cata. Corresp: English, Français. CP: Bologna, 8/17495.

LIBRERIA MARZOCCO, Via Martelli 22 rosso, 50129 Firenze. TN: (055) 24568 and 298575.

CARLA MARZOLI, Corso Porta Nuóva 2, 20121 Milano. TN: (02) 65 38 87. Est: 1947. Office: normal business hours. Spec: Illuminated MSS: Incunabula. Early illustrated. History of Science; Cartography Corresp: English, Français. A.L.A.I., A.B.A.

LIBRERIA MATTEUZZI, Piazza Aldrovandi 5/B, 40125 Bologna TN: (051) 221687. Cata.

LIBRERIA ANTIQUARIA MEDIOLANUM, Via Montebello 30, 20121-Milano. Prop: Dr. Elfo Pozzi. TN: 65 36 37. Established 1928. Shop, early closing Saturday. Very large stock. Spec: old books; autographs; engravings. Corresp: Français. B: Credito Lombardo CTO. 13850/9; C.P. Milano 50751205. L.I.L.A. A.L.A.I.

IL MERCANTE DI STAMPE, Corso Venezia 29, 20121 Milano. TN (02) 704 402. A.L.A.I.

WALTER MICHELONI, Vico Falamonica 15 rosso, 16123 Genova TN: 20 38 21. CP: Genova 4/8256. A.L.A.I.

LIBRERIA G. MICHELOTTI, Corso Roma 18, 5106 Montecatini Terme. TN: (0572) 79 329. A.L.A.I.

LIBRERIA M. MILIANO, Via. B. Croce 60, 80134 Napoli.

LIBRERIA MONTANINI, Via Nino Bixio 58, Parma. Prop: Gian Paolo Montanini. TN: (0521) 68662. Cata. CP: 25/1378.

LIBRERIA ANTIQUARIA MORETTI, Via Lusardi 8, 20122 Milano. TN: (02) 8391 275. Spec: illustrated books; incunabula; atlases and travel. Cata. A.L.A.I.

LIBRERIA A. NANNI, Via Musei 8, 40124 Bologna.

LEO S. OLSCHKI—STUDIO BIBLIOGRAFICO, 52046 Lucignano (Arezzo). Prop: M. and F. Witt. TN: (0575) 846015 TA: Libros Lucignano. Established 1886. Private premises, appointmen necessary. Large stock. Spec: art, architecture; classics, history medicine, science; theology. Corresp: English, Français, Deutsch. B American Express Bank, Florence, No. 7425, A.L.A.I., A.B.A.

LIBRERIA ANTIQUARIA PALMAVERDE, Via Castiglione 35, 40124 Bologna. Prop: dott. Roberto Roversi. TN: 232085. Shop. Large stock. Spec: modern first editions; erudition; philology. Cata: 6 a year. CP: Bologna 8/3319.

LIBRERIA ANTIQUARIA M. PENSO, S. Tomà 2916/a, 30121 Venezia. TN: (041) 38 215. A.L.A.I.

LIBRERIA ANTIQUARIA PERINI, Via A. Sciesa 9, 37100 Verona. TN: (045) 30073. Cata.

DOTT. ADA PEYROT, Via Consolata 8, 10122 Torino. TN: 54 74 38. Spec: illustrated books; topography; economics. A.L.A.I.

LIBRERIA DI PIAZZA S. BABILA, Corso Monforte 2, 20122 Milano. Prop: Peppi Battaglini. TN: (02) 799219. Established 1952. Shop. Old and modern prints. A.L.A.I.

LIBRERIA PIEDMONT, Vice dei Mercanti 22, 10121 Torino.

IL POLIFILO, Via Borgonuovo 3, 20121 Milano. Prop: A. M. Vigevani. TN: 87 11 89. TA: Polifilo Milano. Established 1941. Shop. Spec: old Italian books. Cata. Corresp: English, Français. A.L.A.I.

LIBRERIA ANTIQUARIA PRANDI, Viale Timavo 75, Reggio Emilia. Prop: Dino, and Paolo Prandi. TN: 34973. Established 1927. TA: Libreria Prandi Reggio-E. Spec: fine arts, modern prints, modern illustrated books; philology; folklore. Corresp: English, Français. CP: Reggio Emilia 25/5326. A.L.A.I., S.L.A.M. Chambre Syndicale de l'Estampe-Paris.

LIBRERIA ANTIQUARIA ARTURO PREGLIASCO, Via Accademia Albertina 3 bis, 10123 Torino. TN: (011) 877114. TA: Preliber Torino. Established 1912. Shop, closed Saturday afternoon. Large stock. Spec: old and rare; fine arts, old prints; autographs. Cata: 4–5 a year. Corresp: English, Français. B: Credito Italiano, AG., 7, Torino. CP: Torino 21690102. A.L.A.I.

QUATTRIFOLIO, Via S. Cecilia 2, I-20122 Milano. TN: (02) 781 498. A.L.A.I.

ANTIQUARIATO LIBRARIO RADAELI, Via A. Manzoni 39, 20121 Milano. Prop: dott. Francesco Radaeli. TN: (02) 6590055. Established 1964. Shop, closed Saturday afternoon. Spec: manuscripts; miniatures; Italian XV–XVIII century books. Cata: 2 a year. Corresp: English, Français, Deutsch. Banca 5. Paolo di Brescia, No. 1173. A.L.A.I. V.B.K. (Schweiz)

LIBRERIA L. REGINA, Via Costantinopoli 51, 80138 Napoli. Fine and rare books. Cata.

RICORDI, Negozio di Via Berchet 2, 20121 Milano. Spec: music.

LIBRERIA M. RIGATTIERI, Calle Della Mandola 3713, 30124 Venezia. TN: (041) 31321.

LIBRERIA RIMINESE, Via IV Novembre 46, 47037 Rimini (Forli). TN: (0541) 26417.

RENZO RIZZI, Via Cernaia 4, I–20121 Milano. TN: (02) 655 67 05 TA: Librire Milano. Established 1954. Storeroom, appointment preferred. Small stock. Spec: manuscripts, old Italian books, palaeography. Cata. B: Banca. Pop. Bergamo-Milano. CP: Milano 339 872 07. A.L.A.I., L.I.L.A.

UMBERTO SABA, Via San Nicolo 30, 34121 Trieste. Prop: Carlo Cerne. TN: (040) 631741. Established 1904. Shop, closed Monday. Medium stock, also new books. Spec: old and rare books, incunabula. Cata: 4 a year. Corresp: English, Deutsch. B: Banca Commerciale Italiana, No. 26990. CP: Trieste 11/7847. A.L.A.I.

LIBRERIA ANTIQUARIA DI S. BERNARDINO, via de Servi 49R 50122 Firenze. Prop: Cristiana Lunghetti. TN: 055.295091. Est 1977. Shop, closed Saturday afternoon and Monday morning. Spec rare books. Cata: twice yearly. Corresp: English, Français.

LIBRERIA SALIMBENI S.r.l., Via Matteo Palmieri 14R, 50122 Firenze. Prop: Gustavo & Vitaliano Salimbeni. TN: 29 20 84 and 29 89 05. Spec: fine arts; topography. CP: Firenze 5/16746. A.L.A.I.

SALOTTO DEL BIBLIOFILO, Via Luccoli 21, 16123 Genova. TN (010) 294480. Cata.

E. SERMONETA, Studio Bibliografico, Via C. Battisti 2, I-40122 Bologna. TN: (051) 278 474. A.L.A.I.

LIBRERIA ANTIQUARIA M. SGATTONI, Via Vivaio 22, 20122 Milano. Cata.

SIBRIUM LIBRI E MANOSCRITTI, Via Bigli 21, 20121 Milano. Prop Dr. A. Martegani. TN: 705969. Established 1966. Office, appointment preferred. Small stock. Spec: old and rare books; science. Cata corresp: Français, Deutsch. B: Credito Milanese CC. 1321. A.L.A.I.

LIBRERIA ANTIQUARIA SOAVE, Via Po 48, I–10123 Torino. Prop: Vittorio & Emilio Soave. TN: 011 87 89 57. Established 1935. Shop, closed Monday morning. Large stock. Spec: old books on sciences, history and literature; old prints and engravings. Cata: about twice a year. Corresp: English, Français. CP: Torino 2/28555. A.L.A.I. A.B.A.

BOTTEGA APULJA DI M. SOMMA, Via S. Cognetti 37, 70121 Bari. Cata.

LIBRERIA DELLO STUDENTE, Via Laura 68/A, 50121 Firenze. TN: (055) 24.78.755. A.L.A.I.

LIBRERIA R. TARANTOLA, Via Vitt. Veneto 20, I-33100 Udine. TN: (0432) 23 459.

MATTEO TONINI, Via Antica Zecca 26, 48100 Ravenna. TN: (0544) 30397. Established 1965. Shop. Small stock. Cata: 2 a year. B: Cassa di Risparmio di Ravenna. CP: Ravenna 8/4820. A.L.A.I.

AGENZIA URSO, LIBRI RARI, Via Andrea Verga 4, 20144 Milano. TN: (02) 46.91.690. Postal Business only. Cata.

LIBRERIA VALLERI, Via Ricasoli 68 rosso, 50121 Firenze. Prop: Giovanni Valleri. TN: (055) 296192. Shop. Very large stock. Cata: monthly. Corresp: English, Deutsch. B: Banca Toscana, Firenze. CP: Firenze 5/11097. A.L.A.I.

LIBRERIA ANTIQUARIA ANDREA VALLERINI, Via Dei Mille 7A–13, I-56100 Pisa. TN: (050) 40 393. Est: 1975. Shop, closed Saturday afternoons. Spec: Literature and Classics; early science; architecture; Italian local history. B: Banca Commerciale Italiano, CTO. 3792595-01 A.L.A.I., A.L.I., L.I.L.A.

LIBRERIA SANTO VANASIA, Via M. Macchi 58, 20124 Milano. TN: (02) 266917. Spec: mathematics, physics, chemistry.

ORFEO VIGARANI, Libri Antichi et Stampe, Via Magnani N.6, 40134 Bologna. TN: (051) 414805. Est. 1981. Private premises, closed Saturday. Small stock. Spec: 18th century. Cata: 1–2 a year. Corresp: English, français.

LIBRERIA ANTIQUARIA A. VIGLONGO, Via Genova 266, 10127 Torino. TN: (011) 6060 421. A.L.A.I.

LIBRERIA VINCIANA, Via Monte Napoleone 23, 20121 Milano. TN: (02) 701582. Prop. Alessandro Piantanida. Spec: old and rare books

BANCO LIBRI s.a.s. DI V. ZANNI & C., Via Marsala 6, 40126 Bologna. Local history, religion, travel, militaria, theatre. Cata.

JUGOSLAVIJA

YUGOSLAVIA   JUGOSLAWIEN

BEOGRAD (Belgrade, Belgrad): LJUBLJANA: ZAGREB

ANTIKVARIJAT-KNJIŽARA. NAKLADNOG ZAVODA MATICE HRVATSKE. ILICA 62, 41000 ZAGREB. Prop: Nakladni zavod Matice hrvatske, Zagreb. TN: 00 38 41 442 064. Est. 1962. Shop. Large stock Spec: history; Slavica; Old German literature; new books. Cata occasionally. Corresp. English Deutsch. B: Zagrebačka banka. Aagreb 30105–603–10628. Member: Poslovna zajednica izdavača i knjižara SRH.

CANKARJEVA ZALOZBA, KOPITARJEVA 2, 61001 LJUBLJANA. (P.O Box 201-IV). TN: 323 841. Established 1945. Shop, early closing Saturday. Small stock. Spec: Slavica; rarities. Cata: irregularly Corresp: English, Deutsch. B: Ljubljanska banka.

MATICA HRVATSKA 2 MATICINE, ZAGREB.

ANTIKVARNICA SRPSKE AKADEMIJE NAUKA, KNEZ MIHAJLOVA 11000 BEOGRAD.

SRPSKA KNJIZEVNA ZADRUGA, 19 MARSALA TITA, BEOGRAD.

ANTIKVARIJAT "TIN UJEVIĆ", ZRINSKI TRG. 16, 41000 ZAGREB. Prop Nakladni zavod Znanje, Zagreb. TN: 422 286. Est: 1948. Shop Medium stock sec. and antiq. and low priced new books. Corresp English, Deutsch. B: Zagrebačka banka, Zagreb, 30105–603–10792 Member: Udruženje izdavača i knjižara Jugoslavije, Beograd.

ZALOZBA MLADINSKA KNJIGA "EMKA", 38 CAPOVA, LJUBLJANA.

KYPRIAKI DIMOKRATIA
KIBRIS CUMHURIYETI

CYPRUS   CHYPRE   ZYPERN

NICOSIA

MAM, P.O. Box 1722, NICOSIA. Prop: Mrs. Thelma M. Michaelidou. TN: 72744. TA: Mam Nicosia. Est: 1965. Medium stock. Spec: books about Cyprus. Cata: monthly. B: Greek and English Bank of Cyprus Limited, Account 10-11-055784. Booksellers Association of Cyprus.

LIECHTENSTEIN

VADUZ

INTERLIBRUM ESTABLISHMENT, SCHLOSS-STRASSE 6, FL 9490 VADUZ. (P.O. Box 234). Prop: Walter Alicke. TN: (075) 23261. TA Interlibrum Vaduz. Established 1961. Shop, appointment necessary. Spec: history of science and ideas; illustrated books; Helvetica. Cata 4–6 a year. Corresp: English, Français, Deutsch. B: Bank in Liechtenstein AG., 417 830.0 and Midland Bank Ltd., London 30476285. CP: St. Gallen 90–19707 and Stuttgart 3691–705 S.L.A.M., V.D.A., I.L.A.B.

LUXEMBOURG

MAISON J.-P. KRIPPLER-MULLER, 52A BOULEVARD
GRANDE-DUCHESSE CHARLOTTE, LUXEMBOURG. succ. Michel Gerbes.
TN: 47 03 39. Fondée en 1949. Dépôt. Important stock. Spec: livres
Luxembourgeois de tout genre. Corresp: English, Deutsch. B: Banque
Internationale à Luxembourg. CP: Luxembourg 69304–46.

MAGYARORSZÁG

HUNGARY   HONGRIE   UNGARN

BUDAPEST

KULTURA, P.O. Box 149, H-1389 BUDAPEST. FÖ UTCA. 32, BUDAPEST 1
TN: 388 511. Telex: 22 4441. TA: Kulturpress Budapest. Established
1950. Offices and storerooms, appointment necessary. Closed
Saturday. Very large stock. Spec: scientific and literary books and
journals. Corresp: English, Francçais, Deutsch. B: National Bank of
Hungary 024/7.

The above organisation, Kultura Foreign Trading Company, deals with
the import and export of all books and other printed matter to and from
Hungary.There are no restrictions on the value of books, old or new, that
may be purchased in Hungary, but the export from Hungary of any printed
matter published before 1st January 1957 requires an export licence. The
licence has to be applied for from:

ORSZÁGOS SZÉCHÉNYI KÖNYVTÁR.
BUDAVÁRI PALOTA
"F" épület Disz tér P.O.B. 486 H.-1827, BUDAPEST VIII.

A licence fee of 5% of the value is charged.
Individuals with antiquarian items for sale must submit details to an
official body, which indicates those which must not be sold for export abroad
and those which may. The Department of Manuscripts and Old Books of
the National Library can exercise an embargo on antiquarian books leaving
the country.

The transfer of money is done through the National Bank of Hungary at
the official exchange rate, details of which can be obtained from the local
branch of the Hungarian International Bank.

ANTIKVARBOLTOK, MARTIROK UTJA 44, BUDAPEST II. TN: 151 487.

ANTIKVARBOLTOK, BAJESY-ZSILINSZKY UTJA 13, BUDAPEST I
TN: 116 049.

ANTIKVARBOLTOK, KAROLYI MIHÁLY UTCA 3, BUDAPEST V. TN: 17-
924.

ANTIKVARBOLTOK, MUZEUM KÖRUT 15, BUDAPEST V. TN: 173 514.

ANTIKVARBOLTOK, MUZEUM KÖRUT 17, BUDAPEST V. TN: 174 948.
Spec: Musik.

ANTIKVARBOLTOK, MUZEUM KÖRUT 35, BUDAPEST V, TN: 173 270.

ANTIKVARBOLTOK, BAJESY-ZSILINSZKY UTJA 50, BUDAPEST V. TN: 116 049.

ANTIKVARBOLTOK, VACI UTCA 28, BUDAPEST V. TN: 185 673.

ANTIKVARBOLTOK, NEPKOZTARSASAG UTJA 2, BUDAPEST VI. TN: 315 132.

ANTIKVARBOLTOK, LENIN KÖRUT 20, BUDAPEST VII. TN: 222 670.

ANTIKVARBOLTOK, MAJAKOVSZKIJ UTCA 81, BUDAPEST VII. TN: 223 946.

ANTIKVARBOLTOK, THOKOLY UTJA 5, BUDAPEST VII. TN. 429 562.

ANTIKVARBOLTOK, NEPSZINHAZ UTCA 23, BUDAPEST VIII. TN: 142 050.

ANTIKVARBOLTOK, ULLOI UTJA 11–13, BUDAPEST IX. TN: 183 636.

ANTIKVARBOLTOK, BARTOK B. UTCA 15, BUDAPEST XI. TN: 667 008.
Spec: technical.

ANTIKVARBOLTOK, BARTOK B. UTCA 25 BUDAPEST XI. TN: 665 046.

ANTIKVARBOLTOK CSANADY UTCA 13, BUDAPEST XIII. TN: 296 655.
Spec: Remainders.

MALTA

SLIEMA: VITTORIOSA

PAUL BEZZINA, 114 Saint Lawrence Street, Vittoriosa, Malta. Private premises; appointment necessary. Spec: Maltese books, early maps, engravings: material concerning Malta and the Knights of Malta. Corresp: English, Italiano, Français.

A. LANZEN, 19 Cathedral Street, Sliema, Malta. Spec: local interest books.

FRANK KIRKOP, 106 Blanche Street, Sliema. TN: 513166. Private premises; by appointment only. Very small stock. Spec: antique maps. engravings, colour prints, early books about Malta. Corresp: English. Français, Deutsch, Italiano. B: Bank of Valletta; and Barclays Bank International Limited.

NEDERLAND

NETHERLANDS   HOLLAND
PAYS-BAS   NIEDERLAND

Association: Verband

N.V.A.   =Nederlandsche Vereeniging van Antiquaren, Nieuwe Spiegelstraat 40, 1017
DG Amsterdam. TN: (020) 279982

Public Holidays: Jours de Fête: Feiertage

an. 1: Easter Monday: April 30: May 5: Whitmonday: Dec. 25 and 26.

an. 1. Pâques: Avril 30: Mai 5: lundi de Pentecôte: Dec. 25 et 26.

an. 1: Ostermontag: April 30: Mai 5: Pfingstmontag: Dez. 25 und 26.

I   AMSTERDAM
I   's-GRAVENHAGE (La Haye, The Hague, Den Haag)
II OTHER TOWNS

I   AMSTERDAM

NTIQUARIAAT AMARYL, KONINGINNEWEG 79, 1075–CJ AMSTERDAM.
Prop: W.G. and R. Wildeboer. TN: (020) 799383. Est: 1975. Shop,
closed Mondays. Large stock sec. and antiq. Spec: Dutch and German
literature, history and politics; illustrated; children's; fiction thrillers
and detective. Cata: 1 a year. Corresp: English, Deutsch. B: Postgiro
199338.

MSTERDAMS BOEKHUIS, HAARLEMMERSTRAAT 87, AMSTERDAM. TN:
24 32 55.

NTIQUARIAAT ANTIQUA, HERENGRACHT 159, 1015 BH AMSTERDAM.
Prop: R. van der Peet. TN: (020) 245998. Established 1960. Postal
business only. Medium stock. Spec: History of Science, Philosophy and
Political Economy, Literary History, Old and Rare Books. Cata: 4 a
year. Corresp: English. B: Amro, Amsterdam, No. 46 66 00 100. CP:
Den Haag 258600. N.V.A.

145

A. ASHER & CO., B.V., KEIZERSGRACHT 489–491, AMSTERDAM. Prop Nico Israel. TN: (020) 22 22 55. Telex: 14070. TA: Asherbook Amsterdam. Established 1825. Shop and storeroom. Medium stock Spec: natural history. Cata: 4 a year. Corresp: English, Français Deutsch. B: Hollandse Koopmansbank N.V., Account No. 6 350 14 30. CP: The Hague 511662. N.V.A., S.L.A.M., I.L.A.B.

ATHENAEUM ANTIQUARIAN BOOKSELLERS, REGULIERSGRACH 50, 1017 LT, AMSTERDAM. Prop: Dr. J.B.W. Polak; and B.M.M Hosman, LL.D. TN: (020) 226288. TA: Athbooks Amsterdam. Spec humanistica; autographs. N.V.A.

GEBR. BAKKER, 7 GASTTHUISMOLENSTEEG, AMSTERDAM. TN: 23 97 03.

JOHAN BEEK, HUIDENSTRAAT 24, 1016 ET AMSTERDAM. TN: (020) 23 7 62. Shop, closed Friday and Saturday except by appointment. Mediur stock, Spec: Law, International Law; politics; history: economic an social sciences; philosophy, Cata: 10 a year. Corresp: Deutsch, Englisl B: H.B.U. Amsterdam. Account 623221004. C.C.P. 243279. N N.V.V.A.

JOHN BENJAMINS, B.V., AMSTELDIJK 44, AMSTERDAM. Prop: John I Benjamins. TN: 738156. TA: Benper Amsterdam. Telex: 15798 Established 1964. Storeroom, closed Saturday, appointment necessary Very large stock of periodicals. Spec: periodicals in the domain c liberal arts and social science. Cata: irregularly. Corresp: Englisl Français, Deutsch, Italiano, Español. B: Hollandse Koopmansban CP: Den Haag 289615. N.V.A., I.L.A.B.

VAN BERG ANTIQUARIAAT, OUDE SCHANS 8–10, AMSTERDAM. TN (020) 24 08 48. TA: Bergbooks Amsterdam. Spec: fine ar topography; biography. Cata. CP: Amsterdam 657269.

BERGMANS AND BROUWER ANTIQUARIAN BOOKSELLER: RUSTENBURGERSTRAAT 291, 1073 GE AMSTERDAM. TN: 020 79550 Spec: Rare books, art and architecture 19th and 20th century. N.V.A

DE BOEKERIJ, 122 PRINSENGRACHT, AMSTERDAM. TN: (020) 24 88 54.

TON BOLLAND, PRINSENGRACHT 493, 1002 AMSTERDAM. (Formerly Va Bottenburgs). TN: (020) 22 19 21. Est: 1897. Shop, early closin Saturdays. Medium stock sec. and antiq. books. Spec: humanisr Protestant and Roman Catholic theology; the Reformation and Chur history; also auctioneers. Cata: 4 to 6 a year. M: N.V.A.

NTIQUARIAAT HIERONYMUS BOSCH, LELIEGRACHT 36 (HK KEIZERSGRACHT), 1015 DH AMSTERDAM (P.O. BOX 12018 1100 AA AMSTERDAM S.O.) Prop: P. H. Kerssemakers. TN: (020) 237178. Established 1970. Shop, open 11.00 to 17.00. Large stock, also new books. Spec: fine art. Cata: 8 a year. Corresp: English, Français, Deutsch. CP: Arnhem 166 24 21.

. **VAN BRINK,** LEIDSESTRAAT 30, 1017 PB AMSTERDAM. Spec: Modern art, illustrated books (limited editions) N.V.A.

NTIQUARIAAT BRINKMAN, SINGEL 319, 1012 WJ AMSTERDAM. TN: 020-238353. N.V.A.

NTIQUARIAAT C. BROEKEMA, LEIDSEKADE 68, 1016 DA AMSTERDAM. TN: 020 222126. By appointment only. Spec: Geography, maps, travel. N.V.A.

HARBO'S ANTIQUARIAAT, 75 WILLEMSPARKWEG, AMSTERDAM TN: 76 12 29.

NTIQUARIAAT "DIE SCHMIEDE", BROUWERSGRACHT 4, AMSTERDAM. Prop: A. & G. Leyerzapf. TN: 25 05 01. Est: 1980. Shop open 12.00 to 17.00 hrs, Monday to Friday. Small stock sec. and antiq. Spec: modern German literature; fine printing. Cata: 3 a year. Corresp: English, Français Deutsch. B: AMRO Amsterdam, Account 41 28 24 558. CP: Arnhem 1370757; Frankfurt am Main 300573-600.

. **EMMERING,** N.Z. VOORBURGWAL 304, 1012 RV AMSTERDAM. TN: (020) 231476. Established 1904. Shop and storeroom. Spec: Judaica; Americana (West Indies); Old Master prints. Cata. Corresp: English, Français, Deutsch. B: Algemene Bank Nederland, N.Z. Voorburgwal 304, Amsterdam, No. 54 15 10 037. N.V.A., I.L.A.B.

RASMUS ANTIQUARIAAT EN BOEKHANDEL. SPUI 2, AMSTERDAM. Prop: Dr. A. Horodisch and H. Garnmann. TN: 229147. Established 1934. Shop. Large stock, also new books. Spec: book history and bibliography; history of art; German literature; 16th century books; Judaica. Cata: 5–6 a year. Corresp: English, Français, Deutsch. B: Pierson, Heldring & Pierson, Amsterdam, 24.08.660.0. CP: Den Hag 234079, Milano 7715, München 120134.

J.H. FLINT, Dikninge 119, 1083 VA Amsterdam.

VAN GENDT BOOK AUCTIONS N.V., Keizersgracht 96–98, 1015 C[*] Amsterdam. Prop: W. Hommerson. TN: (020) 23 41 07. T^A Rightbook Amsterdam. Established 1947. Spec: manuscript: incunabula; medicine, old science. Also auctioneers. B: Amro Ban (Nederland), N.V. 46542.

A. GERITS AND SON Rare Books, Hartenstraat 4, 1016 C^I Amsterdam. TN: 120 272285. Spec: Humanities and Social Science N.V.A.

BART GERRITSMA, 350 Herengracht, Amsterdam. TN: 26 14 35.

BERT HAGEN, Herenstraat 38, 1015 CB Amsterdam. TN: (020) 26 3^I 82. Est: 1972. Shop, closed Mondays. Small stock sec. and antiq. Spe old and rare illustrated. 15–19th century, theology, philosophy, histor Cata: 2 a year. Corresp: Deutsch, English, Français. B: AMR(Amsterdam, Account 42 22 38. 848. C.C.P., Arnhem 278 2435. N N.V.V.A.

BERNARD HOUTHAKKER, Rokin 98, Amsterdam. Prop: L. [/] Houthakker. TN: (020) 23 39 39. Shop, closed Saturdays. Spe drawings (15th to 18th centuries); Rembrandt etchings; old paintin B: Amro. CP: Amsterdam 3636. N.V.A.

M. L. HUIZENGA, Oudez. Achterburgwal 156, 1012 D^v Amsterdam. TN: (020) 23 75 66. Est: 1945. Private premises, post business only. Large Stock. Spec: antiquity; philosophy; anthropolog Cata: occasionally. Corresp: English, Deutsch. B: Algemene Ba Nederland, Rokin, Amsterdam. Account No. 540134082. C 's-Gravenhage 644 836. N.V.A., I.L.A.B.

HUMANIORA ANTIQUA, Herengracht 242, Amsterdam, Prop: d[*] A.F. Kan. TN: (020) 261585. Est: 1979. Shop; appointment preferre Small stock sec. and antiq. Spec: Psychology, psychiatry, philosoph Mental Sciences. Cata: 2 a year. Corresp: Deutsch, English, Franca: B: P.C.G.D., Amsterdam. Account 2879006.

B. M. ISRAEL, B.V., Boekhandel en Antiquariaat, N. Voorburgwal 264, 1012 RS Amsterdam. TN: 24 70 40. T[/] Isrealbook Amsterdam. Established 1899. Private premises, op Monday to Friday (Saturday 10.00–13.00 hrs). Large stock. Spec: c and rare; medicine; sciences; travel. Cata: 2–6 a year. Corresp: Englis Français, Deutsch. B: Amro Bank, Head Office, Amsterdam. C Amsterdam 49 03 89. N.V.A. also Printroom, Singel 379.

B. M. ISRAEL, Prentenkabinet, Singel 379, Amsterdam. TN: (020) 22 55 00. N.V.V.A. A.B.A.

MAARTEN J. ISRAEL, P.O. Box 8, 1110 AA Dieman. (Keizersgracht 690, 1017 EV Amsterdam). TN: (020) 261385. TA: Elbok, Dieman. Est: 1980. Stockroom, appointment necessary. Medium stock sec. and antiq. Spec: law, economics, philosophy; old and rare: bibliography. Corresp: English. Français. Deutsch. B: Algemene Bank Nederland, Amsterdam. Account 5403 17 810. CP: 1.267.584. N.V.A.

N. ISRAEL, Keizersgracht 489–491, Amsterdam. TN: (020) 22 22 55. Telex: 14070. TA: Ennibook Amsterdam. Established 1950. Shop and storeroom, Saturday by appointment. Medium stock. Spec: rare books, manuscripts; cartography, travel and voyages. Cata: 1 a year. Corresp: English, Français, Deutsch. B: Hollandse Koopmansbank, Amsterdam, No. 63 50 141 30. CP: Amsterdam 433 275. N.V.A., S.L.A.M., I.L.A.B.

ANTIQUARIAAT JUNK B. V., Van Eeghenstraat 129, 1071 GA Amsterdam. TN: 020 763185. Closed Saturdays. Spec: Old and rare books on natural history. N.V.A.

HISTORISCH ANTIQUARIAAT ANNELIES KEE, Spuistraat 125, 1012 SV Amsterdam. Prop: Annelies Kee. TN: (020) 226682. Established 1980. Shop, closed Saturday, open other days 11.00 to 17.00. Medium stock, also new books. Spec: History. Cata: 10 a year. Corresp: English, Français, Deutsch. CP: 445 6411.

A. KOK EN ZN, 14–18 Oude Hoogstraat, Amsterdam. TN: (020) 231191. Est: 1944. Shops. Very large stock. Spec: Arts, architecture, natural history, Dutch engravings. Cata: 6 a year. Corresp: English, Deutsch. B: Amro Bank, Account 46 67 42–568. CP: 188576.

G.N. LANDRÉ, B.V., Muziekboekhandel & Antiquariaat, Anjelier Sdwarsstraat 36 1015 NR Amsterdam. TN: (020) 24 70 56. Est: 1975. Shop, closed Mondays. Medium stock sec. and antiq. also new books. Spec: music and all connected subjects. Cata: 10 a year. Corresp: English. B: AMRO, Amsterdam. Account 43 50 69 543. CP: 34 82 96.

HANS MARCUS, N. Z. Voorburgwal 284, 1012 RT Amsterdam. TN: (020) 23 45 44. Established 1953. Spec: old illustrated books. B: Amro Bank. CP: 599999. N.V.A.

RUDOLF MULLER INTERNATIONAL BOOKSELLERS, P.O. Box
9016, AMSTERDAM. (Overtoom 487). Managing Director: R. Muller.
TN: 16 59 55. Telex: 12582 (rmbks NL) Est: 1969. Shop, appointment
necessary. Very small sec. and antiq. stock, also new books. Spec:
geography, geology, cartography. Cata: 6 a year. Corresp: English,
Français, Deutsch, Italiano, Español. B: Algemene Bank Nederland,
Amsterdam, and New York. CP: 18 06 019.

GÉ NABRINK & ZOON, BOEKHANDEL EN ANTIQUARIAAT, KORTE
KORSJESPOORTSTRAAT 8, AMSTERDAM–C. Prop: G. and F. R. Nabrink.
TN: (020) 22 30 58. Established 1924. Shop and storeroom, early
closing Saturday. Very large stock, also new books. Spec: Orientalia.
Cata: weekly list and 10 catalogues a year. Corresp: English, Français,
Deutsch. B: Algemene Bank Nederland N.V., Account No. 54 02 75
719. CP: The Hague 114143. N.V.A.

C. P. J. VAN DER PEET, B.V., 33–35 NIEUWE SPIEGELSTRAAT, 1017 DC
AMSTERDAM. TN: (020) 235763. TA: Mobin Amsterdam. Established
1947. Shop, Monday to Friday 9 to 17.00, Saturday 10 to 17 hours.
Large stock, also new books. Spec: Indonesia, Africa, Americana,
Asiatica, Orientalia; Oriental and primitive arts; decorative arts; old
maps and prints. Cata: 2 a month. Corresp: English, Français,
Deutsch. B: A.B.N. Account 54 02 81–239. CP: 529581. N.V.A.,
S.L.A.M. *Also at* 39 JANSWEG, HAARLEM.

G. POSTMA, O.Z. VOORBURGWAL 249, 1012 EZ AMSTERDAM. TN: (020)
24 57 81. Spec: languages. N.V.A.

INEKE SCHIERENBERG ANTIQUARIAAT, LEIDSEGRACHT 42, 1016
CM AMSTERDAM. TN: 020 236178. By appointment only. Spec:
Illustrated books and juveniles, prints, games, curiosities. N.V.A.

DIETER SCHIERENBERG BV. PRINSENGRACHT 485–487, 1016 HP
AMSTERDAM. TN: (0)20 225730. Spec: rare books and periodicals on
natural sciences.

ANTIQUARIAAT W. N. SCHORS, REGULIERSGRACHT 52–54,
AMSTERDAM. TN: (020) 264121 and 250813. Established 1953. Shop,
closed Monday morning, appointment necessary for antiquarian
department. Medium antiquarian stock, also new books on specialities.
Spec: alchemy, comparitive religion, freemasonry, kabbala,
mesmerism, occult,psychology, sexuology, witchcraft. Cata: 5–6 a
year. Corresp: English. Français, Deutsch. B: B.d.B. 236 Singel, 1016
AB Asterdam, Account 85 06 13 590. CP: Den Haag 447730. N.V.A.

ANTIQUARIAAT SCHUHMACHER, Gelderschekade 107, 1011 EM Amsterdam. Prop: Wilma and Max Schuhmacher. TN: (020) 221604. TA: Shoebooks Amsterdam. Established 1952. Shop, Very large stock. Spec: language and literature–Dutch, English, French, German, Avantgarde. Cata: 2 a year. Corresp: English, Français, Deutsch. B: Algemene Bank Nederland, Amsterdam, No. 54 53 10 342. CP: The Hague 388801. N.V.A., I.L.A.B.

JACQUES SCHULMAN, B.V., Keizersgracht 448, 1016 GD Amsterdam-C. TN: (020) 23 33 80. TA: Numismatique Amsterdam. Established 1880. Shop. Numismatics only. Cata: occasionally. Corresp: English, Français, Deutsch, Italiano, Spanish. B: Amro Bank, Amsterdam. CP: Amsterdam 29 73 61. N.V.A. International Association of Professional Numismatists.

J. DE SLEGTE, Kalverstraat 48–52, 1012 PE Amsterdam. TN: (020) 22 59 33. Established 1900. Shop. Very large stock. Spec: art; travels; old maps; views and prints; colour-plate books; remainders. Corresp: English, Français, Deutsch, Espaol. B: Algemene Bank Nederland, Amsterdam. CP: Amsterdam 120646. N.V.A.

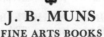

M. SOTHMANN, N.Z. VOORBURGWAL 284, AMSTERDAM. TN: (020) 23 69 20. CP: Amsterdam 513709. N.V.A.

HENK J. STOKKING, C.V., NIEWE SPIEGELSTRAAT 40, 1017 DG AMSTERDAM. TN: (020) 279982. Shop, closed Mondays. Spec: Old master drawings and prints. N.V.A.

VUYK WOUT, 316 SPUISTRAAT, AMSTERDAM. TN: 22 04 61.

II   's-GRAVENHAGE

HET A.B.C. DER BOEKEN, 142 WAGENSTRAAT, 's-GRAVENHAGE. TN: (070) 606044. Shop. Medium stock.

Dr. W. BACKHUYS, OURDORPWEG 12, 3062-RC ROTTERDAM. TN: (010) 123436. Antiq. stock; also new books and publishing. Spec: zoology, botany, geology, paleontology.

JURIDISCH ANTIQUARIAAT, L NOORDEINDE 39, 2514 GC 'S-GRAVENHAGE. Prop: K. P. Jongbloed. TN: (070) 468908. Established 1925. Spec: law, economics. B: Mees & Hope. CP: 's-Gravenhage 114195. N.V.A.

LOOSE, PAPESTRAAT 3, 's-GRAVENHAGE. TN: 460404. Established 1946. Shop. Medium stock. Spec: children's books; topography. Corresp: English, Français, Deutsch. B: Amro Bank, Kneuterdijk, 's-Gravenhage. CP: 's-Gravenhage 170 159. N.V.A.

LELIEFELD MUZIEKANTIQUARIATEN, 212 RIOUWSTRAAT, 'S-GRAVENHAGE. TN: (070) 65 95 56.

ANTIQUARIAAT MINERVA, ZEESTRAAT 48, 's-GRAVENHAGE. (Postbox 1853). Prop: Hans J. Hanselaar. TN: 46 18 11 (After 18h: 55 80 16). Established 1940. Storeroom, open to public, 10 to 17.30 hours, closed Monday morning. Medium stock. Spec: literature; geography; art. Cata: 6 a year. Corresp: English, Français, Deutsch. CP: 35 43 33.

MARTINUS NIJHOFF B.V., P.O. BOX 269, NOORDWAL 4, 2501AX 'S-GRAVENHAGE. TN: (070) 469460. Telex: 34164. TA: Books Hague. Est: 1853. Shop, closed on Saturdays. Very large stock, also new books. Spec: collections; periodicals; humanities in all languages. Cata: 1 general catalogue and 8 subject catalogues a year. Corresp: English, Français, Deutsch. B: Algemene Bank Nederland, 's-Gravenhage, Account No. 51 16 14 403. CP: 4165. K.N.U.B., N.B.B., N.V.A.

J. DE SLEGTE, Spuistraat 9, 2511 BC 's-Gravenhage. TN: (070) 63 97 12. Shop closed Monday mornings. Very large stock, also new books and prints. Spec: Topography. N.V.A.

VAN STOCKUM'S ANT., B.V. Prinsegracht 15, 's-Gravenhage. Prop: C.P. De Jongh and Drs. P.A.G.W.E. Pruimers. TN: (070) 64 98 40 and 64 98 41. Established 1833. Shop. Large stock sec. and antiq. Spec: public auction sales–5 or 6 a year. Corresp. English, Français, Deutsch. B: AMRO Bank. Account 4735 43 664. C.C.P. 5154. N.V.A., I.L.A.B.

MARTIN VEENEMAN, Noordeinde 100, 's-Gravenhage. TN: (070) 11 78 77. TA: Artbooks 's-Gravenhage. Established 1940. Spec: art; old prints. CP: 's-Gravenhage 343020. N.V.A.

H. A. VLOEMANS, Anna Paulownastraat 10, 2518 BE 's-Gravenhage. TN: (070) 607886. Established 1932. House premises, appointment necessary. Spec: modern arts and architecture. Cata: 3 a year. Corresp: English, Français, Deutsch. B: Nederlandsche Middesnstandsbank, No. 66 83 60 070. CP: Den Haag 226330. N.V.A.

III   OTHER TOWNS

ALKMAAR	KAMPEN
APELDOORN	
ARNHEM	LEEUWARDEN
	LEIDEN
BAARN	LISSE
BARNEVELD	LOCHEM
BILTHOVEN	
BLARICUM	MAARSTRICHT
BREDA	MIDDELBURG
BUREN	
BUSSUM	NAARDEN
CASTRICUM	NIEUWKOOP
	NIJMEGEN
DEVENTER	
DIEMAN	RAALTE
DOORNSPIJK	ROTTERDAM
DORDRECHT	
EINDHOVEN	SOEST
ENSCHEDE	TILBURG
GRAVE	UTRECHT
GRONINGEN	
GROUW	VLISSINGEN
HAARLEM	WASSENAAR
's-HERTOGENBOSCH	
HILVERSUM	ZANDVOORT
HOMMERTS	ZUTPHEN
HUYBERGEN	ZWOLLE

DE ACHTERSTRAAT BOEKWINKEL, 44 ACHTERSTRAAT, ALKMAAR TN: (072) 11 75

ALFA ANTIQUARIAN BOOKSELLERS, P.O. BOX 1116, NIJMEGEN (VAN WELDERENSTRAAT 17) *and at* P.O. BOX 26, 5360 AA GRAVE (BRUGSTRAAT S.). Prop: Leo J. H. Kerssemakers. TN: (080) 23 15 6 or (08860) 73966. Established 1970. Two shops. Medium stock. Ol books and prints. Spec: The Middle Ages and comparative religion Cata: 2 a year. Corresp: English, Français, Deutsch, Español. B: Crédi Lyonnais Nederland, Account No. 63 06 05 750. CP: Arnhem 19686 57. N.V.V.A.

ALKMAARS ANTIQUARIAAT, 99 VERDRONKENOORD, ALKMAAR. TN (072) 15 27 25.

ANTIQUARIAAT AMARYL, Tuinbouwstraat 74, 9717-JL Groningen. Prop: W.J. and R. Wildeboer. TN: (050) 778347. Est: 1975. Shop, open Friday and Saturday. Medium stock sec. and antiq. Spec: Dutch literature, history and politics; topography Northern Netherlands. Cata: 1 a year. Corresp: English Deutsch. B: Postgiro 199338. (Also at Amsterdam).

ANTIEKPARADIS, 45 Steenbergsweg, Lepelstraat (Gem. Halsteren). TN: (01641) 63 24.

ARGUS ANTIQUARIAN BOOKSELLERS, Prof. Drionlaan 6, 2670 Baarn. Prop: W. J. Hommerson. TN: (02154) 5820.

H. BECKER, 50 Gierstraat, Haarlem. TN: (023) 31 28 39.

JOHAN BEEK, Graaf Van Lyndenlaan 55, 3771 JB Barneveld TN: (03420) 15118. Private premises: appointment necessary. Medium stock. Spec: Books before 1870; Law: politics: social sciences.

J. L. BEIJERS B.V., Achter Sint Pieter 140, 3512 HT Utrecht. Prop: H. L. Gumbert, E. Franco, Mrs. N. Franco. TN: (030) 310958. TA: Bookbee, Utrecht. Est: 1865. House premises, open 08.30 to 17.00 Monday to Friday. Very large stock sec. and antiq. books; also book auctioneers. Spec: early books; illustrated; history of ideas. Cata: occasionally. Corresp: English, Deutsch, Français. B: Amro Bank Utrecht, Account 45 60 09 035. CP: 7245. N V A

ANTON W. VAN BEKHOVEN. Ruysdaelplein 5, 1411 RD Naarden. TN: 02159 41534. Appointment preferred. Spec: Art, bibliography, religion, philosophy, history, typography, Portugal and Portuguese Colonial activities. N.V.A.

BELROSE BOEKHANDEL GALERIE, Mauritsweg 41, Rotterdam. TN: (010) 14 51 02

ANTIQUARIAAT G. J. BESTEBREURTJE, Lichte Gaard 2, P.O. Box 364 AJ Utrecht. TN: 030 319286 (b.g.g. 03402 63941). Closed Monday mornings. Spec: Voyages and travel, maritime history, East and West-Indies travels. N.V.A.

HET BISSCHOPSHOF, 1 Lichte Gaard, Utrecht. TN: (030) 31 40 93.

DE BOEKENBEURS, 38 Turfkaai, Middelburg. TN: (0180) 3 35 31.

DE BOEKENBOOT, 2 Zuidergrachtswal, Leewarden. TN: (058) 13 96 34.

BOEKENMARKT 'T EZELSOOR, 49 Veemarktstraat, Breda. TN: (076) 22 03 37.

ANTIQUARIAAT DE BOMBERG, 102A SCHOOTSESTRAAT, EINDHOVEN.
TN: (040) 52 8 57.

E. J. BONSET, PATRIJZENSTRAAT 8, 2040-AC ZANDVOORT. (Postbox 136).
TN: (02507) 13906. Established 1955. Private premises. Large stock.
Spec: psychology; social sciences. Also reprints. Cata: 10 a year.
Corresp: all European languages. B: Algemene Bank Nederland. CP:
646 084. N.V.A.

BOUMA'S BOEKHUIS, B.V., TURFSINGEL 3, GRONINGEN. Prop E.
Forsten. TN: (050) 123037. TA: Boumaboek Groningen. Shop, early
closing Saturday. Very large stock, also new books. Spec: philology;
theology; history; philosophy. Cata: 6–8 a year. Corresp: English,
Français, Deutsch. B: Amro Bank, Groningen, Account 44.60 07.730.
CP: Arnhem 806445 and Köln 194840. N.V.A.

D. J. BOUWMEESTER ANTIQUARIAAT, 27–28 GROTE KERKSHOF,
DEVENTER. TN: (05700) 1 41 19.

ANTIQUARIAAT BRABANT, LANGE PUTSTRAAT 14, 5211 KN
'S-HERTOGENBOSCH. Prop: J. F. van Pagée-Selis. TN: (073) 141915.
Spec: History: Illustrated Books; maps & views. N.V.A.

E. J. BRILL, OUDE RIJN 33A, LEIDEN. Manager: W. Backhuys. TN: (071)
146646. Telex: 39296. Established 1683. Spec: Orientalia; Biology;
Ethnography. CP: 's-Gravenhage 13921. N.V.A.

BURGERSDIJK & NIERMANS, NIEUWSTEEG 1, 2311 RW LEIDEN. Prop.
J.H. Douma. TN: 071 121067 Established 1894. Shop. Very large
stock. Spec: antiquity; regional. Cata: 5–6 a year. Corresp: English
Français, Deutsch. B: Algemene Bank Nederland. CP: The Hague
14408. Auctions. N.V.A.

CARPINUS ANTIQUARIAAT, 26 KERKSTRAAT, BUSSUM. TN: (02159)
49 96.

ANTIQUARIAAT VAN COEVORDEN, BEUKENLAAN 3, 8085
DOORNSPIJK. Prop: J. W. van Coevorden. TN: (05258) 1823. TA
Millbooks Soest. Established 1968. House premises, appointmen
necessary. Medium stock. Spec: fine arts, archaeology. Cata: 3 a year
Corresp: English, Deutsch. B: A.B.N. Account 59 90 11 025. CP: 60 0
09. N.V.A.

COSMOS ANTIQUARIAN BOOKS, (P.O. Box 30) MARKET 23, 7240AA LOCHEM. Prop: A. Bouwer. TN: (05730) 4820 or 3693. Est: 1972. Private premises; appointment necessary. Medium stock sec. and antiq. books also new books. Spec: Biological and geological sciences, old and new; history of medicine, chemistry, physics and astronomy. Cata: 3 or 4 a year. Corresp: English, Deutsch, Français. B: Algemene Bank Nederland, Lochem, Account No. 53 27 14 148. CP: Arnhem 22 52 789.

MATTHIJS DE JONGH, JELTEWEI 44–46, 8622 XT HOMMERTS. TN: (05154) 3031. Est: 1975. Private premises; appointment necessary. Very large stock sec. and antiq. Spec: history of ideas; socialism; Dutch and German literature; Dutch history; Indonesia. Corresp: Français, Deutsch, English. B: Ned. Midd. Bank, Account 69 85 06 413. CP: The Hague 121332.

ANTIQUARIAAT DE TILLE B.V., WEERD 11, P.O. Box 233, 8901 BA LEEUWARDEN. Prop: G. S. and S. G. Dykstra. TN: (059) 135500. Telex 46460. Est: 1948. Shop, closed Monday mornings. Medium stock. Spec: history, literature, theology. Cata: 7 a year. B: Rabobank, Leeuwarden. CP: Leeuwarden 3654235. N.V.A.

ANTIQUARIAAT DEVENTER, BRINK 17, 7411 BR DEVENTER. Prop: Mevr. F.J.H. van Pagee. TN: 05700 12735. Spec: Dutch literature, fine arts, illustrated books, prints. N.V.A.

VAN DIJK'S BOEKHUIS B.V., (POSTBOX 23), DIESELSTRAAT 1, 8263 AE KAMPEN. Prop: W. C. van Dijk. TN: (05202) 15757. Est: 1928. Shop, closed Saturdays. Very large stock sec. and antiq., also new books. Spec: books for secondary school pupils and for students. Corresp: English, Deutsche, Français. B: Amro Bank, Kampen, Account No. 47 58 17 508. CP: Arnhem 875004. N.V.A., Vereniging ter Bevordering van de Belangen des Boekhandels.

FORUM B.V., P.O.B. 129, OUDE GRACHT 206, 3511 NR UTRECHT. Prop: S. S. Hesselink. TN: (030) 31 69 77. Telex 47352 (Forum NL). Shop: appointment advisable. Medium stock sec. and antiq., also new books. Spec: Old and rare; history; travel. Geography: Literature, maps and views. Cata: 6 a year. Corresp: Français, Deutsch, English. B: Crediet-en Effectenbank, Utrecht. Account 69 92 11 174. N.V.A. Postgiro: 1882006.

FRISCO ANTIQUARIAT, HOOFDSTRAAT 5, 9001 AM GROUW. Prop: L. and N. Brolsma. TN: (05662) 1316. N.V.A.

A. L. VAN GENDT B.V., Oud Huizerweg 4, 1261 BD Blaricum. TN: 02153 14683. By appointment only. Spec: Bibliography, incunabula, manscripts. N.V.A.

A. GERITS RARE BOOKS, Delilaan 5, 1217 HJ Hilversum. TN: 035 14232. Spec: Humanities, social sciences. N.V.A.

H. G. GERRITSEN, Van Welderenstraat 88, Nijmegen. Prop: A. G. Gerritsen. TN: 224387/224385. Established 1915. Shop, early closing Monday. Large stock. Spec: literature; history; sciences. Cata: 5 a year. Corresp: English, Français, Deutsch. CP: Nijmegen 839095.

ANTIQUARIAAT DE GRAAF, Zuideinde 40, 2421 AK Nieuwkoop. Prop: B. de Graaf. TN: (01725) 1461. TA: Degraaf Nieuwkoop. Established 1959. Private premises, appointment necessary. Medium stock, also new books and publishing. Spec: bibliography; Reformation books; books printed 1500 to 1700. Cata: about 3 a year. Corresp: English, Français, Deutsch, Italiano. B: Rabobank. CP: Nieuwkoop 274 890. N.V.A.

GRON BOEKENBEURS BV., 61/II Oude Ebbingestraat, Groningen. TN: (050) 18 05 08.

GYSBERS EN VAN LOON, Bakkerstraat 7A, Arnhem. TN: (085) 424 421. Established 1942. Shop. Large stock, also new foreign books. Spec: fine arts; folklore; Dutch topography and history; automobiliana. Cata: once a week. Corresp: English Français, Deutsch. B: Algemene Bank Nederland. CP: Arnhem 883 309. N.V.A.

ANTIQUARIAAT BERT HAGEN B.V., Molenweide 24, 1902 CH Castricum. TN: 02518 56734. By appointment. Spec: Old and rare illustrated books from 15th/20th Century, history, topography, children's books. N.V.A.

HISTORISCHE MARITEME BOEKHANDEL, Kleine Houtstraat, Haarlem. TN: (023) 32 53 55.

ANTIQUARIAAT C. HOVINGH & ZN., Kleine Houtstraat 50, 2011DP Haarlem. Prop: C. & C. W. Hovingh. TN: (023) 31 07 14. Established 1940. Shop, closed Monday. Very large stock. Spec: art, history. Cata: 6 a year. Corresp: English, Deutsch, Français, Italiano. B: Mees & Hope, N.V., Haarlem. N.V.A., I.L.A.B.

ANTIQUARIAAT R. DE JONG, Kruisweg 38A 2011 LD Haarlem. Closed Monday mornings. Spec: topography, maps, engravings, local views, decorative prints. N.V.A.

JURIDISCHE BOEKHANDEL AND ANTIQUARIAAT, KLOKSTEEG 4, 2311 SL LEIDEN. Prop: A. Jongbloed and Zoon. TN: 071 122570. Spec: Law, old and modern. N.V.A.

ANTIQUARIAAT FRITS KNUF, P.O.B. 720, 4116-ZJ BUREN. TN: 0 3447 1691. TA: Knuf Buren. Private premises; appointment necessary. Medium stock sec. and antiq., also new books. Spec: bibliography, typography, calligraphy. Cata: 4 a year. N.V.V.A.

BOEKHANDEL ANTIQUARIAAT KRUGER, ACHTER DE HOOFDWACHT 7, NIJMEGEN. Prop: Leo. J.G. Krüger TN: (080) 233715. Spec: books of the 16th to 19th centuries; prints, maps, atlases. B: Commerzbank Kleve Account No. 81 602 00. CP: 3 266

BUBB KUYPER, KLEINE HOUSTRAAT 60, 2011 DP HAARLEM. Prop: F.W. Kuyper. TN: (023) 323986. Est: 1978. Shop, closed Monday morning. Large stook sec. and antiq. Spec: bibliography. typography literature; history; fine and applied arts. Cata: 4 a year. Corresp: English, Deutsch, Français. B: N.M.B., Heemstede, Account 67 11 13 984. CP: 3755327. M: N.V.V.A.

LAMED BOOKSTORE, 11 LANGE HOFSTRAAT, ZUTPHEN. TN: (05750) 1 28 14.

S.C. LEMMERS, VAN BÖNNINGHAUSENLAAN 16, 2161 ET LISSE. TN: 02521 15332. By appointment. Spec: Maps and views, rare books, topography, Natural History. N.V.A.

HET NEDERSAKSISCHE ANTIQUARIAAT, NIEUWSTRAAT 50, 7411 LM DEVENTER. Prop: H. J. & H. Tijenk. TN: 05700 17545. Shop, closed Mondays. Spec: History, topography. N.V.A.

L. M. C. NIERYNCK, VERDILAAN 85, 4384–LD VLISSINGEN. TN: 01184/70172. Private premises, appointment necessary. Spec: early newspapers from 16th to 19th century, and "Illustrated London News". Cata: 1 a year. Corresp: English, Français. B: Algemene Bank Nederland.

P. C. NOTEBAART, POSTBOX 280, 1400 AG. BUSSUM. Established 1967. Postal business only. Small stock. Spec: humaniora; Dutch 17th century books; theology; humaniora; surrealism. Cata: 4 a year. Corresp: English. CP: Amsterdam 12 53 799. N.V.A., I.L.A.B.

P. VAN OS, 68 BAKKERSTRAAT, ARNHEM. TN: (085) 42 44 21.

HENK OLTHUYSEN, 37 STAARTSESTRAAT, HUYBERGEN. TN: (01644) 25 90.

PAPYRUS 2E-HANDS BOEKENWINKEL, 60 NIEUWSTRAAT, DEVENTER. TN: (05700) 1 24 61.

I. H. REEF, 90 HEUVEL, GELDROP. TN: (040) 80 24 32.

REFLEX, P.O. BOX 454, ACHTER SINT PIETER 4, UTRECHT. Prop: A. J. Swertz. TN: (030) 31 52 91. N.V.V.A.

ANTIQUARIAAT DE RIJZENDE ZON, POSTSTRAAT 8, 5038 DH TILBURG. TN: 013 360337. Closed mornings and all day Monday. Spec: Orientalia, Brabantica, ethnology, history, manuscripts. N.V.A.

LUDWIG ROSENTHAL'S ANTIQUARIAAT, BUSSUMERGRINTWEG 4, 1217 BP HILVERSUM. Prop: Mrs. H. B. Rosenthal. TN: 035 47951. TA: Ludros, Hilversum. Est: 1859. Office; appointment preferable, closed Saturdays. Very large stock antiq. books. Spec: Ineunabula; Humanism; Roman Catholic. and Protestant theology, the Reformation. Cata: occasionally. Corresp: English, Francais, Deutsch. B: Algemene Bank Nederland, Hilversum, Account No. 550 711 805. CP: 309 771. N.V.A., V.D.A.

J. DE SLEGTE, JANSTRAAT 28, 6811 GJ ARNHEM. TN: (085) 420 597. Shop, closed Monday mornings. N.V.A.

J. DE SLEGTE, RECHTESTRAAT 36, 5611 GP EINDHOVEN. TN: (040) 44 74 19. Shop, closed Monday mornings. N.V.A.

BOEKHANDEL J. DE SLEGTE B.V., MARKTSTRAAT 13, 7511 GC ENSCHEDE. TN: 053 319200. Closed Monday mornings. Spec: Topography, academic books. N.V.A.

J. DE SLEGTE B.V., HERESTRAAT 33, 9711 LB GRONINGEN. TN: (050) 121422. N.V.A.

J. DE SLEGTE B.V., GROTE HOUTSTRAAT 100, 2011 SR HAARLEM. TN: (023) 31 52 50. N.V.A.

J. DE SLEGTE B.V., BREESTRAAT 73, 2311 CJ LEIDEN. TN: (071) 122007. Shop, closed Monday mornings. N.V.A.

BOEHANDEL J. DE SLEGTE B.V., GROTE STAAT 53, 6211 CV MAASTRIGHT. TN: 043 17296. Closed Monday mornings. Spec: Topography, general sciences, academic books. N.V.A.

J. DE SLEGTE, COOLSINGEL 83, 3012 AE ROTTERDAM. TN: (010) 13 83 05. N.V.A.

J. DE SLEGTE, OUDE GRACHT 121, 3511 AH UTRECHT. TN: (030) 313001. Deutsch. B: A.B.N. Account 54 88 11–180. CP: 120646. N.V.V.A.

BOEKHANDEL J. DE SLEGTE B.V., WEVERSGILDEPLEIN 1-2, 8011 XN ZWOLLE. TN: 038 214408/212789. Closed Monday mornings. Spec: Art, topography, general sciences, academic books. N.V.A.

A SMOORENBURG, 14-16 HOFMEIJERSWEG, RAALTE. TN: (05720) 20 92.

SPHINX, 55 NIEUW BOTERINGESTRAAT, GRONINGEN. TN: (050) 13 72 37.

SWETS & ZEITLINGER, B.V., HEEREWEG 347B LISSE. TN: (02521) 19113. TA: Swezeit Lisse. Est: 1901. Storeroom, appointment necessary. Very large stock. Spec: periodicals, reprints and antiquarian books. Cata: 6 a year. Corresp: English, Français, Deutsch, Español, Portuguese. B: Amro Bank, Amsterdam, Account No. 46.69.74.418. CP: Holland 13984. N.V.V.A.

TAXANDRIA ANTIQUARIAAT, 115 SALESIANENSTRAAT, TILBURG. TN: (013) 67 64 15.

. P. VAN DEN TOL, 94 VOORSTRAAT, DORDRECHT. TN: (078) 13 95 22.

TIMBUCTOO, 6 KLEINE KR. ELLEBOOG, GRONINGEN. TN: (050) 14 31 62.

BOEKHANDEL H. DE VRIES, P.O.B. 274, GED. OUDE GRACHT 27-23 HAARLEM. Prop: J. H. and R. H. C. de Vries. TN: 023 319458. Est: 1905. Shop, closed Mondays. Small sec. and antiq. stock also very large stock new books. Spec: sport and physical education, music. Corresp: English, Deutsch. B: A.B.N., Account 560 919 654 Haarlem. CP: Harlem 5404. N.B.B., N.V.V.A.

ANTIQUARIAAT NIEK WATERBOLK, SCHOUTENSTRAAT 7, 3512 GA UTRECHT. TN: 030 314861. Open afternoons only Tuesday to Saturday. Spec: Illustrated Books (modern), Fine arts after 1800. N.V.A.

H. DE WEERD, Middellaan 34, 7314 GC Apeldoorn. TN: (055) 552181. Established 1961. Private premises, open irregular hours. Small stock, also new books. No catalogues. Corresp: English, Français, Deutsch. B: Amro Bank, Apeldoorn. CP: 11 47 864.

T. WEVER B.V., 16 Zilverstraat, Franeker. TN: (05170) 31 47.

J. WRISTERS, Minrebroederstraat 13, Utrecht. Prop: J. and D. Wristers. TN: 333204. Established 1887. Shop. Large stock, also new books. Spec: theology; medicine. Corresp: English, Deutsch. B: C.E.B.U., Kromme Nieuwe Gracht 6, Utrecht, Account No. 69 90 1 620; Barclays International, 16–18 Brompton Road, London SW, Account 14640681 *and* Barclays International, 100 Water Street, New York, NY 10005. Account 050764250. CP: 'S-Gravenhage 43991 V.B.B., N.B.

GEORGE YNTEMA, 35 Loseweg, Apeldoorn. TN: (055) 21 60 71.

NORGE

NORWAY   NORVÈGE   NORWEGEN

Association: Verband

N.A.B.F.   =Norsk   Antikvarbokhandlerforening
Ullevålsveien 1, OSLO 1. TN: (02) 20
78 05

Public Holidays: Jours de Fête: Feiertage

Jan. 1: Easter: May 1: May 17: Ascension Day; Whitmonday: Dec. 25
and 26.

Jan. 1: Pâques: Mai 1: Mai 17: Ascension: Pentecôte: Dec 25 et 26.

Jan. 1: Karfreitag and Ostermontag: Mai 1: Mai 17: Pfingstmontag: Dez.
25 und 26.

BEKKESTUA: BERGEN: FREDRIKSTAD: OSLO.

ATLANTIS ANTIKVARIAT, FROGNERVEI 30, OSLO. TN: (02) 44 63 55.

BALAKLAVA ANTIKVARIAT, FAERGEPORTGATAN, GAMLEBYEN, 1600
FREDRIKSTAD. TN: (032) 20 122. N.A.B.F.

BØRSUMS FORLAG OG ANTIKVARIAT A-S, FR. NANSENSPLASS 2,
OSLO 1. Prop: Baltzer M. Børsum. TN: 41 04 33. TA: Bokbør Oslo.
Shop and storeroom, early closing Saturday. Very large stock, also new
books. Spec: facsimile editions; marine; old and rare; first editions.
Corresp: English, Français, Deutsch. B: Bergens Privatbank, Oslo. CP:
Oslo 14052. N.A.B.F.

BRUKTBOKA, KIRKEGATAN 70, LILLEHAMMER. TN: (062) 54 249.

J. W. CAPPELENS ANTIKVARIAT, P.O. BOX 350, KIRKEGATAN 15,
N-0101 OSLO 1. Manager: Paul M. Bottn. TN: 42 94 40. Established
1829. Shop, early closing Saturday. Large stock. Spec: old and rare;
maps and views relating to Scandinavia, Iceland and Greenland; travel
and topography. Cata: 8 a year. Corresp: English. B: Christiana Bank
og Kreditkasse, 6001.05.17462. CP: Oslo 5100201. I.L.A.B.

DAMMS ANTIKVARIAT A/S, BOKHUSET, TOLLBODGATA 25, OSLO 2
Prop: Claes Nyegaard. TN: 42 62 75. TA: Dammantikk Oslo. Spec
old and rare; atlases and maps; topography. B: Oslo Sparebank.
Also at: ECKERSBERGSGATEN 14, OSLO. N.A.B.F.

EMBLA BOOKS, P.O. BOX 42, N 5014 BERGEN UNIV. N.A.B.F.

FREDRIKSTAD ANTIKVARIAT, POSTBOKS 169, N-1601 FREDRIKSTAD.

THOR IVERSEN, SKIPPERGATAN 2, OSLO. TN: 20 79 41.

ROLV. LIE ANTIKVARIAT, BERGLYVEIEN 4B, OSLO. TN: (02) 61 20 73
N.A.B.F.

A. LUNGELARSEN, ØYGARDVEIEN 16E, BEKKESTUA. TN: 53 65 06
Private premises, appointment necessary. Spec: Scandinavica; old and
rare. N.A.B.F.

MESSEL & WILDHAGENS ANTIKVARIAT, TVETENVEIEN 32, OSLO
TN: (02) 65 15 23.

OLAF NORLIS BOKHANDEL, UNIVERSITEITSGATAN 18, OSLO. TN: (02
42 91 35.

ROGER TRYGVE OLSEN FORLAG OG ANTIKVARIAT, HAMMERGT. 7
N. OSLO 4, N.A.B.F.

OLSEN & CO., THORNEGATAN 23, DRAMMEN. TN: (03) 53 60 06.

OSLO NYE ANTIKVARIAT, MAJORSTUVN 15, OSLO 3. TN: (02) 46 6
38. N.A.B.F.

BJØRN RINGSTRØMS ANTIKVARIAT, ULLEVALSVEIEN 1, OSLO 1
TN: 20 78 05. Established 1965. Shop, open 10–17, Saturday 9–13
Medium stock. Spec: Norwegian 1st editions and topography; histor
in general. Cata: 8 a year. Corresp: English. B: Bergen Bank 5024.0
17067. CP: Oslo 5 30 09 42. N.A.B.V.

RUUDS ANTIKVARIAT, SIGURDSGATAN 20, OSLO 6. TN: (02) 67 59 21.
Also at ROSTEDSGATAN 16, OSLO 1. TN: 20 20 56. N.A.B.F.

TELEMARKEN ANTIKVARIAT, DRANGEDAL. TN: (036) 36521.

BERGENSANTIKVARIATET K. J. TØSSE, STORE MARKEVEI 8–10
BERGEN. Prop: Olav Tøsse. TN: 21 04 23. Established 1947. Sho
early closing Saturday. Small stock; also new books. Corresp: English.

VINDEREN ANTIKVARIAT, SLEMDALSVEI 63, OSLO. TN: (02) 14 80 75

WANGSMOS ANTIKVARIAT, OLAV TRYGGVASONSGT. 2 A, N-700
TRONDHEIM. N.A.B.F.

ÖSTERREICH

AUSTRIA   AUTRICHE

Association: Verband

V.A.Ö.   =Verband der Antiquare Österreichs
Grünangergasse 4. A-1010 Wien. TN:
(0222) 52 15 35

Public Holidays: Jours de Fête: Feiertage

Jan. 1: Jan. 6: Easter Monday: May 1: Ascension: Whitmonday: Corpus
Christi: Aug. 15: Nov. 1: Dec. 8: Dec. 25 and 26.

Jan. 1: Jan. 6: lundi de Pâques: Mai 1: Ascension: lundi de Pentecôte:
Fête-Dieu: Août 15: Nov. 1: Dec. 8. Dec. 25 et 26.

Jan. 1: Jan. 6: Ostermontag: Mai 1: Christi Himmelfahrt: Pfingstmontag:
Fronleichnam: Aug. 15: Nov. 1: Dez. 8: Dez. 25 und 26.

I

WIEN (Vienna, Vienne)

JOS. ABHEITER, Taborstrasse 11B, 1020 Wien. Laden. Kleiner Vorrat,
auch neue Bücher.

AICHINGER, BERNARD & CO, Weihberggasse L6, Wien. TN: 52 88 53.

GEORG BARTSCH, Lerchenfelderstrasse 138, A-1081 Wien. TN: 43
12 75.

BECK'SCHE UNIVERSITÄTS BUCHHANDLUNG, Währingerstrasse
12, Wien 1009. Laden. Grosser Vorrat, auch neue Bücher.

J. BERGER, Kohlmarkt 3, 1010 Wien. TN: 52 23 60. Spec: Einbände,
Kunst; Archäologie. CP: Wien 53653. V.A.Ö.

ANTIQUARIAT BÖHLAU, Dr. Karl Leuger Ring. 12, A-1014 Wien.

BOSWORTH & CO., LTD., Dr.-Karl-Lueger-Platz 2, A-1010 Wien.
TN: (0222) 52 81 40. Gegründet 1869. Laden, an Samstag in den
Monaten Juli und August geschlossen. Sehr kleiner Vorrat Bücher und
Grosser Vorrat Musikalien (Noten); auch neue Bücher. Spez:
Musikalien und Musikbücher. Corresp: English. B:
Creditanstalt-Bankverein, Kontonummer 62–16592. CP: Wein,
7145.645. M: Hauptverband des Österreichischen Buchhandels.

BOURCY & PAULUSCH, Wipplingerstrasse 5, 1010 Wien. Prop: Otto Bourcy und Hans Paulusch, und Mag. Jörg Treytl. TN: 63 71 49. Gegründet 1917. Laden, Samstag geschlossen. Sehr grosser Vorrat. Spec: Alpinismus; Austriaca; Genealogie; Medizin. Cata. B: Österreichisches Länderbank, Wien. PSK Wien 2319.012 München 1208.87. V.A.Ö.

BÜCHER-ERNST, Gumpendorferstrasse 84, Wien 6. TN: 57 42 57.

DER BUCHFREUND [WALTER SCHADEN], Sonnenfelsgasse 4, 1010 Wien 1. Prop: Rainer Schaden. TN: 52 48 56. Gegründet 1955. Laden. Sehr grosser Vorrat. Spec: Literatur; Kunst; Naturwissenschaften; Reisen. Cata: 2 oder 3 pro Jahr. Corresp: English, Français. B: Erste österr. Spar-Casse, Konto Nr. 400–24229. CP: Wien 1630.149; München 1204 58–803. V.A.Ö.

COTTAGE ANTIQUARIAT R. KNESSL, Gymnasiumstrasse 17, A-1180 Wien. Prop: Renate Knessl. TN: 340133. Laden. Grosser Vorrat, auch neue Bücher. Corresp: English. B: Erste österr. Sparcasse, Kontonummer 048-35700. M: V.A.Ö.

ERWIN A. CUDEK, Die Bücher Fundgruber, Währingerstrasse 24, 1000 Wien IX. TN: 34 21 46. Laden. Mittelgrosser Vorrat. auch Nadlergasse 2/1, 1000 Wien IX. TN: 42 51 70.

F. DEUTICKE, Helferstorferstrasse 4, Wien 1. TN: 63 64 29 und 63 15 35. Spec: Folklore; Kunst; Naturwissenschaften; Philologie; Philosophie. V.A.Ö.

INGEBORG DIEHL, Marzstasse 15, Wien. TN: 95 81 13.

DOBLINGER MUSIKHAUS UND MUSIKVERLAG. Dorotheergasse 10, A-1010 Wien. (Postfach 882). TN: 0222/ 52 35 04. TA: Musikdob, Wien. Gegründet 1876. Laden. Kleiner Vorrat, auch neue Bücher, Bilder und Kuriositäten. Spec: Musikbücher und Musikalien-Früh und Erstdrucke. Cata. Corresp: English, Français. B: Creditanstalt-Bankverein, Konto 52–12360, Wien 1; CP: ÖPSK Wien 7225 235. V.A.Ö.

GEORG FRITSCH, Postfach 883, A-1010 Wien. (Schönlaterngasse 7). TN: 526294. Cata: unregelmässig. Korresp: English. B: Länderbank, 251–106–110. Cata: unregelmässig. Korresp: English, Français, Italiano. B: Länderbank, 251–106–110. CP: 2128–131. V.A.Ö.

GEROLD & CO., Graben 31, 1011 Wien. TN: 52 22 35. TA: Geroldbuch Wien. Laden. Spec: Philologie; Philosophie; Psychologie. CP: Wien 32108. V.A.Ö.

GILHOFER BUCH- UND KUNSTANTIQUARIAT K.G. Bognergasse 2, 1010 Wien. Prop: W. Taeuber und R. Hoffmann. TN: 63 42 85. TA: Gilburg. Wien. Gegründet 1883. Laden. Sehr grosser Vorrat. Spec: Austriaca, Bohemica; Wissenschaften; alte und seltene Bücher; Graphik. Cata. Corresp: English. B: Erste Österreichische Spar-Casse, Konto 002–93385 V.A.Ö., V.D.A.

GODAI BUCHHANDELS Ges.m.b.H., Mariahilfer Strasse 169, 1150 Wien. Prop: Helmut Godai. TN: 83 82 95. Gegründet 1919. Laden; vorzugweise nach Vereinbarung. Kleiner Vorrat, auch neue Bücher. B: Zentralsparkasse, Konto 617 249 909. CP: München 1204 87. Hauptverband des Österr. Buchhandels, I.A.S.V.

F. GOTTSCHALK, Krugerstrasse 10, 1010 Wien. TN: 52 73 32. Spez: Illustrierte Bücher, Kunst: Architektur, Archäologie. *Also:* Mariahilfer Strasse 77–79, 1060 Wien. TN: 93 27 93. *And:* Josefstädter Strasse 71, TN: 43 47 24.

KARL M. HALOSAR, Margaretenstrasse 35, 1040 Wien. TN: 56 13 53. Gegründet 1947. Zwei Läden. Sehr grosser Vorrat, auch neue Bücher. Spec: alte Kinderbücher; illustrierte Bücher; Literatur; Erstausgaben. Cata: unregelmässig. Corresp: English. B: Creditanstalt Bankverein Wien, Konto 64 133 71. CP: Wien 126 1886. V.A.Ö.

A. HARTLEBERN, Schwarzenbergstrasse 6, Wien. TN: 52 62 41.

A. L. HASBACH, Wollzeile 9 und 29, Wien 1. Prop: Dr. Herbert Borufka. TN: 52 88 76 und 52 89 32. Gegründet 1876. Laden und Lagerräume, Samstag Nachmittag geschlossen. Mittelgrosser Vorrat. Spec: Geschichte; Kunst; Sprachwissenschaft. Cata: 1–2 pro Jahr. Corresp: English, Français, Italiano. B: Österreichischer Landerbank 222–103–239. CP: Wien 7041.660. V.A.Ö.

HASSFURTHER, Hohenstaufengasse 7, A-1010 Wien. TN: 63 41 74.

V. A. HECK, Kärntner Ring 14, 1010 Wien. Prop: Dr. Uta Schweger. ø Hans D. Paulusch. TN: 65 51 52. TA: Heckbooks Wien. Gegründet 1870. Laden, Samstag Nachmittag geschlossen. Grosser Vorrat. Spec: Austriaca; Deutsche Literatur; Autographen; alte Landkarten. Cata: 4–6 pro Jahr. Corresp: English, Français. B: Creditanstalt, Konto 66–16999. CP: Wien 7038453 und Frankfurt 3000 10. V.D.A.

RUDOLF HEGER, Wollezeile 2, 1010 Wien 1. Prop: Christl und Olga Wagner. TN: 52 63 98. Laden, Samstag Nachmittag geschlossen. Grosser Vorrat, auch neue Bücher. Spec: Deutsche Literatur; Kunst; Folklore. Cata: 3 pro Jahr. Corresp: English, Français. B: Östereichischer Landerbank, Wien, Konto 2,201,026. CP: Wien 30 903. V.A.Ö.

LEOPOLD HEIDRICH G.m.b.H., Plankengasse 7, Wien 1. TN: 52 37 01 und 52 29 93. Gegründet 1914. Laden, Samstag Nachmittag geschlossen. Mittelgrosser Vorrat, auch neue Bücher. Spec: Kunst; Deutsche Literatur; Austriaca; Viennsia. Cata: 2–4 pro Jahr. Corresp: English, Français. B: Pinschof & Co., Spiegelgasse 3, Wien 1. CP: Wien 103 763, und Frankfurt 300 043. V.A.Ö.

OSKAR HÖFELS, OHG., Seilerstätte 18, 1010 Wien. TN: 52 18 28. V.A.Ö.

KARL HÖLZL, K.G., Seilergasse 3, 1010 Wien. TN: 52 28 96. Spec: Graphik; alte Landkarten; Bibliophile Ausgaben, V.A.Ö. *Auch* Karlsplatzpassage Lokal 14.

INFORMATIO, Seilergasse 19, A-1010 Wien. TN: 52 60 542.

WALTER KLÜGEL, Postfach 40, Wimm 15, Schreiberghof, A-5201 Seekirchen, bei Salzburg und Lager (Fallweise Geöffnet) Gumpendorferstrasse 33, 1060 Wien. TN: (06212) 7133 oder 72274, und Wien: (0222) 5730342. Gegründet 1921 in Wien. Lagerräume Besuche nur mach Vereinbarung. Grosser Vorrat (CA. 50,000). Spec: Krieg und Politik, Geographie, Literatur und Kunst, Bibliophilie, Austriaca, sittengeschte; Bibliophile; Kubiniana. B: Raiffeisenkasse A-5201 Seekirchen, Konto NR. 20.453. C.C.P. Wien 7746.570. V.A.Ö.

R. KREY, Ges.m.b.H., Graben 13, 1010 Wien 1. Laden. Spec: Militaria.

ANTIQUARIAT WALTER KRIEG VERLAG K.G. Kärntnerstrasse 4, 1010 Wien. Prop: Mag. Sigrio Krieg (und Gesellschafter) & Co. TN: 52 11 93. TA: Buchkrieg Wien. Gegründet 1923. Laden, Samstag Geschlossen. Grosser Vorrat, (CA. 50,000), auch neue Bücher. Spec: Bibliophilie; Buchwesen Geschichte. Cata: 2–4 Jährlich. Corresp: English. B: Breisach-Pinschof-Schoeller, A-1010 Wien, Spiegelgasse 3, Konto 304 093 08. CP: Wien 7223 268. V.A.Ö. Osterreichischer Buchhändlerverband.

AKADEMISCHE BUCHHANDLUNG KUPPITSCH, SCHOTTENGASSE 4,
WIEN. Prop: Dr. M. Beer und Dr. Z. Seidl. TN: 63 02 44 and 63 94 30.
Laden, grosser Vorrat auch neue Bücher. Spec: Literatur; Philosophie.
Cata: selten. Corresp: English, Français. B: Creditanstalt-Bankverein,
Wien, Konto 24–96727. CP: Wien 49917 und München 1 201 47.
V.A.Ö.

ERHARD LÖCKER, GLUCKGASSE 3, WIEN. TN: 52 87 42.
Auch ANNAGASSE 5.

FRANZ MALOTA'S ENKELIN A. STERN, WIEDNER HAUPTSTRASSE 22,
WIEN 4. Prop: Anni Stern. TN: 57 92 75. Gegründet 1901. Laden und
Lagerräume, Samstag Nachmittag geschlossen. Sehr grosser Vorrat,
auch neue Bücher. Cata: 4–6 pro Jahr. Corresp: English, Français. CP:
Wien 160 169. V.A.Ö.

MANZ'SCHE VERLAGS- UND UNIVERSITÄTSBUCHHANDLUNG,
KOHLMARKT 16, 1014-WIEN. (Postfach 163). TN: 63 17 85. Laden.
Grosser Vorrat. Spec: Recht.

WILHELM MAUDRICH, LAZARETTGASSE 1, 1091 WIEN. TN: 42 47
12/13. Est. 1904. Lagerräum. Stets Während der Geschäftszeit.
Mittelgrosser   Vorrat.   Spec: Medizin;   Naturwissenschaften.
Corresp: English. CP: Wien 1346–426. V.A.Ö.

CHRISTIAN M. NEBEHAY, ANNAGASSE 18, 1015 WIEN. (Postfach 303).
TN: 52 18 01. TA: Nebehaybooks Wien. V.A.Ö.

ALOIS POXLEITNER-BLASL, STROZZIGASSE 32, 1080 WIEN. TN: 42 82
17. V.A.Ö.

WILHELM PUSKAS, WEIHBURGGASSE 16, 1010 WIEN. TN: 52 88 53.
Spec: Austriaca; Folklore; Geschichte; Philosophie.CP: Wien 39496.

ALOIS REICHMANN, WIEDNER HAUPTSTRASSE 18, WIEN 1040. TN: 57
81 58. Spec: Literaturwissenschaft; Mathematik; Naturwissenschaften;
Spiele; Zeitschriften. CP: Wien 76482. V.A.Ö.

HEINRICH RIMANEK, KAISERSTRASSE 6, 1070 WIEN. TN: 93 98 764.
Spec: Austriaca; Naturwissenschaften; Sprachwissenschaft; Theâter;
Tanz. V.A.Ö.

FRIEDRICH SCHALK, MARIAHILFERSTRASSE 97, WIEN 1006. Gegründe 1895. Laden.

VERLAG Dr. A. SCHENDL, KARLSGASSE 15, A-1041 WIEN.

M. F. STEINBACH, SALMANNSDORFERSTRASSE 64, 1190 WIEN. TN: 44 1 39. Gegründet 1932. Lagerräume, nur nach Vereinbarung. Grosse Vorrat. Spec: Kunst; Literatur; Naturwissenschaften; Graphik. Cata Corresp: English. B: Credit-Anstalt-Bankverein, Wien.

DR. KARL STROPEK, WÄHRINGERSTRASSE 122, 1181 WIEN. Spec: Recht Staatswissenschaften. CP: Wien 28493. V.A.Ö.

J. WELKHAMMER, BURGGASSE 123, 1070 WIEN. (AUC NEUBAUGÜRTEL 48). TN: 93 41 35. V.A.Ö.

WIENER ANTIQUARIAT, SEILERGASSE 16, WIEN. Prop: Ingo Nebehay TN: (0222) 52 54 66. TA: Ingobooks Wien. Gegründet 1962. Laden Samstag Nachmittag geschlossen. Mittelgrosser Vorrat. Spec Autographen; Kunst; Graphik. Cata: 6 pro Jahr. Corresp: English Français, Italiano. B: BPS Bank, Wien, Konto 3060.2303. V.A.Ö.

TH. WILD, MARIAHILFERSTRASSE 158, WIEN 1015. Laden.

WALTER WÖGENSTEIN SINGERSTRASSE 13, WIEN 1. TN: 53 14 72 Spec: Illustuerte Bücher; Kunst. V.A.Ö.

II

GRAZ: INNSBRUCK: LINZ: SALZBURG: ST PÖLTEN: STIF ZWETTL.

EDUARD HÖLLRIGL, SIGMUND HAFFNER GASSE 10, 5010 SALZBURG (Postfach 239). Vorm. Hermann Kerber K.G. Prop: Dr. Gertru Spinnhirn und Helene Stierle. TN: 41 1 46. Gegründet vor 1594 Laden, Samstag Nachmittag geschlossen. Kleiner Vorrat. Spe Salisburgensien; Salzburg. Cata: fallweise. Corresp: English, Françai Italiano. B: Salzburg Sparkasse 16063. CP: Wien 703 86 59; Münche 120 113. Hauptverband d. österr. Buchhandels.

JOS. A. KIENREICH, SACKSTRASSE 6 (im Halbstock), 8011 GRAZ. TN 76441. Spec: Austriaca; Geschichte; Kulturgesschicht Literaturwissenschaft; Philosophie. CP: Wien 45180. V.A.Ö.

PETER MATERN, LINZERGASSE 5, A-5024 SALZBURG. TN: 73 7 95.

MAYRISCHE BUCHHANDLUNG, Theatergasse, 5024 Salzburg. Prop: Werner Neugebauer O.H.G. TN: 73 596. Gegründet circa 1595. Laden und Lagerräume, Samstag Nachmittag geschlossen. Sehr grosser Vorrat, auch neue Bücher. Cata. Corresp: English, Français. B: Spängler Bank. CP: Wien 76 22 508 und München 1,200.72.807. V.A.Ö.

MICHAEL MENZEL, Gertreidegasse 13, A-5022 Salzburg. TN: 41 05 29.

W. NEUGEBAUER, GESm.b.H & CO K.G. Landstrasse 1, 4020 Linz. Prop: Werner, Inge und Walter Neugebauer. TN: (0732) 71766 und 67. Gegründet 1935. Laden. Mittelgrosser Vorrat, auch neue Bücher. Corresp: English, Français. B: Oberbank Linz Konto 401 5699; Sparkasse Linz Konto 127 862. CP: Wien 772 80 93. München 1205 49–806. Verband des Österreichischer Buchhandels. I.A.S.V.

J. G. SYDYS, BUCHHANDLUNG LUDWIG SCHUBERT G.m.b.H., P.O. Box 169, Wienerstrasse 19, 3100 St. Pölten. TN: (02742) 31 89. TA: Sydy St. Pölten. Gegründet 1837. Laden, Mittwochnachmittag geschlossen. Kleiner Vorrat, auch neue Bücher. Spec: Austriaca. Corresp: English. B: Giro-No.0000 018010 Sparkasse St. Pölten. CP: 7116.739 Wien. V.A.Ö., Buchhändlervereinigung österreichs.

Dr. KARL TAUSCH KG, Maria-Theresien-Strasse 1, Innsbruck. TN: (052 22) 244 91.

J. E. THOMA, 3910 Stift Zwettl. Gegründet 1914. Nur Post-Vekehr. Cata. CP: Wien 1831 577.

MATHÄUS TRUPPE, Stubenberggasse 7, 8011 Graz. TN: 79552. Gegründet 1921. Laden, Samstag geschlossen. Kleiner Vorrat. Spec: Graphik: Wissenschaftliche Bücher. Cata: 1 pro jahr. Corresp: English. CP: Wien 1041635. V.A.Ö.

WAGNER'SCHE UNIVERSITÄTS BUCHHANDLUNG OHG., Museumstrasse 4, 6021 Innsbruck. TN: 22316. Spec: Wissenschaften; Dekorative Graphik; Austriaca; Alpinismus. CP: Wien 22316. V.A.Ö.

GALERIE WELZ SALZBURG, Sigmund-Haffnergasse 16, Salzburg. Prop: Prof. Friedrich Welz. TN: 41771. Gegründet 1899. Laden, Samstag Nachmittag geschlossen. Sehr kleiner Vorrat, auch neue Bücher. Spec: Graphik; Kunst. Corresp: English, Français. B: Bankhaus Berger & Co., Salzburg, Konto 1921. CP: Vienna 91.156. V.A.Ö.

L. UND E. WILDNER, Stempfergasse 8, 8010 Graz. Prop: Lilyane und
Edmund Wildner. TN: (0316) 74216. TA: Wildner Graz. Gegründe
1938. Laden, Samstag Nachmittag geschlossen. Sehr grosser Vorrat
Spec: 15–17. Jahrhunderts. Deutsche literatur, erstausgaben
autographen. Cata: Sporadisch. Corresp: English, Français. B
Creditanstalt-Bankverein, Filiale Graz, Konto Nr. 87 75389. V.A.Ö.

POLSKA

POLAND   POLOGNE   POLEN

BYDGOSZCZ (Bromberg): KRAKÓW (Cracovie, Krakau): POZNAŃ
Posen): RADOM: WARSZAWA (Warsaw, Varsovie, Warschau):
WROCLAW (Breslau).

ANTYKWARIAT, 8 PL. UNIVERSYTECKI, WROCŁAW. Shop, secondhand
and antiquarian stock.

ANTYKWARIAT NAUKOWY, ULICA SWIĘTOKRZYSKA 14, WARSZAWA.
Shop, secondhand and antiquarian stock.

ANTYKWARIAT NAUKOWY, ULICA STARY RYNEK 53/54, POZNAN.
Shop, secondhand and antiquarian stock.

ANTYKWARIAT NAUKOWY, ZEROMSKIEGO 89, RADOM. Shop,
secondhand and antiquarian stock.

ANTIKWARIAT NAUKOWY, ULICA SLAWKOWSKA 10, KRAKÓW. Shop,
secondhand and antiquarian stock.

ANTYKWARIAT NAUKOWY, ULICA PODWALE 4, KRAKÓW. Shop,
secondhand and antiquarian stock.

BYDGOSKI ANTYKWARIAT NAUKOWY, "DOM KSIAZKI", STARY
RYNEK 16, 85–105 BYDGOSZCZ. Established 1952. Shop and
storeroom. Very large stock. Spec: humanistic. Cata: 4 a year. Corresp:
English, Esperanto, German, Russian.

DOM KSIAZKI ANTYKWARIAT, 6 RYNEK (kom M.O.I), WROCŁAW.
Shop, secondhand and antiquarian stock.

KSIEGARNIA ANTYKWARYCZNA, NOWY SWIAT 61, WARSZAWA.
Shop, secondhand and antiquarian stock.

PORTUGAL

LISBOA (Lisbon, Lissabon): PORTO.

LIVRARIA ANTIQUARIA, Rua da Misericordia 147, Lisboa. TN: 32 72 72.

LIVRARIA ACADEMICA, Rua Martires da Liberdade 10, Porto. TN: 2 59 88.

AZEVEDO AND BURNAY LDA, Travessa de S. Placido 48-B, 1200 Lisboa, Portugal. TN: 60 69 31. Est. 1982. Shop closed mornings and Saturdays. Medium stock. Spec: natural history; art; auctioneers. Cata: 2 a year. Corresp: English, français, italiano, español. B: Banco do Brasil, Account No. 5557.

LIVRARIA BARATEIRA LDA, 16-A Nv. Trinidad, Lisboa 12. TN: 32 67 55.

BIBLARTE, LIMITADA, Rua de Sao Pedro de Alcantara 71, Lisboa 2. Prop: Ernesto Martins. TN: 363702. Established 1950. Very large stock, also new books. Spec: periodicals; history; art; literature. Cata: 2 a year. Corresp: English, Français, Español.

LIVRARIA A BIBLIÓFILA LTDA., Rua da Misericórdia 102 Lisboa. TN: 33476. Established 1942. Shop. Small stock, also new books. Corresp: English, Français, Italiano, Deutsch. B: 242 Banco Espirito Santo (Camoes).

LIVRARIA BRASÍLIA, Rua da Misericordia 79, Lisboa. TN: 32 03 20.

A. TAVARES DE CARVALHO, Avenida da Republica 46–3°, 100(
Lisboa-1. TN: 77 03 77. Established 1960. House premises
appointment necessary. Large stock. Spec: early rare books on Brazil
Arabia and Persia; sciences; Italian Renaissance; chess. Corresp
English, Français. B: Banco Totta & Açores, No. 907777/001
Midland Bank (Haymarket Branch) London, Account No. 41067893
A.B.A. (Int.).

LIVRARIA CASTRO E SILVA, Rua da Rosa 31, Lisboa. Prop: Ezequie
de Castro e Silva. TN: 367380. Established 1957. Shop and storeroom
Very large stock. Spec: Portuguese literature; history; art; foreign
Cata: 26 a year. Corresp: English, Français, Español. B: Banco
Nacional Ultramarino, (Camoes), 870–5.

LIVRARIA CHAMIN DA MOTA, 37 Flores, Porto. TN: 2 53 80.

DIAS & ANDRADE LDA, LIVRARIA PORTUGAL, Rua do Carmo 70
Lisboa 2. TN: 36 05 82, 32 82 20. Established 1941. Shop. Very larg
stock. Spec: literature; technical; sports. Cata: monthly bibliographica
bulletin. Corresp: English, Français.

LIVRARIA ESQUINA, 126 Av. L. Vieira, Porto. TN: 31 28 21.

LIVRARIA FERIN LDA., Rua Nova do Almada 74, Lisboa. TN: 32 4
22. Prop: Sra. Dias Pinheiro. Est: 1840. Shop, closed Saturda
afternoons. Spec: art; history. Corresp: English, Français. B: Banco
Fonsecas e Burnay, rua do Comercio, Lisboa 2. A.P.E.L.

LIVRARIA HISTÓRICA E ULTRAMARINA LDA [J. C. SILVA
Travessa da Queimada 28, 1200– Lisboa 2. Prop: José Maria d
Costa e Silva. TN: 368 589. Established 1951. Shop. Very large stock
Spec: Africana; Judaica; history; engravings; maps; manuscripts. Cata
monthly. Corresp: English, Français, Español. B. Banco Naciona
Ultramarino and Banco Espirito Santo e Commercial de Lisboa
A.B.A.

LIVRARIA LUSA, 477 Cadofeita, Porto.

LIVRARIA MARINHO, 215 Almada, Porto. TN: 2 66 50.

AMERICO F. MARQUES, Rua da Misericordia 92–1, Lisboa. TN: 3
49 77. Shop.

LIVRARIA EDUARDO ANTUNES MARTINHO, Rua Voz do Operário 7-B, Lisboa 2. TN: 86 64 86. Est: 1942. Shop. Large stock sec. and antiq. Spec: Theatre; politics; medicine. Cata: monthly. Corresp: English, Français. B: Banco Português do Atlântico, Account No. 516 1118560. Associacao Portuguesa dos Editures e Livreiros de Portugal.

LIVRARIA D. PEDRO V., Rua d. Pedro V. 16, Lisboa. TN: 36 89 04.

R. B. ROSENTHAL, Rua do Alecrim 47-4° Salas D, Lisboa 2. TN: 32 31 44. TA: Rosliber, Lisboa. Est: 1958. Storeroom, open normal business hours Monday to Friday. Stock of about 70,000 sec. and antiq. books. Spec: old Portugese and Spanish books and manuscripts; Africana. Corresp: English, Deutsch, Français, Español.

JOAQUIM GUEDES DA SILVA & CA., LDA., Livraria Academica, Rua Martires da Liberdade 8–12, Porto. TN: 25988. Large Stock. Spec: rare books, engravings and maps. A.B.A.

J. A. TELLES DA SYLVA, Travessa Marquês sá da Bandeira, 19-3° Esq. Lisboa 1. Prop: Dom José António Telles da Sylva. TN: 778754 or 211 6870 (Private). TA: Telsil, Lisboa. Est: 1966. Shop, closed Saturdays. Medium stock sec. and antiq., also new books. Spec: Portugese and Spanish travels; Braziliana; fine books. Cata: 4 a year. Corresp: English, Français, Italiano. Español. B: Banco Espírito Santo e Comercial de Lisboa, Agência da Av. de Berna, Account No. 3171. A.B.A.

ROMINA

ROUMANIA   ROUMANIE   RUMANIEN

BRAŞOV (Kronstadt): BUCUREŞTI (Bucharest, Bukarest): CONSTANTA.

In Romania the control of important antiquarian books and manuscripts is exercised mainly through the Central State Commission for the National Cultural Heritage. In general the export will not be permitted of items that were in Romanian territory prior to 1700, books printed in Romania prior to 1830, or of certain printings since that date, including *Dacia literara* and other 19th century periodicals, the Ion Creanga princeps editions, the Mihai Eminescu princeps edition, and even, owing to the small number printed Calinescu's *History of Romanian Literature*.

The export abroad of books purchased in Romania is permitted (subject to the consent of the customs offices) if they were printed in Romania after 1952, or printed abroad after 1970 and bought from a bookshop in Romania. For books printed abroad after 1800 which are translations from world fiction; any other printings from Romania or abroad if a copy exists in the Central State Library, the Library of the National Academy, or in a specialised or county library; or any kind of exerpts as long as they bear the number of the publication of which they are a part, a permit to export must be obtained from one of the Departments for the National Cultural Heritage. For certain works printed in Romania before 1952 an ideological certificate regarding their contents is also necessary, and this too may be obtained from the Departments for the National Cultural Heritage.

The export abroad of manuscripts, typescripts and other copies requires the consent of the appropriate body: For fictional works, the Writers' Union or the publishing house where the work was presented for publication.; for musical compositions, the Composers' Union and certain specialised publishing houses; for scientific works, that of the institution that made use of the results of the research or of the publishing house where it was presented for publication; for doctoral theses, the Ministry of Education; for other works in manuscript or typescript, that of a County Department of the State General Archives.

ANTICARIAT C.L.D.C., STRADA REPUBLICII 24, BRAŞOV. Shop.

ANTICARIAT UNITATEA Nr. 18, TOMIS STRADA, CONSTANTA. Shop.

ANTICARIATUL BUCUREȘTI, Lipscani 6, Bucureşti. TN: 14 47 61. Established 1950. Shop and storeroom, open 7–15 hours. Very large stock. Spec: Roumania–history, law, economics, etc. Corresp: Français Deutsch. B: Banca Româna de Comert Exterior.

ANTICARIATUL Nr. 2, Bulevardul Republicii 5, Bucureşti. TN: 15 87 61. Shop.

ANTICARIATUL Nr. 3, Bulevardul General Magheru 2, Bucureşti TN: 15 52 96. Shop. Medium stock, Roumainian and foreign. Hours 9–13 and 16–20.

ANTICARIATUL Nr. 4, Bis Enei 16, Bucureşti. TN: 15 48 83. Shop.

ANTICARIATUL Nr. 6, Calea Victoriei 45, Pasaj Kretzulescu Bucureşti. TN: 13 08 97. Shop, open 8–13.30 and 17–19.30 Monday Thursday and Saturday, 8–14 Tuesday, Wednesday and Friday. Very large stock, also new books and maps, engravings and prints.

ANTICARIATUL Nr. 9, Polizii 2, Bucureşti. TN: 15 35 93. Shop.

S.S.S.R   (C.C.C.P.)

SOYUZ SOVYETSKIH SOZIALISTICHESKIH RESPUBLIK

U.S.S.R.   U.R.S.S.   U.d.S.S.R.

LENINGRAD: MOSKVA (Kyrillic=MOCKBA) Moscow: Moscou: Moskau: RIGA.

MOSCOW

"BUKINIST", Stoleshnikov Lane, Moscow. Shop. Secondhand and antiquarian stock.

MAGAZIN No. 1. AKADEMKNIGA (BUKINISTICHESKI), Ulitsa Gorkogo d.8, Moscow.

MAGAZIN No. 7 (BUKINISTICHESKI), Ulitsa Sretyenka d.9, Moscow.

MAGAZIN No. 9 (BUKINISTICHESKI), Ulitsa Kirova d.13, Moscow.

MAGAZIN No. 14 (BUKINISTICHESKI), Proyezd Khydojestvevenogo Teatra d.5, Moscow.

MAGAZIN No. 28 (BUKINISTICHESKI), Stoleshnikov Perbylok d.14, Moscow.

MAGAZIN No. 32 (BUKINISTICHESKI), Kutaiski Proyezhd d.1, Moscow.

MAGAZIN No. 34 (BUKINISTICHESKI), Dobrininskaya Ulitsa d.32/2, Moscow.

MAGAZIN No. 35 (BUKINISTICHESKI), Ulitsa Arbat d.10, Moscow.

MAGAZIN No. 36 (BUKINISTICHESKI), Ulitsa Arbat d.8, Moscow.

MAGAZIN No. 45 (BUKINISTICHESKI), Prospekt Marksa d.1, Moscow. Spec: antiquarian.

MAGAZIN No. 54 (BUKINISTICHESKI), Ulitsa Chernishevskogo d.50, Moscow.

MAGAZIN No. 121 (BUKINISTICHESKI), Leninski Prospekt d.69, Moscow.

LENINGRAD

LENKNIGI MAGAZIN No. 10 (BUKINISTICHESKI), Ulitsa Zhukovskogo 2, Leningrad. TN: 63 33 84.

LENKNIGI MAGAZIN No. 26 (BUKINISTICHESKI), Bolshoi Prospekt 19, Leningrad. TN: 32 17 65.

LENKNIGI MAGAZIN No. 40 (BUKINISTICHESKI), Vasilevski Ostrov, Leningrad. TN: 13 43 47.

LENKNIGI MAGAZIN No. 53 (BUKINISTICHESKI), Ulitsa Gertsena 12, Leningrad. TN: 19 78 62.

LENKNIGI MAGAZIN No. 61 (BUKINISTICHESKI), Liteini Prospekt 59, Leningrad. TN: 62 97 14.

RIGA, LATVIAN S.S.R.

ANTIKVARIATS, Peteris Stuckas Ilea 5, Riga. Shop, new and secondhand stock.

CENTRALIS ANTIKVARIATS, Lenina Ilea 46, Riga. Shop, new and secondhand stock.

SUISSE SCHWEIZ SVIZZERA

SWITZERLAND

Languages—Langues—Sprache Français, Deutsch, Italiano

Associations: Verbände

SLACES   =Syndicat de la Librairie Ancienne et du Commerce de l'Estampe en Suisse.

VEBUKU   =Vereinigung der Buchantiquare und Kupferstichhandler der SCHWEIZ Bälliz 64, CH-3601 THUN. TN: (033) 22 19 22

SBVV   =Schweizer Buchhändler und Verleger Verband

SKV   =Schweizer Kunsthandelsverband.

SLESR   =Société des Libraires et Editeurs de la Suisse Romande.

SZBV   =Schweizer und Zürcher Buchhändlervereine.

VSAK   =Verband Schweizer Antiquare und Kunsthändler.

VWB   =Verband Wissenschaftlichen Buchhandlungen.

Public Holidays: Jours de Fête: Feiertage

Jan. 1: Good Friday: Ascension Day: Dec. 25.

Jan. 1: Vendredi-Saint: Ascension: 25 Déc.

Jan. 1: Karfreitag: Christi Himmelfahrt: Weihnachstag.

English	Français	Deutsch	Italiano
—	ARAN	—	—
—	—	BADEN	—

English	Français	Deutsch	Italiano
BASLE	BALE	BASEL	BASILEA
—	BERNE	BERN	—
—	—	BURGDORF	—
—	—	FRIBÓURG	—
GENEVA	GENÈVE	GENF	GINEVRA
—	—	KREUZLINGEN	—
—	LAUSANNE	—	LOSANNA
—	—	LIESTAL	—
—	—	—	LUGANO
—	LUCERNE	LUZERN	—
—	NEUCHATEL	—	—
—	—	OLTEN	—
—	SAINT GALLEN	—	—
—	SAINT PREX	—	—
—	—	THUN	—
—	—	WINTERTHUR	—
—	YVERDON	—	—
—	—	ZÜRICH	ZURIGO

ABC ANTIQUARIAT, ZÄHRINGERSTRASSE 31, CH-8001 ZÜRICH. TN: 262 71 45.

ROBERT ALDER, JUNKERNGASSE 41, BERN. TN: (031) 22 41 02. Gegründet 1936. Etagengeschäft, 2. Stock (Aufzug). Grosses Lager. Spec: Geisteswissenschaften; Geschichte; Kunst; Literatur; Helvetica. Corresp: Français. B: Kantonalbank von Bern, und Bank von Ernst & Cie, A.G., Bern. CP: 30 10 955. VEBUKU.

ALTSTADT ANTIQUARIAT, RUE D'OR 16, CH-170° FRIBOURG. TN (037) 22 38 08. Prop: Ben A. Harteveld. Laden; Dienstag geschlossen. Spec: alte Bücher; Topographie. M: Vebuku.

L'ART ANCIEN S.A., SIGNAUSTRASSE 6, 8008 ZÜRICH. TN: 479229. TA Artancien Zürich. Lagerräume, Samstag geschlossen. Wertvolle Bücher, Graphik und Zeichnungen grosser Meister. Cata: 2–3 a year. Corresp: English, Français. B: Julius Baer & Cie., Postfach, 8022 Zřich. CP: Zürich 80–29905. VEBUKU, SBVV, ZBV, VSAK, SKV. ABA.

LIBRAIRIE ANCIENNE "L'AUTOGRAPHE", S.A., 6 Chemin de Grange Canal, CH-1208 Genève. TN: (022) 36 10 44. Fondée: 1959. Bureau, ouvert sur rendez-vous. vente par catalogue. Stock très important. Seulement autographes: lettres, photos signées et livres dedicaces. inscrit. Cata: 5 par an. Corresp: English, Deutsch, Italiano, Française. M: S.L.A.M. Manuscript Society.

WILLY BENZ, Universitätstrasse 31, CH-8006 Zürich. TN: 47 79 54.

FÉLIX BLOCH, 10 Route de Rolle, 1162 Saint-Prex. (Boite Postale 58). TN: (021) 76 16 62. Fondée en 1973. Domicile, sur rendez-vous. Restreint stock. Spec: Histoire de la médecine et science. Cata: 1 par an. Corresp: English, Deutsch. B: Banque cantonale vaudoise, Lausanne. Swiss Bank Corporation, New York. CP: 10 323 52. S.L.A.C.E.S., S.L.E.S.R.

HANS BOLLIGER BÜCHER UND GRAFIK, Lenggstrasse 14, Zürich. TN: (01) 53 58 88. Gegründet 1970. Wohnung; nur nach Vereinbarung. Vorrat ca. 5.000 Bände. Spec: Illustrierte Bücher; Kunst; Erstausgaben. Cata: 1 pro Jahr. Corresp: English, Deutsch; Français. B: Schweizer. Bankgesellschaft Zürich. Konto Nr. 253 340 01 J. CP: 80–64559 Zürich. V.E.B.U.K.U.

LIVRES ANCIENS MAURICE BRIDEL, S.A., Avenue du Tribunal-Fédéral 5, 1002 Lausanne. TN: (021) 23 77 35. TA: Livrancien Lausanne. Fondée en 1948. Boutique fermé samedi apres-midi. Restreint stock, aussi les livres neufs. Spec: beaux livres anciens et modernes; equitation. Cata: mensuel. Corresp: English. B: Société de Banque Suisse, Lausanne. CP: Lausanne 10–9155. SLACES, SLAM.

BUCHANTIQUARIAT BRITSCHGI, Rämistrasse 33, 8000 Zürich. Prop: Armin Troesch. TN: (051) 575632. Gegründet 1941. Laden. Mittelgrosser Vorrat. Spec: Alpinismus, Reisen, Literatur, Kunst, Geschichte, Philosophie, Psychologie. Corresp: English, Français. CP: Zrich VIII 80–29990. VEBUKU.

BÜCHER-SCHMIDT ANTIQUARIAT, Torgasse 4, 8000 Zürich. Prop: Max Schmidt. TN: (051) 32 85 27. TA: Bucherschmidt Zürich. Geründet 1913. Laden. Grosser Vorrat, auch neue Bücher. Spec: Zoologie; Botanik; Philosophie. B: Schweiz Bankverein, Depka Bellevue, Zürich. CP: Zürich 80–25354. VEBUKU.

ZUM BÜCHERWURM AG, Gerbergässlein 12, Basel. TN: (061) 25 73 58. Laden. Mittlerer Vorrat.

CACHET, Munsterberg 13, CH-4051 Basel. Prop: H. Seckinger. TN: (061) 23 35 94. Laden. Spec: Helvetica; dekorative Graphik. VEBUKU.

LIBRAIRIE DE LA CORRATERIE, 20 rue de la Corraterie, CH-1211 Genève (Case Postale 181). Prop: Claude Martingay. TN: (022) 2807 08. Boutique fermé le lundi matin. Spec: editions originales; livres anciens; livres illustrés. M: S.L.A.C.E.S.

GALERIE GÉRALD CRAMER, 13 rue de Chantepoulet, Genève. TN: (022) 31 47 31. TA: Bibliocramer Genève. Fondée 1945. Galerie. Spec: éstampes modernes et livres de peintres modernes; sculptures modernes. Cata. Corresp: English. B: Société de Banques Suisse, Agence Cornavin, Genève. SLACES, SKV.

PATRICK CRAMER, rue de Chantepoulet 13, CH-1201 Genève. TN: (022) 32 54 32. TA: Pacrame, Genève. Galerie. Spec: Éstampes; livres illustrés. M: S.L.A.C.E.S.

PAUL DESCOMBES, rue du Vieux-Collège 6, 1204 Genève. TN: (022) 240443. SLACES.

GALERIE ENGELBERTS, 11 Grand Rue, CH-1204 Genève. Prop: Edwin Engelberts. TN: 28 37 32. TA: Cantabile, Genève. Fondée en 1960. Galerie, fermée lundi. Spec: art contemporain; tableaux, dessins, gravures, livres illustrés par les peintres. B: Banque Gutzwiler, Kurz, Bungener SA Case postale 51 CH–1211 Genève 11. CP: Genève XII–579. SLACES.

LA FIERA DEL LIBRO, Via Marconi 2, 6900 Lugano. TN: (034) 22 60 44. TN: 227649. Est: 1948. Shop. Spec: books fine arts, maps and views, prints and drawings. Corresp: English, Deutsch, Français, Italiano.

EDUARD FINK, Metzergasse 18, 3400 Burgdorf. TN: (034) 224711. SLACES.

PAUL & ARTHUR FISCHER, Haldenstrasse 19, 6006 Luzern. TN: (041) 225772. SLACES.

LYDIA FREISTADT, Brunngasse 11, CH-8001 Zürich. TN: 261 15 18.

FUCHS & REPOSO, Librairie Wega, Via Nassa 21, 6900 Lugano. TN: (091) 23 16 06. TA: Wega Lugarno. Fondée en 1935. Boutique, early closing Saturday. Moyen stock. Spec: moderne bibliophile. Corresp: English, Français, Deutsch, Italiano. B: Unione de Banche Svizzere. CP: Lugano 69 1911. SBVV, VEBUKU.

GILHOFER & RANSCHBURG G.m.b.H., Sternegg 5, 6005 Luzern. Leiter: Axel Erdmann. TN: (041) 44 10 18. TA: Gilhag, Luzern. Laden, aber vorzugsweise nach Vereinbarung. Gegründet 1924. Kleiner Vorrat. Spec: Inkunabeln; XVI Jahrhundert; Manuskripte; Geschichte d. Wissenschaften und Medizin. Cata: 2 pro Jahr. Corresp: Deutsch, Français, English, Italiano. B: Schweiz. Kreditanstalt, Luzern. CP: 60 2786. ILAB, VEBUKU.

ANTIQUARIAT HEINRICH GILSING, Neuensteinerstrasse 17, 4053 Basel. Prop: Ingrid Gilsing. TN: (061) 50 74 66. TA: Gilsingbuch, Basel. Gegründet 1957. Wohnung; Beouche nur nach Vereinbarung. Mittelgrosser   Vorrat.   Spez: Geschichte;   Theologie; Geisteswissenschaften; Kata: 5–8 pro Jahr. Korresp: English, Deutsch, Français. B: Schweiz. Bankverein, Basel, Filiale Tellplatz; Konto Nr. 20–200 735. CP: Basel 40–26 125.

CLAUDE GIVAUDAN, rue du Soleil Levant 3, CH-1204 Genève. TN: (022) 29 91 61. Boutique; fermé le Lundi matin. Spec: livres illustrés; relieures romantiques; éditions originales du 15e–20e siecles. M: S.L.A.C.E.S.

LIBRAIRIE DU GRAND-CHÊNE, Chemin de Montagny, 1603 Aran. Prop: Ernest Abravanel. TN: (021) 99 25 21. Domicile, sur rendez-vous. Restreint stock. Spec: Stendhal, Balzac, Proust, Rilke; critique littéraire. Cata: 6 par an. Corresp: English, Français, Deutsch. B: Banque populaire suisse, Lausanne, Compte 167 160. CP: Lausanne 10 177 69. VEBUKU, LILA, SLESR.

DAS GUTE BUCH, Rosengasse 10, 8001 Zürich. Prop: Sigmund Seidenberg. TN: 2517072. Gegründet 1940. Laden. Sehr grosser Vorrat. Spec: alle Gebiete; Okkulta. Schweizer Kreditanstalt, Rathaus, Zürich. CP: Zürich 80 22853. Schweizische Buchhändlervereinigung.

ANTIQUARIAT ALBERT GUNTERN. Luzern, Hertensteinstrasse 17. TN: 041 38817. Gegründet 1975. Laden. Sehr kleiner Vorrat.

DR. ANNEMARIE GUYER-HALTER, Auf Der Mauer 1, 8000 Zürich 1. TN: (011) 47 33 43. Spec: Geschichte; Philosophie; Wissenschaften. B: Schweiz. Kreditanstalt. CP: Zürich 80–33053. VEBUKU.

HANS HAUBENSACK, Froschaugasse 11, CH-8001 Zürich. TN: 251 26 18.

HAUS DER BÜCHER, AG, "ERASMUSHAUS", BÄUMLEINGASSE 18, 4000 BASEL. Dir: Alain F. Moirandat, Lic. Phil. TN: 23 30 88. TA: Buchhaus Basel. Spec: Auktionen; alte Bücher; Autographen. B: Crédit Suisse.

HEGNAUER UND SCHWARZENBACH, KRAMGASSE 16, 3011 BERN, Prop: Eduard Hegnauer und Christoph Schwarzenbach. TN: (031) 22 64 15 und 22 74 00. Gegründet 1944. Laden, Montag geschlossen. Sehr grosser Vorrat. Corresp: English, Française, Deutsch. B: Schweizer Creditanstalt, Konto 0094–339175–91. Schweizerische Bankgessellschaft, Konto 364.090.01 P. CP: 30 15595. VEBUKU, LILA.

HEINIMANN & CO., KIRCHGASSE 17, 8000 ZÜRICH 1, (ehemals HANS RAUNHARDT). Prop: Gerhard Heinimann. TN: (01) 251 13 68. TA: Raunhardtbuch Zürich. Spec: Recht, Wirtschaft, Medizin. B: Schweiz. Kreditanstalt (Depka Rathausplatz) Zürich. CP: Zürich 80905. V.E.B.U.K.U.

P. H. HEITZ, POSTFACH 80, BASEL 4006. TN: 42 88 60. TA: Heitzverlag Basel. Gegründet 1483 (Strasbourg, France). Domicile, par rendez-vous seulement. Spec: Helvetica; Alsatica; Incunabula. Corresp: English, Français, Italiano. B: Schweizer Kreditanstalt, Basel. CP: V 8905 Basel. SLAM.

ARNOLD HESS, GALERIE ZUR KRONE, ZÜRCHERSTRASSE 183, CH-8500 FRAUENFELD. TN: (054) 73604. Laden; Montag geschlossen. Spec: Helvetica; Graphik und Ansichtenwerke. M: VEBUKU.

M. UND R. HOFER, MÜNSTERGASSE 56, CH-3011 BERN. TN: (031) 22 78 97. Laden. Spec: Helvetica; alte Ansichten und Landkarten; dekorative Graphik. M: VEBUKU.

ANTIQUARIAT IBERIA, HIRSCHENGRABEN 6, 3001 BERNE. Prop: Jaime Romagosa. TN: 25 59 43. Fondée 1950. Boutique. Moyen stock. Littérature espagnole, littérature générale, philosophie. Corresp: English, Français, Deutsch, Español, Italiano. B: Union de Banque Suisse, Berne. CP: Berne 30–22065. SLACES.

HEINZ HUBERTUS KAMPF, WASSERWERKGASSE 31, POSTFACH 246. CH-3011 BERN. TN: (031) 22 33 73. Besuch nur nach Vereinbarung. Spec: alte Medizin; Geschichte der Wissenschaften. M: VEBUKU.

KORNFELD & CO., LAUPENSTRASSE 41, CH-3008 BERN. Prop: Eberhard W. Kornfeld. TN: 031 25 46 73. TA: Artus, Bern. Est: 1867 (formerly Kornfeld & Klipstein). Shop. Spec: fine arts; old and modern prints and drawings. Corresp: English, Français, Deutsch. B: Kantonalbank vo Bern; Konto 550.471.04. V.E.B.U.K.U.; Swiss Art Dealers' Association.

KREBSER A.G., BÄLLIZ 64, 3601 THUN. Prop: Markus Krebser. TN: 22 19 22. TA: Krebserag Thun. Spec: Veduten; Naturwissenschaft; illustrierte Bücher. B: Spar und Leihkasse, Thun; Schweizerische Bankgesellschaft, Thun. Postcheck, Konto Nr. 30–5181. V.E.B.U.K.U.

HERBERT LANG & CIE A.G., MÜNZGRABEN 2, 3000 BERN 7. TN: (031) 22 88 71. TA: Librilang, Bern. Gcgründet 1921. Lagerraäume; Samstag geschlossen, Besuche vorzugweise nach Vereinbarung. Sehr grosser Vorrat. Spec: Rechts-, Wirtschafts- und Sozialwissenschaften; Philosophie; Geschichte. Cata: 8–10 pro Jahr. Corresp: English, Français, Italiano. B: Schweiz. Kreditanstalt Bern Konto Nr. 429500–11; Dresdner Bank Hamburg Konto Nr. 966058600; Crédit Lyonnais, Paris Compte 6212 H; Crédir Suisse, New York. CP: Bern 30–4108; Frankfurt am Main 3003 76–607. S.L.A.C.E.S.S., V.D.A., I.L.A.B.

ANTIQUARIAT WOLFGANG LANGER, POSTFACH 521, 8001 ZÜRICH. TN: 01 252 69 50. Montag geschlossen. Corresp: Deutsch, Franais, English. B: SKA/Filiale Rathausplatz 652 729 01. CP: Zürich 80 57856 4.

AUGUST LAUBE, TRITTLIGASSE 19, 8001 ZÜRICH. TN: (01) 251 85 50. TA: Buchlaube Zürich. Spec: Illustrierte Bücher, alte und moderne Graphik; B: Schweizerische Kreditanstalt, Zürich. CP: Zürich 80–9245. VEBUKU, SLACES.

BUCHANTIQUARIAT MADLIGER-SCHWAB, POSTFACH 8022, TIEFENHÖFE (BEIM PARADEPLATZ) 8001 ZÜRICH. Prop: H. und R. Madliger-Schwab. TN: (01) 221 06 86. TA: Madligerschwab Zürich. Gegründet 1951. Laden, Montagvormittag und Samstagnachmittag geschlossen (January-November). Sehr grosser Vorrat, auch neue Bücher. Spec: Bibliographie; Kunst; Geschichte; Helvetica. Corresp: Deutsch, Français. B: Schweiz. Kreditanstalt, Zürich, Konto Nr. 359 738–41. CP: 80–37 276–6.

KARL MOHLER, RHEINSPRUNG 7, CH-4051 BASEL. Prop: U. Wenger-Mohler. TN: (061) 25 98 82. Laden, Montag geschlossen. Spec: Helvetica; alte Landkarten und Ansichten; dekorative Graphik. VEBUKU.

MOLENES S.A., Librairie Quentin, 7 Place de la Fusterie, CH-1204 Geneve. TN: (022) 21 14.33. Fondée: 1979. Boutique. Restreint stock: aussi livres neufs. Spec: manuscrits; beaux livres anciens et modernes. Cata: 5 par an. Corresp: English. B: Banque Suisse de Credit et de Dépôts, Compte U6 428 1760. CP: Genève 12–6656. M: L.I.L.A., C.L.E.F., S.L.A.C.E.S.

EDUARD MÜLLER, Universitätstrasse 19, CH-8006 Zürich. TN: 47 04 25.

HENRY MÜLLER, Postfach 55, 8405 Winterthur. Spec: Illustrierte Bücher.

GALERIE ANNIE MURISET, 4 Place du Molard, 1204 Genève. TN (022) 21 60 01. Spec: gravures anciennes; géographie. SLACES.

F. SCHEIBER, Denkmalstrasse 8, Luzern. TN: (041) 36 4823. Laden. Kleiner Vorrat.

ANNEMARIE PFISTER, Petersgraben 18, 4051 Basel. TN: (061) 2: 75 02. Gegründet 1974. Laden. Kleiner Vorrat, auch neue Bücher. Spec: Klassiker; Kunst; Geisteswissenschaften. Corresp: English Français. B: Schweiz. Bankverein. CP: 40 36 232.

ANTIQUARIAT PINKUS GENOSSENSCHAFT, Froschaugasse 7, 800 Zürich. (Postfach 8025 Zürich). Prop: Studienbibliothek zu Geschichte der Arbeiterbewegung. TN: 251 26 47. TA: Desiderat Zürich. Gegründet 1940. Laden und Lagerräume (Antiquaria Montag geschlossen). Grosser Vorrat, auch neue Bücher. Spec Literatur in Erstausgaben; Reisebeschreibungen, alte Drucke illustrierte Bücher; Politik, alter Kinderbücher; Philosophie kulturgeschichte. Cata: 6 pro Jahr. Corresp: Deutsch, Français English. B: Schweizer Kreditanstalt Depositenkasse, Rathausplatz 8022 Zürich. CP: Zürich 80 25 787. Stuttgart 5004. SBVV.

MARCO PINKUS, ABC Antiquariat, Zähringerstrasse 31 CH-800 Zürich. TN: (01) 252 71 45. Laden. Spec: Bibliographie; Kunst. M V.E.B.U.K.U.

GALERIE PULITZER & KNÖLL AG., Junkerngasse 17, CH-3011 Bern Prop: Elsbeth Haudenschild. TN: (031) 22 56 91 und 22 93 33. Laden. VEBUKU.

LAURENT RASTELLO, Place Bourg-de-Four 22, CH-1204 Genève.

ANTIQUARIAT UND GALERIE IM RATHAUSDURCHGANG Postfach 72, CH-8402 Winterthur.

MADAME EUGÈNE REYMOND, 14 FAUBOURG DE L'HÔPITAL, CH-2000 NEUCHATEL. TN: (038) 25 45 15. TA: Libremon Neuchâtel. Fondée 1927. Fermé Lundi. Spec: érudition, documentation tous sujets. Cata. Corresp: English. B: Société de Banque Suisse. CP: Neuchâtel 20–2036. SLACES.

RIBAUX BUCHHANDLUNG UND ANTIQUARIAT, BAHNHOFSTRASSE 2, CH-9001 ST GALLEN. TN: (071) 22 16 04. Laden. Spec: Helvetica; Belletristik; Zeitgeschichte. M: V.E.B.U.K.U.

HANS ROHR, OBERDORFERSTRASSE 5, 8024 ZÜRICH 1. TN: (01) 251 36 36. Filmbuchhandlung, Oberdorsfstr. 3, TN: (01) 25 136 36, Filiale Torgasse 4, TN: (01) 251 36 36. Gegründet 1921. Laden und Lagerräume, Montag Geschlossen. Sehr grosser Vorrat, auch neue Bücher. Spec: Altphilologie; Philosophie; Psychologie; Helvetica; Literatur; Film. Corresp: English, Français. B: Zurcher Kantonalbank; Credit Suisse, New York; Deutsche Bank, Frankfurt a/M; Midland Bank, Oversea Div., London. CP: Zürich 80/9613 und Stuttgart 107 30–705. VEBUKU.

HENRI SACK, GRAND-RUE 1, 1204 GENÈVE. Prop: Louis Porte. TN: (022) 21 1212. TA: Librisack. Boutique. Spec: éditions originales; autographes. CP: Genève 12–3985. S.L.A.C.E.S.

JÖRG SCHÄFER, ALFRED-ESCHER-STRASSE 76, 8002 ZÜRICH. TN: (01) 202 69 75. TA: Schaeferbuch Zürich. Gegründet 1971. Laden; Besuche nach Vereinbarung. Spec: Bücher des 15. und 16. Jahrhunderts; Geschichte der Wissenschaften. Cata: 3 pro Jahr. Corresp: English, Français. B: Julius Bär & Co., Zürich. CP: Zürich 80–69515. V.E.B.U.K.U., I.L.A.B., V.D.A.

HENRY SCHELLER, SEEFELDSTRASSE 73, CH-8008 ZÜRICH. TN: 252 45 00.

SCHLÖHLEIN G.m.b.H., SCHÜTZENMATTSTRASSE 15, CH-4003 BASEL. TN: (061) 25 43 17. Prop: Heinz Kyburz und Marianne Wehrli. Laden, Montag geschlossen. Spec: Musikliteratur, Musikalische Erst- und Fruhdrucke. VEBUKU.

HELLMUT SCHUMANN, AG., RÄMISTRAASE 25, 8024 ZÜRICH. Manager: Hans Neubauer. TN: (01) 2510272. Telex: 816484. TA: Schumannbush Zürich. Gegründet 1828. Laden, Montag Geschlossen. Sehr grosser Vorrat. Spec: Bücher, Graphik. Cata: 6 pro Jahr. Corresp: English, Francçais, Italiano. B: Swiss Credit, Zürich, Branch Seefeld. CP: Zürich 80–2932–2. VEBUKU.

PHILIPP SEIDENBERG, BÜCHERLADEN, BRUNNGASSE 4, 8001 ZÜRICH.

RENE SIMMERMACHER A.G., Kirchgasse 25, CH-8024 Zürich. TN: (01) 2525512. Ladengeschäft. Sehr kleine Vorrat. Spec: Kunstwissenschaft; Griechenland frühe lithographien. CP: Zürich 80–10427. B: Bank Lev AG Konto: 13018–1

RENÉ SIMMERMACHER, Talstrasse 5, 7800 Zürich. TN: (0761) 73676. Wohnung. Sehr kleiner Vorrat, auch neue Kunstbücher. Spec: Kunst, Griechenland. Cata. Corresp: English, Français. B: Sparkasse Freiburg/Breisgau, Konto 2013105. CP: Karlsruhe 3276-751. V.D.A. Kunst-und Antiquitäten Händler Verband.

M. SLATKINE ET FILS, 5 rue des Chaudronniers, 1211 Genève. Prop: Michel Slatkine. TN: 20 04 76. TA: Slatlivre, Genève. Fondée en 1914. Boutique et depôt. Très important stock. Spec: Romanica, Helvetica, périodiques. Cata: 5 par an. Corresp: English, Deutsch, Français. B: Crédit Suisse, Genève. CP: Genève 12 3238. SLACES.

MUSIK & THEATER ANTIQUARIAT ARMIN TRÖSCH, Rämistrasse 33, 8001 Zürich. TN: (01) 47 56 32. Gegründet 1978. Laden. Mittelgrosser Vorrat. Spec: Musik- und Theaterliteratur; Musiknoten; Tanz, Ballett, Film. Corresp: English, Deutsch, Français. B: Schweiz. Kreditanstalt Hauptsitz, 8021 Zürich, Konto PK 20104–8.

LOUIS VUILLE, rue Maison-Rouge 5, 1400 Yverdon. TN: (24) 21 25 44. Fondée 1853. Magasin, fermé samedi après-midi. Restreint stock. Spec: Helvetica; voyages et gravures décoratives. Cata: 1 par an. Corresp: Deutsch, Français. B: Banque vaudoise de Crédit. CP: Lausanne 10–12464. S.L.A.C.E.S.

OTTO WASER-ALBIEZ, Rümelinsplatz 15, Basel. TN: 237318. Laden. Kleiner Vorrat, auch neue Bücher.

R. & I. WANNER-ZANDER, Kronengasse 35, 5400 Baden. TN: (056 22 30 93. TA: ISIBOOK. Gegründet 1971. Etage geschlossen Montag. Mittelgrosser Vorrat. Spez: Geschichte; Literatur. Helvetica. Corresp: English; Deutsch; Français. CP: 50–9645. B: Schweiz. Bankgesellschaft, Baden. VEBUKU, SBVV.

ANTIQUARIAT H. U. WEISS BIBLIOTHECA GASTRONOMICA, Winzerstrasse 5, CH-8049 Zürich. TN: (01) 56 97 84. Besuch nach Vereinbarung. Spec: Gastronomie, Oenologie, Alimentation; Voyages, Tourisme.

GALERIE WIDMER, Neugasse 35, 9000 St. Gallen. Prop: Carl
Widmer. TN: (071) 22 16 26. Gegründet 1936. Laden. Spec:
Kupferstiche; Landkarten; Helvetica. B: St. Gallische Creditanstalt,
Marktplatz 1, St. Gallen. CP: St. Gallen 90–2364. VEBUKU.

ALEXANDER WILD, Rathausgasse 30, 3011 Bern. TN: (031) 22 44 80.
TA: Wildbuch, Bern. Gegründet 1963. Laden, Montag Vormittags
geschlossen. Sehr grosser Vorrat. Spez: Wissenschaften, Philosophie
Theologie; Recht; Geschichte Korresp: English; Française, Deutch. B:
Kantonalbank, Bern. Kontonummer 958 291 0.02 CP: Bern 30–30284;
Stuttgart 86 15–702; Wien 7759 952; 's-Gravenhage 114 75.
V.E.B.U.K.U., S.B.V.V., V.W.B.

GERHARD ZÄHRINGER, Hauptstrasse 90, CH-8280 Kreuzlingen.
Prop: Ruth Zähringer. TN: (072) 72 12 71. Telex: 882149. Zach CH.
Laden; Montag geschlossen. Spec: Architektur; Kunstwissenschaft;
illustrierte   Bücher;   Pressendrucke;   Bibliographie;
Buckbinderei-Literatur. M: V.E.B.U.K.U.

SUOMI

FINLAND   FINLANDE   FINNLAND

Languages: Langues: Sprache
Finnish and Swedish.

Association: Verband
F.A.F.   = Finska Antikvariatforeningen
Suomen Antikoariaa
Norra Magasinsgatan 6, Helsingfors.

Public Holidays: Jours de Fete: Feiertage
Easter Monday: May 1: Whitmonday: Dec. 6: Dec. 25.

lundi de Pâques: May 1: lundi de Penticôte: Dec. 6: Dec. 25

Ostermontag: Mai 1: Pfingstmontag: Weihnachtstag

HELSINKI = HELSINGFORS: KERAVA: LAHTI: TURKU: VALKEAKOSKI

ANTIIKKI-KIRJA, KALEVANKATU 25, 00100 HELSINKI 10. Prop: Jan Strang. TN: (90) 611 775. Shop and stockrooms. Large stock sec. and antiq. also new books. Spec: Finno-ugric linguistics; topography and travel (Finland, Russia); periodicals. Cata: 2 a year. Corresp: English, Deutsch, Français, Russian. B: Union Bank of Finland. Account 205938–14094. CP: 6457 73–8. M: Suomen antikvariaattiyhdistys.

ANTIKVAARINEN   KIRJAKAUPPA   KAARLE   ERVASTI, TORKKELINKATU 4, 00500 HELSINKI. Prop: K. Ervasti. TN: 7530509.

HAGELSTAMIN ANTIKVAARINEN KIRJAKAUPPA, FREDRIKINKATU 35, HELSINKI 12. TN: (90) 649 291. F.A.F.

HELSINGIN   ANTIKVARIAATTI, MECHELININKATU 19, 00100 HELSINKI. Prop: K. Salmevaara and Mr. S. Salmevaara. TN: (90) 407656.

ANTIKVAARINEN   KIRJAKAUPPA   SEPPO   HILTUNEN.
VIHERNIEMENKATU 3, HELSINKI 53. Prop: Seppo Hiltunen. TN: (90)
753 6435. Est: 1930. Shop. Medium stock sec. and antiq. Spec:
History; political science; sociology. Corresp: English. CP: 85806–1
M: Suomen Antikvariaattiyhdistys.

ANTIKVARIA A. HONKANEN, VIRONKATU 8, HELSINKI. TN: 663 839.

KAMPINTORIN ANTIKVARIAATTI, FREDRIKINKATU 63, HELSINKI
TN: 63 99 61. CP: Helsinki 77452. F.A.F.

KAUPPAMAKASIIN, VUORIMIEHENKATU 10, HELSINKI. TN: 628 004.

KESKUSTAN ANTIKVARIAATTI, 1 YRJÖNKATU, HELSINKI. F.A.F.

KIRJA-KETTUNEN, TUUSULANTIE 2, 04200 KERAVA. Prop: M. Kettunen
TN: 245725.

KIRJAKUJA KY, UUDENMAANKATU 4–6, HELSINKI. Prop: Hyytiäinen &
Viljakainen. TN: 633396. Est: 1922. Shops, closed Saturdays i
Summer. Very large stock sec. and antiq. Corresp: English, Français
Deutsch. F.A.F.

KVARIAATTI, HAMEENKATU 16, 20500 TURKU. Prop: T. Vinkala. TN
(921) 331668.

LAHDEN ANTIKVAARINEN KIRJAKAUPPA, VESIJÄRVENKATU 12
15110 LAHTI. Prop: P. Suuronen. TN: (918) 40295.

NORDISKA ANTIVARISKA BOKHANDELN, NORRA MAGASINGATAN 6
HELSINGFORS. Prop: Mrs. Tove Nilsson. TN: 62 63 52. TA: Antiqv:
Helsingfors. Shop. Large stock. Spec: maps; travels; rare books
Russia, Scandinavia; prints. B: H.A.B., Helsingfors. CP: Helsingfor:
13. F.A.F., S.A.F., I.L.A.B.

ANTIKVAARINEN   KIRJAKAUPPA   B.   SAMALETDIN,   IS(
ROOBERTINKATU 9, 00120 HELSINKI. Prop: B. Samaletdin. TN: (90
645886.

TAPIOLA-ANTIKVARIAATTI, MALMINRINNE 3, 00100 HELSINKI. Prop
H. Mela. TN: (90) 6944779.

VALKEAKOSKEN KIRJA-ANTIKVARIAATTI, VALTAKATU 20, 3760(
VALKEAKOSKI. Prop: L. Saarinen. TN: (937) 46940.

SVERIGE

SWEDEN   SUÈDE   SCHWEDEN

Association: Verband

S.A.F.   =Svenska Antikvariatforeningen
Birger   Jarlsgatan   32,   11429
Stockholm.

Public Holidays: Jours de Fête: Feiertage

Jan. 1: Jan. 12: Good Friday and Easter Monday: May 1: Ascension Day: Whitmonday: Saturday between July 21 and 28: First Saturday of November: Dec. 25 and 26.

Jan. 1: Jan. 12: Pâques: May 1: Ascension: Pentecôte, 2 jours: Samedi entre Juillet 21 et 28: Premier Samedi du Novembre: Dec. 25 and 26.

Jan. 1: Jan. 12: Karfreitag und Ostermontag: Mai 1: Himmelfahrt: Pfingsten 2 Tage: Samstag zwischen July 21 and 28: Erstex Samstag November: Dez. 25 und 26.

ESLÖV: FALKOPING: GÖTEBORG HELSINGBORG: (Gothenburg): KARLSTAD: LANDSKRONA: LIDINGÖ: LOBERÖD: LUND: MALMÖ: NORRKÖPING: ÖSTERBYMO: RÖNNINGE: STOCKHOLM: UMEA: UPPSALA: VÄSTERAS: VÄSTRA FRÖLUNDA

ÅKARPS ANTIKVARIAT, Box 1129, KLOSTERGATAN 11, 221 04 LUND. Prop: P. Dethorey. TN: (046) 11 24 99. Established 1867. Shop, early closing Saturday. Very large stock. Corresp: English, Deutsch, Español. S.A.F., I.L.A.B.

ANDREASSONS ANTIKVARIAT, OPALGATAN 61, S-421 62, VÄSTRA FRÖLUNDA. Spec: bibliography; history of books and libraries, reference works and history of literature.

ANTIKVARIAT ANTIQUA, KARLAVÄGEN 12, 114 31 STOCKHOLM. TN: 08 10 09 96. Open Tuesday to Friday afternoons. Spec: applied art, antiquities and architecture. S.A.F.

197

ANTIQUARIAT ATHENAEUM, NARVAVAGEN 23, BOX 5852, 102 48 STOCKHOLM. TN: 08 67 78 40. Spec: old books; maps and views; voyages; history; biographies and topography in Swedish and foreign languages. S.A.F.

ANTIQUARIA BOK- & BILDANTIKVARIAT, KRISTINELUNDSGATAN 7, 41137 GÖTEBORG. TN: (031) 16 14 15.

ASPINGTONS ANTIKVARIAT AB, VÄSTERLÅNGGATTAN 54, 11129 STOCKHOLM. Prop: Inga Lisa Aspington. TN: 20 11 00. Shop. B: Skandinaviska Enskilda Banken 794–7906. CP: 45 86 46–7. S.A.F.

ANTIKVARISKA BOKHANDELN AB, GUSTAF ADOLFS TORG 41, 21139 MALMÖ. Prop: Bo Sörlin. TN: 97 97 28. Established 1942. Shop, early closing Saturday. Very large stock, also new books and remainders. Cata: occasionally. Corresp: English, Deutsch. B: Svenska Handelsbanken, Malmö, Account No. 6776–3338. VP: Malmö 87–6350. S.A.F.

BJÖRCK & BÖRJESSON, KINDSTUGATAN 2, POSTBOX 5405, 11131 STOCKHOLM. TN: (08) 215842. TA: Bokbörje Stockholm. Shop and storeroom. Very large stock. Spec: old and rare; voyages; natural history; scientific periodicals; Swedish literature; old science. Cata: 2–3 a year. Corresp: English, Deutsch, Français. B: Svenska Handelsbanken, 73–4061. CP: Stockholm 2717. S.A.F., A.B.A.

ANTIKVARIAT BÖCKER, LUNTMAKARGATAN 50, STOCKHOLM.

BOKER BOKSAMARBETE, TEGNERGATAN 17, STOCKHOLM.

BÖRJESONS ANTIKVARIAT, JÄRNVÄGSGATAN 47, 21614 MALMÖ. TN: 040 159518. S.A.F.

A. CEDERBERGS EFTR. AB, SYSSLOMANSGATAN 8, 752 23 UPPSALA. Prop: Sven P. Ullberg. TN: (018) 13 80 08. S.A.F. TA: Upsalabok Uppsala. Established 1903. Shop, early closing Saturday. Large stock. also new books. Corresp: English, Français, Deutsch. Svenska Handelsbanken, 802–6478. CP: Uppsala 378565–6. S.A.F., I.L.A.B.

CENTRAL ANTIKVARIATET OLOF PETERSON, DROTTNINGGATAN 73B, 11136 STOCKHOLM. TN: (08) 11 91 36. S.A.F.

DAHLSTRÖMS ANTIKVARIAT AB, STORGATAN 31, LANDSKRONA. TN 11464.

ENHÖRNINGEN ANTIKVARIAT, STOCKHOLMSVÄGEN 60, 18142 LIDINGÖ. Prop: Bo Lowenstrom. TN: 08–767 64 11. S.A.F.

198

ERA ANTIKVARIAT Drottninggatan 102, (Box 45511) 10430 Stockholm. TN: (08) 11 08 91. S.A.F.

GRAFIK-ANTIKVARIATET, Skomakargatan 24, 111 29 Stockholm. TN: 08 32 75 05. Spec: old prints; maps and views; rare books; old photographs. S.A.F.

HAGELIN ANTIKVARIAT AB, P.O. Box 3321, 10366 Stockholm. TN: (08) 327 505. Hagelin books. Private Premises. Appointment necessary. Spec: Linnaeus and his disciples; natural history; history of science and medicine; travels. Cata: 2 a year. Corresp: English, Deutsch, Français. CP: 757005–4.

HALLENS ANTIKVARIAT, Köpmangatan 4, 11131 Stockholm. TN: 08–20 0270. Spec: first editions and prints. Cata: occasionally. S.A.F.

ANTIKVARIAT CARL HELLMOR, Box 648 52101 Falköuping, (Aschebergsgatan 34) (41133 Göteburg). TN. (515) 197 07. Cata: S.A.F.

GRETA HOLMS ANTIKVARIAT, Norrlandsgatan 16, Stockholm-C. Prop: Eva Margareta Holm. TN: 11 59 64. B: Skandinaviska Banken. CP: Stockholm 35–6417.

GUNNAR JOHANSON-THOR, AB., Ellinge, 24100 Eslöv. TN: (0413) 601 00. Private premises, appointment necessary. Spec: old Swedish books; topography; old science; history; old prints and maps. Cata: 5–6 a year. Corresp: English, Français, Deutsch. B: Eslöv-Onsjö Bank 277–9031. S.A.F.

JONES ANTIKVARIAT, Nortullsgatan 3, 11329 Stockholm. Prop: Ragnar Jones. TN: 30 76 97. Spec: illustrated books; first editions; fine arts. B: Göteborgs Bank. S.A.F.

KARLSTAD ANTIKVARIAT, Östra Torggatan 1, 652 24 Karlstad. TN: 54342. S.A.F.

LEANDERS ANTIVARIAT, Storagatan 44-B, 72212 Västeras. TN: 021 11 99 00.

LENGERTZ' ANTIKVARIAT-BOKHANDEL I LUND AB, St. Gråbrödersgatan 13, 222 22 Lund. Prop: Kjell-Åke Askagården. TN: (046) 110345. Established 1922. Large stock. Corresp: English, Deutsch. B: Bankgiro 869–2659. CP: 53 84 69–8. S.A.F.

LENGERTZ' ANTIKVARIAT GÖSTA JANSON, Regementsgatan 6, 211 42, Malmö. TN: 040 12 22 65. Spec: Fine bindings; illustrated books. S.A.F.

LIBRIS ANTIKVARIATET, Kommendörsgatan 14, 10243 Stockholm. (P.O. Box 5123). Prop: Ake Andersson. TN: 62 21 31 and 60 92 62. TA: Librisantik Stockholm. Established 1960. Shop, early closing Saturday. Medium stock. Spec: old and rare books; bindings; humanities. Cata: 6–8 a year. Corresp: English. B: Skandinaviska Banken, account 57 5754. CP: Stockholm 6074–86. S.A.F.

LILLA ANTIKVARIATET, Södra Förstadsgatan 20, 21143 Malmö-C. Prop: G. Jansson. TN: 12 04 83. CP: Malmö 43–5604. S.A.F.

LINDBERGHS ANTIKVARIAT, Tegnérgatan 10, 113 58 Stockholm. Prop: Nils Lindbergh. TN: 31 20 20. Established 1952. Shop, early closing Saturday. Large stock. Corresp: English, Deutsch. CP: Stockholm 50 05 85. S.A.F.

5. LUNDGRENS ANTIKVARIAT Romares Stiftelse, Romares Väg, Box 3010, 250 03 Helsingborg. TN: (042) 11 73 86. S.A.F.

LUNDQUISTS ANTIKVARIAT, Geijersgatan 5, 411 34 Göteborg. Prop: Sten Lundquist. TN: (031) 189719. Est: 1973. Shop. Medium stock sec. and antiq. Corresp: English. B: SE-Banken Account 701–7874. CP: 42828–4. S.A.F.

KARNA MATCHTMEISTER BILDANTIKVARIAT, De Geersgatan 12, 11529 Stockholm. TN: (08) 61 91 97. Spec: old maps, prints and views, engravings etc. S.A.F.

REDINS ANTIKVARIAT, Box 150 49 S-75015 Uppsala. (Drottninggatan 11). Prop: Johan Redin. TN: (018) 117000. Est: 1974. Stockroom, open normal business hours, large stock sec. and antiq. Spec: history; economics; philology. Cata: 5 to 8 a year. Corresp: English, Français Deutsch. B: PK-Banken. Account 205–4559. CP: 859114–1. S.A.F.

OVE G. RENQVIST, Grafik-Antikvariatet, Skomakargatan 24. 11129 Stockholm. TN: (08) 21 80 75. S.A.F.

RÖNNELLS ANTIKVARIAT, AB, Birger Jarlsgatan 32, 11429 Stockholm. TN: 20 21 63 and 11 54 11. TA: Roennellbok Stockholm. Established 1930. Shop. Very large stock, also new books. Spec: scholarly and scientific books and periodicals in many languages; old Swedish views and maps. Cata: occasionally. Corresp: English, Français, Deutsch. B: Jämtlands Folkbank, 476–9287. CP: Stockholm 50040–5. S.A.F., V.D.A.

RYÖS ANTIKVARIAT AB, Hantverkargatan 21, 112 21 Stockholm
TN: (08) 54 80 86. Est: 1977. Shop. Large stock sec. and antiq., also a
few new books. Spec: art books; first editions. Cata: 4 or 5 a year
Corresp: English. B: Handelsbanken, Account No. 344 889 971. CP: 1
72 38–7. S.A.F., I.L.A.B.

NILS SABELS ANTIVARIAT, Box 1049, 15024 Rönninge 1
(Storskogsv. 1). TN: 753 506 82. Spec: illustrated books; topography
and travels; history. Cata. S.A.F.

SAMLAREN ANTIKVARIAT & KONSTHANDEL, Korsgatan 2, 41116
Göteborg. Prop: S. Grauers. TN: 13 18 07. Spec: first editions
(Swedish literature); fine arts; topography. CP: Göteborg 47061
S.A.F.

SCHULTZ ANTIKVARIAT AB, Bergsgatan 4, 211 54 Malmö. TN: 040
97 83 10; 97 66 36. Open Wed. to Fri. afternoons, Sat. morning. Cata.
S.A.F.

SETTERGARDS ANTIKVARIAT, Birger Jarlsgatan 44.
Stockholm-Ö. TN: 20 23 84.

SKANSTULIS ANTIKVARIAT, Götgatan 99, 11662 Stockholm. TN
08 42 43 66.

SÖRHUUS ANTIKVARIAT AB, Riddargatan 23, 114 57 Stockholm.
TN: 08 60 61 02. Spec: modern books in first and illustr. edns.
architecture; art; cinema; theatre; music; photography; literary
criticism; philosophy. Cata. S.A.F.

THULIN & OHLSON, Kungsgatan 9B, 41119 Göteborg. Prop: T
Ohlson. TN: 118974 and 118975. TA: Antiqva Göteborg. Established
1918. Shop. Very large stock. Spec: old Swedish children's books
Cata: 2 a year. Corresp: English. B: Skandinavska Enskilda Banken
Bankgiro No. 500–2340. CP: Göteborg 12408–1. S.A.F.

THULINS ANTIKVARIAT, AB., 57060 Österbymo. Prop: R. Du Rietz
TN: (0140) 83021. Very large stock. Spec: early printed; old science
Corresp: English, Français, Deutsch. S.A.F.

ANTIKVARIAT BLÅ TORNET, Drottninggatan 85, Stockholm
Prop: Harald Hult. TN: 20 21 43 and 7673111 (private). Established
1967. Shop, early closing Saturday. Large stock. Spec: old and rare
books; old and new illustrated books. Cata: 1 or 2 a year. Corresp
English. CP: Stockholm 407158–5. S.A.F.

UMEA ANTIKVARIAT, Västra Esplanaden 6, 90248 Umea. Prop: Roger Jacobsson. TN: 090–13 58 50. Spec: Lapland and Northern Scandinavia. S.A.F.

VARIA-ANTIKVARIAT, Tibble, Leksand. Prop: Gunnar Alfvén. TN: 62 76 83. Established 1943. Shop. Large stock. Corresp: English, Deutsch. B: Skandinaviska Banken, Account No. 57–5758. CP: Stockholm 55 28 36. S.A.F.

ALPHABETICAL LIST

LISTE ALPHABÉTIQUE
ALPHABETISCHE LISTE

ALPHABETICAL LIST

LISTE ALPHABÉTIQUE
ALPHABETISCHE LISTE

A

A.B.C. der Boeken (Het), 142 Wagenstraat, 's-Gravenhage, Nederland.
A.M.O. Antikvariat & Forlag, Ordr. Jagtory 91, København, Danmark.
Aabenhus (H.)=Bøckmann's Antikvariat, DK-8000 Aarhus-C, Danmark.
l'Abbaye (Librairie de), 27 rue Bonaparte, 75006 Paris, France.
Abbe Girard (Librairie), 6 rue de l'Abbe Girard, 63000 Clermont-Ferrand, France.
Abc Antiquariat, zähringerstrasse 31, CH-8001 Zürich, Schweiz.
Abela (Jo Charles), 11 rue Pierre-Démours, 75017 Paris, France.
Abelard, 7 rue F. Dons, 1050 Bruxelles, Belgium.
Abheiter (Jos.), Taborstrasse 11B, 1020 Wien, Österreich.
Abrams-Books (Harvey), an den Huberthausern 21, 1000 Berlin 38, Deutschland.
Abravanel (Ernest)=Librairie du Grand-Chêne, Aran, Schweiz.
Academic Bookstore, Hippocratus Street 33, Athens, Ellas.
Academica (Livraria), Rua Martires da Liberdade 10, Porto, Portugal.
"Achille" di A. Misan (Libreria), Piazza Vecchia 4, 34121 Trieste, Italia.
Achterstraat Boekwinkel (De), 44 Achterstraat, Alkmaar, Nederland.
Ackermann (Theodor), Ludwigstrasse 7, 8000 München, Deutschland.
Adaen (P.), 210 Torhoutstr, Oostende, Belgium.
Adam, 42 rue Mellery, 1020 Bruxelles, Belgium.
Adler (Arno), Hüxstrasse 55, 2400 Lübeck. (Postfach 2048), Deutschland.
Adler (Marcel), 3 Quai Malaquais, 75006 Paris, France.
Aesse (Studio Bibliografico), Via Castiglione, 30, 40124 Bologna, Italia.
Aichinger, Bernard & Co, Weihberggasse 16, Wien, Österreich.
Åkarps Antikvariat, Box 1129, Klostergatan 11, 221 04 Lund, Schweden.
Albertina (Libreria), Via Carlo Alberto 7, I-10123 Torino, Italy.
Albizi (A. Degli), Piazza Duomo 22r, Firenze, Italia.
Alder (Robert), Junkerngasse 41, Bern, Schweiz.
Aldus (Antikvariatet), S. Boulevarden 38, København, Danmark.
Alessandria (Libreria), Via Alessandria 216/a, Roma, Italia.
Alfa Antiquarian Booksellers, P.O. Box 1116, Nijmegen. (Van Welderenstraat 17)
    and at P.O. Box 26, 5360 AA Grave (Brugstraat S.), Nederland.
Alicke (Walter)=Interlibrum Establishment, Vaduz, Liechtenstein.
Alkmaars Antiquariaat, 99 Verdronkenoord, Alkmaar, Nederland.
Allanegui (Señora Herminia)=Libreria Mirto, Madrid, Spain.
Allegretti (Danilo), 17 Viale Rosselli, 22100 Como, Italia.
Alpes (Librairie des), 6 rue de Seine, 75006 Paris, France.
Alpina (Libreria), Via C. Coronedi-Berti 4, 40137 Bologna, Italia.
Altstadt Antiquariat, rue d'Or 16, CH-170° Fribourg, Schweiz.
Amager Bøger & Billeder, Amagerboulevarden 118, København, Denmark.
Amaryl (Antiquariaat), Tuinbouwstraat 74, 9717-JL Groningen, Nederland.
Amaryl (Antiquariaat), Koninginneweg 79, 1075–CJ Amsterdam, Netherlands

l'Amateur d'Art, 38 rue de Vaugirard, 75006 Paris, France.
Amateurs de Livres (Aux), 62 Avenue de Suffren, 75015 Paris, France.
Amatteis (Maurice), 12 Avenue Lys, Dammarie le Lys, France.
Ambrosiana (Bottega), Via Vitruvio 47, 20124 Milano, Italia.
Amelang (Antiquariat), Cranachstrasse 45, 2000 Hamburg 52, Deutschland.
American Bookshop, Largo Cairoli, Milano, Italia.
Amis du Livre (Les), 9 Valaoritou Street, Athens 134, Ellas.
Amsterdams Boekhuis, Haarlemmerstraat 87, Amsterdam, Netherlands.
Andersen (Carl), Å-Boulevarden 60, 2200 København-n, Danmark.
Andersen (Frode)=Art & Print, København, Denmark.
Andersen (Kristian)=Bog-Borsen, 1455 København-K, Danmark.
Andersen (Oda)=Martins Antikvariat, Københaven, Danmark.
Andersen (Peter)=Carl Andersen, 2200 København-n, Danmark.
Andersens Antikvariat (S.C.), Alhambravej 22, 1826, København-v, Danmark.
Andersson (Ake)=Libris Antikvariatet, Stockholm, Schweden.
Andraeas (Walter), Wischhofstieg 5, 2000 Hamburg 65, Deutschland.
André (Jean-Pierre), A L'Homme de Fer 2 rue Jean-Baptiste Salle, France.
André (Simone), 111 Avenue Victor Hugo, 75016 Paris, France.
Andreassons Antikvariat, Opalgatan 61, S-421 62, Västra Frölunda, Sverige.
l'Ane d'Or, Boite Postale 6, 95450 Vigny, France.
Anselot (Noël), Hamaide 102, 6914 Redu, Belgium.
Antiekparadis, 45 Steenbergsweg, Lepelstraat (Gem. Halsteren), Nederland.
Antigua y Moderna (Libreria), Calle De Los Libreros 2, Madrid 13, Spain.
Antiikki-Kirja, Kalevankatu 25, 00100 Helsinki 10, Finland.
Antikvarboden, Gammel Jernbanevej 4, København, Danmark.
Antikvarboltok, Lenin Körut 20, Budapest VII, Magyarország
Antikvarboltok, Muzeum Körut 15, Budapest V, Magyarország
Antikvarboltok, Bartok B. Utca 25 Budapest XI, Magyarország
Antikvarboltok, Karolyi Mihály Utca 3, Budapest V, Magyarország
Antikvarboltok, Martirok Utja 44, Budapest II, Magyarország
Antikvarboltok, Thokoly Utja 5, Budapest VII, Magyarország
Antikvarboltok, Bajesy-zsilinszky Utja 50, Budapest V, Magyarország
Antikvarboltok, Vaci 28, Budapest V, Magyarország
Antikvarboltok, Nepkoztarsasag Utja 2, Budapest VI, Magyarország
Antikvarboltok, Bartok B. Utca 15, Budapest XI, Magyarország
Antikvarboltok, Ulloi Utja 11–13, Budapest IX, Magyarország
Antikvarboltok, Nepszinhaz Utca 23, Budapest VIII, Magyarország
Antikvarboltok, Muzeum Körut 35, Budapest V, Magyarország
Antikvarboltok, Majakovszkij Utca 81, Budapest VII, Magyarország
Antikvarboltok Csanady Utca 13, Budapest XIII, Magyarország
Antikvarboltok, Muzeum Körut 17, Budapest V, Magyarország
Antikvariat 70, Ordrupvej 70A, København, Danmark.
Antikvariat, Istedvej 49, København, Danmark.
Antikvariat Antiqua, Karlavägen 12, 114 31 Stockholm, Sverige.
Antikvariat (Boghallens)=Arcade Prints, København, Danmark.
Antikvariatet, Elmegade 24, København, Denmark.
Antikvarijat-Knjižara. Nakladnog Zavoda Matice Hrvatske. Ilica 62, 41000 Zagreb
    Jugoslavija
Antikvariska Bokhandeln AB, Gustaf Adolfs Torg 41, 21139 Malmö, Schweden.
Antikvarni Knigi, 19 Ulitsa Graf Ignatiev, Sofia, Bulgaria.
Antiqua (Antiquariaat), Herengracht 159, 1015 BH Amsterdam, Nederland.
Antiqua Libri, Via Borgo Nuovo 27 2, I-20121 Milano, Italy.

Antiquaria Bok- & Bildantikvariat, Kristinelundsgatan 7, 41137 Göteborg, Schweden.
Antiquaria (Livraria), Rua da Misericordia 147, Lisboa, Portugal.
Antiquariat Aix la Chappelle, Pontstrasse 10, D-5100 Aachen, Deutschland.
Antiquariat (Altonaer), Am Felde 91, 2000 Hamburg 50, Deutschland.
Antiquariat an den Ceciliengärten, Rubensstr. 14, D-1000 Berlin-Friedenau 41, Germany.
Antiquariat Athenaeum, Narvavagen 23, Box 5852, 102 48 Stockholm, Sverige.
Antiquariat im Hinterhaus, Königswortherstrasse 19, D-3000 Hannover, Deutschland.
Antiquariat unter den Linden, Unter Den Linden 37/45, 108 Berlin, DDR.
Antiquariats-Buchhandlung, Friedrichstrasse 127, DDR-104 Berlin, DDR.
Antiquariats-Buchhandlung, Münzstrasse 1, DDR-102 Berlin, DDR.
Apollo Galeries, 23–24 Place St. Gudule, 1000 Bruxelles, Belgium.
Arbicone (Libreria Antiquaria M.), Via Spalato 43, 00198 Roma, Italia.
Arcade Prints, City Arkaden, Østergade 32, København, Danmark.
Archives S.A. 76 rue de la Montagne, 1000 Bruxelles, Belgium.
Ardy (Libreria Giuridica), Piazza Sauli 4–2, 16123 Genova, Italia.
Arendrup (Aage)=Frederiksborg Antikvariat, DK-3400 Hillerød, Denmark.
Arenthon (Librairie-Galerie), 3 Quai Malaquais, 75006 Paris. France
'Argences (Librairie), 38 rue Saint-Sulpice, 75006 Paris, France.
Argonautes (Les), 74 rue Seine, 75006 Paris, France.
Argus Antiquarian Booksellers, Prof. Drionlaan 6, 2670 Baarn, Nederland.
Arioso S.A.R.L., 6 rue Lamartine, 75009 Paris, France.
Aristeucos (Libreria Anticuaria), Paseo de la Bonanova 14, G. Barcelona 080 22, España.
Armarium Buchhandlung und Antiquariat, Zum See 10, 2313 Raisdorf Über Kiel, Deutschland.
Armarium" Buchhandlung und Antiquariat, Jahnstrasse 116, 4000 Düsseldorf 1, Deutschland.
'Archivolto s.a.s. (Libreria), Via Marsala 2, 20121 Milano, Italia.
'Argus du Livre. 17 Avenue de la Bourdonnais, 75007 Paris, France.
Ars Graphica, 14 Winkelgalerij, Botermarkt, 2800 Mechelen, Belgium.
'Art Ancien S.A., Signaustrasse 6, 8008 Zürich, Schweiz.
Art de Voir, 166 Boulevard Haussmann, 75008 Paris, France.
Art & Print, Kompagnistraede 25, København, Denmark.
'Arte Antica, Via A. Volta 2, 10121 Torino, Italia.
Arts et Lettres, "Le Vieux Chateau", 83330 le Castellet, France.
Arts et Metiers (Librairie des), 20 rue de Verdun, Lormaye, 28210 Nogent le Roi, France.
Arts et Philatélie, Place Guerin, 26 rue Bugeaud, 29200 Brest, France.
Asanin (M.), Schellingstrasse 58, München 40, Deutschland.
Asher & Co., (A), Keizersgracht 489–491, Amsterdam, Nederland.
Askagården (Kjell-Åke)=Lengertz' Antikvariat-Bokhandel i Lund AB, Lund, Sverige.
'Aspect, "La Legende" (Jacques), 58 rue d'Aubagne, 13001, Marseille, France.
Aspingtons Antikvariat AB, Västerlånggattan 54, 11129 Stockholm, Schweden.
Athenaeum Antiquarian Booksellers, Reguliersgracht 50, 1017 LT, Amsterdam, Nederland.
Atika Books, P.O. Box 1086, Yannai Street 3, Jerusalem, Israel
Atlantis Antikvariat, Frognervei 30, Oslo, Norge.
L'Autographe", S.A. (Librairie Ancienne), 6 Chemin de Grange Canal, CH-1208 Genève, Suisse.

Auvermann und Reiss Kg, Zum Talblick 2, 6246 Glashütten, Deutschland.
Axelsen Booksellers ApS., Østergade 44, København, Danmark.
Azathoth et Cie, 107 rue Saint-Dominique, 75007 Paris, France.
Azevedo and Burnay Lda, Travessa de S. Placido 48-B, 1200 Lisboa, Portugal, Portugal.

B

B.M.C.F. Antiquariat, AM Rain 23, 7936 Almendingen, Deutschland.
Babendererde (Peter), Grosse Burgstrasse 35, 2400 Lübeck, Deutschland.
Bach (Susanne), Jakob-Klar-Strasse 10, 8000 Munchen 40, Deutschland.
Bachelier (Pierre), 6 rue Neuve-des-Capucins, 44000 Nantes, France.
Backhuys (W.)=E.J. Brill, Leiden, Nederland.
Backhuys (Dr. W.), Ourdorpweg 12, 3062-RC Rotterdam, Netherlands.
Bader (Winfried)=Heinrich Kerler, 7900 Ulm, Deutschland.
Bado E Mart (Antiquariato Librario), Via Dietro Duomo 14 Int 1, 35100 Padova, Italy.
Baer (Alexandre), 2–6 rue Livingstone, 75018 Paris, France.
Bakker (Gebr.), 7 Gastthuismolensteeg, Amsterdam, Nederland.
Balaklava Antikvariat, Faergeportgatan, Gamlebyen, 1600 Fredrikstad, Norge.
Baland (Torsten), Spielhagenstr. 13, D-1000 Berlin-Charlottenburg 10, Deutschland.
Balberghe (Emile Van), Rue Vautier 4, B-1040 Bruxelles, Belgium.
Baldassari (Philippe)=Librairie Delamain, Paris, France.
Bancarella (Libreria la), Via Cavour 119, Roma, Italia.
Banzi (Libreria Antiquaria Luigi), Via Borgonuovo 10, 40125 Bologna, Italia.
Barasch (Rüdiger), Hähnelstr. 5, D-1000 Berlin-Friedenau 41, Germany.
Barateira Lda (Livraria), 16-A Nv. Trinidad, Lisboa 12, Portugal.
Barbazan (Beneit J.), Calle de los Libreros 4, Madrid, España
Barbero (Blazqez), Call Moyano 5, Madrid, España
Barbier (Michel), Bibliomax-Office, 7 rue de l'Enfer, 55140 Chalaines, France.
Bardini (Libreria S.), Via XII Ottobre, 16121 Genova, Italia.
Bardon (Luis), Plaza de San Martin 3, Madrid. (Apartado Postal 7092), España.
Bärenreiter Antiquariat, Heinrich-Schutz-Allee 35, 3500 Kassel-Wilhelmshöhe, Deutschland.
Barme (Antiquariat), Krumdal 24, 2000 Hamburg 55, Deutschland.
Barrera (Dott. Angelo)=Bottega d'Erasmo, Torino, Italy.
Barth (R.), Fürther Strasse 89, Nürnberg 80, Deutschland.
Bartkowiak (Antiquariat), Körnerstrasse 24, 2000 Hamburg 60, Deutschland.
Bartsch (Erika), Gottfried-Keller-Strasse 10, 7505 Ettlingen, Deutschland.
Bartsch (Georg), Lerchenfelderstrasse 138, A-1081 Wien, Österreich.
Baruch (Jacques)=Librairie-Editions Thanh-Long, 1040 Bruxelles, Belgie.
Bassenge (Galerie Gerda), Erdenerstrasse 5 A, D-1000 Berlin 33, Deutschland.
Bât d'Argent et du Chariot d'Or (Librairie du), 38 rue des Remparts d'Ainay, 69002 Lyon, France.
Bataille (Paul), "Calendal", 14 rue Châteauredon, 13 Marseille, France.
Bateau-Livre (LE), 14 rue des Eperonniers, 1000 Bruxelles, Belgie.
Batlle y Tejedor (Angel), Calle de la Paja 23, Barcelona (2), España.
Battaglini (Peppi)=Libreria de Piazza S. Babila, Milano, Italia.
Baudoin (Dominique)=Librairie Stendhal, 75006 Paris, France.
Baudry (Alain), 60 Avenue de Suffren, 75015 Paris, France.
Bauer (Arthur), Nestorstrasse 1, 1000 Berlin 31, Deutschland.
Bauer (Brigitte), Ofenerstrasse 17, 2900 Oldenburg, Deutschland.

Bauer (Galerie J.-H.), Burgstrasse 25, 3000 Hannover, Deutschland.
Bayarre (Fabrice), 21 rue de Tournon, 75006 Paris, France.
Bayssat (M.)=Librairie Abbe Girard, 63000 Clermont-Ferrand, France.
Beaufils (Fernand), 169 avenue Victor-Hugo, 75016 Paris, France.
Beck'sche Universitäts Buchhandlung, Währingerstrasse 12, Wien 1009, Österreich.
Becker (H.), 50 Gierstraat, Haarlem, Nederland.
Becker (I.), Lister Meile 49, D-3000 Hannover, Deutschland.
Beek (Johan), Huidenstraat 24, 1016 ET Amsterdam, Netherlands.
Beek (Johan), Graaf Van Lyndenlaan 55, 3771 JB Barneveld Netherlands.
Beer (Dr. M.)=Akademische Buchhandlung Kuppitsch, Wien, Österreich.
Behrens (Antiquariat), Leibnizstrasse 47, D-1000 Berlin 12, Deutschland.
Behrens (Stefan)=Antiquariat Behrens, D-1000 Berlin 12, Deutschland.
Beijers B.V. (J. L.), Achter Sint Pieter 140, 3512 HT Utrecht, Nederland.
Beisler (Hermann), Oskar-v. Miller-Ring 33, 8000 München 2, Deutschland.
Bekart (Ch.)=Librairie des Chercheurs, 1000 Bruxelles, Belgie.
Bekhoven. (Anton W. van) Ruysdaelplein 5, 1411 RD Naarden, Nederland.
Bellanger (A.), 6 et 8 Passage Pommeraye, 44000 Nantes, France
Belle (Librairie Jean Michel), 16 Boulevard Jean Jaurès, 06300 Nice, France.
Belrose Boekhandel Galerie, Mauritsweg 41, Rotterdam, Nederland.
Benecke (Hans)=Antiquariat Amelang, 2000 Hamburg 52, Deutschland.
Benedetti (Madame Michelle)=Librairie de l'Escurial, Nice, France.
Benelli (Jacques), 244 rue Saint-Jacques, 75005 Paris, France.
Benjamins, B.V., (John), Amsteldijk 44, Amsterdam, Nederland.
Benz (Willy), Universitätstrasse 31, CH-8006 Zürich, Schwerz.
Berche et Pagis, 60 rue Mazarine, 75006 Paris, France.
Berchi (Libreria Jose A. Fernandez), Claudio Moyano 26, Madrid, Spain.
Berès (Pierre), 14 avenue de Friedland, 75008 Paris, France
Berg Antiquariaat (Van), Oude Schans 8–10, Amsterdam, Nederland.
Berger (J.), Kohlmarkt 3, 1010 Wien, Österreich.
Bergmans and Brouwer Antiquarian Booksellers, Rustenburgerstraat 291, 1073 GE
     Amsterdam, Nederland.
Berisio (Libreria Vincenzo), Via Port'Alba 28–29, 80134 Napoli, Italia.
Berliner Antiquariat, Rheinstrasse 6, D-1000 Berlin-Friedenau 41, Germany.
Berliner Musikantiquariat, Pestalozzistr. 23. D-1000 Berlin-Charlottenburg 12,
     Deutschland.
Bernardino (S. Libreria Antiquaria di), via de Servi 49R, 50122 Firenze, Italia.
Bernardo (Libreria San), Calle San Bernardo 63, Madrid 8, Spain.
Berruto (Libreria Antiquaria), Via San Francesco da Paola 10 bis, 10123 Torino,
     Italia.
Berthier (Georges)—"Vieille France", Arcachon, France.
Bertocchi (Felice)=Libreria la Bancarella, Roma, Italia.
Bertocchi (Libreria), Strada Maggiore 70, 40125 Bologna, Italia.
Bertola & Locatelli Musica, Via Alba 53, 12100 Cuneo, Italia.
Bertran (Étienne), 110 rue Molière, 76000 Rouen. France.
Bessières (André), 12 rue Delambre, 75014 Paris, France.
Bestebreurtje (Antiquariaat G. J.), Lichte Gaard 2, P.O. Box 364 Aj Utrecht,
     Nederland.
Bezzina (Paul), 114 Saint Lawrence Street, Vittoriosa, Malta, Malta.
"Bianchino del Leone" (Libreria Antiquaria), Piazza Ansidei 4, 06100 Perugia. (C.P.
     25), Italia

Biblarte, Limitada, Rua de Sao Pedro de Alcantara 71, Lisboa 2, Portugal.
Bibliófila Ltda. (Livraria A), Rua da Misericórdia 102 Lisboa, Portugal.
Bibliofilo (Il), Via Roma 45, I-53100 Siena, Italy.
"Bibliographicum", Hauptstrasse 194, 6900 Heidelberg, Deutschland.
Bibliophage (Le), 17 rue de l'Etuve, 4000 Liege, Belgium.
Bibliophile Russe (Le), 12 rue Lamartine, 75009 Paris, France.
Bickhardt'sche Buchhandlung, Karl-Marx-Strasse 168, 1000 Berlin-Neukölln 44 Deutschland.
Bienvault (Mme.), 31 rue de Bordeaux, 37000 Tours (Indre-et-Loire), France.
Billesberger (Siegfried)=Galerie Zur Mühle, 8059 Moosinning, Deutschland.
Birland (J.)=Amager Bøger & Billeder, København, Denmark.
Bisey (Paul), 35 Place de la Réunion, 68100 Mulhouse, France.
Bisschopshof (Het), 1 Lichte Gaard, Utrecht, Nederland.
Björck & Börjesson, Kindstugatan 2, Postbox 5405, 11131 Stockholm, Sverige.
Bjørklunds Antivariat, Amagerbrogade 12, København, Denmark
Bjørnvig, Holm & Møller ApS, Odden Hovedgård, Mygdal, DK-9800 Hjørring Denmark.
Blaagaardsplads Antikvariat, Blaagaardsgade 25, København, Denmark.
Blackburn (Charles)=Ex-Libris, Paris, France.
Blaizot S.A. (Librairie Auguste), 164 Faubourg Saint-Honoré, 75008 Paris, France.
Blanchard (A.), 9 rue de Mèdicis, 75006 Paris, France.
Blancheteau (Marcel)=Aux Amateurs de Livres, Paris, France.
Blank (Herbert), Melonenstrasse 54, 7000 Stuttgart 75, Deutschland.
Blattermann (Annette)=Antiquariat M. Hofweg, 2000 Hamburg 76, Deutschland.
Bloch (Félix), 10 Route de Rolle, 1162 Saint-Prex. (Boite Postale 58), Suisse.
Bloch (Mrs. Maria)=Branners Bibliofile Antikvariat ApS, 1260 København-K Danmark.
Blöcker (Thomas), Nürnberger Strasse 50–56, D-Berlin-Charlottenburg 30 Deutschland.
Blot (Étienne), 42 rue Sortier, 75020 Paris, France.
Blumes Antikvariat, Vaernedamsvej 9, København, Denmark.
Böcker (Antikvariat), Luntmakargatan 50, Stockholm, Sweden.
Bøckmann's Antikvariat, Rosensgade 11, DK-8000 Aarhus-C, Danmark.
Bodo (P.le)=Mme. Bienvault, 37000 Tours (Indre-et-Loire), France.
Boekenbeurs (De), 38 Turfkaai, Middelburg, Nederland.
Boekenboot (De), 2 Zuidergrachtswal, Leewarden, Nederland.
Boekenmarkt 't Ezelsoor, 49 Veemarktstraat, Breda, Nederland.
Boekerij (De), 122 Prinsengracht, Amsterdam, Nederland.
Boerner (C.G.), Kasernenstrasse 14, 4000 Düsseldorf, Deutschland.
Bog-Borsen, Studiestraede 10, 1455 København-K, Danmark.
Bogantikvaren, † Farimagsgade 59, København, Denmark.
Boghallens Antikvariat, Raadhuspladsen 37, DK 1585 København-V, Danmark.
Boghytten (Antikvariatet), Absalonsgade 28, København, Danmark.
Böhlau (Antiquariat), Dr. Karl Leuger Ring. 12, A-1014 Wien, Österreich.
Böhringer (Heinrich), Marktplatz 2, 8592 Wunsiedel, Deutschland.
Boisgerault (Marcel), 31 Fossés saint-Marcel, 75005 Paris,
Bokavarden, Hverfisgotu 52, Simi 29720, Reykjavik, Iceland.
Boker Boksamarbete, Tegnergatan 17, Stockholm, Sweden.
Boldi (Lea)=Studio Bibliografico Lidis, Genova, Italia.
Bolland (Ton), Prinsengracht 493, 1002 Amsterdam. Nederland.

212

oloukhère (J.)=Librairie des Galeries, 1000 Bruxelles, Belgique.
omberg (Antiquariaat De), 102a Schootsestraat, Eindhoven, Nederland.
on (Michel), 4 rue Frederic-Sauton, 75005 Paris, France.
onaparte, S.A.R.L., (Librairie), 31 rue Bonaparte, 75006 Paris, France.
onfanti (Libreria), Via Macedonio Melloni 19, 20129 Milano, Italia.
onnefoy (Henri), 36 Avenue Villemain, 75014 Paris, France.
onnefoy (Ivan)=l'Envers du Miroir, Paris, France.
onset (E. J.), Patrijzenstraat 8, 2040-AC Zandvoort. (Postbox 136), Nederland.
onvallet (Jean-Louis)=Librairie Elbe, 75007 Paris, France.
ook Market, Rue de la Madeleine 47, B-1000 Bruxelles, Belgium.
orgne Agasse (La), 18 rue de l'Athenee, 1050 Bruxelles, Belgium.
örjesons Antikvariat, Järnvägsgatan 47, 21614 Malmö, Sverige.
orreani (Laurent), 11 Cours Saint-Louis, 13100 Aix-en-Provence, France.
ørsums Forlag og Antikvariat A-S, Fr. Nansensplass 2, Oslo 1, Norge.
orufka (Dr. Herbert)=A. L. Hasbach, Wien 1, Österreich.
osch (Antiquariaat Hieronymus), Leliegracht 36 (hk) Keizersgracht). 1015 DH
    Amsterdam, Nederland.
osch. (Libreria) Carlos Arniches 15, Madrid, Spain.
osworth & Co., Ltd., Dr.-Karl-Lueger-Platz 2, A-1010 Wien, Österreich.
ottega Apulja di Mario Somma, Via Salvatore Cognetti 37, I-70121 Bari, Italy.
ottin, Librairie Nicoise (Jean Claude), 2 rue Défly, 06 Nice, France.
ottn (Paul M.)=J. W. Cappelens Antikvariat, N-0101 Oslo 1, Norge.
ouma's Boekhuis, B.V., Turfsingel 3, Groningen, Nederland.
ouquinerie de l'Institut S.A., 12 rue de Seine, 75006 Paris, France.
ouquinerie (La), 89 rue de Lyon, 89200 Avallon, France.
ouquineur (Le), 10 rue Gambetta, 37000 Tours, France.
ouquiniste (Le), 18 rue Lakanal, 38000 Grenoble, France.
ouquiniste (Le), 162 Grand-rue, 86000 Poitiers, France.
ouquiniste (Le), Via Principe Amedeo 29, 10123 Torino, Italia.
ouquins, rue de Boigne 13, 73000 Chambéry, France.
ourcy & Paulusch, Wipplingerstrasse 5, 1010 Wien, Österreich.
ourguignat (Librairie), 10 bis Rue de Chateaudun, 75009 Paris, France.
ourlot (Bice), Piazza Castello 9, Torino, 10123, Italia.
ourlot (Libreria Antiquaria), Piazza San Carlo 183, I-10123 Torino, Italia.
ouvier Universitätsbuchhandlung G.m.b.H., am Hof 32, 5300 Bonn, Deutschland.
ouwer (A.)=Cosmos Antiquarian Books, 7240AA Lochem, Nederland.
ouwmeester Antiquariaat (D. J.), 27–28 Grote Kerkhof, Deventer, Nederland.
raatz (R.), Knooper Weg 28, 2300 Kiel, Deutschland.
rabant (Antiquariaat), Lange Putstraat 14, 5211 KN 's-Hertogenbosch,
    Nederland.
randes (W.), Postfach 1660, Wolfenbüttlerstrasse 12, 3300 Braunschweig,
    Deutschland.
ranners Bibliofile Antikvariat ApS, Bredgade 10, 1260 København-K, Danmark.
rasch (F.H.)=Bogantikvaren, København, Denmark.
raun-Elwert (Dr. Wilhelm)=.N.G. Elwert Universitätsbuchhandlung, 3550
    Marburg (Lahn), Deutschland.
raune (Dr) and Mrs. Peter=Frédéric van Hoeter, Bruxelles 1040 Belgie.
remer und Schlak (Antiquariat), Kornmarkt 4–5, 3340 Wolfenbüttel, Deutschland.
retonne (Librairie-Galerie), 1 rue des Fossés, 35000 Rennes, France.
ridel, S.A. (Livres Anciens Maurice), Avenue du Tribunal-Fédéral 5, 1002
    Lausanne, Schweiz.
ieux (Alain), 48 rue Jacob, 75006 Paris, France.

Brighenti (Libreria Antiquaria), Via Malpertusoi 40123 Bologna. Italia.
Brill (E. J.) Oude Rijn 33A, Leiden, Nederland.
Brincken (Klaus Von), Theresienstrasse 58 und Pacellistrasse 2, 8000 München 2, Deutschland.
Brink (J. van), Leidsestraat 30, 1017 PB Amsterdam, Nederland.
Brinkman (Antiquariaat), Singel 319, 1012 WJ Amsterdam, Nederland.
Brissaud (Daniele)=Le Bouquiniste, Poitiers, France.
Britschgi (Buchantiquariat), Rämistrasse 33, 8000 Zürich, Schweiz.
Brocéliande, rue de la Reine Bérengère 21, 72000 Le Mans, France.
Brockhaus Antiquarium, Am Wallgraben 127, 7000 Stuttgart 80. (Postfach 800 205), Deutschland.
Broekema (Antiquariaat C.), Leidsekade 68, 1016 DA Amsterdam, Nederland.
Brolsma (L. and N.)=Frisco Antiquariat, 9001 AM Grouw, Nederland.
Brøndum Antikvariat, St. Brondum Gl. Skole, DK-9520 Skørping, Denmark.
Brønshøj Antikvariat, Frederikssundsvej 128H, København, Danmark.
Brotrini (G.)=Libreria Antiquaria M.T., Roma, Italia.
Bruktboka, Kirkegatan 70, Lillehammer, Norge.
Brumme Frankfurt (Galerie), Braubachstr. 34, 6000 Frankfurt-am-Main, Deutschland.
Brumme (Siegfried), Kirschgarten 11, 6500 Mainz, Deutschland.
Brun, Édition et Diffusion M.P. (Daniel), 6 rue Clodion, 75015 Paris, France.
Bub (Hermann), Postfach 5328, Kürschnerhof 7, 8700 Würzburg 1, Deutschland.
Bücgerfass I (Das), Pfalzburger Strasse 12, Berlin-Wilmersdorf 15, Deutschland.
Buch-Dienst G.m.b.H., Apostel-Paulus-Strasse 18, 1000 Berlin, Deutschland.
Buch und Kunst, Münzgasse 16, 7750 Konstanz, Deutschland.
Bücher-Ernst, Gumpendorferstrasse 84, Wien 6, Österreich.
Bücher-Schmidt Antiquariat, Torgasse 4, 8000 Zürich, Schweiz.
Bücherfass II (Das), Hertelstr. 5, Postfach 209, D-1000 Berlin-Friedenau 41, Germany.
Bücherhaus (Das), Wiesenstrasse 21, 3012 Langenhagen, Deutschland.
Bücherkabinett, Türkenstrasse 21 (Innenhof), 8000 München 40, Deutschland.
Bücherkabinett (Das), Poststrasse 14–16, 2000 Hamburg 36, Deutschland.
Bücherkeller, Hauptstrasse 103, D-1000 Berlin-Schöneberg 62, Deutschland.
Bücherlaube (Die), Weimarer Str. 29, D-1000 Berlin-Charlottenburg 12, Germany.
Bücherstube am See, Kreuzlingerstrasse 11, 7750 Konstanz-Bodensee, Deutschland.
Bücherwurm AG (Zum), Gerbergässlein 12, Basel, Schweiz.
Buchfreund [Walter Schaden] (Der), Sonnenfelsgasse 4, 1010 Wien 1, Österreich.
Bucklein (Dr. Heide)=Margot Lörcher o.H.G., 7000 Stuttgart 1, Deutschland.
Bucklein (Dr. Heide)=Margot Loürcher, 8000 München, Deutschland.
Buffet (Claude), 7 rue Saint-Sulpice, 75006 Paris, France.
Bugnard (André)=Librairie Montmartroise, Paris, France.
Buisson (Madame J.)=Librairie Bonaparte, Paris, France.
Bülow (Rolf)=Fantask ApS., København-K, Danmark.
Burchard (Friedrich), Sonnbornerstrasse 144, 5600 Wuppertal-Sonnborn, Deutschland.
Burgersdijk & Niermans, Nieuwsteeg 1, 2311 RW Leiden, Nederland.
Burollaud (Michel)=Galerie Vauquelin, Dieppe, France.
Busck (Arnold), Fiolstraede 24, 1171 København-K, Danmark.
Buzzanca (Giampaolo), Piazzeta Pedrocchi 5, 35100 Padova, Italia.
Byens Antikvariat, Smedebakken 7, 1455 København-K, Danmark.

C

Cabinet de l'Estampe et du Livre Ancien (Le), S.A.M. 51 rue Grimaldi, le Panorama, Monaco, Principaute de Monaco, France.
Cabinet der Geschichte, Esplanade 17, 2000 Hamburg 36, Deutschland.
Cachet, Munsterberg 13, CH-4051 Basel, Schweiz.
Cadéo de Iturbide (Mme A.)=Arts et Lettres, le Castellet, France.
Cadre d'Art (Le), rue St. Paul 33, 4000 Liege, Belgium.
Caldini (Libreria Internazionale C.), Via Tornabuoni 89/91r., 50123 Firenze, Italia.
Callejon (Libreria el), Calle Preciados 2, Madrid, Spain.
Camée (Librairie du 34 rue Serpente, 75006 Paris, France.
Candide, 7 rue Montault, 49000 Angers, France.
Cankarjeva Zalozba, Kopitarjeva 2, 61001 Ljubljana. (P.O. Box 201-IV), Jugoslavija.
Cappelens Antikvariat (J. W.), P.O. Box 350, Kirkegatan 15, N-0101 Oslo 1, Norge.
Cappellini (Libreria Antiquaria), Corso Tintori 31r. I-50122 Firenze, Italy.
Caracedo (Libreria Anticuaria Angel), Pelayo 76, Madrid, Spain.
Carbonnel (M.)=Thélème, Marseille 13005, France.
Carel (Gilbert), 45 Avenue Saint-Mandé, 75012 Paris, France.
Carmes (La Bouquinerie des), rue St. Paul 35, 4000 Liege, Belgium.
Carpaneto (Luigi), Via Burlamacchi 31, 55100 Lucca, Italia.
Carpinus Antiquarlaat, 26 Korkstraat, Bussum, Nederlands.
Carrillo (Francisco), 86 Faubourg Saint-Antoine, 75012 Paris, France.
Carvalho (A. Tavares de), Avenida da Republica 46–3°, 1000 Lisboa-1, Portugal.
Casalini Libri, Via Benedetto Da Maiano 3, I-50114 Fiesole (Firenze), Italy.
Case de la Troya (La), Luna 21 (portada roja), Madrid, España.
Casella (Libreria Gaspare), Piazza Municipio 84, 80133 Napoli, Italy.
Cassini (Giocondo), Via XXII Marco San Marco 2424, 30124 Venezia, Italia.
Castaing (Michel)=Maison Charavay, Paris, France.
Castells-Plandiura (Mariano)=Libreria Anticuaria Aristeucos, Barcelona 22, España.
Castro E Silva (Livraria), Rua da Rosa 31, Lisboa, Portugal.
Cau (Jean), 22 rue Peyras et Bouquinerie Balaran, 52 rue du Taur, 31000 Toulouse, France.
Cause (Jean-Marie), 36 rue Provence, 75009 Paris, France.
Cavalieri d'Oro, Via Mazzini 84, 44022 Comacchio, Italia.
Cavriolo (Libreria Antiquaria), Via Capriolo 16/D, 25100 Brescia, Italia.
Cayla (Robert), 28 rue Saint-Sulpice, 75006 Paris, France.
Cederbergs EFTR. AB (A.), Sysslomansgatan 8, 752 23 Uppsala, Schweden.
Central Antikvariatet Olof Peterson, Drottninggatan 73B, 11136 Stockholm, Schweden.
Cerne (Carlo)=Umberto Saba, Trieste, Italia.
Cevenole (Bouquinerie), 10 rue Porte de France, Nîmes (Gard), France.
Chabaneix (Philippe), 33 rue Mazarine, 75006 Paris, France.
Chabanne (M.), 26B rue du Fort, Bruxelles, Belgium.
Chalvert (Maurice)—Librairie Davis, 75008 Paris, France.
Chambefort (Librairie Ancienne), 26 Place Bellecour, 69 Lyon, France.
Chamin da Mota (Livraria), 37 Flores, Porto, Portugal.
Chaminade (Jacques), 8 rue de l'Isle, 74000 Annecy, France.
Chamonal (François et Rodolphe), 40 rue le Peletier, 75009 Paris, France.
Champavert (Librairie), 2 rue du Perigord, 31000 Toulouse, France.
Chanoine=Librairie du Miroir, 7000 Mons, Belgium.

Chanut (François), Place de la Madeleine, 89310 Noyers-Sur-Serein, France.
Charavay (Maison), 3 rue de Furstenberg, 75006 Paris, France.
Charbo's Antiquariaat, 75 Willemsparkweg, Amsterdam Nederland.
Charmoy (Librairie Xavier), 9 rue Guizot, F30000 Nîmes, France.
Chartier (Pascal)=Librairie du Bât d'Argent et du Chariot d'Or, Lyon, France.
Chassaniol (Robert)=A la Recherche du Passe, 56370 Sarzeau, France.
Chastenay (Florence de), 76 rue Gay-Lussac, 75005 Paris, France.
Chauny (A.)=Librairie Duchemin, Paris, France.
Chauvin (Georges), 78 rue Mazarine, 75006 Paris, France.
Chellini (Pietro)=Libreria Oreste Gozzini di Pietro Chellini, Firenze, Italy.
Chenu (Jean-Paul)=Bouquinerie Comtoise S.A.R.L., Besançon, France.
Chercheurs (Librairie des), Galerie du Commerce 66-68, 1000 Bruxelles, Belgie.
Chevalier (Librairie), 176A rue Blaes, 1000 Bruxelles, Belgique.
Chevaux Lëgers (Les), 34 rue Vivienne, 75002 Paris, France.
Chezubina (Michetti)=Libreria S. Agostino, Roma, Italia.
Chiesa (Carlo Alberto), Via Bigli 11, 20121 Milano, Italy.
Chiverto (Antonio)=Libreria San Bernardo, Madrid 8, Spain.
Chmeljuk (Librairie I.), 1 rue de Fleurus, 75006 Paris, France.
Chrétien (Pierre), 178 Faubourg Saint-Honoré, 75008 Paris, France.
Chrispeels (Carl F.), Combahnstrasse 15, 5300 Bonn 3, Deutschland.
"Christo" (Antiquariat), Alte Gasse 67, Frankfurt M, Deutschland.
Chwat (Gerard), 2 Place Saint-Pierre, 83170 Brignoles, France.
Cicerano (Libreria), Via G. Bausan 58, I-80121 Napoli, Italy.
Cicerone (Libreria Antiquaria M.T.), Via Cicerone 39–41, 00193 Roma, Italia.
Cimes (Librairie des), Square Steurs 15, 1030 Bruxelles, Belgium.
Cité des Vieux Livres, 139 Grande Rue, 25000 Besançon, France.
Claassen (Aribert D.), Buch- und Kunstantiquariat, Hardstrasse 8, 5483 Ba
Neuenahr 1, Deutschland.
Clavreuil, 37 rue Saint-André-Des-Arts 75006 Paris, France.
Clavreuil (Bernard)=Librairie Thomas-Scheler, Paris, France.
Clerc (Librairie Pierre), 13 rue Alexandre Cabanel, 34000 Montpellier, France.
Cluzel (René), 61 Rue de Vaugirard, 75006 Paris, France.
Cobet (Antiquariat), Eysseneckstrasse 40, D-6000 Frankfurt am Main
Deutschland.
Coevorden (Antiquariaat van), Beukenlaan 3, 8085 Doornspijk, Nederland.
Colas (Gaston), 84 boulevard Raspail, 75006 Paris, France.
Colas (Pierre), 38 rue de Vaugirard, 75006 Paris, France.
Colbert (Librairie), 11 bis rue Colbert (Place du Chateau), 78000 Versailles, Franc
"Il Collezionista" (Libreria), Via Madonnina 9, 20121 Milano, Italia.
Collin (Gérard)=Bouquinerie du Languedoc, Montpellier, France.
Colonnese (Libreria), 33 Via S. Pietro A Majella, 80138 Napoli. P.O. Box 14
Italia.
Comellas (Mme. Françoise), 7 rue du Petit Saint-Pierre, 72000 le Mans, France.
Commerzcabinett, Humboldtstrasse 125, 2000 Hamburg 76, Deutschland.
Comtoise, S.A.R.L. (Bouquinerie), 9 rue Morand, 25000 Besançon (Doubs), France
Conradt (Dr. Maria)=Das Bücherkabinett, 2000 Hamburg 36, Deutschland.
Cornaro (Galleria Regina), Via Regina Cornaro 214, I-31011 Asolo (Treviso), Italy
Cornic Art Bookshop (Jullien), 118 rue du Faubourg Saint Honore, 75008 Par
France.
Corraterie (Libriarie de la), 20 rue de la Corraterie, CH-1211 Genève, Suisse.

Cosmos Antiquarian Books, (P.O. Box 30) Market 23, 7240AA Lochem, Nederland.
Cottage Antiquariat R. Knessl, Gymnasiumstrasse 17, A-1180 Wien, Österreich.
Coulet & A. Faure (C.), 5 rue Drouot, 75006 Paris, France.
Coulet, 1 rue Dauphine, 75006 (Jean), Paris. France.
Cournand (Gilberte), 14 rue de Beaune, 75007 Paris, France.
Couturier (Madame), 7 rue de Duras, 75008 Paris, France.
Cramer (Galerie Gérald), 13 rue de Chantepoulet, Genève, Schweiz.
Cramer (Patrick), rue de Chantepoulet 13, CH-1201 Genève, Suisse.
Crozemarie (R.)=Art de Voir, 75008 Paris, France.
Crucis (Gerard), rue St. Jean 33, 1000 Bruxelles, Belgium.
Cudek (Erwin A.), Die Bücher Fundgruber, Währingerstrasse 24, 1000 Wien IX, Österreich.
Cuisinier, Cookbooks (Le), P.O. Box 17221, Tel Aviv, Israel.
Cuppers (Joachim)=Frankfurter Kunstkabinett, 6000 Frankfurt-am-Main, Deutchland.
Curt (Yves), 119 rue Saint-Denis, 75001, France.

D

Daake (F. von), Lothringer 32, D-3000 Hannover, Deutschland.
Dahlströms Antikvariat AB, Storgatan 31, Landskrona, Schweden.
Dallai (Libreria Antiquaria), Piazza de Marini 11 rosso, 16123 Genova, Italy.
Dam (Ole)=Boghallens Antikvariat, DK 1585 København-V, Danmark.
Dambournet (Maurice)=l'Argus du Livre, 75007 Paris, France,
Damms Antikvariat A/S, Bokhuset, Tollbodgata 25, Oslo 2, Norge.
Danigo (Henri), 17 rue Marc-Sangnier, 29000 Quimper, France.
Dansk Bogservice, Amagerfaelledvej 9, DK-2300, København, Danmark.
Dardoize (Véronique), 30 rue de la Ferrage, F-30000 Nîmes, France.
Dargent (G. et A.), 11 rue Alain-Blanchard, 76000 Rouen, France.
Dasté (Francis), 16 rue de Tournon, 75006 Paris, France.
Davis (Librairie), 12 avenue Franklin-Roosevelt, 75008 Paris, France.
Dawson-France, S.A., zone Industrielle "la Prairie", 91121 Villebon-sur-Yvette. (B.P. 40), France.
De Jongh (C.P.)=Van Stockum's Ant., B.V., 's-Gravenhage, Nederland.
De Jongh (Matthijs), Jeltewei 44–46, 8622 XT Hommerts, Netherlands.
De Profundis Antiquariat, Postfach 21H, D-8012 Ottobrunn, Deutschland.
De Tille B.V. (Antiquariaat), Weerd 11, P.O. Box 233, 8901 BA Leeuwarden, Nederland.
Degheldere (W.), 2 Smedenstr, Brugge 1, Belgium.
Degreef (R.)=Libráric Simonson, 1060 Bruxelles, Belgium.
Delamain (Librairie), 155 rue Saint-Honoré, 75001 Paris, France.
Delatte (Max-Philippe), 15 rue Gustave Courbet, 75116 Paris, France.
Delbès (Alain)=Librairie Rieffel, Paris, France.
Il Delfino' (Libreria Antiquaria), Via Cesare Battisti 19A, 10123 Torino, Italia.
Delon (Librairie Jean-Paul), 74150 Marigny-Saint Marcel. TN: 01 29 14, France.
Dempwolf (Ursula), Damaschkeweg 19A, D-4830 Gütersloh, Deutschland.
Denis (Librairie), 50 rue de la Scellerie, 37000 Tours, France.
Deny (Georges A.), rue du Chêne 5, 1000 Bruxelles, Belge.
Depadt (Fr.)=Libraire des Cimes, Bruxelles, Belgium.
Bücherwurm (Der), Ottenser Hauptstrasse 60, 2000 Hamburg 50, Deutschland.
Derryx dit Derks (Mme.)=De Renaissance van het Boek, 9000 Gent, Belgie.
Desalmand (L.)=Librairie-Galerie Arenthon, 75006 Paris, France.

Deschamps (Jean), 22 rue Visconti, 75006 Paris, France.
Descombes (Paul), rue du Vieux-Collège 6, 1204 Genève, Schweiz.
Deuticke (F.), Helferstorferstrasse 4, Wien 1, Österreich.
Deutsch (Harri), Gräfstrasse 47, 6000 Frankfurt am Main, Deutschland.
Deux Gares. (Librairie des) 76 Boulevard de Magenta, 75010 Paris, France.
Deventer (Aniquariaat), Brink 17, 7411 BR Deventer, Nederland.
Devroe (Antiquariaat Johan), L. Vanderkelenstraat 43, 3000 Leuven, Belgium.
Devroe (Philippe)=Antiquariaat Sanderus, 8510 Kortrijk, Belgium.
Dhennequin (Michele), 76 rue du Cherche-Midi, 75006 Paris, France.
Dhouailly=Librairie Galerie 89, 89200 Avallon, France.
Dias & Andrade Lda, Livraria Portugal, Rua do Carmo 70, Lisboa 2, Portugal.
Didier Cart-Tanneur, 11 bis rue Vauquelin, 75005 Paris, France.
"Die Schmiede" (Antiquariaat), Brouwersgracht 4, Amsterdam, Netherlands.
Diehl (Ingeborg), Marzstasse 15, Wien, Österreich.
Dijk's Boekhuis B.V. (Van), (Postbox 23), Dieselstraat 1, 8263 AE Kampen, Netherlands.
Dinter (Jürgen), Antiquariat für Philosophie, Buchholzstrasse 8–10, Köln, Deutschland.
Doblinger Musikhaus und Musikverlag. Dorotheergasse 10, A-1010 Wien, Österreic▮
'Docet', Via A. Righi 9/A, 40126 Bologna, Italia.
Documents (Galerie), rue de Seine 53, 75006 Paris, France.
Domizlaff (Helmuth), Hocherlach 35, 8212-Übersee (Chiemsee), Deutschland.
Domplatz (Buch- und Kunstantiquariat am), Domplatz-Luragogasse. 8390 Passau Deutschland.
Dorbon Ainé =Le Bouquineur, Tours, France.
Dörling (F.), Neuer Wall 40, 2000 Hamburg 36, Deutschland.
Dössinger (F.), Hohennzollernstrasse 156, München 40, Deutschland.
Dotti (Libreria), Via Della Scrofa 58, 00186 Roma, Italia.
Douma (J.H.)=Burgersdijk & Niermans, 2311 RW Leiden, Nederland.
Draghi-Randi (Libreria Int) Via Cavour 17–19 I-35122 Padova, Italy.
Dresdener Antiquariat, Bautzner Strasse 27, 806 Dresden, DDR.
Dresdner Antiquariat Paul Alicke, Kurt-Schumacher-Strasse 33–35, D-6000 Frankfurt am Main, Deutschland.
Du Rietz (R.)=Thulins Antikvariat, AB, Österbymo, Sverige.
Dubouchet (Librairie), 2 rue Général Foy, 42000 Saint-Étienne (Loire), France.
Duchemin (Librairie), 18 rue Soufflot, 75005 Paris, France.
Dudragne (Librairie), 86 rue Maubeuge 75010 Paris, France.
Dupont (Henri), 141 boulevard de la Liberté, 59000 Lille, France.
Durance (Gabriel), 5 Allée d'Orléans, 44000 Nantes, France.
Durand-Noel (Yves), 38 rue de Normandie, 35510 Thorigne-sur-Vilaine, France.
Dutel (Jean-Pierre), 17 rue Mazarine, 75006 Paris, France.
Düwal (Eckard), Schlüterstr. 17, D-1000 Berlin-Charlottenburg 12, Germany.
Dykstra (G.S. & S.G.)=Antiquariaat De Tille B.V., Leeuwarden, Nederland.

E

Eché (Librairie Ancienne), 19 rue André Délieux, 31400 Toulouse, France.
Eclictica (Libreria), Piazza Cavana, Trieste, Italia.
Edelmann (M.), Postfach 9360, Breitegasse 52 und 54, 8500 Nürnberg–11 Deutschland.
Egenolf (Herbert)=Ukiyo-E Galerie, 4000 Düsseldorf 1, Deutschland.
Elbé. (Librairie) 213bis, boulevard Saint Germain, 75007 Paris, France.

Elchlepp (Alice), Schillerstrasse 14, 3360 Osterode a. Harz, Deutschland.
Elephants (Librairie des), Place Van Meenen 19, 1000 Bruxelles, Belgium.
Eluard-Valette (Cecile), 43 rue Sous Barri, OMM 06800 Haut de Cagnes, France.
Elwert (N.G.), Reitgasse 7–9, 3550 Marburg (Lahn), Deutschland.
Embla Books, P.O. Box 42, N 5014 Bergen Univ, Norge.
Emmering (S.), N.Z. Voorburgwal 304, 1012 RV Amsterdam, Nederland.
Encrenaz (Olivier), 8 rue des Deux-Haies, 49000 Angers, France.
Endres (B.), Utzschneiderstrasse 10, München 5, Deutschland.
Engelberts (Galerie), 11 Grand Rue, CH-1204 Genève, Schweiz.
Engelbrecht (K-Th.), Laves 76, D-3000 Hannover, Deutschland.
Enghave Plads Antikvariat, Enghaveplads 3, København, Danmark.
Engholst (Frede), Studiesstraede 35, 1455 København-K, Danmark.
Enhörningen Antikvariat, Stockholmsvägen 60, 18142 Lidingö, Sweden.
l'Envers du Miroir, 19 rue de Seine, 75006 Paris, France.
Eppe (Paul), 49 rue de Provence, 75009 Paris, France.
Eppendorfer Antiquariat, Gärtnerstrasse 31, 2000 Hamburg 20, Deutschland.
Era Antikvariat Drottninggatan 102, (Box 45511) 10430 Stockholm, Sweden.
d'Erasmo (Bottega), Via Gaudenzio Ferrari 9, 10124 Torino, Italia.
Erasmus Antiquariaat en Boekhandel. Spui 2, Amsterdam, Nederland.
Erdlen (George J.), Obermarkt 5, Postfach 1109, 8110 Murnau am Staffelsee, Deutschland.
Erdlen (Paul E.)=Antiquariat J. Reinhardt, D–802 Halle (Westf.), Deutschland.
Erdmann (Axel)=Gilhofer & Ranschburg, Luzern, Schweiz.
Erlemann (Hartmut), Münsterstrasse 71, 4700 Hamm 1, Deutschland.
Ervasti (Antikvaarinen Kirjakauppa Kaarle), Torkkelinkatu 4, 00500 Helsinki, Suomi.
l'Escurial (Librairie de), 29 rue Alphonse Karr, 06000 Nice, France.
Espagnon et Lebret, 1 rue de Fleurus, 75006 Paris, France.
Esquina (Livraria), 126 Av. L. Vieira, Porto, Portugal.
Esslingen (Kunstgalerie), Possartstrasse 12, D-8000 München 80, Deutschland.
Evangelische Buchhandlung Max Müller, Ernst-Thälmann-Strasse 23, Postfach 229, 9010 Karl-Marx-Stadt, DDR.
Ewald (Antiquariat Georg), Grosse Bockenheimer Strasse 29, 6000 Frankfurt 1, Deutschland.
Ex-Libris, 11 rue Victor Cousin, 75005 Paris, France.
l'Ex Libris, 57 rue des Recollets, 30400 Villeneuve les Avignon, France.

F

Fach (Joseph), Fahrgasse 8, 6000 Frankfurt-am-Main. 1, Deutschland.
Faculté Des Sciences (Librairie De La), rue des Ursulines. 75005 Paris, France.
Fantask ApS., Sankt Pedersstraede 18, DK-1453 København-K, Danmark.
Fauché (Madame)=Arts et Philatélie, 29200 Brest, France.
Favereaux (Librairie), 19ter rue de l'Hôpital-Militaire, 59000 Lille, France.
"La Fenice" (Studio Bibliografico), Calle del Frutariol-S. Marco, 1850, 30124 Venezia, Italia.
Ferin Lda. (Livraria), Rua Nova do Almada 74, Lisboa, Portugal.
Ferrari (Louis), 140 rue Belleville, 75020 Paris, France.
Ferraton (Le Libraire Alain), Rue Ernest Allard 39, B-1000 Bruxelles, Belgium.
Feucht (Rainer G.), B.M.C.F. Antiquariat, am Rain 23, D-7936 Allmendingen, Deutschland.
Feucht (Rainer)=B.M.C.F. Antiquariat, 7901 Ulm-Gögglingen, Deutschland.

Feurer (Dr. Reto), Wanningerstrasse 7, D-8201 Obing/Oberbayern, Deutschland.
Fiammenghi (Libreria C.), Via Malcontenti 11, 40126 Bologna, Italia.
Fiammenghi (Maria)=Garisenda Libri & Stampe, S.A.S., Bologna, Italia.
Fiera del Libro (La), Via Marconi 2, 6900 Lugano, Schweiz.
Fillet (Louis)=Bouquins, Chambéry, France.
Fink (Eduard), Metzergasse 18, 3400 Burgdorf, Schweiz.
Finzi (Luigi), Foro Buonaparte 12, 20121 Milano, Italia.
Fiol, Llibres, OMS 45–A, Palma de Mallorca, 07003, España.
Fiorentino (Libreria Fausto), Calata Trinita Maggiore 36, 80134 Napoli, Italia.
Fischer (Paul & Arthur), Haldenstrasse 19, 6006 Luzern, Schweiz.
Flammarion (Librairie), 4 rue Casimir Delavigne, 75006 Paris, France.
Fleury (Gérard), Librairie François, 1er, 34 Avenue Montaigne, 75008 Paris, France.
Flint (J.H.), Dikninge 119, 1083 VA Amsterdam, Nederlands.
Floesser (Jean Michel de), 28 rue des Remparts, 33000 Bordeaux (Gironde), France.
Flumen Dantis di P. Zali (Libreria), Piazza Mazzini 12/1, 16043 Chivari (Genova), Italia.
Fog (Dan), Graabrødretorv 7, 1154 København-K, Danmark.
Fornbokaverzlun Kristjanssonar, Hverfisgotu 26, Reykjavík, Island.
Fornbokverzlunin, Klapperstig 37, Reykjavík, Island.
Forni Editore s.p.a. (A.), Via Gramsci 164, 40010 Sala Bolognese (Bologna), Italia.
Forsetn (E.) =Bouma's Bockhuis, B.V., Groningen, Nederland.
Fortuna (Studio Bibliografico), Via de' Pucci 4, I-50122 Firenze, Italy.
Forum B.V., P.O.B. 129, Oude Gracht 206, 3511 NR Utrecht, Netherlands.
Founès (Daniel)=Antoine Grandmaison, Paris, France.
Fournier (Librairie-Galerie Jean), 44 rue Quincampoix, 75004 Paris, France.
Frachon (Jacqueline)=Librairie de Montbel, Paris, France.
France (E. & Mrs N.)=J.L. Beijers B.V., 3512 HT Utrecht, Nederland.
Francis (Etienne)=Les Vieux Ordinaires, 83000 Toulon, France.
François (Librairie le), 91 boulevard Saint-Germain, 75006 Paris, France.
Franken (Klaus)=Rotkäppchen, D-1000 Berlin-Wedding 65, Deutschland.
Frankfurter Bücherstube, Börsenstrasse 2–4, 6000 Frankfurt-am-Main, Deutschland.
Frankfurter Kunstkabinett, Hanna Bekker vom Rath, G.m.b.H., Börsenplatz 13-15, 6000 Frankfurt-am-Main, Deutschland.
Franz (H.), Jakobstrasse 8, 7000 Stuttgart 1, Deutschland.
Frederiksberg Antikvariat, Gammel Kongevej 120, 1850 København-V, Danmark.
Frederiksborg Antivariat, Blehaven 10, DK-3400 Hillerød, Denmark.
Frederiksdal (Antikvariatet), Kongevejen 43, DK-2840 Holte, Danmark.
Fredrikstad Antikvariat, Postboks 169, N-1601 Fredrikstad, Norveg.
Freistadt (Lydia), Brunngasse 11, CH-8001 Zürich, Schweiz.
Fricke (Antiquariat M. und R.), Poststrasse 3, 4000 Düsseldorf 1, Poststrasse 3, 4000 Düsseldorf 1, Deutschland.
Friedländer & Sohn G.m.b.H. (R.), Dessauer Strasse 28–29, 1000 Berlin 61, Deutschland.
Frimanns Antikvariat, Strandboulevarden 166, København, Danmark.
Frisco Antiquariat, Hoofdstraat 5, 9001 AM Grouw, Nederland.
Fritsch (Georg), Postfach 883, A-1010 Wien. (Schönlaterngasse 7), Österreich.
Fritsche (Rüdiger)=Antiquariat Paul Hennings, 2000 Hamburg 1, Deutschland.
Fuchs & Reposo, Librairie Wega, Via Nassa 21, 6900 Lugano, Schweiz.
Fuentes (Patrick), 11 Pourtour des Halles, 8000 Amiens, France.
Fundgruber für Bücherfreunde, Dammtordamm 4, 2000 Hamburg 36, Deutschland.

Furgeri (D.)="Docet", 40126 Bologna, Italia.

G

Gabay (Jacques), 151 bis. rue Saint-Jacques, 75005 Paris, France.
Gabinetto Delle Stampe (Il), Via Montenapoleone 3, 20121 Genova, Italia.
Gaitanides (R.), Wagenburgstrasse 111, 7000 Stuttgart A, Deutschland.
Galantaris (Christian), 15 rue des Saints-Pères, 75006 Paris, France.
Galcante (La), 2 rue Temple, 79000 Niort, France.
Galerie 89 (Librairie), rue de Lyon 89, 89200 Avallon, France.
Galignani (Librairie Française et Étrangère), 224 rue de Rivoli, 75001 Paris, France.
Gallimard (Librairie), 15 boulevard Raspail, 75007 Paris, France.
Gallini, Via Del Conservatorio 17, 20122 Milano, Italia.
Gangloff (Librairie), 13 Auguste Wicky, 68100 Mulhouse, France.
Gangloff (Louis), 20 Place de la Cathédrale, 67000 Strasbourg, France.
Ganseforth (Antiquariat), Hohestrasse 47, 4000 Düsseldorf-Altstadt, Deutschland.
Garisenda Libri & Stampe, S.A.S., Strada Maggiore 14/A, 40125 Bologna, Italia.
Garnier Arnoul (Librairie du Spectacle), 39 rue de Seine, 75006 Paris, France.
Garnman (H.)=Erasmus Antiquariaat en Boek handel, Amsterdam, Nederland.
Gärtner (Bernd)—Kreuzberger Antiquariat, Berlin-Kreuzberg 61, Germany.
Gärtner (Heinz), Marienstrasse 105, D-300 Hannover, Deutschland.
Gason (Pierre-M.), 8 Place de la Victoire, 4880 Anhel, Belgium.
Gätjens (Dieter), Antiquariat, Brahmsallee 28, D-2000 Hamburg 13,
Gauthier (André), 68 rue Faubourg Montmartre, 75009 Paris, France.
Gauthier S.A. (Andre), B.P. 373–09, F 75424 Paris Cedex 09, France.
Gautron (Roberte), 10 rue Sophie-Germain, 75014 Paris, France.
Geisenheyner (Winfried), Postfach 480155, Roseneck 6, D-4400 Münster-Hiltrup,
    Deutschland.
Gelbert (Antiquariat Gundel), St. Apern Strasse 4, 5000 Köln 1, Deutschland.
Geley (Jean-Philippe), 229 rue de Tolbiac 75013, Paris, France.
Gendt B.V. (A. L. van), Qud Huizerweg 4, 1261 BD Blaricum, Nederland.
Gendt Book Auctions N.V. (van), Keizersgracht 96–98, 1015 CV Amsterdam,
    Nederland.
George (Albert)=Cité des Vieux Livres, Besançon, France.
Georgiou & Company (Panayiotis), P.O. 622, Athens, Ellas.
Gerbes (Michel)=Maison J.-P.) Krippler-Muller, Luxembourg.
Gerits Rare Books (A.), Delilaan 5, 1217 HJ Hilversum, Nederland.
Gerits and Son (A.) Rare Books, Hartenstraat 4, 1016 CB Amsterdam, Nederland.
Gerling (Rolf-Peter), Fedelhören 89. 2800 Bremen, Deutschland.
Gerlinghaus (Rainer)=Das Graphik-Kabinett, 4000 Düsseldorf 1, Deutschland.
Gerold & Co., Graben 31, 1011 Wien, Österreich.
Gerritsen (H. G.), Van Welderenstraat 88, Nijmegen, Nederland.
Gerritsma (Bart), 350 Herengracht, Amsterdam, Nederland.
Gerry (Ephraim)=Le Cuisinier, Cookbooks,
Gess (Karl), Kanzleistrasse 5, 7750 Konstanz. (Postfach 190), Deutschland.
Geuthner S.A. 12 rue Vavin, 75006 Paris, France.
Gevaert (Yves), rue du Pinson 160, 1170 Bruxelles, Belgium.
Gibert Jeune, 23 Quai Saint-Michel, 75005 Paris, France.
Giglio (Libreria), Via Convenevole 37, 50047 Prato (Firenze), Italia.
Gilhofer Buch und Kunstantiquariat K G. Bognergasse 2, 1010 Wien, Österreich.
Gilhofer & Ranschburg G.m.b.H., Sternegg 5, 6005 Luzern, Schweiz.
Gilquin (Raymond), 34 rue Charonne, 75011 Paris, France.
Gilsing (Antiquariat Heinrich), Neuensteinerstrasse 17, 4053 Basel, Schweiz.

Gilsing (Ingrid)=Antiquariat Heinrich Gilsing, Basel, Schweiz.
Girand (François), 76 rue de Seine, 75006 Paris, France.
Giraud-Badin (Librairie), 22 rue Guynemer, 75006 Paris, France.
Givaudan (Claude), rue du Soleil Levant 3, CH-1204 Genève,
Gladsaxe Antikvariat, Søborg Hovedgade 195, København, Danmark.
Glavey (M.)=Parsifal [S.A.R.L.], 75006 Paris. France.
Godai Buchhandels Ges.m.b.H., Mariahilfer Strasse 169, 1150 Wien, Österreich.
Goerigk (W.)=F. Dörling, 2000 Hamburg 36, Deutschland.
Goffin (Adrienne)=Librairie au Vieux Quarter, B-5000 Namur, Belgium.
Goldau (Gerard), Gasteig 4, 8022 Grünwald, Deutschland.
Gomis (Libreria Angel), Luna 17 Y Estrella 6, Madrid 13, Spain.
Gomis (Libreria Francisco), Claudio Moyano 27, Madrid 7, Spain.
Gonnelli & Figli (Luigi), Via Ricasoli 14 rosso, Firenze, Italia.
Gonot (René), Librairie Saint-Augustin, 99 boulevard Haussmann, 75008 Paris, France.
Goossens (Paul), Greenhillstraat 45, 8320 Brugge, Belgium.
Gothier, Librairie Universitaire (Fernand), place du 20 Août 11, 4000 Liège, Belgie.
Gothier (Paul), rue Bonne Fortune 3 et 5, Liège, Belgie.
Göttinger Antiquariat, Mauerstrasse 16/17, 3400 Göttingen, Deutschland.
Gottschalk (F.), Krugerstrasse 10, 1010 Wien, Österreich.
Götz (Antiquariat), Nernstrasse 16, 2800 Bremen 33, Deutschland.
Govi (Libreria Alberto), C.P. 321 Centro, I-41100 Modena, Italy.
Gozzini di Pietro Chellini (Libreria Oreste), Via Ricasoli 49, 50122 Firenze, Italia.
Graaf (Antiquariaat de), Zuideinde 40, 2421 AK Nieuwkoop, Nederland.
Grafik-Antikvariatet, Skomakargatan 24, 111 29 Stockholm, Sverige.
Granata (Libreria), Reyes Carolicos 8, Almeria, España.
Grand-Chêne (Librairie du), Chemin de Montagny, 1603 Aran, Schweiz.
Grandmaison (Antoine), Librairie "Les Arcades", 8 rue de Castiglione, 75001 Paris, France.
Granier G.m.b.H. (Antiquariat), Welle 9, 4800 Bielefeld 1, Deutschland.
Granier (Jochen), Buch und Kunstauktionen, Gadderbaumer Strasse 22, 4800 Bielefeld 1, Deutschland.
Graphik-Kabinett (Das), Humboldtstrasse 80, 4000 Düsseldorf 1, Deutschland.
Grauers (S.)=Samlaren Antikvariat & Konsthandel, Göteborg, Schweden.
Gravüre (Die), Rüttenschneider Strasse 56, 4300 Essen 1, Deutschland.
Gregoriades (B.N.), Rue Phidias 2. Athènes 142, Ellas.
Greiser (Galerie Olaf), Schröderstrasse 14, 6900 Heidelberg, Deutschland.
Grenier à Livres, 50 Passage Jouffroy, 75009 Paris, France.
Grenier du Collectionneur (Le), avenue Orban 238, 1150 Bruxelles, Belgie.
Grifoni (G. C.), Via Emilia Levante 13, 40139 Bologna, Italia.
Gron Boekenbeurs BV., 61/II Oude Ebbingestraat, Groningen, Nederlands.
Gross (Erich)=Göttinger Antiquariat. 3400 Göttingen, Deutschland.
Grubb's Antikvariat (J.), Nørregade 47, Dk-1165 København-K, Danmark.
Grundmann (Herbert)=Bouvier Universitätsbuchhandlung G.m.b.H., 5300 Bonn, Deutschland.
Gruppo (Gerald), 13 rue Puech Beringuier, 81000 Albi, France.
Gsellius'sche Buch-, Antiquar- und Globenhandlung G.m.b.H., Hertastrasse 16, 1000 Berlin 37, Deutschland.
Guénégaud, S.A.R.L. (Librairie), 10 rue de l'Odéon, 75006 Paris, France.
Guida (Libreria A.), Via Port'Alba, 20/24, I-80134 Napoli, Italia.
Guillaume & Cie., S.A.R.L. (Michel), Librairie Generale du Calvados, 98 rue Saint-Pierre, 14000 Caen, France.

Guillaume (Mme.)=La Maison du Livre, Angoulême, France.
Gumbert (H.L.) =J. L. Beijers B.V., 3512 HT Utrecht, Nederland.
Guntern. (Antiquariat Albert) Luzern, Hertensteinstrasse 17, Schweiz.
Günther (Max), Charlottenbrunnerstrasse 5a, 1000 Berlin 33, Deutschland.
Gustafsson (J.), Volden 12, 8000 Aarhus-C, Danmark.
Gustavsson (Sigurdur), Gardastracti 40, 101 Reykjavík, Island.
Gute Buch (Das), Rosengasse 10, 8001 Zürich, Schweiz.
Gutenberg Buchhandlung (Johannes), Grosse Bleiche 29, 6500 Mainz. (Auch In der Universität). Prop: Josef A. Kohl, Deutschland.
Guyer-Halter (Dr. Annemarie), Auf Der Mauer 1, 8000 Zürich 1, Schweiz.
Guzman (Antonio de)=Libreria Antigua y Moderna, Madrid, Spain.
Gysbers en van Loon, Bakkerstraat 7A, Arnhem, Nederland.

H

Habelt, G.m.b.H. (Dr. Rudolf), am Buchenhang 1, 5300 Bonn. (Postfach 150104), Deutschland.
Hafen (Antiquariat am), Bernhardt-Nacht-Strasse 95, 2000 Hamburg 4,
Hagelin Antikvariat AB, P.O. Box 3321, 10366 Stockholm, Schweden.
Hagelstamin Antikvaarinen Kirjakauppa, Fredrikinkatu 35, Helsinki 12, Finland.
Hagen B.V. (Antiquariaat Bert), Molenweide 24, 1902 CH Castricum, Nederland.
Hagen (Bert), Herenstraat 38, 1015 CB Amsterdam, Nederland.
Hagenstein (E.), Schleisheimerstrasse 9, München 2, Deutschland.
Hakkert (Adolf M.), Calle Alfambra 26, Las Palmas España.
Habelt (Antiquariat Gero), Königsheimstrasse 12, 5300 Bonn 1, Deutschland.
Hallens Antikvariat, Köpmangatan 4, 11131 Stockholm, Sweden.
Halosar (Karl M.), Margaretenstrasse 35, 1040 Wien, Österreich.
Hamburgensien-Meyer, Poststrasse 2-4, 2000 Hamburg 36, Deutschland.
Hamecher (Horst), Goethestrasse 74, 3500 Kassel, Deutschland.
Hammerstein (H.), Türkenstrasse 37, München 40, Deutschland.
Hampartz (Edouard), l'Epi de Blé, 90 rue de Lévis, 75017 Paris, France.
Hamre (J.I.)=Antikvariatet Frederiksdal, København, Danmark.
Hamre (Jens)=Holte Antikvariat, DK-2840 Holte, Denmark.
Hankard (Jean-Jacques), 25 rue de la Paix, 1050 Bruxelles, Belgie.
Hannak (Antiquariat), Schlossbergstrasse 4 D-8110 Murnau, Deutschland.
Bolliger Bücher und Grafik (Hans), Lenggstrasse 14, Zürich, Suisse.
Hanselaar (Hans J.)=Antiquariaat Minerva, 's-Gravenhage, Nederland.
Hansen (Erik)=Gladsaxe Antikvariat, København, Danmark.
Harcks Antikvariat, Fiolstraede 34, 1171 København-K, Danmark.
Harlinghausen (Antiquariat), Arndtstrasse 5, 4500 Osnabrück, Deutschland.
Harms (Ernst und Jochen D.)=W. Mauke Söhne, 2000 Hamburg 36, Deutschland.
Harrassowitz (Otto), Taunusstrasse 5, 6200 Wiesbaden, Deutschland.
Hartlebern (A.), Schwarzenbergstrasse 6, Wien, Österreich.
Hartmann (Gebrüder), Schwarzer Bär 7, D-3000 Hannover, Deutschland.
Hartmund (Nils), Gammel Kongevej 163, DK-1850 København, Danmark.
Hartung (Karl)=Karl & Faber, 8000 München 2, Deutschland.
Hartung und Karl, Karolinenplatz 5A, 8000 München 2, Deutschland.
Hartwig (Robert), Pestalozzistr. 23, D-1000 Berlin-Charlottenburg 12, Germany.
Hasbach (A. L.), Wollzeile 9 und 29, Wien 1, Österreich.
Haschtmann (W.), Antiquariat für Rechtswissenschaft, Knüll 15, 2306 Schonberg, Deutschland.
Hase (Anna-Maria)=August Hase, 6000 Frankfurt-am-Main, Deutschland.

Hase (August), im Trutz 2, 6000 Frankfurt-am-Main, Deutschland.
Hassfurther, Hohenstaufengasse 7, A-1010 Wien, Österrich.
Haubensack (Hans), Froschaugasse 11, CH-8001 Zürich, Schweitz.
Haudenschild (Elsbeth)=Galerie Pulitzer und Knöll, CH-3011 Bern, Schweiz.
Haus der Bücher, AG, "Erasmushaus", Bäumleingasse 18, 4000 Basel, Schweiz.
Hauser (Elsa), Schellingstrasse 17, 8000 München 13, Deutschland.
Hauswedell und Nolte, Pöseldorferweg 1, 2000 Hamburg 13, Deutschland.
Hauvette (Bernard et Natasha)=Librairie Rivarès, Pau, France.
Heck (V. A.), Kärntner Ring 14, 1010 Wien, Österreich.
Heckenhauer (J.J.), Holzmarkt 5, 7400 Tübingen. (Postfach 1728), Deutschland.
Hedenborg's Antikvariat, Dronning Margarethesvej 4, Roskilde, Danmark.
Heger (Rudolf), Wollezeile 2, 1010 Wien 1, Österreich.
Hegnauer und Schwarzenbach, Kramgasse 16, 3011 Bern, Schweiz.
Heidrich G.m.b.H. (Leopold), Plankengasse 7, Wien 1, Österreich.
Heinen (P.), Dehnhaide 1, 2000 Hamburg 76, Deutschland.
Heinimann & Co., Kirchgasse 17, 8000 Zürich 1, (ehemals Hans Raunhardt), Schweiz.
Heinze (Walter), Bismarckstrasse 23, 2900 Oldenburg, Deutschland.
Heinzelmann und Herrmann, Alexanderstrasse 157, 7000 Stuttgart 1, Deutschland.
Heitz (P. H.), Postfach 80, Basel 4006, Schweiz.
Hellmor (Antikvariat Carl), Box 648 52101 Falkoüping, Sweden.
Helluin (Serge), 11 rue Leon-Blum, 80000 Amiens, France.
Helsingin Antikvariaatti, Mechelininkatu 19, 00100 Helsinki, Suomi.
"Hemus", 6 Rouski Boulevard, Sofia, Bulgariya.
Henke (Manfred), Motzstr. 59, D-1000 Berlin-Schöneberg 30, Germany.
Henle (Mady)=Zeil-Antiquariat, 6000 Frankfurt-am-Main, Deutschland.
Henner (Librairie), 9 rue Henner, 75009 Paris, France.
Hennies und Zinkelsen, Marienstrasse 14 und 18, D-3000 Hannover, Deutschland.
Hennig (Theodor), Motzstr. 25, D-1000 Berlin-Schöneberg 30, Germany.
Hennings (Antiquariat Paul), Altstädter Strasse 15, 2000 Hamburg 1, Deutschland.
Hennwack (Antiquariat), Langenscheidtstrasse 4, D-1000 Berlin-Schöneberg 62, Deutschland.
Herbinet (Jacques), 39 rue de Constantinople, 75008 Paris, France.
Hermans (Elisabeth)=Hendrik van Veldeke, 3500 Hasselt, Belgium.
Hermes (Elke)=Buchhandlung Kubiak, Berlin-Schöneberg 62, Germany.
Hero (Hans-Erich), Wielandstrasse 13, 1000 Berlin 12, Deutschland.
Hertling (Edmund), Zum Wingert 15, D-620g Aarbergen, Deutschland.
Haffner (Hervé), 6 rue Serane, 34000 Montpellier, France.
Hervé (Librairie Ancienne), 62 rue Pierre Larousse, 75014 Paris, France.
Hesperia (Libreria), Plaza de Los Sitios 10, Zaragoza. Espanña.
"Hesperus", Jakobstrasse 20, D-3000 Hannover, Deutschland.
Hess (Arnold), Galerie zur Krone, Zürcherstrasse 183, CH-8500 Frauenfeld, Schweiz.
Hesselink (S. S.)=Forum B.V., Utrecht, Netherlands.
Heuberger (Antiquariat), Düppelstrasse, Köln-Deutz 21, Deutschland.
Heybutzki (Werner), Pfeilstrasse 8, 5000 Köln 1, Deutschland.
Hiard (Bernard)=l'Intermédiaire du Livre, Paris, France.
Higny (D.)=La Bouquinerie des Carmes, 4000 Liege, Belgium.
Higny (D.)=Varia Librairie, 4000 Liege, Belgium.
Hilderbrandt (Helmut)=Struppe und Winckler, 1000 Berlin 30, Deutschland.

Hill (Theo), Schildergasse 107, 5000 Köln, Deutschland.
Hillenbrand (E.), Rindermarkt 10, München 2, Deutschland.
Hillerød Antikvariat, Slotsgade 57, DK-3400 Hillerød, Denmark.
Hiltunen (Antikvaarinen Kirjakauppa Seppo), Viherniemenkatu 3, Helsinki 53, Finland.
Hirlam (R. & G.)=Librairie des Deux Gares, 75010 Paris, France.
Histórica e Ultramarina LDA [J. C. Silva] (Livraria), Travessa da Queimada 28, 1200– Lisboa 2, Portugal.
Historische Mariteme Boekhandel, Kleine Houtstraat, Haarlem, Nederland.
Hobbeling (Theo.)=Th. Stenderhoff & Co., 4400 Münster, Deutschland.
Hobucher (D.) Alt Rödcllgeun 13, 6000 Frankfurt am Main 90,
Höchtberger. Mauerkircherstr. 28, 8000 München 80, Deutschland
Hoeter (Frédéric van), 61 Rue Saint-Quentin, Bruxelles 1040, Belgie.
Höfels, OHG. (Oskar), Seilerstätte 18, 1010 Wien, Österreich.
Hofer (M. und R.), Münstergasse 56, CH-3011 Bern, Schweiz.
Hoffmann (Ernst), Weissadlergasse 3, 6000 Frankfurt-am-Main, Deutschland.
Hoffmann (R.)=Gilhofer Buch- und Kunstantiquariat K.G., 1010 Wien, Österreich.
Hofmann (Wilhelm), Bismarckstrasse 98, 6700 Ludwigshafen, Deutschland.
Hofner (Gerhard), Kleinweidenmühle 10, Nürnberg 90, Deutschland.
Höfs (Johannes), Gertrudenstrasse 33, Köln 1, Deutschland.
Hofweg (Antiquariat A M), Hofweg 57, 2000 Hamburg 76, Deutschland.
Hollmann (Klaus)=Antiquariat im Kudamm-Karree, D-1000 Berlin-Charlottenburg 15, Deutschland.
Höllrigl (Eduard), Sigmund Haffner Gasse 10, 5010 Salzburg. Österreich.
Holms Antikvariat (Greta), Norrlandsgatan 16, Stockholm-C, Schweden.
Holstein Antiquariat G.m.b.H. (Jürgen), Postfach 68, Feldafingerstrasse 37, 8134 Pöcking, Deutschland.
Holte Antikvariat, Kongevej 43, DK-2840 Holte, Denmark.
Hölzl, K.G. (Karl), Seilergasse 3, 1010 Wien, Österreich.
Hommerson (W. J.)=Argus Antiquarian Booksellers, 2670 Baarn, Nederland.
Hommerson (W.)=van Gendt Book Auctions N.V. Amsterdam, Nederland.
Honkanen (Antikvaria A.), Vironkatu 8, Helsinki, Finland.
Horodisch (Dr. A.)=Erasmus Antiquariaat en Boekhandel, Amsterdam, Nederland.
Hosman (Dr. B.M.M.)=Athenaeum Antiquarian Booksellers, Amsterdam, Nederland.
Houthakker (Bernard), Rokin 98, Amsterdam, Nederland.
Hovingh & Zn. (Antiquariaat C.), Kleine Houtstraat 50, 2011DP Haarlem, Nederland.
Huetz de Lemps (J.), 70 rue du Cherche-Midi, 75006 Paris, France.
Hüfner (A.), Theresienpl 1, Nürnberg 1, Deutschland.
Hugendubel (H.), Salvatorplatz 2, 8000 München 2, Deutschland.
Hugues. 1 rue de Furstenberg, 75006 Paris, France.
Huillet, Manoir de Beaupre (Yvette), Route de Monts, 37250 Veigne, France.
Huizenga (M. L.), Oudez. Achterburgwal 156, 1012 DW Amsterdam, Nederland.
Hult (Harald)=Antikvariat Blå Tornet, Stockholm, Sverige.
Humaniora Antiqua, Herengracht 242, Amsterdam, Netherlands.
Krippler-Muller (Maison J.-P.), 52A boulevard Grande-Duchesse Charlotte, Luxembourg, Luxembourg.
Hüning (Antiquariat B.), Rothenburg 52, 4400 Münster, Deutschland.
Huret (Jean-Étienne)=Le Tour du Monde, Paris, France.

Hyytiäinen=Kirjakuja Ky, Helsinki, Suomi.

I

Iberia (Antiquariat), Hirschengraben 6, 3001 Berne, Schweiz.
Iliu (Alte Graphik Julia F.), Barer Strasse 46, 8000 München 40, Deutschland.
Dell'Impero (Libreria Antiquaria), Corso Rinascimento 63, 00186 Roma, Italia.
In den Eenhoorn, Ezelstraat 84, Bruges, Belgie.
Informatio, Seilergasse 19, A-1010 Wien, Österreich.
Interlibrum Estalishment, Schloss-Strasse 6, Fl 9490 Vaduz. Liechtenstein.
l'Intermédiaire du Livre, 88 rue Bonaparte, 75006 Paris, France.
l'Invitation au Voyage, 15 Quai Saint-Michel, 75005 Paris, France.
Israel (B. M.), Prentenkabinet, Singel 379, Amsterdam, Netherlands.
Israel, B.V. (B. M.), Boekhandel en Antiquariaat, N.Z. Voorburgwal 264, 1012 RS Amsterdam, Nederland.
Israel (Maarten J.), P.O. Box 8, 1110 AA Dieman, Netherlands.
Israel (N.), Keizersgracht 489–491, Amsterdam, Nederland.
Israel (Nico)=A. Asher & Co., B.V., Amsterdam, Nederland.
Iversen (Thor), Skippergatan 2, Oslo, Norge.

J

Jacobs (Antoine)=Librairie des Elephants, 1000 Bruxelles, Belgium.
Jadis et Naguère, 166 Faubourg Saint-Honoré, 75008 Paris, France.
Jäger (Antiquariat Ruthild), Steinweg 17, 2120 Lüneburg-Oedeme, Deutschland.
Jamin (Anneliese)=Ed. Walz, 8000 München 22, Deutschland.
Jammes (Paul), 3 rue Gozlin, 75006 Paris, France.
Jansson (G.)=Lilla Antikvariatet, Malmö-C, Schweden.
Jaugeon (Andre)=Morvran, Bretagne, France.
Javelle (Claude), 32 rue de Provence, 75009 Paris, France.
Jean-Léo=Le Grenier du Collectionneur, 1150 Bruxelles, Belgie.
Jehanno (Xavier), 4 Place de l'Eglise, 78430 Louveciennes, France.
Jensen (Helge), Bogensevej 485, 5270 Odense N, Denmark.
Jensen (N.)=Brønshøj Antikvariat, København, Danmark.
Jensen (Solv.), Borgbjervej 11, København, Denmark.
Jentsch (Ralph D.I.)=Kunstgalerie Esslingen, D-8000 München 80, Deutschland.
Jeschke (Hans-Joachim), Winterfeldstrasse 51, D-1000 Berlin-Schöneberg 30, Germany.
Jeske (Wolfgang)=Weddinger Antiquariat, Berlin-Wedding 65, Germany.
Jessen (Jess T.)=Nansensgade Antikvariat, København, Denmark.
Johanson-Thor, AB. (Gunnar), Ellinge, 24100 Eslöv, Sverige.
Joly (Librairie J.), 6 rue Victor-Cousin, 75005 Paris, France.
Jones Antikvariat, Nortullsgatan 3, 11329 Stockholm, Schweden.
Jong (Antiquariaat R. de), Kruisweg 38a 2011 LD Haarlem, Nederland.
Jongbloed (A.)=Juridische Boekhandel and Antiquariaat, 2311 SL Leiden, Nederland.
Jongbloed (K. P.)=Juridisch Antiquariaat, 's-Gravenhage, Nederland.
Jonsson & Co. H. F. (Snaebjorn), Hafnarstraeti 4 Reykjavík. (P.O. Box 1131), Island.
Jørgensen (H.)=Antikvariatet Boghytten, København, Danmark.

Joyaux (Camille), 55 rue de la Scellerie, 37000 Tours, France.
Juhel-Douet (Mme.), 3 rue d'Angleterre, 41000 Blois, France.
Junk B. V. (Antiquariaat), Van Eeghenstraat 129, 1071 GA Amsterdam, Nederland.
Jürdens (J.E.) Hillmannplatz, 2800 Bremen, Deutschland.
Juridisch Antiquariaat, L Noordeinde 39, 2514 GC 'S-Gravenhage, Nederland.
Juridische Boekhandel and Antiquariaat, Kloksteeg 4, 2311 SL Leiden, Nederland.

K

Kaabers Antikvariat, Skindergade 34, 1159 København-K, Danmark.
Kaak (Antiquariat), Ole Hoop 9, 2000 Hamburg 55, Deutschland.
Kairôs (Libreria Filosofica), Studio d'Arte, 11219 Milano-Isola, via Baldinucci 6, 20158 Milano, Italia.
Kaldewey (Antiquariat Gunnar), Poststrasse 3, 4000 Düsseldorf 1, Deutschland.
Kaldewey (Sibylle), Poststrasse 3, D-4000 Düsseldorf 1, Deutschland.
Kampf (Heinz Hubertus), Wasserwerkgasse 31, Postfach 246. CH-3011 Bern, Schweiz.
Kampintorin Antikvariaatti, Fredrikinkatu 63, Helsinki, Suomi.
Kan (Drs. A.Γ.)=Humaniora Antiqua, Amsterdam, Nederland.
Kapp (Adolf), Bahnhofstrasse 17, 7407 Rottenburg. (Postfach 46), Deutschland.
Karavias (Dion P.), 67 Aschpiou Street, 10680 Athens, Ellas.
Karl & Faber, Karolinenplatz 5A, 8000 München 2, Deutschland.
Karl-Marx-Buchhandlung (Antiquariat der), Karl-Marx-Allee 78–84, DDR-1017 Berlin, DDR.
Karl Marx Buchhandlung, G.m.b.H., Jordanstrasse 11, 6000 Frankfurt 90, Deutschland.
Karlstad Antikvariat, Östra Torggatan 1, 652 24 Karlstad, Schweden.
Karsch (Florian)=Galerie Nierendorf, 1000 Berlin 12, Deutschland.
Katsicalis (Christos), Zambakis Bookshop, 14 Massalias Street, Athens, Ellas.
Katzbichler (Dr. Emil), Wilhelm-ring 7. 8201 Frasdorf, Deutschland.
Kauffmann (Librarie), 28 Stadium Street, Athens-132, Ellas.
Kauppamakasiin, Vuorimiehenkatu 10, Helsinki, Finland.
Kee (Annelies), Spuistraat 125, 1012 SV Amsterdam, Nederland.
Keip, KG Wissenschaftliches Antiquariat Hainerweg 46–48, 6000 Frankfurt-am-Main 70, Deutschland.
Kellermann (Elisabeth)=Die Gravüre, 4300 Essen 1, Deutschland
Kemmer (Antiquariat), Eppendorferweg 248, 2000 Hamburg 20, Deutschland.
Kerangué et Pollès, 34 rue Vivienne, 75002 Paris, France.
Kerangué (Pierre de)=Les Chevau Légers, Paris, France.
Kerler (Heinrich), Platzgasse 26, 7900 Ulm. (Postfach 2668), Deutschland.
Kern (Elsa)=Elsa Hauser, 8000 München 13, Deutschland.
Kerssemakers (Leo J. H.)=Alfa Antiquarian Booksellers, Nijmegen, Nederland.
Kerssemakers (P.H.)=Antiquariaat Hieronymus Bosch, Amsterdam, Nederland.
Keskustan Antikvariaatti, 1 Yrjönkatu, Helsinki. F.A.F, Suomi.
Ketterer (Galerie Wolfgang), Briennerstrasse 25, 8000 München 2, Deutschland.
Kettunen (M.)=Kirja-Kettunen, 04200 Kerava, Suomi.
Ketz (Hans-Jürgen), Scharnhorststrasse 92, D-4400 Münster, Deutschland.
Kiefer (Antiquariat Peter), Kirchstrasse 4, D-7537 Remchingen-Wilferdingen, Deutschland.
Kieffer (Librairie René), 46 rue Saint-André des Arts, 75006 Paris, France.

Kienreich (Jos. A.), Sackstrasse 6 (im Halbstock), 8011 Graz, Österreich.
Kiepert G.m.b.H. Hardenbergstrasse 4–5, 1000 Berlin 12, Deutschland.
Kirja-Kettunen, Tuusulantie 2, 04200 Kerava, Suomi.
Kirjakuja Ky, Uudenmaankatu 4–6, Helsinki, Suomi.
Kirkop (Frank), 106 Blanche Street, Sliema, Malta.
Kistner (E. und R.), Weinmarkt 6, 8500 Nürnberg, Deutschland.
Kistner (Heiko)=M. Edelmann, 8500 Nürnberg 1, Deutschland.
Kitzinger (J.), Schellingstrasse 25, 8000 München, Deutschland.
Kjaer (Ole), Blaagaardsplads Antikvariat, København, Denmark.
Klaussner (Antiquariat), Professor-Kurt-Huber-Strasse 19, 8032 Gräfelfing (München), Deutschland.
Kleinert (Rudolf), Alladorf No. 66, D-8656 Thurnau, Deutschland.
Klette & Kölsch (Antiquariat), Markelstrasse 58, D-1000 Berlin-Steglitz 41, Deutschland.
Klittich-Pfankuch (Antiquariat A.), Kleine Burg 12, 3300 Braunschweig, Deutschland.
Klügel (Walter), Postfach 40, Wimm 15, Schreiberghof, A-5201 Seekirchen, bei Salzburg, Österreich.
Knagsteds Antikvariat, Kompagnistraede 8, 1208 København-K, Danmark.
Knapps (Gertrud)=Max Günther, 1000 Berlin 33, Deutschland.
Knessl (Renate)=Cottage Antiquariat R. Knessl, A-1180 Wien, Österreich.
Knödler (Karl), Katherinenstrasse 8–10, 7410 Reutlingen, Deutschland.
Knudsen (J.)=Cabinet der Geschichte, 2000 Hamburg 36, Deutschland.
Knuf (Antiquariaat Frits), P.O.B. 720, 4116-ZJ Buren, Netherlands.
Kobberstikhuset, Kronprinsensgade 4, København, Danmark.
Köbelin. Schellingstrasse 99, 8000 München 40, Deutschland.
Koch (Antiquariat Jürgen), 1 Mittelweg 9, Frankfurt am Main, Deutschland.
Koch (Hans Horst), Kurfürstendamm 216, 1000 Berlin 15, Deutschland.
Kocher-Benzing (Dr. F.)=Stuttgarter Antiquariat, 7000 Stuttgart 1, Deutschland.
Koerner G.m.b.H. (Valentin), H.-Sielckenstrasse 36, 7570 Baden-Baden, Deutschland.
Kohl (Joseph A.)=Johannes Gutenberg Buchhandlung, 6500 Mainz, Deutschland.
Kohlhauer (Carl-Ernst), Graser Weg 2, 8805 Feuchtwangen, Deutschland.
KOK en Zn (A.), 14–18 Oude Hoogstraat, Amsterdam, Nederland.
Kolb (Otto), Von-Mann-Strasse 2, 8670 Hof, Deutschland.
König (Antiquariat), Untere Schmiedgasse 8, Nürnberg 70, Deutschland.
Körner (V.), Kettenhofweg 57, Frankfurt am Main 1, Deutschland.
Kornfeld & Co., Laupenstrasse 41, CH-3008 Bern, Schweiz.
Köhl (Peter H.), Dudweiler Strasse 10, 6600 Saarbrücken 3, Deutschland.
Kowallik (Brigitta), Klarissenstrasse 5, 4040 Neuss, Deutschland.
Kraemer und Hansen (Antiquariat), Arndstrasse 7, D-4500 Osnabrück, Deutschland.
Kraus-Thompson-Organization=Dr. Martin Sändig G.m.b.H., 6200 Wiesbaden, Deutschland.
Krebser A.G., Bälliz 64, 3601 Thun, Schweiz.
Kreuzberger Antiquariat, Yorckstr. 75, D-1000 Berlin-Kreuzberg 61, Germany.
Krey, Ges.m.b.H. (R.), Graben 13, 1010 Wien 1, Österreich.
Krieg Verlag K.G. Kärntnerstrasse 4, 1010 Wien, Österreich.
Kristjonsson, Antikvariat (Bragi), P.O. Box 775, Skolavördustigur 20, Reykjavík, Island.
Kruger (Boekhandel Antiquariaat), Achter de Hoofdwacht 7, Nijmegen, Netherlands.

Ksiegarnia Antykwaryczna, Nowy Swiat 61, Warszawa, Polska.
Kuballe (Reinhard), Sutthauser Strasse 19, D-4500 Osnabrück, Deutschland.
Kubiak (Buchhandlung), Martin-Luther-Str. 125, D-1000 Berlin-Schöneberg 62, Germany.
Kudamm-Karree (Antiquariat im), Kurfürstendamm 206-208, D-1000 Berlin-Charlottenburg 15, Deutschland.
Kuhn, Breitscheidstrasse 49, Nürnberg 40, Deutschland.
Kühn (Carlos)=Carl Wegner, 1000 Berlin 62, Deutschland.
Kuhrdt (Wilhelm), Paulusstrasse 28, 4800 Bielefeld, Deutschland.
Kullman (Hermann)=Armarium Buchhandlung und Antiquariat, 2313 Raisdorf über Kiel, Deutschland.
Kullmann (H.), Zum See 10, 2313 Raisdorf, Deutschland.
Kullmann (Hermann)="Armarium" Buchhandlung und Antiquariat, 4000 Düsseldorf 1,
Kultura, P.O. Box 149, H-1389 Budapest. Fö Utca. 32, Budapest 1, Magyarország.
Kuppitsch (Akademische Buchhandlung), Schottengasse 4, Wien, Österreich.
Küsters (Karl-Heinz), Gustav-Adolf-Strasse 12, 3000 Hannover, Deutschland.
Kuttner (Walter), Lohmühler Berg 31, 5620 Velbert-:Neviges 15, Deutschland.
Kuyper (Bubb), Kleine Houstraat 60, 2011 DP Haarlem, Netherlands.
Kvariaatti, Hameenkatu 16, 20500 Turku, Suomi.
Kyburz (Heinz)=Schlöhlein G.m.h.H., CH-4003 Basel, Schweiz.
Kyrieleis (Hans-Werner)=R. Friedländer & Sohn G.m.b.H., 1000 Berlin 61, Deutschland.

L

Laatzen (Hermann), Warburgstrasse 18, 2000 Hamburg 36, Deutschland.
Lacaze (M.-J.)=Pont Traversé, 75006 Paris, France.
Laffitte (Jeanne), 25 Cours d'Estienne-d'Orves, 13001 Marseille, France.
Laffitte Libraire (Henri), 13 rue de Buci, 75006 Paris, France.
Laget (Jaques)=Librair des Arts et Metiers, 28210 Nogent le Roi, France.
Laget (Librairie Leonce), 75 rue de Rennes, 75006 Paris, France.
Lagnel-Tastemain, 25 Boulevard Marechal-Leclerc, 14300 Caen, France.
Lahden Antikvaarinen Kirjakauppa, Vesijärvenkatu 12, 15110 Lahti, Suomi.
Lamed Bookstore, 11 Lange Hofstraat, Zutphen, Nederland.
Lammens (Charles)=Librairie A. Rombaut, 9000 Gent, Belgie.
Lamongie (Georges), 2 rue de la Nation, 24000 Perigueux, France.
Landré (G.N.), Muziekboekhandel & Antiquariaat, Anjeller Sdwarsstraat 36 1015 NR Amsterdam, Netherlands.
Lang & Cie A.G. (Herbert), Münzgraben 2, 3000 Bern 7, Schweiz.
Lange und Springer G.m.b.H. & Co., Antiquariat, Otto-Suhr-Allee 26–28, D-1000 Berlin 10, Deutschland.
Langer (Antiquariat Wolfgang), Postfach 521, 8001 Zürich, Schweiz.
Langlais (Roger), 47 ter rue Orsel, 75018 Paris, France.
Languedoc (Bouquinerie du), 12 rue de l'Université, 34000 Montpellier, France.
Lanzen (A.), 19 Cathedral Street, Sliema, Malta, Malta.
Lapiccirella (Leonardo), 3 via Tornabuoni, 50123 Firenze, Italia.
Lardanchet (Librairie), 100 rue de Faubourg Saint-Honoré, 75008 Paris, France.
Lardanchet (Librairie), 5 Route de Limonest, 69370 Saint-Didier au Mont d'Or, France.

Larsen (Kjeld), Enghavevej 5, København, Danmark.
Lassare (Edmond), 1 bis rue de la Chaise, 75007 Paris, France.
Laube (August), Trittligasse 19, 8001 Zürich, Schweiz.
Laucournet (Marcel), 45 boulevard Carnot, 87000 Limoges, France.
Leanders Antivariat, Storagatan 44-B, 72212 Västeras, Sweden.
Lecointre et Denis Ozanne (Didier), 9 rue de Tournon, 75006 Paris, France.
Lecomte (Marcel), 17 rue de Seine, 75006 Paris, France.
Lefebvre, 38 rue de la Paroisse, 78000 Versailles, France.
Lefebvre (Librairie), 1 rue Lucien-Pean, 45750 Saint-Pryvé-Saint-Mesmin, France.
Legende (La), 58 rue d'Aubagne, 13001 Marseille, France.
Liebmann (Dr. Konrad), Lortzingstrasse 1, 4500 Osnabrück, Deutschland.
Leissle (Peter), Daiserstrasse 40, München 70, Deutschland.
Leisten (Günther), St. Engelbertstrasse 24, D-5068 Odenthal-Voiswinkel, Deutschland.
Lelant (Pierre), 18 rue Bertin, 49000 Angers, France.
Leliefeld Muziekantiquariaten, 212 Riouwstraat, 's–Gravenhage, Nederland.
Lemmers (S.C.), van Bönninghausenlaan 16, 2161 Et Lisse, Nederland.
Lengertz' Antikvariat-Bokhandel i Lund AB, St. Gråbrödersgatan 13, 222 22 Lund, Sverige.
Lengertz' Antikvariat Gösta Janson, Regementsgatan 6, 211 42, Malmö, Sverige.
Lequeltel (Gerard), 6 rue d'Amboise, 75002 Paris, France.
Lerner (Hartmut)=Libresso, Antiquariat an der Universität, 2000 Hamburg 13, Deutschland.
'Les Arcades' (Librairie), 8 rue de Castiglione, F-75001 Paris, France.
Lester (Maurice), 13 bis rue du Cygne (Marché aux Fleurs), 28000 Chartres, France.
Lestringant, 123 rue Général-Leclerc, 76000 Rouen, France.
Leuner (Antiquariat), Bishofsnadel 15, 2800 Bremen, Deutschland.
Leuwer (Franz), Am Wall 171, 2800 Bremen, Deutschland.
Levilliers (Arnold), 118 route de Chartres (RN 188), 91400 Gometz-le-Chatel (Essone), France.
Levy (Jacques), 46 rue d'Alésia, 75014 Paris, France.
Lévy (Yves)=l'Ane d'Or, Vigny, France.
Leyerzapf (A. & G.)=Antiquariaat "Die Schmiede", Amsterdam, Netherlands.
Librairie des Galeries, Galerie du Roi, 2, 1000 Bruxelles, Belgique.
Librairie des Victoires, 4 bis Place des Petits Pères, 75002 Paris, France
Librairie du Pont Neuf R.G., 1 rue Dauphine, 75006 Paris, France.
Librairie K, 17 rue Mazarine, 13100 Aix en Provence, France.
Libresso, Antiquariat an der Universität, Binderstrasse 24, 2000 Hamburg 13, Deutschland.
Libri, 20 rue du Pont, 71000 Macon, France.
Libris Antikvariatet, Kommendörsgatan 14, 10243 Stockholm. (P.O. Box 5123), Schweden.
Licosa Antiquariato, Via Lamarmora 45, 50121 Firenze, Italia.
Lidis (Studio Bibliografico), Foro Bonaparte 12, 20121 Genova, Italia.
Lie Antikvariat (Rolv.), Berglyveien 4b, Oslo, Norge.
Liebermann (B.)=Société Hébraica Judaica, Paris, France.
Liebing G.m.b.H. & Co.. Postfach 5840, Werner-von-Siemmens-Strasse 5, 8700 Würzburg, Deutschland.
Lilla Antikvariatet, Södra Förstadsgatan 20, 21143 Malmö-C, Schweden.

Lincke (Claus), Königsallee 96, 4000 Düsseldorf, Deutschland.
Lindberghs Antikvariat, Tegnérgatan 10, 113 58 Stockholm, Schweden.
List (Kunstantiquariat Stephan), Barer Strasse 39, 8000 München 40, Deutschland.
List (Maria), Eisenacher Str. 111, D-1000 Berlin-Schöneberg 30, Germany.
Livraria Brasília, Rua da Misericordia 79, Lisboa, Portugal.
Livres, 105, rue Faubourg Saint Denis, 75010 Paris, France.
Löcker (Erhard), Gluckgasse 3, Wien, Österreich.
Lodovico (Silvestri)=Libreria Antiquaria "Bianchino del Leone", Perugia, Italia.
Loeb-Larocque (Louis), 36 rue le Peletier, 75009 Paris, France.
Loewy (Alexandre), 85 rue de Seine, 75006 Paris, France.
Logos Bookshop, 38 Ben Yehuda Street, Tel Aviv, Israel.
Lohmann (G.), Talstrasse 10, D-4802 Halle (Westfalen), Deutschland.
Loliée (Bernard), 72 rue de Seine, 75006 Paris, France.
Loliée (Librairie Marc), 40 rue des Saints-Pères, 75007 Paris, France.
Lombardi (Libreria Luigi), Via Constantinopoli 4 bis, 80138 Napoli, Italia.
Lombardi (Libreria Pasquale), Via San Eufemia 11, 00187 Roma, Italia.
Loock (A. van), rue Saint Jean 51, 1000 Bruxelles, Belgie.
Loose, Papestraat 3, 's-Gravenhage, Netherlands.
Lörcher o.H.G. (Margot), Heubergstrasse 42, 7000 Stuttgart 1, Deutschland.
Lörcher o.H.G. (Margot), Meyerbeerstrasse 53, 8000 München, 60, Deutschland.
Lorieul (Jules), Normania, 3 Place du Castel, 50580 Port Bail, France.
Lusson (Charles)=Paradis des Chercheurs, B-1060 Bruxelles, Belgium.
Lowenstrom (Bo)=Enhörningen Antikvariat, Stockholmsvägen 60, Sweden.
Lucas (Librairie Charles), 10 rue Armengaud, 92210 Saint-Cloud, France.
Lucenay (G. de), 15 rue Petite-Fusterie, 84000 Avignon, France.
Lüders (Axel), Heussweg 33, 2000 Hamburg 19, Deutschland.
Lummert (Christa), Skalitzer Str. 75, D-1000 Berlin-Kreuzberg 36, Germany.
Lundgrens Antikvariat (S.) Romares Stiftelse, Romares Väg, Box 3010, 250 03 Helsingborg, Schweden.
Lundquists Antikvariat, Geijersgatan 5, 411 34 Göteborg, Sweden.
Lungelarsen (A.), Øygardveien 16e, Bekkestua, Norge.
Lunghetti (Christiana)=Libreria Antiquaria di S. Bernardino, 50122 Firenze, Italia.
Lusa (Livraria), 477 Cadofeita, Porto, Portugal.
Lyngby Antikvariat, Jernbanev 1A, 2800 Lyngby, Danmark.
Lynge & Son, Silkegade 11, 1113 København, Danmark.

M

Maccono (Dott. Carla Viotto)=Le Bouquiniste, Torino, Italy.
Mackensen & Niemann, Utrechter Strasse 42, D-1000 Berlin-Wedding 65, Deutschland.
Mader (Alfred), 67 rue Saint-Jacques, 75005 Paris, France.
Madliger-Schwab (Buchantiquariat), Postfach 8022, Tiefenhöfe (Beim Paradeplatz) 8001 Zürich, Schweiz.
Maeght (Galerie), 13 rue de Téhéran, 75008 Paris, France.
Mafart (Librairie C.), 9 rue Maître Albert, 75006 Paris, France.
Magis (Jean-Jacques), 47 rue Saint André-des-Arts, 76006 Paris, France.
Magister Tinius, Hackerstr. 4, D-1000 Berlin-Friedenau 41, Germany.
Maille (Bernard), 3 rue Dante, 75005 Paris, France.
Maison du Livre (La), 24 rue de la Cloche Verte, 16000 Angoulême, France.
Maisonneuve (Adrien), 11 rue St. Sulpice, 75006 Paris, France.
Makrocki (Achim), Quellenstrasse 14, 3500 Kassel, Deutschland.

Malota's Enkelin A. Stern (Franz), Wiedner Hauptstrasse 22, Wien 4, Österreich.
MAM, P.O. Box 1722, Nicosia, Cyprus.
Manterola (Libreria), Manterola 8, San Sebastian,
Mantua (Libreria Antiquaria), Via A. Doria 6, 10123 Torino, Italia.
Manusé (Gaetano), Via Hoepli 3, Milano, Italia.
Manz'sche Verlags- und Universitätsbuchhandlung, Kohlmarkt 16, 1014-Wien, Österreich.
Marcus (Hans), N. Z. Voorburgwal 284, 1012 RT Amsterdam, Nederland.
Marcus (Hans), Ritterstrasse 10, 4000 Düsseldorf, Deutschland.
Maréchal (Boekhandel Jos.), Mariastraat 10, 8000 Brugge, Belgie.
Margotat (Yves), 8 rue de l'Odéon, 75006 Paris, France.
Marinho (Livraria), 215 Almada, Porto, Portugal.
Maronne (Mme. E.), 37 rue Bouffard, 33000 Bordeaux, France.
Marques (Americo F.), Rua da Misericordia 92–1, Lisboa, Portugal.
Marquina y Marin (Luis)=Libreria Hesperia, Zaragoza, Espanña.
Martegani (Dr. A.)=Sibrium Libri e Manoscritti, Milano, Italy.
Martelli (Libreria Antiquaria), Via Santo Stefano 43, 40125 Bologna, Italia.
Martin-Brès (Henri), 60 rue Grignan, 13001 Marseille, France.
Martin (Dr. Paul C.)=Commerzcabinett, 2000 Hamburg 76, Deutschland.
Martinez (Fernand), 97 rue de Seine, 75006 Paris, France.
Martinez (Jean-Claude), 21 rue Saint-Sulpice, 75006 Paris, France.
Martingay (Claude)=Librairie de la Corraterie, CH-1211 Genève, Suisse.
Martinho (Livraria Eduardo Antunes), Rua Voz do Operário 7-B, Lisboa 2, Portugal.
Martins Antikvariat, Falkonerallé 65, København, Danmark.
Martins (Ernesto)=Biblarte, Limitada, Lisboa 2, Portugal.
Marzocco (Libreria), Via Martelli 22 rosso, 50129 Firenze, Italia.
Marzoli (Carla), Corso Porta Nuova 2, 20121 Milano, Italia.
Matarasso (Librairie-Galerie Jacques), 2 rue Longchamp, 06000 Nice, France.
Matchtmeister Bildantikvariat (Karna), De Geersgatan 12, 11529 Stockholm, Sweden.
Matern (Peter), Linzergasse 5, A-5024 Salzburg, Österreich.
Matica Hrvatska 2 Maticine, Zagreb, Jugoslavija.
Matlofsky (S.), Alfasi 7, Jerusalem 92302, Israel.
Matteuzzi (Libreria), Piazza Aldrovandi 5/B, 40125 Bologna, Italia.
Matussek (Hans K.), Marktstrasse 13, 4054 Nettetal, Deutschland.
Maudrich (Wilhelm), Lazarettgasse 1, 1091 Wien, Österreich.
Mauke Söhne (W.), Karl-Muck-Platz 12, 2000 Hamburg 36, Deutschland.
Maurel (Isabelle)=librairie des Victoires, Paris, France.
Maurel (Librairie-Galerie Paul), 27–29 boulevard Albert 1er, 06600 Antibes, France.
Mayer Limited (Ludwig), Shlomzion Hamalka 4, Jerusalem, Israel.
Mayrische Buchhandlung, Theatergasse, 5024 Salzburg, Osterreich.
Mazo (Alain), 15 rue Guénégaud, 75006 Paris, France.
Mazo (Alain)=Bouquinerie de l'Institut S.A., Paris, France.
Mecklenburg (Günther und Klaus)=J.A. Stargardt, 3550 Marburg, Deutschland.
Mediolanum (Libreria Antiquaria), Via Montebello 30, 20121-Milano, Italia.
Mehrdorf (Renate), Karl-Jäger-Strasse 6, D-7100 Heilbronn, Deutschland.
Mehren (F. und A.), Telgenweg 8, 4400 Münster, Deutschland.
Meichsner und Dennerlein, Dreieichstrasse 52, Frankfurt am Main 70, Deutschland.
Meilleurs Livres (Les), 18 boulevard Saint-Michel, 75006 Paris, France.

Meinke (Herbert), Stubenrauchstrasse 70, D-1000 Berlin-Friedenau 41, Deutschland.
Mela (H.)=Tapiola-Antikvariaatti, 00100 Helsinki, Suomi.
Menagé (Jean)=Librairie Stendhal, Grenoble, France.
Menetret (Claude)=l'Invitation au Voyage, Paris, France.
Menger (A.), Albrechtstrasse 122, D-1000 Berlin-Tempelhof 42, Deutschland.
Mennenöh (Ina)=C. Roemke & Cie, 5000 Köln, Deutschland.
Menzel (Michael), Gertreidegasse 13, A-5022 Salzburg, Österreich.
Mercante di Stampe (Il), Corso Venezia 29, 20121 Milano, Italia.
Mercier (H.)=La Proue, 1000 Bruxelles, Belgie.
Mergenthaler (Antiquariat Walter), Textorstrasse 22, 8700 Würzburg, Deutschland.
Meris (Visano)=Libreria Antiquaria 'Il Delfino', Torino, Italia.
Messel & Wildhagens Antikvariat, Tvetenveien 32, Oslo, Norge.
Metais (Henri), 2 Place Barthelemy, 76000 Rouen, France.
Metra (Guy), 13 Grand-Rue Chauchien, 71400 Autun, France.
Meur, S.A.R.L. Librairie le, 12 Place du Theâtre, 21000 Dijon, France.
Meuschel (Konrad), Kaiserplatz 5, 5300 Bonn, Deutschland.
Meyer (Franz H.)=Hamburgensien-Meyer, 2000 Hamburg 36, Deutschland.
Michaelidou (Mrs. Thelma M.)=MAM, Nicosia, Cyprus.
Michalek (Eva)=Bücherkabinett, 8000 München 40, Deutschland.
Michel (R.-G.), 17 Quai Saint-Michel, 75005 Paris, France.
Micheloni (Walter), Vico Falamonica 15 rosso, 16123 Genova, Italia.
Michelotti (Libreria G.), Corso Roma 18, 5106 Montecatini Terme, Italia.
Mielke (M.), Schlägerstrasse 33, D-3000 Hannover, Deutschland.
Migliorini (Giorgio)=Libreria Internazionale C. Caldini, Firenze, Italia.
Miliano (Libreria M.), Via. B. Croce 60, 80134 Napoli, Italia.
Minerva (Antiquariaat), Zeestraat 48, 's-Gravenhage. (Postbox 1853), Nederland.
Mingardi (Gastone & Mario)=Libreria Alpina, Bologna, Italia.
Miroir (Librairie du), rue du Miroir 9–11, 7000 Mons, Belgium.
Miron (Galerie Francois), 62 rue Francois Miron, 75004 Paris, France.
Mirto (Libreria), Ruiz de Alarcon 27, Madrid 14, España
Misasi (Carlo)=Libreria Alessandria, Roma, Italia.
Mohler (Karl), Rheinsprung 7, CH-4051 Basel, Schweiz.
Moirandat (A.F.)=Haus der Bücher, Basel, Schweiz.
Molenes S.A., Libriarie Quentin, 7 Place de la Fusterie, CH-1204 Geneve, Suisse.
Molina (Gabriel), Travesia del Arenal 1, Madrid, España
Monaco-Gravures, B.P.89, 32 Boulevard des Moulins, Monte-Carlo, Principaute de Monaco, France.
Monfort (Gérard), St.-Pierre-de-Salerne, 27800 Brionne, France.
Monge (Librairie), 5 rue de L'Echaudé, 75006 Paris, France.
Montanini (Libreria), Via Nino Bixio 58, Parma, Italia.
Montbarbon (S.A.R.L. Bouquinerie), 1 rue R. Andricu, 83100 Toulon, France.
Montbel et Cie (Librairie de), 1 rue Paul Cézanne, 75008 Paris, France.
Montenegro (Libreria Antiquaria), Via Dei Gracchi 291/a, 00192 Roma, Italia.
Montmartroise (Librairie), 29 rue Durantin, 75018 Paris, France.
Moorthamers (Librairie Louis), rue Lesbroussart 124, 1050 Bruxelles, Belgie.
Moorthamers (M.), 5 Wapper, Antwerpen, Belgium.
Morcrette (Daniel), 4 avenue Joffre, 95270 Luzarches. (B.P. 26), France.
Morel de Westgaver (Alain), rue Saint-Jean, 1000 Bruxelles, Belgium
Morel (Jean), 33 rue du Dr Caron, 76420 Rouen, France.
Moreno (Antonio)=Libreria Granata, Almeria, España.
Moretti (Libreria Antiquaria), Via Lusardi 8, 20122 Milano, Italy.

233

Morin (Charles), 102 rue de Cherche-Midi, 75006 Paris, France.
Morin (Charles), 9 rue Auvray, 72000 Le Mans, France.
Mørk (Antikvariat), Teglgårdsstraede 6, København, Danmark.
Mornet (Franck-Noel)=Quartier Latin, la Rochelle, France.
Mortensen (Aage)=Antikvarboden, København, Danmark.
Morvran, Boite Postale 22, Brignou en Berrien, 29218 Huelgoat, Bretagne, France.
Moscow S.S.S.R.
Moser (Kunstantiquariat Otto), Tölzer Strasse 24, 8022 Grünwald, Deutschland.
Mühle (Galerie Zur), Billesberger Hof, 8059 Moosinning, Deutschland.
Müller (Clemens), Kapellenweg 59, 5600 Wuppertal-Barmen, Deutschland.
Müller & Gräff, Calwerstrasse 54, 7000 Stuttgart-1, Deutschland.
Muller (Rudolf) International Booksellers, P.O. Box 9016, Amsterdam. (Overtoom 487), Nederland.
Munari (Rene), 9 rue Bayard, 38000 Grenoble, France.
Muriset (Galerie Annie), 4 Place du Molard, 1204 Genève, Schweiz.
Murr (Antiquariat Karlheinz), Karolinenstrasse 4, 8600 Bamberg. Deutschland.
Musica Antiqua, Alleen 54, København, Danmark.
Mussejong, 201 Provinciestr, Antwerpen, Belgium.
Muthmann (Ruth-Maria)=C.G. Boerner, 4000 Düsseldorf, Deutschland.
Müller (Eduard), Universitätstrasse 19, CH-8006 Zürich, Schweiz.
Müller (Henry), Postfach 55, 8405 Winterthur, Schweiz.

N

Nabrink & Zoon (Gé), Korte Korsjespoortstraat 8, Amsterdam–C, Nederland.
Naert (Mme Janine)=Saffroy, Paris, France.
Naestved Antikvariat, Vinhusgade 13, København, Denmark.
Nancon, 184 rue Saint-Maur (Bernadette), 75010 Paris. laa Aaaaa France.
Nanni (Libreria A.), Via Musei 8, 40124 Bologna, Italia.
Nansensgade Antikvariat, Nansensgade 70, 1366 København-K, Denmark.
Nantaise Y. Vachon. 3 Place de la Monnaie, 44000 Nantes, France.
Nardecchia, S.r.l. (Libreria Gia), Piazza Cavour 25, 00193 Roma, Italy.
Neal, Booksellers (Michael and Gwenola), 16 le Bosquet, 91940 les Ulis, France. France
Nebehay (Christian M.), Annagasse 18, 1015 Wien. (Postfach 303), Österreich.
Nebehay (Ingo)=Wiener Antiquariat, Wien, Österreich.
Nedersaksische Antiquariaat (Het), Nieuwstraat 50, 7411 LM Deventer, Nederland
Neidhardt (Fritz), Relenbergstrasse 20, 7000 Stuttgart, Deutschland.
Neser (Peter), Kreuzlingerstrasse 11, 7750 Konstanz-Bodensee, Deutschland.
Neser (Peter)=Bücherstube am See, 7750 Konstanz-Bodensee, Deutschland.
Neuf Muses (Les), 41 Quai des Grands-Augustins, 75006 Paris, France.
Neugebauer (Inge)–W Neugebauer Ges.m.b.H. & Co K.G., 4020 Linz, Österreich.
Neugebauer (Walter)=I Neugebauer Ges.m.b.H. & Co K.G., 4020 Linz, Österreich
Neugebauer (Werner)=Meyrische Buchhandlung, Salzburg, Österreich.
Neugebauer (W.), Landstrasse 1, 4020 Linz, Österreich.
Nicaise S.A. (Librairie), 145 boulevard Saint Germain, 75006 Paris, France.
Nickel-Zadow, Plobenhofstrasse 4, Hauptmarkt, Nürnberg, Deutschland.
Nielsen (Bjarne)=Antikvariat Pinkerton, 1366 København-K, Denmark.
Nielsen (Hans Arne), Nørre Farimagsgade 31, København, Danmark.
Nielsen (Ove), Valdemarsgade 30, København, Danmark.
Nierendorf (Galerie), Hardenbergstrasse 19, 1000 Berlin 12, Deutschland.

Nierynck (L. M. C.), Verdilaan 85, 4384–LD Vlissingen, Nederland.
Nijhoff B.V. (Martinus), P.O. Box 269, Noordwal 4, 2501AX 's-Gravenhage, Netherlands.
Nilsson (Mrs Tove)=Nordiska Antivariska Bokhandeln, Helsingfors, Suomi.
Nizet (A.G.)=Au Plaisir du Texte, 75005 Paris, France.
Nizet (Librairie A.-G.), 3 bis Place de la Sorbonne, 75005 Paris, France.
Nobele (F. de), rue Bonaparte 35, 75006 Paris, France.
Nobis (Günter), Forststrasse 12, 6200 Wiesbaden, Deutschland.
Nociti (Guiseppe)=Libreria Antiquaria Martelli, Bologna, Italia.
Noelle Gemälde (Dr. Margarethe), Meinekestrasse 11, 1000 Berlin 15, Deutschland.
Nolte (Ernst)=Hauswedell und Nolte, 2000 Hamburg 13, Deutschland.
Nørballe (Leif)=Frederiksberg Antikvariat, 1850 København-V, Danmark.
Norddeutsches Antiquariat, Kröpeliner Strasse 14, DDR-25 Rostock. DDR.
Nordiska Antivariska Bokhandeln, Norra Magasingatan 6, Helsingfors, Suomi.
Nørgart (H.C.), Fiolstraede 15, 1171 København-K, Danmark.
Norlis Bokhandel (Olaf), Universiteitsgatan 18, Oslo, Norge.
Nørrebro Antikvariat, Griffenfeldsgade 45, DK-2200 København, Danmark.
Notabene, Østerbrogade 96, København, Danmark.
Notebaart (P. C.), Postbox 280, 1400 AG. Bussum, Nederland.
Nyegaard (Claes)=Damms Antikvariat A/S, Oslo 1, Norge.

O

Ober (Peter H.)=Magister Tinius, Berlin-Friedenau 41, Germany.
Oberle (Gerard), Manoir de Pron, Montigny a. Canne. 58340 Circy-la-Tour, France.
Occitania (Librairie), 46 rue du Taur, 31000 Toulouse, France.
Octopus (Dr.), Aahusgade 2, København, Denmark.
Offermann und Schmitz, Antiquariat, Wittelsbacherstrasse 31, 5600 Wuppertal 2, Deutschland.
Ohlson (T.)=Thulin & Olson, Göteborg, Sverige.
Ole Hos Antikvariat, Jagtvej 51, København, Danmark.
Oleff (M.C.)=Posada Art Books, 1000 Bruxelles, Belgium.
Olschki (Leo S.)—Studio Bibliografico, 52046 Lucignano (Arezzo), Italia.
Olsen Forlag og Antikvariat, Hammergt. 7, N. Oslo 4, Norge.
Olsen (Hans)=Marinus Olsen, 1455 København-K, Denmark.
Olsen (Marinus), Studiestraede 41, 1455 København-K, Danmark.
Olsen & Co., Thornegatan 23, Drammen, Norge.
Olthuysen(Henk), 37 Staartsestraat, Huybergen, Nederland.
Omo (Hanne)=Hillerød Antikvariat, DK-3400 Hillerød, Denmark.
Onkel Buttes Eftf, Fredriksborgvej 29, København, Denmark.
Les' Ordinaires, 8 rue Baudin, 83000 Toulon, France.
Or Du Temps, 89 rue Octavie-Duchellier, 80730 Dreuil-les-Amiens, France.
Orangerie-Reinz Galerie, Helenenstrasse 2, 5000 Köln 1, Deutschland.
Origarani (Orfeo), Libri Antichi et Stampe, Via Magnani N.6, 40134 Bologna, Italia.
Os (P. van), 68 Bakkerstraat, Arnhem, Nederland.
Oslo Nye Antikvariat, Majorstuvn 15, Oslo 3, Norge.
Ott (W.), Frankfurter Strasse 56, 6050 Offenbach (Main), Deutschland.

P

Pabel (Antiquariat Reinhold), Krayenkamp 10b, D-2000 Hamburg 11, Deutschland.

Pabian, 4 rue de Clichy, 75009 Paris, France.

Page (Mevr. F.J.H. van)=Antiquariaat Deventer, 7411 BR Deventer, Nederland.

Pagée-Selis (J. F. van)=Antiquariaat Brabant, 's-Hertogenbosch, Nederland.

Palladio (Librairie), 66 rue du Cherche-Midi, 75006 Paris, France.

Palmaverde (Libreria Antiquaria), Via Castiglione 35, 40124 Bologna, Italia.

Paludan (Erik), Fiolstraede 10, 1171 København-K, Danmark.

Pankow (Antiquariat), Schönholzer Strasse 1, DDR-110 Berlin, DDR.

Papon, les Rivaux (Bernard), B.P. 12, 24006 Trelissac-Perigueux, France.

Papyrus 2e-Hands Boekenwinkel, 60 Nieuwstraat, Deventer, Nederland.

Para Bibliofilos, Pl. San Martin 3, Madrid, España.

Paradis des Chercheurs, 245 Chaussée de Charleroi, B-1060 Bruxelles, Belgium.

Parrot (J.-P.), 59 rue de Rennes, 75006 Paris, France.

Parsifal [S.A.R.L.], 80 Boulevard Raspail, 75006 Paris, France.

Pasini-Picard (Chantal)=Editions A. & J. Picard, 75006, Paris, France.

Patzer (Rudolf), Mainzer Berg 23, 6739 Weidenthal, Deutschland.

Paulusch (Hans)=Bourcy & Paulusch, 1010 Wien, Österreich.

Paulusch (Hans D.)=V. A. Heck, 1010 Wien, Österreich.

Pedersen (Soren)=Fantask ApS., København-K, Danmark.

Pedro V. (Livraria D.), Rua d. Pedro V. 16, Lisboa, Portugal.

Peet, B.V. (C. P. J. van der), 33–35 Nieuwe Spiegelstraat, 1017 DC Amsterdam, Nederland.

Peet (R. van der)=Antiquariaat Antiqua, Amsterdam, Nederland.

Pegasus, Blaagaardsgade 3, København, Denmark.

Pels-Leusden (Hans), Kurfürstendamm 59–60, D-1000 Berlin-Charlottenburg 15, Germany.

Penso (Libreria Antiquaria M.), S. Tomà 2916/a, 30121 Venezia, Italia.

Perini (Libreria Antiquaria), Via A. Sciesa 9, 37100 Verona, Italia.

Perre (Francine van der), rue de la Madeleine 23, 1000 Bruxelles, Belgie.

Perrin (Andre)=Le Bouquiniste, 38000 Grenoble, France.

Persson (Stellan)=Skakhuset [The Chess House], 1455 København-K, Denmark.

Petersen (O.B.)=Nørrebro Antikvariat, København, Danmark.

Petersen (V. Severin)=Kobberstikhuset, København, Danmark.

Petit-Siroux (Albert), 45, 46, 47 Galerie Vivienne, 75002 Paris, France.

Petitot (Pierre), 234 boulevard Saint-Germain, 75007 Paris, France.

Peyrot (Dott. Ada), Via Consolata 8, 10122 Torino, Italia.

Peyrotte (Gérant)=Arioso S.A.R.L., Paris, France.

Peysson (Jean), 7 rue du Plat, 69002 Lyon, France.

Pfister (Annemarie), Petersgraben 18, 4051 Basel, Schweiz.

Philographicon, Galerie für Alte Graphik im Antic-Haus, Neuturmstrasse 1, 8000 München 2, Deutschland.

Piantanida (Alessandro)=Libreria Vinciana, Milano, Italia.

Piazza S. Babila (Libreria di), Corso Monforte 2, 20122 Milano, Italia.

Picard (Editions A. & J.), 82 rue Bonaparte, 75006 Paris, France.

Picard Fils (Henri), 126 Faubourg Saint-Honoré, 75008 Paris, France.

Picard (Pierre), 60 boulevard Malesherbes, 75008 Paris, France.

Piedmont (Libreria), Vice dei Mercanti 22, 10121 Torino, Italia.

Piermont (Antiquariat), Rolandstrasse 13, 5480 Remagen-Rolandswerth, Deutschland.

Pilegaard (Gunnar), Algade 65, Aalborg, Danmark.

Pinault (J.-H.), 36 rue Bonaparte, 75006 Paris, France.

Pinczower (F.), 83 Sokolow Street, Tel Aviv. (P.O. Box 6008), Israel.
Pinheiro (Sra. Dias)=Livraria Ferin Lda., Lisboa, 1200 Portugal.
Pinkerton (Antikvariat), Nansensgade 68, 1366 København-K, Denmark.
Pinkus Genossenschaft (Antiquariat), Froschaugasse 7, 8001 Zürich. (Postfach 8025 Zürich), Schweiz.
Pinkus (Marco), ABC Antiquariat, Zähringerstrasse 31 CH-8001 Zürich, Schweiz.
Pique-Puces, 204 Chausee de Wavre, 1050 Bruxelles, Belgium.
Pixi (Antikvariat), Enghavsvej 28B, København, Denmark.
Plähn (Gisela), Innsbrucker Str. 4, D-1000 Berlin-Schoneberg, Germany.
Plaisir du Texte (Au), 8 Rue des Fossés St.-Jacques, 75005 Paris, France.
Plas (Jean-Marie van de), 10 rue des Eperonniers, 1000 Bruxelles, Belgie.
Plöger (Traute), Ostfeuerbergstrasse 35, 2800 Bremen, Deutschland.
Polak (Dr. J.B.W.)=Athenaeum Antiquarian Booksellers, Amsterdam, Nederland.
Polak (Jean), 8 rue de l'Échaudé, 75006 Paris, France.
Pölck (Rainer), Antiquariat-Grafikum, Alt Rödelheim 15, Frankfurt am Main 90, Deutschland.
Polifilo (Il), Via Borgonuovo 3, 20121 Milano, Italia.
Pollès (Malo)=Les Chevau Légers, Paris, France.
Pont Traversé, 8 rue de Vaugirard, 75006 Paris, France.
Porte Étroite (La), 10 rue Bonaparte, 75006 Paris, France.
Porte (Louis)=Henri Sack, Genève, Schweiz.
Porter-Libros, Avenida Puerta del Ángel 9, Barcelona. A.B.A, España.
Posada Art Books S.P.R.L., rue de la Madeleine 27, 1000 Bruxelles, Belgium.
Posse (Libreria de Estanislao Rodriguez), San Bernardo 27, Madrid 8, Spain.
Post (Antiquariat Constantin), Zülpicher Strasse 16, 5000 Köln 1, Deutschland.
Postma (G.), O.Z. Voorburgwal 249, 1012 EZ Amsterdam, Nederland.
Poursin, Cite Noël (Librairie), 22 rue Rambuteau, 75003 Paris, France.
Poxleitner-Blasl (Alois), Strozzigasse 32, 1080 Wien, Österreich.
Pozzi (Dr. Elfo)=Libreria Antiquaria Mediolanum, Milano, Italia.
Prandi (Libreria Antiquaria), Viale Timavo 75, Reggio Emilia, Italia.
Pregliasco (Libreria Antiquaria Arturo), Via Accademia Albertina 3 bis, 10123 Torino, Italy.
Preidel (H.), Postfach 1128, Bismarckstrasse 20, 3007 Gehrden/Hannover, Deutschland.
Preminger, Ltd. (Nissen), 9 Montefiore Street, Tel Aviv. (P.O. Box 29001), Israel.
Pressler (Dr. Cristine)=Robert Wölfle OHG., 8000 München 40, Germany.
Pressler (Dr. Karl H.), Römerstrasse 7, 8000 München 40, Deutschland.
Prinz (Walter) und Siegfried Unverzagt, Limburgerstrasse 14–16, 5000 Köln 1, Deutschland.
Privat (Librairie Georges), 162 boulevard Haussmann, 75008 Paris, France.
Pro-Francia (V.R.I.L.L.E. Editions), 3 rue Saint-Philippe du Roule, 75008 Paris, France.
Pro Libro, Pariser Str. 14, D-1000 Berlin-Wilmersdorf 15, Germany.
Prouc (La), 6 rue des Eperonniers, 1000 Bruxelles, Belgie.
Prouté (Guy), 15 rue du 18-Juin, 92210 Saint-Cloud, France.
Prouté (Robert), 12 rue de Seine, 75006 Paris, France.
Prouté S.A. (Paul), 74 rue de Seine, 75006 Paris, France.
Pruimers (Drs. P.A.G.W.E.)=van Stockum's Ant., B.V., 's-Gravenhage, Nederland.
Pruss (Wolfgang)=Eppendorfer Antiquariat, 2000 Hamburg 20, Deutschland.
Pudlich (Klaus D.)=Die Bücherlaube, Berlin-Charlottenburg 12, Germany.
Pugno (Librairie), 19 Quai des Grandes-Augustins, 75006 Paris, France.
Pulitzer & Knöll AG. (Galerie), Junkerngasse 17, CH-3011 Bern, Schweiz.
Puskas (Wilhelm), Weihburggasse 16, 1010 Wien, Österreich.

Puzin (Librairie), 30 rue de la Paroisse, 78000 Versailles, France.

Q

Quartier Latin, 21 rue Albert-1er, 17000 la Rochelle, France.
Quattrifolio, Via S. Cecilia 2, I-20122 Milano, Italy.
Quinsac (P.)=Librairie Duchemin, Paris, France.

R

Radaeli (Antiquariato Librario), Via A. Manzoni 39, 20121 Milano, Italia.
Raffy (G.), 85 rue des Rosiers (Stand 83 Marché Biron), 93400 Saint-Ouen (Seine-St. Denis), France.
Raoust (Librairie), 11 rue Neuve, 59000 Lille, France.
Rappaport (Libreria Antiquaria C.E.), Via Sistina 23, 00187 Roma, Italia.
Rasmussen (Peter Holm)=Bjørnvig, Holm & Møller ApS, DK-9800 Hjørring, Denmark.
Rastello (Laurent), Place Bourg-de-Four 22, CH-1204 Genève, Schweiz.
Rathausdurchgang (Antiquariat und Galerie im), Postfach 72, CH-8402 Winterthur, Schweiz.
Rauhut (Rainer)=Philographicon, Galerie für Alte Graphik im Antic-Haus, 8000 München 2, Deutschland.
Rebeyrol (Bernard)=Brocéliande, le Mans, France.
Recherche du Passe" ("A la), Saint-Colombier, 56370 Sarzeau, France.
Redins Antikvariat, Box 150 49 S-75015 Uppsala. (Drottninggatan 11), Sweden.
Reef (I. H.), 90 Heuvel, Geldrop, Nederland.
Reflex, P.O. Box 454, Achter Sint Pieter 4, Utrecht, Netherlands.
Regina (Libreria L.), Via Costantinopoli 51, 80138 Napoli, Italia.
Reichmann (Alois), Wiedner Hauptstrasse 18, Wien 1040, Österreich.
Reinhardt (Antiquariat J.), Kirchplatz 10, D–802 Halle (Westf.), Deutschland.
Reinz (Gerhard F.)=Orangerie-Reinz, Galerie und Verlag, 5000 Köln 1, Deutschland.
Reiss und Auvermann, Buch- und Kunstantiquariat, Zum Talblick 2, 6246 Glashütten im Taunus, Deutschland.
Remy (Librairie A.), 25 rue Stanislas, 54000 Nancy, France.
Renacimiento (el), Huertes 49, Madrid, Spain.
Renaissance van het Boek (De), Walpoortstraat 7, 9000 Gent, Belgie.
Renner (Antiquariat Gerh.), An d. Unteren Berg (Fuchsfarm), Postfach 1648, 7470 Albstadt 2, Deutschland.
Renner (Klaus), 8021 Hohenschaeftlarn, Deutschland.
Renqvist (Ove G.), Grafik-Antikvariatet, Skomakargatan 24. 11129 Stockholm, Sweden.
Reymond (Madame Eugène), 14 Faubourg de l'Hôpital, CH-2000 Neuchatel, Schweiz.
Ribaux Buchhandlung und Antiquariat, Bahnhofstrasse 2, CH-9001 St Gallen, Schweiz.
Riccardi (Claude), 7 rue Meyerbeer, 06000 Nice, France.
Riccardi (Libreria Maresca), Via Banco S. Spirito 61, 00186 Roma, Italia.
Richter (Günter), Breite Strasse 29, 1000 Berlin 33, Deutschland.
Rico (Antonia Molina)=Gabriel Molina-Sucesora, Madrid, Spain.
Ricordi, Negozio di Via Berchet 2, 20121 Milano, Italia.
Rieffel (Librairie), 15 rue de l'Odéon, 75006 Paris, France.

Rigattieri (Libreria M.), Calle Della Mandola 3713, 30124 Venezia, Italia.
Rijzende Zon (Antiquariaat de), Poststraat 8, 5038 DH Tilburg, Nederland.
Rimanek (Heinrich), Kaiserstrasse 6, 1070 Wien, Österreich.
Riminese (Libreria), Via IV Novembre 46, 47037 Rimini (Forli), Italia.
Ringstrøms Antikvariat (Bjørn), Ullevålsveien 1, Oslo 1, Norge.
Ripoll (Libreria), San Miguel 12, (Apartado 338), Palma de Mallorca, España.
Rivares (Librairie), 3 rue Rivares, 64000 Pau, France.
Rizzi (Renzo), Via Cernaia 4, I–20121 Milano, Italia.
Roberg (Franz), Friedrichstrasse 45, 4000 Düsseldorf, Deutschland.
Robichon (Anne-Marie), 16 Quai de la Loire, 37210 Rochecorbon/Vouvray, France.
Roemke & Cie. (C.), Apostelnstrasse 7, 5000 Köln, Deutschland.
Rogers Turner Books Ltd., 24 rue du Buisson Richard, 78600 le Mesnil-le-Roi, France.
Rohr (Hans), Oberdorferstrasse 5, 8024 Zürich 1, Schweiz.
Röhrscheid G.m.b.H. (Ludwig), am Hof 28, 5300 Bonn, Deutschland.
Romagosa (Jaime)=Antiquariat Iberia, Berne, Schweiz.
Romana. (Libreia) Via del'Prefetti 16, 00186 Roma, Italia.
Romand (Jean-Claude)=Sagot le Garrec & Cie, Paris, France.
Romand (Michel)=Galerie Documents, Paris, France.
Rombaut (Librairie A.), Lievestraat 14, 9000 Gent, België.
Rönnells Antikvariat, AB, Birger Jarlsgatan 32, 11429 Stockholm, Schweden.
Rosenberg (H.)=Antiquariat am Hafen, 2000 Hamburg 4, Deutschland.
Rosenkilde og Bagger, 3 Kron-Prinsens-Gade, P.O. Box 2184, DK-1017 København, Danmark.
Rosenthal (R. B.), Rua do Alecrim 47-4° Salas D, Lisboa 2, Portugal.
Rosenthal's Antiquariaat (Ludwig), Bussumergrintweg 4, 1217 BP Hilversum, Nederland.
Rossignol (Louis Daniel)=Libraire Rossignol, 06400 Cannes, France.
Rossignol (Emile), 8 rue Bonaparte, 75006 Paris, France.
Rossignol (Librairie), 1 rue Jean Daumas, 06400 Cannes, France.
Rossignol (Librairie Eugéne), 4 rue de l'Odéon, 75006 Paris, France.
Röth (L. G.), Pfarrstrasse 21, 7000 Stuttgart 1, Deutschland.
Roth-Wölfle (Dr. Lotte)=Robert Wölfle OHG., 8000 München 40, Germany.
Rotkäppchen, Brusseler Strasse 14, D-1000 Berlin-Wedding 65, Deutschland.
Rouam (Maurice), 29 rue Mazarine, 75006 Paris, France.
Rouillon (Jean-Paul), Galerie J.P.R., 27 rue de Seine, 75006 Paris, France.
Roulleau (Paul), 108 rue Saint-Honoré, 75001 Paris, France.
Rousseau-Girard (Librairie), 2 ter rue Dupin, 75006 Paris, France.
Roux-Devillas (Olivier), 12 rue Bonaparte, 75006 Paris, France.
Roversi (dott. Roberto)=Libreria Antiquaria Palmaverde, Bologna, Italia.
Rozza (Dr. Edoardo)=Libreria Filosofica Kairòs, 20158 Milano, Italia.
Ruel (André)=Libri, Macon, France.
Ruff (Edgar A.)=Das Bücherfass II, Berlin-Friedenau 41, Germany.
Ruff (Edgar A.)=Das Bücherfass I, Berlin-Wilmersdorf 15, Deutschland.
Rumbler (Kunsthandlung Helmut H.), Braubachstrasse 36, 6000 Frankfurt-am-Main, Deutschland.
Ruuds Antikvariat, Sigurdsgatan 20, Oslo 6, Norge.
Ryös Antikvariat AB, Hantverkargatan 21, 112 21 Stockholm, Sverige.

S

Saarinen (L.)=Valkeakosken Kirja-Antikvariaatti, 37600 Valkeakoski, Suomi.
Saba (Umberto), Via San Nicolo 30, 34121 Trieste, Italia.
Sabels Antivariat (Nils), Box 1049, 15024 Rönninge 1, (Storskogsv. 1), Sweden.
Sack (Henri), Grand-Rue 1, 1204 Genève, Schweiz.
Sack (Hermann), Bahnstrasse 61, 4000 Düsseldorf, Deutschland.
Saffroy, 3 Quai Malaquais, 75006 Paris, France.
Saffroy (Gaston), 4 rue Clément, 75006 Paris, France.
Saggiori. (Renata) Mas du Pin Perdu, Le Col de Gordes, 84200 Gordes, France.
Sagot le Garrec & Cie, 24 rue du Four, 75006 Paris, France.
S. Agostino (Libreria), Via S. Agostino 17/A, Roma, Italia.
Saint-Jacques (Librairie), 10 rue Saint-Jacques, 64500 Saint-Jean-de-Luz, France.
Sainte-Marie (Jean-Louis), B.P. 24. 6 rue Guileran, 82200 Moissac, France.
Salamon (Harry)=Il Gabinetto Delle Stampe, Genova, Italia.
Salamon (Teresa)=l'Arte Antica, Torino, Italia.
Salfelt (R.), Gammel Kongevej 146, København, Danmark.
Salimbeni S.r.l. (Libreria), Via Matteo Palmieri 14R, 50122 Firenze, Italia.
Salmevaara (K. & S.)=Helsingin Antikvariaatti, 00100 Helsinki, Suomi.
Salon du Livre d'Occasion (Le), 26 rue du Grand-Four, 13300 Salon-de-Provence, France.
Salotto del Bibliofilo, Via Luccoli 21, 16123 Genova, Italia.
Samaletdin (Antikvaarinen Kirjakauppa B.), Iso Roobertinkatu 9, 00120 Helsinki, Suomi.
Samlaren Antikvariat & Konsthandel, Korsgatan 2, 41116 Göteborg, Schweden.
Samtleben (Manfred)=Reiss und Auvermann, 6246 Glashütten im Taunus, Deutschland.
Samuelian (Librairie Orientale H.), 51 rue Monsieur-le-Prince, 75006 Paris, France.
Sanderus (Antiquariaat), Brugsestraat 88, 8510 Kortrijk, Belgium.
Sändig G.m.b.H. (Dr. Martin), Kaiser-Friedrich-Ring 70, 6200 Wiesbaden, Deutschland.
Sapir (Mrs. H.)=Atika Books, Jerusalem, Israel.
Sartoni-Cerveau, 13 Quai Saint-Michel, 75005 Paris, France.
Sauer (Georg), Gerichtsstrasse 7, 6240 Königstein im Taunus, Deutschland.
Savine (André)=La Bibliophiie Russe, 75009 Paris, France.
Sawhney (Christiane), Winterfeldtstrasse 44, D-1000 Berlin-Schöneberg 30, Deutschland.
Scarpignato (Guiseppe), Via Ripetta 156, 00186 Roma, Italia.
Scelles (Roger)=Librairie Delamain, Paris, France.
Schaden (Rainer)=Der Buchfreund, 1010 Wien 1, Österreich.
Schäfer (Bernhard), Conradistrasse 2, 3522 Karlshafen, Deutschland.
Schäfer (Jörg), Alfred-Escher-Strasse 76, 8002 Zürich, Schweiz.
Schäfer (Lutz), Johann-Sigismund Str. 15, D-1000 Berlin-Wilmersdorf 31, Germany.
Schalk (Friedrich), Mariahilferstrasse 97, Wien 1006, Österreich.
Scharioth'sche Antiquariat, Huyssenallee 58, D–4300 Essen 1, Deutschland.
Schebella (Wolfgang), Zeltinger Pl. 9/13, D-1000 Berlin-Frohnau 28, Germany.
Scheiber (F.), Denkmalstrasse 8, Luzern, Schweiz.
Scheler (Lucien)=Librairie Thomas-Scheler, Paris, France.
Scheller (Henry), Seefeldstrasse 73, CH-8008 Zürich, Schweiz.
Schendl (Verlag Dr. A.), Karlsgasse 15, A-1041 Wien, Österreich.
Scheppler (Gerhard), Giselastrasse 25, 8000 München 40, Deutschland.

Scheringer (Georg)=Buch und Kunst, 7750 Konstanz, Deutschland.
Scheringer (R.)=Gsellius'sche Buchhandlung, 1000 Berlin 37, Deutschland.
Schierenberg Antiquariaat (Ineke), Leidsegracht 42, 1016 CM Amsterdam, Nederland.
Schierenberg BV. (Dieter) Prinsengracht 485–487, 1016 HP Amsterdam, Nederland
Schikowski (Richard), Motzstrasse 30, D-1000 Berlin-Schöneberg 30, Germany.
Schiller (Ludwig Helmut), am Birkenrain 28, 7811 St. Peter, Deutschland.
Schilling (Kurt)=Scientia Verlag und Antiquariat, 7080 Aalen, Deutschland.
Schindegger (Antiquariat Paul), Heidenpoint 26, 8228 Freilassing, Deutschland.
Schlöhlein G.m.b.H., Schützenmattstrasse 15, CH-4003 Basel, Schweiz.
Schmidt (Geschwister), Karl-Marx-Strasse 15, 6750 Kaiserslautern, Deutschland.
Schmidt (H.) und C. Günther, Ubierstrasse 20, 6238 Hofheim, Deutschland.
Schmidt (Kunstantiquariat Monika), Türkenstrasse 48, 8000 München 40, und Schloss Haimhausen, 8048 Haimhausen, Deutschland.
Schmidt (Max)=Bücher-Schmidt Antiquariat, 8000 Zurich, Schweiz
Schmidt Periodicals G.m.b.H., Dettendorf, 8201 Bad Feilnbach 2, Deutschland.
Schmidt. (Sigismund) Eppendorfer Marktplatz 15, 2000 Hamburg 20, Deutschland
Schmitz (Hans-Martin)=Offermann und Schmitz, 5600 Wuppertal 2, Deutschland.
Schneider (Ulrich)=W. Brandes, 3300 Braunschweig, Deutschland.
Schneider (Dr. Gerhard), Rhode-Goldsiepen 12, 5960 Olpe, Deutschland.
Schneider (Hans), Mozartstrasse 6, 8132 Tutzing Über München, Deutschland.
Schneider (Karl Friedrich), Seltersweg 38, 6300 Giessen, Deutschland.
Schomaker & Niederstrasser, Bundesallee 221, D-1000 Berlin-Wilmersdorf 15, Germany.
Schöningh (Ferdinand), Domhof 4c, 4500 Osnabrück. (Postfach 4060), Deutschland.
Schors (Antiquariaat W. N.), Reguliersgracht 52–54, Amsterdam, Nederland.
Schrage (Antiquariat), Schaumburgerstrasse 20, D-6252 Diez, Deutschland.
Schramm (Bernd), Dänische Strasse 26, 2300 Kiel, Deutschland.
Schrepf (R.), Nürnberger Strasse 31, 8510 Fürth, Deutschland.
Schreyer (Hartmut R.), Auf Dem Kreuz 9, D-8900 Augsburg, Deutschland.
Schreyer (Hanno), Euskirchenerstrasse 57–59, 5300 Bonn 1, Deutschland.
Schroeder (Erika), Winterfeldstr. 46, D-1000 Berlin-Schöneberg 30, Germany.
Schroeder und Weise (Antiquariat), Lehrterstrasse, 3000 Hannover-Anderten, Deutschland.
Schrotter (Alain)=La Bouquincric, Avallon, France.
Schrotter=Librairie Galerie 89, 89200 Avallon, France.
Schuhmacher (Antiquariaat), Gelderschekade 107, 1011 EM Amsterdam, Nederland.
Schulman, B.V. (Jacques), Keizersgracht 448, 1016 GD Amsterdam-C, Nederland.
Schultz Antikvariat AB, Bergsgatan 4, 211 54 Malmö, Sverige.
Schulze (Wigbert)="Hesperus", D-3000 Hannover, Deutschland.
Schumann, AG. (Hellmut), Rämistraase 25, 8024 Zürich, Schweiz.
Schumann (Richard)=Frankfurter Bücherstube, 6000 Frankfurt-am-Main, Deutschland.
Schutt (H.), Arnsburger Strasse 76, Frankfurt am Main 60, Deutschland.
Schwarz (Peter), Eisenacher Str. 43, D-1000 Berlin-Schöneberg 62, Germany.
Schweger (Dr. Uta)=V. A. Heck, 1010 Wien, Österreich.
Schwilden (Tristan), Galerie Bortier 5, 1000 Bruxelles, Belgium.
"Sciences Nat" (Librairie), 2 rue Andre-Mellenne, Venette, 60200 Compiegne, France.
Scientia Verlag und Antiquariat, Adlerstrasse 65, 7080 Aalen (Württemberg), Deutschland.

Screpel (Michel)=l'Amateur d'Art, 75006 Paris, France.
Seacombe (Elisabeth & James)=Libreria Antiquaria C.E. Rappaport, Roma, Italia.
Seckinger (H.)=Cachet, CH-4051, Basel, Schweiz.
Seidenberg (Philipp), Bücherladen, Brunngasse 4, 8001 Zürich, Schweiz.
Seidenberg (Sigmund)=Das Gute Buch, Zürich, Schweiz.
Seidenfadens Antikvariat, Vaerndamsvej 5, København, Danmark.
Seidl (Dr. Z.)=Akademische Buchhandlung Kuppitsch, Wien, Österreich.
Seiffert (S.), Höhenstrasse 43, Frankfurt am Main 60, Deutschland.
Senzel (Gerhard), Knesebeckstrasse 13/14, D-1000 Berlin-Charlottenburg 12, Deutschland.
Serignan (Philippe), 15 rue Joseph-Vernet, 84000 Avignon, France.
Sermoneta (E.), Studio Bibliografico, Via C. Battisti 2, I-40123 Bologna, Italy.
Settergards Antikvariat, Birger Jarlsgatan 44, Stockholm-Ö, Schweden.
Seuffer (Walter), Steglitzer Damm 57, 1000 Berlin 41, Deutschland.
Severin (Matthias), Meraner Strasse 6, D-1000 Berlin-Schoneberg 62, Deutschland.
Severin (Peter)=Bickhardt'sche Buchhandlung, 1000 Berlin-Neukölln 44, Deutschland.
Seze (Librairie C. et O. de), 6 Place du General Leclerc, 24000 Perigueux, France.
Sforzini (Libreria), Via Della Vite 43, 00187 Roma, Italia.
Sgattoni (Libreria Antiquaria M.), Via Vivaio 22, 20122 Milano, Italia.
Sheftl (E.)=Zohar, Tel Aviv, Israel.
Shiavo (Dott. Guido Lo)=Libreria Gaspare Casella, Napoli, Italy.
Sibrium Libri e Manoscritti, Via Bigli 21, 20121 Milano, Italia.
Sieber (Dr. Maria)=Wiener Bücherstube, 6000 Frankfurt-am-Main, Deutschland.
Siebert (Werner)=Franz Leuwer, 2800 Bremer, Deutschland.
Sieg (Manfred), Fasanenstr. 45, D-1000 Berlin-Wilmersdorf 15, Germany.
Sieur (Pierre), 3 rue de la Universitée, 75007 Paris, France.
Silva & Ca., Lda. (Joaquim Guedes da), Livraria Academica, Rua Martires da Liberdade 8–12, Porto, Portugal.
Simmermacher (René), Talstrasse 5, 7800 Zürich, Switzerland.
Simmermacher A.G. (Rene), Kirchgasse 25, CH-8024 Zürich, Schweiz.
Simon (Carlota)=Das Bücherkabinett, 2000 Hamburg 36, Deutschland.
Simonsen (C.F.)=Arnold Busck, København-K, Danmark.
Simonson (Librairie), Chaussée de Charleroi 227, 1060 Bruxelles, Belgium.
Sindern (A.), Jungbrunnenweg 15, 4800 Bielefeld, Deutschland.
Sion (M.), 15 Steendam, Gent, Belgium.
Skafte(K.E.), DK-4800 Nykobing Falster, Danmark.
Skakhuset [The Chess House], 24 Studiesstraede, 1455 København-K, Danmark.
Skandinavisk Antiquariat, Gammel Strand 48, København, Danmark.
Skanstulis Antikvariat, Götgatan 99, 11662 Stockholm, Sweden.
Skovle & Skovle (Antikvariat), Dag Hammerskjoldallee 42, København, Danmark.
Skovle (Stefan), Nørrebrogade 8, København, Danmark.
Skutta (D.), Humboldtstrasse 80, 4000 Düsseldorf 1, Deutschland.
Slatkine et Fils (M.), 5 rue des Chaudronniers, 1211 Genève, Schweiz.
Slegte B.V. (Boehandel J. de), Grote Staat 53, 6211 CV Maastright, Nederland.
Slegte B.V. (Boekhandel J. de), Weversgildeplein 1-2, 8011 XN Zwolle, Nederland.
Slegte B.V.(Boekhandel J. de), Marktstraat 13, 7511 GC Enschede, Nederland.
Slegte B.V. (J. de), Grote Houtstraat 100, 2011 SR Haarlem, Nederland.
Slegte B.V. (J. de), Breestraat 73, 2311 CJ Leiden, Nederland.
Slegte B.V. (J. de), Herestraat 33, 9711 LB Groningen, Nederland.
Slegte (J. de), Janstraat 28, 6811 GJ Arnhem, Nederland.
Slegte (J. de), Kalverstraat 48–52, 1012 PE Amsterdam, Nederland.

Slegte (J. de), Coolsingel 83, 3012 AE Rotterdam, Nederland.
Slegte (J. de), Spuistraat 9, 2511 BC 's-Gravenhage, Nederland.
Slegte (J. de), Rechtestraat 36, 5611 GP Eindhoven, Nederland.
Slegte (J. de), Oude Gracht 121, 3511 AH Utrecht, Nederland.
Slot (Mary)=Lyngby Antikvariat, 2800 Lyngby, Danmark.
Smoorenburg (A), 14-16 Hofmeijersweg, Raalte, Nederland.
Snuffelaar (De), Ketelpoort, 9000 Gent, Belgium.
Soave (Fiammetta), Via Guiseppe Cuboni 12, 00197 Roma, Italia.
Soave (Fiammetta), Via Leccosa 4, Roma, Italia.
Société Hébraica Judaica, 12 rue des Hospitalières St.-Gervais, 75004 Paris, France.
Société Livres & Musique, 6 rue Lamartine, 75009 Paris, France.
Soete (Edgar), Librairie Salet, 5 Quai Voltaire, 75007 Paris, France.
Sol i de la Lluna (La Libreria Del), Carrer de la Canuda 24, Barcelona 2, Spain.
Somma (Bottega Apulja Di M.), Via S. Cognetti 37, 70121 Bari, Italia.
Sonnenthal (Thomas), Cauerstrasse 20/21, Berlin-Charlottenburg 10, Deutschland.
Sonnewald-Heckenhauer, Waldhof 1, 7947 Mengen, Deutschland.
Sonnewald (Herbert Friedrich)=J.J. Heckenhauer, 7400 Tübingen, Deutschland.
Sorel, 6 Square Jules Chéret (Jacqueline), 75020 Paris.   aaaaa A1aaa France.
Sørensen (Birgit Møller)=Brøndum Antikvariat, DK-9520 Skørping, Denmark.
Sørensen (Richard)=Byens Antikvariat, København-K, Danmark.
Sörhuus Antikvariat AB, Riddargatan 23, 114 57 Stockholm, Sverige.
Sörlin (Bo)=Antikvariska Bokhandeln AB, Malmö, Schweden.
Sor& Antikvariat, Frederiksbergvej 8, 4180, Sorø, Danmark.
Sothmann (M.), N.Z. Voorburgwal 284, Amsterdam, Nederland.
Spaducci (Renato), Piazza S. Giovanni in Laterano 18/B, 00184 Roma, Italia.
Spandonaro (Julia & Augusto)=Les Amis du Livre, Athens, Ellas.
Speeckaert (E.), 53 Boulevard Saint-Michel, B-1040 Bruxelles, Belgium.
Sphinx, 55 Nieuw Boteringestraat, Groningen, Nederland.
Spinnhirn (Dr. Gertrud)=Eduard Höllrigl, 5010 Salzburg, Österreich.
Springer (Rudolf J.), Fasenenstrasse 13, 1000 Berlin 12, Deutschland.
SRPSKA Knjizevna Zadruga, 19 Marsala Tita, Beograd, Jugoslavija.
SRPSKE Akademije Nauka (Antikvarnica), Knez Mihajlova, 11000 Beograd, Jugoslavija.
St. Gertrude (Antiquariat), Gertruden Kirchhof 2, 2000 Hamburg 1, Deutschland.
Stadelmann (Antiquariat B.F.), Dieselstrasse 5, 6070 Langen, Deutschland.
Stadelmann (Burkhard F.), Dieselstrasse 5, 6070 Langen Deutschland.
Stangl (Galerie), Briennerstrasse 11, 8000 München, Deutschland.
Stargardt (J.A.), Radestrasse 10, 3550 Marburg, Deutschland.
Staschen (Wolfgang), Potsdamer Str. 138, 1000 Berlin 30, Deutschland.
Stavridis (Stavros), Panaghitsas 18, Kifisia, 14562 Athens, Greece.
Steinbach (Antiquariat Michael), Demollstrasse 1/I 8000 München 19, Deutschland.
Steinbach (M. F.), Salmannsdorferstrasse 64, 1190 Wien, Österreich.
Steinernen Kreuz (Antiquariat Beim), 2800 Bremen 1, Deutschland.
Steinkopf (J.F.), Postfach 1116, Marienstrasse 3, 7000 Stuttgart, Deutschland.
Stenderhoff & Co. (Th.), Alter Fischmarkt 21, 4400 Münster, Deutschland.
Stendhal (Librairie), 41 rue Mazarine, 75006 Paris, France.
Stendhal (Librairie), 4 rue de Sault, 38000 Grenoble, France.
Stern (Anni)=Franz Malota's Enkelin, Wien 4, Österreich.
Stern-Verlag Janssen & Co., Postfach 7820, Friedrichtustrasse 26, 4000 Düsseldorf, Deutschland.

Sternberg (Leon), Lange Leemstraat 27, 2018 Antwerpen, Belgium.
Stierle (Helene)=Eduard Höllrigl, 5010 Salzburg, Österreich.
Stockum's Ant. (Van), B.V. Prinsegracht 15, 's-Gravenhage, Nederland.
Stöhr (U.)=Gsellius'sche Buchhandlung, 1000 Berlin 37, Deutschland.
Stokking, C.V. (Henk J.), Niewe Spiegelstraat 40, 1017 DG Amsterdam, Netherlands.
Stolzenberg (Kurt G.), Gr. Seestrasse 63, Frankfurt am Main 90, Deutschland.
Storm (Antiquariat), Hakenstrasse 2A, 2800 Bremen, Deutschland.
Stoven (Jacques), 53 rue du Mail, 49000 Angers, France.
Strang (Jan)=Antiikki-Kirja, 00100 Helsinki 10, Finland.
Streisand (Hugo), Eislebener Strasse 4, 1000 Berlin 30, Deutschland.
Streng (Ingelore), Landwehrstrasse 2, 8000 München 2, Deutschland.
Stropek (Dr. Karl), Währingerstrasse 122, 1181 Wien, Österreich.
Struck (Antiquariat Nikolaus), Wilhelmstrasse 5, 5449 Pfalzfeld, Deutschland.
Struppe und Winckler, Potsdamerstrasse 103, 1000 Berlin 30, Deutschland.
Studente (Libreria Dello), Via Laura 68/a, 50121 Firenze, Italia.
Stuttgarter Antiquariat, Rathenaustrasse 21, 7000 Stuttgart 1, Deutschland.
Sundby (Antikvariat), Middelgrundsvej 5, København, Danmark.
Suuronen (P.)=Lahden Antikvaarinen Kirjakauppa, 15110 Lahti, Suomi.
Svensson (Bengt)=Librairie du Spectacle Garnier Arnoul, Paris, France.
Swertz (A. J.)=Reflex, Utrecht, Netherlands.
Swets & Zeitlinger, B.V., Heereweg 347B Lisse, Nederland.
Sydys, Buchhandlung Ludwig Schubert G.m.b.H. (J. G.), P.O. Box 169, Wienerstrasse 19, 3100 St. Pölten, Österreich.
Sylva (J. A. Telles da), Travessa Marquês sá da Bandeira, 19-3° Esq. Lisboa 1, Portugal.
Sylvie (Librairie), 26 Place Vòsges, 75003 Paris, France.
Symanczyk (Wolfgang), Hubertusweg 32, 4040 Neuss, Deutschland.

T

Tacke (Friedrich)=C. Roemke & Cie, 5000 Köln, Deutschland.
Taeuber (W.)=Gilhofer Buch- und Kunstantiquariat K.G., 1010 Wien, Österreich.
Talke (Eberhard B.)=Antiquariat Aix la Chapelle, D-5100 Aachen, Germany.
Tamburello (Dott. Mario)=Libreria Antiquaria Luigi Banzi, Bologna, Italia.
Tapiola-Antikvariaatti, Malminrinne 3, 00100 Helsinki, Suomi.
Tarantola (Libreria R.), Via Vitt. Veneto 20, I-33100 Udine, Italy.
Tausch KG (Dr. Karl), Maria-Theresien-Strasse 1, Innsbruck, Österreich.
Tausky (Théodore), 33 rue Dauphine, 75006 Paris, France.
Taxandria Antiquariaat, 115 Salesianenstraat, Tilburg, Nederland.
Technisches Antiquariat, Lauteschlagerstrasse 4, 6100 Darmstadt, Deutschland.
Telemarken Antikvariat, Drangedal, Norge.
Tenner (E.), Hauptstrasse 194, 6900 Heidelburg, Deutschland.
Tenner (Erna)="Bibliographicum", 6900 Heidelberg, Deutschland.
Tenner K.G. (Dr. Helmut), Sofienstrasse 5, 6900 Heidelburg, Deutschland.
Terroy (Didier), 39 rue de Douai, Paris 75009, France.
Thanh-Long (Librairie-editions), 34 rue Dekens, 1040 Bruxelles, Belgie.
Theimann (Dr. S.), Violenstrasse 33–35, 2800 Bremen, Deutschland.
Thelem Antiquariat, Mölkereistrasse 19, Postfach 50, 8399 Rotthalmünster, Deutschland.
Thélème, rue St. Savournin No. 29, Marseille 13005, France.
Thérond (André), 40 rue Victor Hugo, 81100 Castres, France.

Thoma (J. E.), 3910 Stift Zwettl, Österreich.
Thomas (G. L.)=Librairie-Galerie Bretonne, Rennes, France.
Thomas, Marche Vernaison (Simone), Allee 3/7, Stand 146, 136, Avenue Michelet, 93400 Saint-Ouen, France.
Thomas-Scheler (Librairie), 19 rue de Tournon, 75006 Paris, France.
Thourel (Claude)=Librairie Occitania, Toulouse, France.
Thuesens Antikvariat, Fiolstraede 23, 1171 København-K, Danmark.
Thulin & Ohlson, Kungsgatan 9B, 41119 Göteborg, Sverige.
Thulins Antikvariat, AB., 57060 Österbymo, Sverige.
Tiedmann (H.-H.)=Altonaer Antiquariat, 2000 Hamburg 50, Deutschland.
Tijenk (H. J. & H.)=Het Nedersaksische Antiquariaat, Deventer, Nederland.
Timbuctoo, 6 Kleine Kr. Elleboog, Groningen, Nederland.
"Tin Ujević" (Antikvarijat), Zrinski trg. 16, 41000 Zagreb, Jugoslavija.
Tiraspolsky (Wladimir), 69 avenue Victor-Cresson, 92130 Issy-les-Moulineaux.
    Spec: langues étrangères; France.
Tode (Riewert Q.), Dudenstr. 22, D-1000 Berlin-Kreuzberg 61, Germany.
Tol (J. P. van den), 94 Voorstraat, Dordrecht, Nederland.
Tonini (Matteo), Via Antica Zecca 26, 48100 Ravenna, Italia.
Tornet (Antikvariat Blå), Drottninggatan 85, Stockholm, Sverige.
Tour du Monde (Le), 9 rue de la Pompe, 75116 Paris, France.
Toussaint (Gilbert A.)=Book Market, B 1000 Bruxelles, Belgium.
Touzot (Jean), 38 rue Saint-Sulpice, 75278 Paris, France.
Traineau (Jean-Baptiste), 33 rue Royale, 78000 Versailles, France.
Trefpunt, 98 Boterlaarbn, 2100 Deurne-Zuid, Belgium.
Tresor am Römer, Galerie, Buch und Kunst Antiquariat, Braubachstrasse 15, Passage Techn. Rathaus, Frankfurt 1, Deutschland.
Treytl (Jörg)=Bourcy & Paulusch, 1010 Wien, Österreich.
Triantafyllou (Efthimiou D.)=Academic Bookstore, Athens, Ellas.
Triaud, Domaine de Choisy, ABZAC, 33230 Coutras, France.
Trochon (Michel)=Librairie du Camee, Paris, France.
Trochon (Michel)=Librairie du Camee, 75006 Paris, France.
Trojanski (Hans), Blumenstrasse 11, 4000 Düsseldorf, Deutschland.
Trösch (Musik & Theater Antiquariat Armin), Rämistrasse 33, 8001 Zürich, Schweiz.
Truppe (Mathäus), Stubenberggassc 7, 8011 Graz, Österreich.
Tulkens (Fl.), 21 rue du Chêne, Bruxelles 1, Belgie.
Tøsse (Bergensantikvariatet K. J.), Store Markevei 8–10, Bergen, Norge.

U

Ukiyo-E Galerie, Citadellstrasse 14, 4000 Düsseldorf 1, Deutschland.
Ullberg (Sven P.)=A. Cederbergs Eftr, AB, Uppsala, Schweden.
Umea Antikvariat, Västra Esplanaden 6, 90248 Umea, Sweden.
Unteregger (Alfons)=Adolf Kapp, 7407 Rottenburg, Deutschland.
Urbs & Orbis, Göddertzgarten 42, 5309 Meckenheim-Merl, Deutschland.
Urso, Libri Rari (Agenzia), Via Andrea Verga 4, 20144 Milano, Italia.
Utzt (Inge), Taubenheimerstrasse 30, 7000 Stuttgart-Bad Canstatt 30, Deutschland.

V

Vaisson (Patrick), 3 rue Moines, 75017 Paris, France.
Vaisson (Patrick), 67 rue Saint-Charles, 75015 Paris, France.
Valentien (Galerie), Königsbau, 7000 Stuttgart, Deutschland.
Valentien (H.)=Kunstantiquariat Valentien, 4800 Bielefeld, Deutschland.
Valentien (Kunstantiquariat), Niederwall 14, 4800 Bielefeld, Deutschland.
Valette (Librairie Robert D.), 11 rue de Vaugirard, 75006 Paris, France.
Valkeakosken Kirja-Antikvariaatti, Valtakatu 20, 37600 Valkeakoski, Suomi.
Valleri (Libreria), Via Ricasoli 68 rosso, 50121 Firenze, Italia.
Valleriaux (Librairie), 98 Boulevard Voltaire, 75011 Paris, France.
Vallerini (Libreria Antiquaria Andrea), Via Dei Mille 7A–13, I-56100 Pisa, Italy.
Vanasia (Libreria Santo), Via M. Macchi 58, 20124 Milano, Italia.
Vanasia (Santo), Calle Victor Hugo 1, Madrid 4, Spain.
Vandevelde (A.W.), Dweersstraat 6, 8000 Bruges, Belgie.
Vandevelde (Titia)=In den Eenhoorn, Bruges, Belgie.
Vanlaecken (Mireille), Bloemendalestraat 73, 8030 Beernem (bij Brugge), Belgium.
Varia Librairie, rue Soeurs de Hasque 15, 4000 Liege, Belgium.
Vauquelin (Galerie), 4 rue Vauquelin, 76200 Dieppe, France.
Vedrines (Josiane), 38 rue de Richelieu, 75001 Paris, France.
Veeneman (Martin), Noordeinde 100, 's-Gravenhage, Nederland.
Veldeke (Hendrik van), 50 B.10, Guffenslaan, 3500 Hasselt, Belgium.
Velden (E. von den), Neureuther Strasse 1. 8000 München 40, Deutschland.
Venator, KG., Cäcilienstrasse 48 (im Kunsthaus Lempertz) 5000 Köln, Deutschland.
Venator (Rolf)=Venator, K.G., 5000 Köln, Deutschland.
Verbeke (Christian F.), Bloemendalestraat 73, 8030 Beernem (bij Brugge), Belgium.
Vester (Dr. Helmut), Friedrichstrasse 7, 4000 Düsseldorf, Deutschland.
Vestergarrd (G.)=Antikvariat Mørk, København, Danmark.
Viaducto (Liberia Anticuaria el), Plaza Cruz Verde 1, Madrid, Spain.
Viardot (Jean), 15 rue de l'echaudé, 75006 Paris, France.
Vibert-Guigue (Elise)=Librairie des Alpes, Paris, France.
"Vieille France", 65 boulevard Général-Leclerc, 33120 Arcachon, France.
Viesel (Hansjörg)=Magister Tinius, Berlin-Friedenau 41, Germany.
Vieux Quartier (Librairie au), Rue des Fripiers 11, B-5000 Namur, Belgium.
Vigevani (A. M.)=Il Polifilo, Milano, Italia.
Viglongo (Libreria Antiquaria A.), Via Genova 266, 10127 Torino, Italia.
Vigna (Nicolas)=Monaco-Gravures, Principaute de Monaco, France.
Vigneron (René), Les Argonautes, 74 rue de Seine, 75006 Paris, France.
Vilain (M.), 287 Ten Eekhovelei, 2100 Deurne, Belgium.
Viljakainen=Kirjakuja Ky, Helsinki, Suomi.
Vinciana (Libreria), Via Monte Napoleone 23, 20121 Milano, Italia.
Vinderen Antikvariat, Slemdalsvei 63, Oslo, Norge.
Vinkala (T.)=Kvariaatti, 20500 Turku, Suomi.
Violet (Librairie), 41 rue Violet, 75015 Paris, France.
Vloemans (H. A.), Anna Paulownastraat 10, 2518 BE 's-Gravenhage, Nederland.
Voerster (J.), Relenberg Strasse 20, 7000 Stuttgart, Deutschland.
Voigt (Rainer Gerd), Langerstrasse 2/IV, D-8000 München 80, Deutschland.
Voltaire (A.F.), 30 rue Adolphe-Thiers, 13001 Marseille, France.
Vömel (Alex. und Edwin)=Galerie Vömel, 4000 Düsseldorf, Deutschland.
Vömel (Galerie), Königsallee 30, 4000 Düsseldorf, Deutschland.
Vonderbank, K.G., (Karl), Goethestrasse 11, 6000 Frankfurt-am-Main, Deutschland.

Vötterle (Dr. Karl)=Bärenreiter Antiquariat, 3500 Kassel-Wilhelmshöhe, Deutschland.
Vries (Boekhandel H. de), P.O.B. 274, Ged. Oude Gracht 27-23 Haarlem, Netherlands.
Vrin (J), 6 Place de la Sorbonne, 75005 Paris, France.
Vuille (Louis), rue Maison-Rouge 5, 1400 Yverdon, Suisse.
Vulin (Ribot), 8 rue de Rome, 75008 Paris, France.
Vuyk Wout, 316 Spuistraat, Amsterdam, Nederland.

W

Wäger (Antiquariat Hans), Lavesstrasse 6, 3000 Hannover, Deutschland.
Wagner (Christl und Olga)=Rudolf Heger, 1010 Wien 1, Österreich.
Wagner (Karl Dieter), Rothenbaumchaussee 1, 2000 Hamburg 13, Deutschland.
Wagner'sche Universitäts Buchhandlung OHG., Museumstrasse 4, 6021 Innsbruck, Österreich.
Wahle et Compagnie S.P.R.L., rue du Méry 14a, 4000 Liege, Belgium.
Walz (Ed.), Lerchenfeldstrasse 4, 8000 München 22, Deutschland.
Wangsmos Antikvariat, Olav Tryggvasonsgt. 2 a, N-7000 Trondheim, Norge.
Wanner-Zander (R. & I.), Kronengasse 35, 5400 Baden, Schweiz.
Waser-Albiez (Otto), Rümelinsplatz 15, Basel, Schweiz.
Wasmuth Buchhandlung & Antiquariat KG., Hardenbergstrasse 9a, 1000 Berlin 12, Deutschland.
Waterbolk (Antiquariaat Niek), Schoutenstraat 7, 3512 GA Utrecht, Nederland.
Weber (Peter), Kunstantiquariat, Eichstrasse 12, 7570 Baden-Baden, Deutschland.
Weddinger Antiquariat, Willdenowstr. 5b/E. Burgsdorfstr., D-1000 Berlin-Wedding 65, Germany.
Weerd (H. de), Middellaan 34, 7314 GC Apeldoorn, Nederland.
Wegner (Carl), Martin-Luther-Strasse 113, 1000 Berlin 62, Deutschland.
Wegner (Margrit)=Frankfurter Kunstkabinett, Hanna Bekker vom Rath, G.m.b.H., 6000 Frankfurt-am-Main, Deutschland.
Wehrli (Marianne)=Schlöhlein G.m.b.H., CH-4003 Basel, Schweiz.
Weick (Werner), Sternstrasse 2, Am Markt, 5300 Bonn 1, Deutschland.
Weigel (Felix Oswald)=Otto Harrassowitz, 6200 Wiesbaden, Deutschland.
Weil (D.), 1 rue du Dragon, 75006 Paris, France.
Weiss Bibliotheca Gastronomica (Antiquariat H. U.), Winzerstrasse 5, CH-8049 Zürich, Schweiz.
Weissert (Freidrich), Charlottenstrasse 21c, 7000 Stuttgart 1, Deutschland.
Weissert (M. F.)=Cabinet de l'Estampe et du Livres Ancien, Monaco, France.
Welkhammer (J.), Burggasse 123, 1070 Wien. (Auch Neubaugürtel 48), Österreich.
Wellm (Horst), Bennigserweg 1, D-3017 Pattensen 1, Deutschland.
Wellnitz (Elisabeth), Sachsenstrasse 35, 6100 Darmstadt, Deutschland.
Wellnitz (Rudolf)=Technisches Antiquariat, 6100 Darmstadt, Deutschland.
Welz Salzburg (Galerie), Sigmund-Haffnergasse 16, Salzburg, Österreich.
Wendt (Bernhard), Hauptstrasse 29, 8084 Inning-Buch/Ammersee, Über München, Deutschland.
Wengen-Mohler (U.)=Karl Mohler, CH-4051 Basel, Schweiz.
Wenner (H. Th.), Postfach 4307, Hegerstrasse 2-3, 4500 Osnabrück, Deutschland.
Wever BV. (T.), 16 Zilverstraat, Franeker, Nederland.
Widmer (Galerie), Neugasse 35, 9000 St. Gallen, Schweiz.
Wiedebusch (Max), Dammtorstrasse 20, 2000 Hamburg 36, Deutschland.
Wiedenroth (Hermann)=Das Bücherhaus, 3012 Langenhagen, Deutschland.

Wiehe (Antiquariat Irene), Hildersheimerstrasse 46, 3000 Hannover, Deutschland.
Wiele (Marc van de), St. Salvatorkoorstraat 3, 8000 Brugge, Belgium.
Wiener Antiquariat, Seilergasse 16, Wien, Österreich.
Wiener Bücherstube, Eschersheimer Landstrasse 18, 6000 Frankfurt-am-Main
  Deutschland.
Wild (Alexander), Rathausgasse 30, 3011 Bern, Schweiz.
Wild (Th.), Mariahilferstrasse 158, Wien 1015, Österreich.
Wildeboer (W.G. & R.)=Antiquariaat Amaryl, 1075-CJ Amsterdam.
Wildeboer (W.J. & R.)=Antiquariaat Amaryl, 9717-JL Groningen.
Wildner (L. und E.), Stempfergasse 8, 8010 Graz, Österreich.
Wiluzanski (Z.), P.O. Box 3183, 58 Ben Jehuda Street, Tel Aviv 61031, Israel.
Winterberg (Arno), Buch und Kunstantiquariat, Blumenstrasse 15, 6900 Heidelberg,
  Deutschland.
Wirnitzer (Galerie Elfriede), Lilienmattstrasse 6, Haus Lauschan, 7570
  Baden-Baden, Deutschland.
Wissenschaftliches Antiquariat, Humboldtstrasse 6, 2800 Bremen, Deutschland.
Wissenschaftliches Antiquariat und Buchvertriebs GmbH, Sandweg 115, Frankfurt
  am Main 1, Deutschland.
Witt (M. & F.)=Leo S. Olschki—Studio Bibliografico, (Arezzo), Italia.
Wögenstein (Walter) Singerstrasse 13, Wien 1, Österreich.
Wohlers & Co. (Dr. Robert), Lange Reihe 68, 2000 Hamburg 1, Deutschland.
Wölfle OHG. (Robert), Amalienstrasse 65, 8000 München 40, Deutschland.
Wristers (J.), Minrebroederstraat 13, Utrecht, Nederland.
Wünnenberg (Eckhard), Hollestrasse 1, Haus D. Tecknik, D-4300 Essen,
  Deutschland.
Wünschmann (Heinz), Wasserturmstrasse 14, 8520 Erlangen, Deutschland.
Wyngaert (Ch. de), 129A rue R. Vandevelde, B-1030 Bruxelles, Belgium.

Y

Yntema (George), 35 Loseweg, Apeldoorn, Netherland.

Z

Zadek (Walter)=Logos Bookshop, Tel Aviv, Israel.
Zagreb (Nakladni zavod Znanje)=Antikvarijat 'Tin Ujević', Zagreb, Jugoslavija.
Zähringer (Gerhard), Hauptstrasse 90, CH-8280 Kreuzlingen, Suisse.
Zale (Jean), rue Mazelle 37, 5700 Metz, France.
Zalozba Mladinska Knjiga "Emka", 38 Capova, Ljubljana, Jugoslavija.
Zambakis (Angelos), Le Bibliophile, 14 Massalis, Athens 144, Ellas.
Zanni & C. (Banco Libri s.a.s. Di V.), Via Marsala 6, 40126 Bologna, Italia.
Zeil-Antiquariat, Zeil 24, 6000 Frankfurt-am-Main, Deutschland.
Zentralantiquariat der DDR. Talstrasse 29, 701 Leipzig. (Postfach 1080), DDR.
Zentrales Antiquariat Berlin, Rungerstrasse 20, DDR-102 Berlin, DDR.
Zimmerling. (Gunter) Johanniswall 3, 2000 Hamburg 1, Deutschland.
Zisska & R. Kistner (Buch und Kunstauktionshaus F.), Unterer Anger 15, 8000
  München 2, Deutschland.
Zlatin (Madame S.), 46 rue Madame, 75006 Paris, France.
Zohar, 1 Nachlat-Benjamin, Tel Aviv. (P.O. Box 4814.) Israel.
Zoon=Juridische Boekhandel and Antiquariaat, 2311 SL Leiden, Nederland.
Zukunft (Bjarne)=Sor& Antikvariat, Sorø, Danmark.
Zyssman (G.)=Librairie Monge, Paris, France.

SPECIALITIES

SPECIALITIES SPECIALITÉS:
SPEZIALITÄTEN

Specialities are arranged under the following heads:

1. AUCTIONEERS: Ventes aux Enchères: Auktionen
2. AUTOGRAPHS and MANUSCRIPTS: Autographes et Manuscrits: Autographen und Handschriften
3. BIBLIOGRAPHY: Bibliographie: Buchwesen
4. COLLECTING: Livres pour Collectionneurs: Bücher für Sammler
5. CRAFTS and USEFUL ARTS: Arts et Mêtiers: Kunstgewerbe
6. ENTERTAINMENTS: Théâtre et Cinéma: Theater und Kino
7. EROTIC and CURIOUS: Curiosités et Érotique: Erotik
8. FINE and RARE: Beaux livres: Schöne und Seltener Bücher
9. JUVENILE: Livres d'Enfants: Kinderbücher
10. HISTORY: Histoire: Geschichte
11. LANGUAGES: Langues: Sprache
12. LAW and CRIMINOLOGY: Droit et criminologie: Recht
13. MEDICINE: Médecine: Medizin
14. MUSIC: Musique: Musik und Noten
15. NATURAL HISTORY: Sciences naturelles: Naturwissenschaften
16. PERIODICALS: Périodiques: Zeitschriften
17. PICTORIAL ART: Beaux Arts: Kunst und Graphik
18. RELIGION and PHILOSOPHY (I): RELIGIONS and PHILOSOPHIE (I): THEOLOGIE UND PHILOSOPHIE (I)
19. RELIGION and PHILOSOPHY (II): Religions et Philosophie (II): Theologie und Philosophie (II)
20. REMAINDERS and OVERSTOCKS: Soldes: Restauflage
21. SOCIOLOGY: Sociologie: Soziologie
22. SPORTS, GAMES and PASTIMES: Sports et Jeux: Sport und Spiele
23. TECHNICAL and EDUCATIONAL: Technique et Érudition: Technik
24. SCIENCE: Sciences: Wissenschaften
25. TOPOGRAPHY and TRAVEL: Régionalsime et voyages: Topographie und Reisen

SPECIALITIES

SPECIALITIES SPECIALITÉS:
SPEZIALITÄTEN

1. AUCTIONEERS: VENTES AUX ENCHÉRES: AUKTIONEN

Azevedo and Burnay Lda, Travessa de S. Placido 48-B, 1200 Lisboa, Portugal, Portugal.

J. L. Beijers B.V., Achter Sint Pieter 140, 3512 HT Utrecht, Nederland.

W. Brandes, Postfach 1660, Wolfenbüttlerstrasse 12, 3300 Braunschweig, Deutschland.

Christian Galantaris, 15 rue des Saints-Pères, 75006 Paris, France.

Librairie Giraud-Badin, 22 rue Guynemer, 75006 Paris, France.

Hartung und Karl, Karolinenplatz 5A, 8000 München 2, Deutschland—*Auktionen.*

Haus der Bücher, AG, "Erasmushaus", Bäumleingasse 18, 4000 Basel, Schweiz.

Hauswedell und Nolte, Pöseldorferweg 1, 2000 Hamburg 13, Deutschland.

August Laube, Trittligasse 19, 8001 Zürich, Schweiz.

Reiss und Auvermann, Buch- und Kunstantiquariat, Zum Talblick 2, 6246 Glashütten im Taunus, Deutschland.

J. A. Stargardt, Radestrasse 10, 3550 Marburg, Deutschland.

Van Stockum's Ant., B.V. Prinsegracht 15, 's-Gravenhage, Nederland.

Dr. Helmut Tenner K.G., Sofienstrasse 5, 6900 Heidelburg, Deutschland.

Venator, KG., Cäcilienstrasse 48 (im Kunsthaus Lempertz) 5000 Köln, Deutschland.

2. AUTOGRAPHS AND MANUSCRIPTS: AUTOGRAPHES ET MANUSCRITS: AUTOGRAPHEN UND HANDSCHRIFTEN

Librairie de l'Abbaye, 27 rue Bonaparte, 75006 Paris, France.

Athenaeum Antiquarian Booksellers, Reguliersgracht 50, 1017 LT, Amsterdam, Nederland—*autographs.*

Librairie Ancienne "L'Autographe", S.A., 6 Chemin de Grange Canal, CH-1208 Genève, Suisse—*autographes et les livres inscrit.*

Émile Van Balberghe, Rue Vautier 4, B-1040 Bruxelles, Belgium—*manuscrits.*

Libreria Antiquaria Luigi Banzi, Via Borgonuovo 10, 40125 Bologna, Italia.

Galerie Gerda Bassenge, Erdenerstrasse 5 A, D-1000 Berlin 33, Deutschland.

Fabrice Bayarre, 21 rue de Tournon, 75006 Paris, France—*manuscrits.*

Pierre Berès, 14 avenue de Friedland, 75008 Paris, Franc—*manuscrits.*

Libreria Antiquaria 'Bianchino del Leone", Piazza Ansidei 4, 06100 Perugia. (C.P. 25), Italia—*autographs.*

Librairie Auguste Blaizot S.A., 164 Faubourg Saint-Honoré, 75008 Paris, France —*manuscrits et autographes.*

Boghallens Antikvariat, Raadhuspladsen 37, DK 1585 København-V, Danmark —*manuscripts.*

Libreria Internazionale C. Caldini, Via Tornabuoni 89/91r., 50123 Firenze, Italia —*manuscripts, incunabula.*

Cavalieri d'Oro, Via Mazzini 84, 44022 Comacchio, Italia—*autographs.*

Maison Charavay, 3 rue de Furstenberg, 75006 Paris, France—*autographes et documents historiques.*

Pierre Chrétien, 178 Faubourg Saint-Honoré, 75008 Paris, France—*manuscrits.*

Commerzcabinett, Humboldtstrasse 125, 2000 Hamburg 76, Deutschland.

Librairie Davis, 12 avenue Franklin-Roosevelt, 75008 Paris, France—*autographes.*

Antiquariaat Johan Devroe, L. Vanderkelenstraat 43, 3000 Leuven, Belgium.

Cecile Eluard-Valette, 43 rue Sous Barri, OMM 06800 Haut de Cagnes, France —*autographes.*

Frederiksborg Antikvariat, blehaven 10, DK-3400 Hillcrød, Denmark—*documents, manuscripts.*

van Gendt Book Auctions N.V., Keizersgracht 96–98, 1015 CV Amsterdam, Nederland—*manuscripts*.

Gilhofer & Ranschburg G.m.b.H., Sternegg 5, 6005 Luzern, Schweiz —*Manuskripte*.

Librairie Giraud-Badin, 22 rue Guynemer, 75006 Paris, France—*Manuscrits*.

Hartung und Karl, Karolinenplatz 5A, 8000 München 2, Deutschland —*Autographen*.

August Hase, im Trutz 2, 6000 Frankfurt-am-Main, Deutschland—*Autographen*.

V. A. Heck, Kärntner Ring 14, 1010 Wien, Österreich—*Autographen*.

Livraria Histórica e Ultramarina LDA [J. C. Silva], Travessa da Queimada 28, 1200– Lisboa 2, Portugal—*manuscripts*.

Jean Hugues. 1 rue de Furstenberg, 75006 Paris, France—*manuscrits*.

N. Israel, Keizersgracht 489–491, Amsterdam, Nederland—*manuscripts*.

Librairie Lardanchet, 5 Route de Limonest, 69370 Saint-Didier au Mont d'Or, France—*manuscrits*.

Bernard Loliée, 72 rue de Seine, 75006 Paris, France.

Librairie Marc Loliée, 40 rue des Saints-Pères, 75007 Paris, France.

Carla Marzoli, Corso Porta Nuova 2, 20121 Milano, Italia—*illuminated manuscripts*.

Libreria Antiquaria Mediolanum, Via Montebello 30, 20121-Milano, Italia.

Konrad Meuschel, Kaiserplatz 5, 5300 Bonn, Deutschland.

Molenes S.A., Librairie Quentin, 7 Place de la Fusterie, CH-1204 Geneve, Suisse— *manuscrits*.

Daniel Morcrette, 4 avenue Joffre, 95270 Luzarches. (B.P. 26), France.

Les Neuf Muses, 41 Quai des Grands-Augustins, 75006 Paris, France.

Libreria Antiquaria Arturo Pregliasco, Via Accademia Albertina 3 bis, 10123 Torino, Italy—*autographs*.

Antiquariato Librario Radaeli, Via A. Manzoni 39, 20121 Milano, Italia —*manuscripts, miniatures*.

Libreria Ripoll, San Miguel 12, (Apartado 338), Palma de Mallorca, España.

Renzo Rizzi, Via Cernaia 4, I–20121 Milano, Italia—*manuscripts, palaeography*.

Emile Rossignol, 8 rue Bonaparte, 75006 Paris, France—*manuscrits*.

Librairie Rossignol, 1 rue Jean Daumas, 06400 Cannes, France—*autographes*.

Olivier Roux-Devillas, 12 rue Bonaparte, 75006 Paris, France.

Henri Sack, Grand-Rue 1, 1204 Genève, Schweiz—*Autographes*.

Saffroy, 3 Quai Malaquais, 75006 Paris, France—*autographs, documents historiques*.

Gaston Saffroy, 4 rue Clément, 75006 Paris, France.

Renata Saggiori. Mas du Pin Perdu, Le Col de Gordes, 84200 Gordes, France.

Sibrium Libri e Manoscritti, Via Bigli 21, 20121 Milano, Italia.

Pierre Sieur, 3 rue de la Universitée, 75007 Paris, France.

Librairie Simonson, Chaussée de Charleroi 227, 1060 Bruxelles, Belgium.

E. Speeckaert, 53 Boulevard Saint-Michel, B-1040 Bruxelles, Belgium.

J.A. Stargardt, Radestrasse 10, 3550 Marburg, Deutschland.

Leon Sternberg, Lange Leemstraat 27, 2018 Antwerpen, Belgium.

Théodore Tausky, 33 rue Dauphine, 75006 Paris, France—*autographes, manuscrits, documents historiques*.

Librairie Robert D. Valette, 11 rue de Vaugirard, 75006 Paris, France.

Wiener Antiquariat, Seilergasse 16, Wien, Österreich—*Autographen*.

3. BIBLIOGRAPHY: BIBLIOGRAPHIE: BUCHWESEN

Andreassons Antikvariat, Opalgatan 61, S-421 62, Västra Frölunda, Sverige.

Rüdiger Barasch, Hähnelstr. 5, D-1000 Berlin-Friedenau 41, Germany.
Anton W. van Bekhoven. Ruysdaelplein 5, 1411 RD Naarden, Nederland.
Libreria Antiquaria Berruto, Via San Francesco da Paola 10 bis, 10123 Torino, Italia.
Libreria Antiquaria Brighenti, Via Malpertusoi 40123 Bologna. (P.O. Box 506), Italia.
Das Bücherfass II, Hertelstr. 5, Postfach 209, D-1000 Berlin-Friedenau 41, Germany.
Arnold Busck, Fiolstraede 24, 1171 København-K, Danmark.
La Bouquinerie des Carmes, rue St. Paul 35, 4000 Liege, Belgium.
Francis Dasté, 16 rue de Tournon, 75006 Paris, France.
Dresdener Antiquariat, Bautzner Strasse 27, 806 Dresden, DDR.
Eckard Düwal, Schlüterstr. 17, D-1000 Berlin-Charlottenburg 12, Germany.
Erasmus Antiquariaat en Boekhandel. Spui 2, Amsterdam, Nederland.
Librairie Giraud-Badin, 22 rue Guynemer, 75006 Paris, France.
Fernand Gothier, place du 20 Août 11, 4000 Liège, Belgie—*documentation.*
Antiquariaat de Graaf, Zuideinde 40, 2421 AK Nieuwkoop, Nederland.
Gsellius'sche Antiquariat, Hertastrasse 16, 1000 Berlin 37, Deutschland.
Max Günther, Charlottenbrunnerstrasse 5a, 1000 Berlin 33, Deutschland.
H. Hugendubel, Salvatorplatz 2, 8000 München 2, Deutschland.
Maarten J. Israel, P.O. Box 8, 1110 AA Diemen (Keizersgracht 690, 1017 EV Amsterdam), Netherlands.
Paul Jammes, 3 rue Gozlin, 75006 Paris, France—*typographie; bibliographie; estampes.*
Hans-Joachim Jeschke, Winterfeldstrasse 51, D-1000 Berlin-Schöneberg 30, Germany.
Walter Klügel, Postfach 40, Wimm 15, Schreiberghof, A-5201 Seekirchen, bei Salzburg und Lager (Fallweise Geöffnet) Gumpendorferstrasse 33, 1060 Wien, Österreich.
Antiquariaat Frits Knuf, P.O.B. 720, 4116-ZJ Buren, Netherlands.
Hans Horst Koch, Kurfürstendamm 216, 1000 Berlin 15, Deutschland.
Antiquariat Walter Krieg Verlag K.G. Kärntnerstrasse 4, 1010 Wien, Österreich.
Henri Laffitte Libraire, 13 rue de Buci, 75006 Paris, France.
Buchantiquariat Madliger-Schwab, Postfach 8022, Tiefenhöfe (Beim Paradeplatz) 8001 Zürich, Schweiz.
Yves Margotat, 8 rue de l'Odéon, 75006 Paris, France.
Müller & Gräff, Calwerstrasse 54, 7000 Stuttgart-1, Deutschland.
Rudolf Patzer, Mainzer Berg 23, 6739 Weidenthal, Deutschland.
Marco Pinkus, ABC Antiquariat, Zähringerstrasse 31 CH-8001 Zürich, Schweiz.
Dr. Karl H. Pressler, Römerstrasse 7, 8000 München 40, Deutschland.
Rosenkilde og Bagger, 3 Kron-Prinsens-Gade, P.O. Box 2184, DK-1017 København, Danmark.
Maurice Rouam, 29 rue Mazarine, 75006 Paris, France.
Edgar Soete, Librairie Salet, 5 Quai Voltaire, 75007 Paris, France.
E. Speeckaert, 33 Boulevard Saint Michel, B-1040 Bruxelles, Belgium.
Wolfgang Symanczyk, Hubertusweg 32, 4040 Neuss, Deutschland—*Philologie.*
Varia Librairie, rue Soeurs de Hasque 15, 4000 Liege, Belgium.
Josiane Vedrines, 38 rue de Richelieu, 75001 Paris, France.
Horst Wellm, Bennigserweg 1, D-3017 Pattensen 1, Deutschland.
Gerhard Zähringer, Hauptstrasse 90, CH-8280 Kreuzlingen, Suisse.

4. COLLECTING: LIVRES POUR COLLECTIONNEURS: BÜCHER FÜR SAMMLER

Michel Bon, 4 rue Frederic-Sauton, 75005 Paris, France—*Numismatique.*

Galerie Documents, rue de Seine 53, 75006 Paris, France—*affiches originales, fin de siecle.*

Alice Elchlepp, Schillerstrasse 14, 3360 Osterode a. Harz, Deutschland—*Militaria.*

Le Grenier du Collectionneur, avenue Orban 238, 1150 Bruxelles, Belgie—*toys, childrens books, printed ephemera.*

Bouquinerie du Languedoc, 12 rue de l'Université, 34000 Montpellier, France —*numismatique.*

Nissen Preminger, Ltd., 9 Montefiore Street, Tel Aviv. (P.O. Box 29001), Israel —*horology.*

Rogers Turner Books Ltd., 24 rue du Buisson Richard, 78600 le Mesnil-le-Roi, France—*horlogerie.*

Gaston Saffroy, 4 rue Clément, 75006 Paris, France—*histoire généalogie.*

Bernhard Schäfer, Conradistrasse 2, 3522 Karlshafen, Deutschland—*Ex-libris, Bookplates.*

Jacques Schulman, B.V., Keizersgracht 448, 1016 GD Amsterdam-C, Nederland —*Numismatics.*

Pierre Sieur, 3 rue de la Universitée, 75007 Paris, France—*numismatique.*

K.E. Skafte, DK-4800 Nykobing Falster, Danmark—*arms & armour, horology, portrait miniatures.*

Josiane Vedrines, 38 rue de Richelieu, 75001 Paris, France—*Numismatique.*

"Vieille France", 65 boulevard Général-Leclerc, 33120 Arcachon, France —*curiosités.*

Les' Vieux Ordinaires, 8 rue Baudin, 83000 Toulon, France—*affiches.*

5. CRAFTS AND USEFUL ARTS: ARTS ET MÉTIERS: KUNSTGEWERBE

Libreria Anticuaria Aristeucos, Paseo de la Bonanova 14, G. Barcelona 080 22, España—*gastronomy.*

Dr. Reto Feurer, Wanningerstrasse 7, D-8201 Obing/Oberbayern, Deutschland —*Film und Fotografie.*

Frederiksberg Antikvariat, Gammel Kongevej 120, 1850 København-V, Danmark.

Antiquariat M. und R. Fricke, Poststrasse 3, 4000 Düsseldorf 1, Poststrasse 3, 4000 Düsseldorf 1, Deutschland—*fotographie*

Le Grenier du Collectionneur, avenue Orban 238, 1150 Bruxelles, Belgie—*food and drink.*

Antiquariat Gunnar Kaldewey, Poststrasse 3, 4000 Düsseldorf 1, Deutschland.

Didier Lecointre et Denis Ozanne, 9 rue de Tournon, 75006 Paris, France —*Photographie.*

Arnold Levilliers, 118 route de Chartres (RN 188), 91400 Gometz-le-Chatel (Essone), France.

Daniel Morcrette, 4 avenue Joffre. 95270 Luzarches. France—*gastronomie.*

Bernd Schramm, Dänische Strasse 26, 2300 Kiel, Deutschland.

Edgar Soete, Librairie Salet, 5 Quai Voltaire, 75007 Paris, France—*gastronomie.*

Antiquariat H. U. Weiss Bibliotheca Gastronomica, Winzerstrasse 5, CH-8049 Zürich, Schweiz—*Gastronomie.*

6. ENTERTAINMENTS: THÉÂTRE ET CINÉMA: THEATER UND KINO

Librairie Bonaparte, 31 rue Bonaparte, 75006 Paris, France—*Théâtre, danse, cinema.*

Bücherkabinett, Türkenstrasse 21 (Innenhof), 8000 München 40, Deutschland
—*Tanz; Theater, Film, Zircus.*
Gilberte Cournand, 14 rue de Beaune, 75007 Paris, France—*danse, ballet.*
Luigi Finzi, Foro Buonaparte 12, 20121 Milano, Italia—*theatre.*
Librairie du Spectacle Garnier Arnoul, 39 rue de Seine, 75006 Paris, France
—*théâtre, ballet, cirque, mime.*
Robert Hartwig, Pestalozzistr. 23, D-1000 Berlin-Charlottenburg 12, Germany
—*Theater, Film.*
Livraria Eduardo Antunes Martinho, Rua Voz do Operário 7-B, Lisboa 2, Portugal
—*Theatre*
Pro Libro, Pariser Str. 14, D-1000 Berlin-Wilmersdorf 15, Germany—*Theater.*
Heinrich Rimanek, Kaiserstrasse 6, 1070 Wien, Österreich—*Theâter, Tanz.*
Libreria S. Agostino, Via S. Agostino 17/A, Roma, Italia.
Sörhuus Antikvariat AB, Riddargatan 23, 114 57 Stockholm, Sverige—*Theatre.*
Didier Terroy, 39 rue de Douai, Paris 75009, France.
Musik & Theater Antiquariat Armin Trösch, Rämistrasse 33, 8001 Zürich, Schweiz
—*Theater.*
Carl Wegner, Martin-Luther-Strasse 113, 1000 Berlin 62, Deutschland—*Theater.*
Gerhard Zähringer, Hauptstrasse 90, CH-8280 Kreuzlingen, Suisse
—*Buckbinderei-Literatur.*
Banco Libri s.a.s. Di V. Zanni & C., Via Marsala 6, 40126 Bologna, Italia—*Theatre.*
Madame S. Zlatin, 46 rue Madame, 75006 Paris, France—*théâtre, danse, cirque,
marionnettes.*

7. EROTIC AND CURIOUS: CURIOSITÉS et ÉROTIQUE: EROTIK

B.M.C.F. Antiquariat, Am Rain 23, 7936 Almendingen, Deutschland—*Magica und
Curiosa: Erotica.*
Walter Klügel, Postfach 40, Wimm 15, Schreiberghof, A-5201 Seekirchen, bei
Salzburg, Österreich.
Gabriel Molina, Travesia del Arenal 1, Madrid, España—*curious.*

8. FINE AND RARE: BEAUX LIVRES: SCHÖNE UND SELTENER
   BÜCHER

Alstadt Antiquariat, rue d'Or 16, CH-170 Fribourg, Schweiz.
l'Amateur d'Art, 38 rue de Vaugirard, 75006 Paris, France—*Editions originales.*
Antiquariat Amelang. Cranachstrasse 45, 2000 Hamburg 52, Deutschland
—*Pressendrucke.*
Noël Anselot, Hamaide 102, 6914 Redu, Belgium.
Antiquariaat Antiqua, Herengracht 159, 1015 BH Amsterdam, Nederland.
Antiqua Libri, Via Borgo Nuovo 27 2, I-20121 Milano, Italy—*15th & 16th
centuries.*
Antiquariat Athenaeum, Narvavagen 23, Box 5852, 102 48 Stockholm, Sverige.
Arts et Lettres, "Le Vieux Chateau", 83330 le Castellet, France—*anciens.*
Alexandre Baer [J. Baer & Co.], 2–6 rue Livingstone, 75018 Paris, France.
Émile Van Balberghe, Rue Vautier 4, B-1040 Bruxelles, Belgium.
Antiquariat Behrens, Leibnizstrasse 47, D-1000 Berlin 12, Deutschland.
J. L. Beijers B.V., Achter Sint Pieter 140, 3512 HT Utrecht, Nederland.

Pierre Berès, 14 avenue de Friedland, 75008 Paris, Franc—*livres illustrés; belles reliures.*

Bergmans and Brouwer Antiquarian Booksellers, Rustenburgerstraat 291, 1073 GE Amsterdam, Nederland.

Libreria Antiquaria Di S. Bernardino, via de Servi 49R, 50122 Firenze, Italia.

Libreria San Bernardo, Calle San Bernardo 63, Madrid 8, Spain.

Björck & Börjesson, Kindstugatan 2, Postbox 5405, 11131 Stockholm, Sverige.

Bjørnvig, Holm & Møller ApS, Odden Hovedgård, Mygdal, DK-9800 Hjørring, Denmark.

Herbert Blank, Melonenstrasse 54, 7000 Stuttgart 75, Deutschland*Pressendrucke.*

Bøckmann's Antikvariat, Rosensgade 11, DK-8000 Aarhus-C, Danmark—*first editions.*

Boghallens Antikvariat, Raadhuspladsen 37, DK 1585 København-V, Danmark —*fine, old, bound sets.*

Børsums Forlag og Antikvariat A-S, Fr. Nansensplass 2, Oslo 1, Norge—*old and rare.*

Jean Claude Bottin, Librairie Nicoise, 2 rue Défly, 06 Nice, France—*éditions originales.*

Le Bouquiniste, Via Principe Amedeo 29, 10123 Torino, Italia—*old and rare.*

Libreria Antiquaria Bourlot, Piazza San Carlo 183, I–10123 Torino, Italia—*old and rare.*

Bouvier Universitätsbuchhandlung G.m.b.H., am Hof 32, 5300 Bonn, Deutschland —*Bibliophilie.*

Branners Bibliofile Antikvariat ApS, Bredgade 10, 1260 København-K, Danmark —*old, rare, fine.*

Livres Anciens Maurice Bridel, S.A., Avenue du Tribunal-Fédéral 5, 1002 Lausanne, Schweiz.

Buch und Kunst, Münzgasse 16, 7750 Konstanz, Deutschland.

J. W. Cappelens Antikvariat, P.O. Box 350, Kirkegatan 15, N-0101 Oslo 1, Norge —*old and rare.*

Carlo Alberto Chiesa, Via Bigli 11, 20121 Milano, Italy—*old and rare.*

René Cluzel, 61 Rue de Vaugirard, 75006 Paris, France*16ème au 19ème cent.*

Libreria Colonnese, 33 Via S. Pietro A. Majella, 80138 Napoli, Italia—*first editions.*

Galleria Regina Cornaro, Via Regina Cornaro 214, I-31011 Asolo (Treviso), Italy.

C. Coulet & A. Faure, 5 rue Drouot, 75006 Paris, France—*editions originales.*

Damms Antikvariat A/S, Bokhuset, Tollbodgata 25, Oslo 2, Norge.

Max-Philippe Delatte, 15 rue Gustave Courbet, 75116 Paris, France—*éditions originales.*

Librairie Denis, 50 rue de la Scellerie, 37000 Tours, France.

Georges A. Deny, rue du Chêne 5, 1000 Bruxelles, Belge.

Antiquariaat Johan Devroe, L. Vanderkelenstraat 43, 3000 Leuven, Belgium.

Antiquariaat "Die Schmiede", Brouwersgracht 4, Amsterdam, Netherlands—*fine printing.*

Jürgen Dinter, Antiquariat für Philosophie, Buchholzstrasse 8–10, Köln, Deutschland—*Inkunabeln.*

'Docet', Via A. Righi 9/A, 40126 Bologna, Italia—*old and rare.*

Helmuth Domizlaff, Hocherlach 35, 8212-Übersee (Chiemsee), Deutschland—*15 und 16 Jahrhunderts.*

Librairie Dubouchet, 2 rue Général Foy, 42000 Saint-Étienne (Loire), France —*livres anciens.*

Erasmus Antiquariaat en Boekhandel. Spui 2, Amsterdam, Nederland—*16th century*.

Espagnon et Lebret, 1 rue de Fleurus, 75006 Paris, France—*Editions originales*.

Librairie Flammarion, 4 rue Casimir Delavigne, 75006 Paris, France—*éditions originales*.

Gérard Fleury, Librairie François, 1er, 34 Avenue Montaigne, 75008 Paris, France —*reliures*.

Forum B.V., P.O.B. 129, Oude Gracht 206, 3511 NR Utrecht, Netherlands.

Frederiksborg Antikvariat, Blehaven 10, DK-3400 Hillerød, Denmark—*first editions*.

Christian Galantaris, 15 rue des Saints-Pères, 75006 Paris, France—*éditions originales*.

Winfried Geisenheyner, Postfach 480155, Roseneck 6, D-4400 Münster-Hiltrup, Deutschland.

Antiquariat Gundel Gelbert, St. Apern Strasse 4, 5000 Köln 1, Deutschland.

A. L. van Gendt B.V., Qud Huizerweg 4, 1261 BD Blaricum, Nederland —*Incunabula*.

van Gendt Book Auctions N.V., Keizersgracht 96–98, 1015 CV Amsterdam, Nederland—*incunabula*.

Gilhofer Buch- und Kunstantiquariat K.G. Bognergasse 2, 1010 Wien, Österreich.

Gilhofer & Ranschburg G.m.b.H., Sternegg 5, 6005 Luzern, Schweiz—*Inkunabeln, XVI Jahrhundert*.

Claude Givaudan, rue du Soleil Levant 3, CH-1204 Genève—*relieures romantiques*.

Luigi Gonnelli & Figli, Via Ricasoli 14 rosso, Firenze, Italia—*old and rare*.

Paul Gothier, rue Bonne Fortune 3 et 5, Liège, Belgie.

Göttinger Antiquariat, Mauerstrasse 16/17, 3400 Göttingen, Deutschland.

Grafik-Antikvariatet, Skomakargatan 24, 111 29 Stockholm, Sverige.

Librairie du Grand-Chêne, Chemin de Montagny, 1603 Aran, Schweiz—*Stendhal, Balzac, Proust, Rilke*.

Max Günther, Charlottenbrunnerstrasse 5a, 1000 Berlin 33, Deutschland.

Antiquariaat Bert Hagen B.V., Molenweide 24, 1902 CH Castricum, Nederland —*15–20 centuries*.

Hallens Antikvariat, Köpmangatan 4, 11131 Stockholm, Sweden—*first editions*.

Hartung und Karl, Karolinenplatz 5A, 8000 München 2, Deutschland*fine & rare*.

P. H. Heitz, Postfach 80, Basel 4006, Schweiz—*Incunabula*.

Librairie Henner, 9 rue Henner, 75009 Paris. France—*Editions originales; reliures*.

Werner Heybutzki, Pfeilstrasse 8, 5000 Köln 1, Deutschland—*Erstausgaben*.

Hans Höchtberger. Mauerkircherstr. 28, 8000 München 80, Deutschland—*Erstausgaben*.

Ernst Hoffmann, Weissadlergasse 3, 6000 Frankfurt-am-Main, Deutschland —*Inkunabeln, Holzschnittbücher*.

Yvette Huillet, Manoir de Beaupre, Route de Monts, 37250 Veigne, France —*éditions originales, reliures*.

B. M. Israel, B.V., Boekhandel en Antiquariaat, N.Z. Voorburgwal 264, 1012 RS Amsterdam, Nederland.

N. Israel, Keizersgracht 489–491, Amsterdam, Nederland—*rare*.

Camille Joyaux, 55 rue de la Scellerie, 37000 Tours, France—*réliures*.

Antiquariaat Junk B. V., Van Eeghenstraat 129, 1071 GA Amsterdam, Nederland.

Sibylle Kaldewey, Poststrasse 3, D-4000 Düsseldorf 1, Deutschland.

Christos Katsicalis, Zambakis Bookshop, 14 Massalias Street, Athens 144TN, Ellas.

Librairie René Kieffer, 46 rue Saint-André des Arts, 75006 Paris, France—*éditions originales*.

E. und R. Kistner, Weinmarkt 6, 8500 Nürnberg, Deutschland.

Hans Horst Koch, Kurfürstendamm 216, 1000 Berlin 15, Deutschland.

Boekhandel Antiquariaat Kruger, Achter de Hoofdwacht 7, Nijmegen, Netherlands *16th–19th centuries.*

l'Argus du Livre. 17 Avenue de la Bourdonnais, 75007 Paris, France.

Librairie Lardanchet, 5 Route de Limonest, 69370 Saint-Didier au Mont d'Or, France—*Incunabula; reliures.*

Librairie Lefebvre, 1 rue Lucien-Pean, 45750 Saint-Pryvé-Saint-Mesmin, France —*éditions originales.*

Dr. Konrad Liebmann, Lortzingstrasse 1, 4500 Osnabrück, Deutschland —*Erstausgaben.*

Günther Leisten, St. Engelbertstrasse 24, D-5068 Odenthal-Voiswinkel, Deutschland.

S.C. Lemmers, van Bönninghausenlaan 16, 2161 Et Lisse, Nederland.

Lengertz' Antikvariat Gösta Janson, Regementsgatan 6, 211 42, Malmö, Sverige —*fine bindings.*

Librairie K, 17 rue Mazarine, 13100 Aix en Provence, France—*éditions originales.*

Libris Antikvariatet, Kommendörsgatan 14, 10243 Stockholm. (P.O. Box 5123), Schweden.

Claus Lincke, Königsallee 96, 4000 Düsseldorf, Deutschland—*Alte und seltene Bücher.*

Librairie Marc Loliée, 40 rue des Saints-Pères, 75007 Paris, France— *kelivres.*

A. van Loock, rue Saint Jean 51, 1000 Bruxelles, Belgie.

Lynge & Son, Silkegade 11, 1113 København, Danmark—*rare.*

Libreria Manterola, Manterola 8, San Sebastian,

Yves Margotat, 8 rue de l'Odéon, 75006 Paris, France—*rare*

Libreria Antiquaria Martelli, Via Santo Stefano 43, 40125 Bologna, Italia —*incunabula.*

Henri Martin-Brès, 60 rue Grignan, 13001 Marseille, France—*livres anciens.*

Carla Marzoli, Corso Porta Nuova 2, 20121 Milano, Italia—*Incunabula.*

Libreria Antiquaria Mediolanum, Via Montebello 30, 20121-Milano, Italia.

Konrad Meuschel, Kaiserplatz 5, 5300 Bonn, Deutschland.

Librairie du Miroir, rue du Miroir 9–11, 7000 Mons, Belgium—*XVIme-XVIIIme siècle.*

Molenes S.A., Librairie Quentin, 7 Place de la Fusterie, Ch-1204 Geneve, Suisse —*beaux livres.*

Gabriel Molina, Travesia del Arenal 1, Madrid, España

Daniel Morcrette, 4 avenue Joffre, 95270 Luzarches. (B.P. 26), France.

Libreria Antiquaria Moretti, Via Lusardi 8, 20122 Milano, Italy—*incunabula.*

Het Nedersaksische Antiquariaat, Nieuwstraat 50, 7411 LM Deventer, Nederland.

Les Neuf Muses, 41 Quai des Grands-Augustins, 75006 Paris, France—*éditions originales.*

Orfeo Vigarani, Libri Antichi et Stampe, Via Magnani N.6, 40134 Bologna, Italia —*18th century.*

Paradis des Chercheurs, 245 Chaussée de Charleroi, B-1060 Bruxelles, Belgium —*Bandes dessinées.*

Hans Pels-Leusden, Kurfürstendamm 59–60, D-1000 Berlin-Charlottenburg 15, Germany—*Pressendrucke.*

Henri Picard Fils, 126 Faubourg Saint-Honoré, 75008 Paris, France—*beaux livres anciens.*

Antiquariat Pinkus Genossenschaft, Froschaugasse 7, 8001 Zürich. (Postfach 8025 Zürich), Schweiz.

Pont Traversé, 8 rue de Vaugirard, 75006 Paris, France—*éditions originales modernes.*

Libreria Antiquaria Arturo Pregliasco, Via Accademia Albertina 3 bis, 10123 Torino, Italy.

Dr. Karl H. Pressler, Römerstrasse 7, 8000 München 40, Deutschland.

Librairie Puzin, 30 rue de la Paroisse, 78000 Versailles, France—*livres anciens, gravures.*

Antiquariato Librario Radaeli, Via A. Manzoni 39, 20121 Milano, Italia —*incunabula.*

"A la Recherche du Passe", Saint-Colombier, 56370 Sarzeau, France—*livres anciens.*

Libreria Ripoll, San Miguel 12, (Apartado 338), Palma de Mallorca, España.

Ludwig Röhrscheid G.m.b.H., am Hof 28, 5300 Bonn, Deutschland.

Rosenkilde og Bagger, 3 Kron-Prinsens-Gade, P.O. Box 2184, DK-1017 København, Danmark.

Ludwig Rosenthal's Antiquariaat, Bussumergrintweg 4, 1217 BP Hilversum, Nederland—*Incunabula.*

Emile Rossignol, 8 rue Bonaparte, 75006 Paris, France—*incunables; editions anciennes.*

Maurice Rouam, 29 rue Mazarine, 75006 Paris, France—*éditions originales.*

Umberto Saba, Via San Nicolo 30, 34121 Trieste, Italia—*incunabula; old and rare.*

Jean-Louis Sainte-Marie, B.P. 24. 6 rue Guileran, 82200 Moissac, France—*livres anciens.*

Antiquariaat Sanderus, Brugsestraat 88, 8510 Kortrijk, Belgium.

Jörg Schäfer, Alfred-Escher-Strasse 76, 8002 Zürich, Schweiz—*15. und 16. Jahrhunderts.*

H. Schmidt und C. Günther, Ubierstrasse 20, 6238 Hofheim, Deutschland —*Pressendrucke.*

Sibrium Libri e Manoscritti, Via Bigli 21, 20121 Milano, Italia.

Joaquim Guedes da Silva & Ca., Lda., Livraria Academica, Rua Martires da Liberdade 8–12, Porto, Portugal—*rare.*

Librairie Simonson, Chaussée de Charleroi 227, 1060 Bruxelles, Belgium.

Fiammetta Soave, Via Leccosa 4, Roma, Italia.

Edgar Soete, Librairie Salet, 5 Quai Voltaire, 75007 Paris, France—*reliures.*

Sörhuus Antikvariat AB, Riddargatan 23, 114 57 Stockholm, Sverige—*first editions.*

E. Speeckaert, 53 Boulevard Saint-Michel, B-1040 Bruxelles, Belgium—*reliures.*

Th. Stenderhoff & Co., Alter Fischmarkt 21, 4400 Münster, Deutschland—*Alte.*

Librairie Stendhal, 41 rue Mazarine, 75006 Paris, France—*reliures.*

Stuttgarter Antiquariat, Rathenaustrasse 21, 7000 Stuttgart 1, Deutschland —*Erstausgaben.*

Thelem Antiquariat, Mölkereistrasse 19, Postfach 50, 8399 Rotthalmünster, Deutschland.

Librairie Thomas-Scheler, 19 rue de Tournon, 75006 Paris, France—*incunables.*

Thulins Antikvariat, AB., 57060 Österbymo, Sverige—*early printed.*

Riewert Q. Tode, Dudenstr. 22, D-1000 Berlin-Kreuzberg 61, Germany —*Erstausgaben, Schöne Literatur d. 20. Jh.*

Antikvariat Blå Tornet, Drottninggatan 85, Stockholm, Sverige.

Jean Touzot, 38 rue Saint-Sulpice, 75278 Paris, France—*incunabula; reliures.*

Fl. Tulkens, 21 rue du Chêne, Bruxelles 1, Belgie—*old bindings.*

Librairie Robert D. Valette, 11 rue de Vaugirard, 75006 Paris, France —*incunabulae; reliures*

Jean Viardot, 15 rue de l'Echaudé, 75006 Paris, France—*éditions originales*.
Libreria Vinciana, Via Monte Napoleone 23, 20121 Milano, Italia—*old and rare*.
Bernhard Wendt, Hauptstrasse 29, 8084 Inning-Buch/Ammersee, Uber München, Deutschland—*Inkunabeln*.
Angelos Zambakis, Le Bibliophile, 14 Massalis, Athens 144, Ellas.
Buch und Kunstauktionshaus F. Zisska & R. Kistner, Unterer Anger 15, 8000 München 2, Deutschland—*Alte Drucke*.

9. JUVENILE: LIVRES D'ENFANTS: KINDERBÜCHE

Antiquariaat Amaryl, Koninginneweg 79, 1075–CJ Amsterdam, Netherlands
Antiquariat Erika Bartsch, Gottfried-Keller-Strasse 10, 7505 Ettlingen, Deutschland.
René Cluzel, 61 Rue de Vaugirard, 75006 Paris, France.
Olivier Encrenaz, 8 rue des Deux-Haies, 49000 Angers, France.
Antiquariaat Bert Hagen B.V., Molenweide 24, 1902 CH Castricum, Nederland.
Karl M. Halosar, Margaretenstrasse 35, 1040 Wien, Österreich—*alte Kinderbücher*.
Holte Antikvariat, Kongevej 43, DK-2840 Holte, Denmark.
Jacques d'Aspect, "La Legende", 58 rue d'Aubagne, 13001, Marseille, France.
Didier Lecointre et Denis Ozanne, 9 rue de Tournon, 75006 Paris, France.
Librairie des Victoires, 4 bis Place des Petits Pères, 75002 Paris, France
Loose, Papestraat 3, 's-Gravenhage, Netherlands.
Librairie Palladio, 66 rue du Cherche-Midi, 75006 Paris, France.
Antiquariat Pinkus Genossenschaft, Froschaugasse 7, 8001 Zürich. Schweiz.
Rotkäppchen, Brusseler Strasse 14, D-1000 Berlin-Wedding 65, Deutschland.
Thulin & Ohlson, Kungsgatan 9B, 41119 Göteborg, Sverige—*Swedish*.
Le Tour du Monde, 9 rue de la Pompe, 75116 Paris, France.

10. HISTORY: HISTOIRE: GESCHICHTE

Robert Alder, Junkerngasse 41, Bern, Schweiz.
Alfa Antiquarian Booksellers, P.O. Box 1116, Nijmegen. *and at* P.O. Box 26, 5360 AA Grave, Nederland—*Middle Ages*.
Antiquariaat Amaryl, Koninginneweg 79, 1075–CJ Amsterdam, Netherland —*Netherlands and Germany*.
Antiquariaat Amaryl, Tuinbouwstraat 74, 9717-JL Groningen, Nederland —*Netherlands*.
l'Amateur d'Art, 38 rue de Vaugirard, 75006 Paris, France.
Noël Anselot, Hamaide 102, 6914 Redu, Belgium—*spacial*.
Libreria Antigua y Moderna, Calle De Los Libreros 2, Madrid 13, Spain.
Antiquariat Athenaeum, Narvavagen 23, Box 5852, 102 48 Stockholm, Sverige.
Librairie d'Argences, 38 rue Saint-Sulpice, 75006 Paris, France.
"Armarium" Buchhandlung und Antiquariat, Jahnstrasse 116, 4000 Düsseldorf 1, Deutschland—*historische Hilfswissenschaften*.
Armarium Buchhandlung und Antiquariat, Zum See 10, 2313 Raisdorf Über Kiel, Deutschland.
B.M.C.F. Antiquariat, AM Rain 23, 7936 Almendingen, Deutschland —*Folkloristica*.
Librairie du Bât d'Argent et du Chariot d'Or, 38 rue des Remparts d'Ainay, 69002 Lyon, France.
Anton W. van Bekhoven. Ruysdaelplein 5, 1411 RD Naarden, Nederland.
Berche et Pagis, 60 rue Mazarine, 75006 Paris, France.

J. Berger, Kohlmarkt 3, 1010 Wien, Österreich—*Archäologie*.
Berliner Antiquariat, Rheinstrasse 6, D-1000 Berlin-Friedenau 41, Germany.
André Bessières, 12 rue Delambre, 75014 Paris, France.
Antiquariaat G. J. Bestebreurtje, Lichte Gaard 2, P.O. Box 364 Aj Utrecht,
   Nederland—*Maritime*.
Biblarte, Limitada, Rua de Sao Pedro de Alcantara 71, Lisboa 2, Portugal.
Ton Bolland, Prinsengracht 493, 1002 Amsterdam, Nederland—*Reformation and
   Church history*.
Michel Bon, 4 rue Frederic-Sauton, 75005 Paris, France.
Book Market, Rue de la Madeleine 47, B-1000 Bruxelles, Belgium.
Bouma's Boekhuis, B.V., Turfsingel 3, Groningen, Nederland—*history*.
La Bouquinerie, 89 rue de Lyon, 89200 Avallon, France.
Le Bouquiniste, Via Principe Amedeo 29, 10123 Torino, Italia.
Bourcy & Paulusch, Wipplingerstrasse 5, 1010 Wien, Österreich—*Genealogie*.
Antiquariaat Brabant, Lange Putstraat 14, 5211 KN 's-Hertogenbosch, Nederland.
Librairie Galerie Bretonne, 1 rue des Fossés, 35000 Rennes, France—*folklore*.
Buchantiquariat Britschgi, Rämistrasse 33, 8000 Zürich, Schweiz.
Daniel Brun, Edition et Diffusion M.P., 6 rue Clodion, 75015 Paris, France.
Die Bücherlaube, Weimarer Str. 29, D-1000 Berlin-Charlottenburg 12, Germany.
Bücherstube am See, Kreuzlingerstrasse 11, 7750 Konstanz-Bodensee, Deutschland.
Claude Buffet, 7 rue Saint-Sulpice, 75006 Paris, France.
Livraria Castro e Silva, Rua da Rosa 31, Lisboa, Portugal.
Jean Cau, 22 rue Peyras et Bouquinerie Balaran, 52 rue du Taur, 31000 Toulouse,
   France.
Librairie Ancienne Chambefort, 26 Place Bellecour, 69 Lyon, France.
Jacques Chaminade, 8 rue de l'Isle, 74000 Annecy, France.
Georges Chauvin, 78 rue Mazarine, 75006 Paris, France.
Librairie Chevalier, 176A rue Blaes, 1000 Bruxelles, Belgique.
Carl F. Chispeels, Combahnstrasse 15, 5300 Bonn 3, Deutschland—*15. Jahrhundert*.
Antiquariat "Christo", Alte Gasse 67, Frankfurt M, Deutschland.
Clavreuil, 37 rue Saint-André-des-Arts 75006 Paris, France.
Librairie Pierre Clerc, 13 rue Alexandre Cabanel, 34000 Montpellier, France.
Librairie Colbert, 11 bis rue Colbert (Place du Chateau), 78000 Versailles, France
   117
Commerzcabinett, Humboldtstrasse 125, 2000 Hamburg 76, Deutschland—*Sozial.
   Finanzgeschichte*.
Gerard Crucis, rue St. Jean 33, 1000 Bruxelles, Belgium.
Francis Dasté, 16 rue de Tournon, 75006 Paris, France—*Paris*.
Matthijs De Jongh, Jeltewei 44–46, 8622 XT Hommerts, Netherlands—*Dutch
   history, History of ideas*.
Antiquariaat De Tille B.V., Weerd 11, P.O. Box 233, 8901 BA Leeuwarden,
   Nederland.
Librairie Denis, 50 rue de la Scellerie, 37000 Tours, France.
Librairie des Deux Gares. 76 Boulevard de Magenta, 75010 Paris, France.
Alice Elchlepp, Schillerstrasse 14, 3360 Osterode a. Harz, Deutschland.
N.G. Elwert Universitätsbuchhandlung, Reitgasse 7–9, 3550 Marburg (Lahn),
   Deutschland.
Olivier Encrenaz, 8 rue des Deux-Haies, 49000 Angers, France.
Frede Engholst, Studiesstraede 35, 1455 København-K, Danmark.
Livraria Ferin Lda., Rua Nova do Almada 74, Lisboa, Portugal.
Le Libraire Alain Ferraton, Rue Ernest Allard 39, B-1000 Bruxelles, Belgium
   —*Moyen age*.

Forum B.V., P.O.B. 129, Oude Gracht 206, 3511 NR Utrecht, Netherlands.
Pierre-M. Gason, 8 Place de la Victoire, 4580 Aubel, Belgium.
H. G. Gerritsen, Van Welderenstraat 88, Nijmegen, Nederland.
Karl Gess, Kanzleistrasse 5, 7750 Konstanz, Deutschland.
Gerard Goldau, Gasteig 4, 8022 Grünwald, Deutschland—*Militaria*.
René Gonot, Librairie Saint-Augustin, ·99 boulevard Haussmann, 75008 Paris, France.
Paul Goossens, Greenhillstraat 45, 8320 Brugge, Belgium.
Fernand Gothier, place du 20 Août 11, 4000 Liège, Belgie.
Libreria Oreste Gozzini di Pietro Chellini, Via Ricasoli 49, 50122 Firenze, Italia.
Antoine Grandmaison, Librairie "Les Arcades", 8 rue de Castiglione, 75001 Paris, France.
J. Grubb's Antikvariat, Nørregade 47, Dk-1165 København-K, Danmark.
Michel Guillaume & Cie., S.A.R.L., Librairie Generale du Calvados, 98 rue Saint-Pierre, 14000 Caen, France.
Dr. Annemarie Guyer-Halter, Auf der Mauer 1, 8000 Zürich 1, Schweiz.
Gysbers en van Loon, Bakkerstraat 7A, Arnhem, Nederland—*Dutch*.
Antiquariaat Bert Hagen B.V., Molenweide 24, 1902 CH Castricum, Nederland.
Bert Hagen, Herenstraat 38, 1015 CB Amsterdam, Nederland.
Adolf M. Hakkert, Calle Alfambra 26, Las Palmas España—*Ancient history: Byzantium*
Jean-Jacques Hankard, 25 rue de la Paix, 1050 Bruxelles, Belgie.
J.J. Heckenhauer, Holzmarkt 5, 7400 Tübingen, Deutschland.
Rudolf Heger, Wollezeile 2, 1010 Wien 1, Osterreich—*Folklore*.
Serge Helluin, 11 rue Leon-Blum, 80000 Amiens, France.
Theodor Hennig, Motzstr. 25, D-1000 Berlin-Schöneberg 30, Germany.
Antikvaarinen Kirjakauppa Seppo Hiltunen, Viherniemenkatu 3, Helsinki 53, Finland.
Livraria Histórica e Ultramarina Lda [J. C. Silva], Travessa da Queimada 28, 1200–Lisboa 2, Portugal.
Antiquariaat C. Hovingh & Zn., Kleine Houtstraat 50, 2011DP Haarlem, Nederland.
M. L. Huizenga, Oudez. Achterburgwal 156, 1012 DW Amsterdam, Nederland—*antiquity*.
l'Intermédiaire du Livre, 88 rue Bonaparte, 75006 Paris, France.
Xavier Jehanno, 4 Place de l'Eglise, 78430 Louveciennes, France.
Karl Marx Buchhandlung, G.m.b.H., Jordanstrasse 11, 6000 Frankfurt 90, Deutschland.
Historisch Antiquariaat Annelies Kee, Spuistraat 125, 1012 SV Amsterdam, Nederland—*General and Church history*.
Keip, KG Wissenschaftliches Antiquariat, Hainerweg 46–48, 6000 Frankfurt-am-Main 70, Deutschland.
J. Kitzinger, Schellingstrasse 25, 8000 München, Deutschland.
Antiquariat A. Klittich-Pfankuch, Kleine Burg 12, 3300 Braunschweig, Deutschland.
Kreuzberger Antiquariat, Yorckstr. 75, D-1000 Berlin-Kreuzberg 61, Germany.
Antiquariat Walter Krieg Verlag K.G. Kärntnerstrasse 4, 1010 Wien, Österreich.
Wilhelm Kuhrdt, Paulusstrasse 28, 4800 Bielefeld, Deutschland.
Bubb Kuyper, Kleine Houstraat 60, 2011 DP Haarlem, Netherlands.
Henri Laffitte Libraire, 13 rue de Buci, 75006 Paris, France.
Georges Lamongie, 2 rue de la Nation, 24000 Perigueux, France.
Herbert Lang & Cie A.G., Münzgraben 2, 3000 Bern 7, Schweiz.

Librairie Lardanchet, 5 Route de Limonest, 69370 Saint-Didier au Mont d'Or, France.
Lestringant, 123 rue Général-Leclerc, 76000 Rouen, France.
Jacques Levy, 46 rue d'Alésia, 75014 Paris, France.
Libreria Luigi Lombardi, Via Constantinopoli 4 bis, 80138 Napoli, Italia.
Jules Lorieul, Normania, 3 Place du Castel, 50580 Port-Bail, France.
Christa Lummert, Skalitzer Str. 75, D-1000 Berlin-Kreuzberg 36, Germany.
Yves Margotat, 8 rue de l'Odéon, 75006 Paris, France—*XVe au XVIIIe siècle*.
Libreria Antiquaria Martelli, Via Santo Stefano 43, 40125 Bologna, Italia—*folklore, history*.
Libreria Antiquaria Montenegro, Via Dei Gracchi 291/a, 00192 Roma, Italia —*Fascism*.
Müller & Gräff, Calwerstrasse 54, 7000 Stuttgart-1, Deutschland.
Nansensgade Antikvariat, Nansensgade 70, 1366 København-K, Denmark.
Librairie Nantaise Y. Vachon. 3 Place de la Monnaie, 44000 Nantes, France —*guerre de Vendée*.
Peter Neser, Kreuzlingerstrasse 11, 7750 Konstanz-Bodensee, Deutschland.
Nordiska Antivariska Bokhandeln, Norra Magasingatan 6, Helsingfors, Suomi.
Leo S. Olschki—Studio Bibliografico, 52046 Lucignano (Arezzo), Italia.
Librairie Palladio, 66 rue du Cherche-Midi, 75006 Paris, France.
J.-P. Parrot, 59 rue de Rennes, 75006 Paris, France.
Parsifal [S.A.R.L.], 80 Boulevard Raspail, 75006 Paris, France.
Francine van der Perre, rue de la Madeleine 23, 1000 Bruxelles, Belgie—*genealogy, heraldry*.
Albert Petit-Siroux, 45, 46, 47 Galerie Vivienne, 75002 Paris, France.
Editions A. & J. Picard, 82 rue Bonaparte, 75006 Paris, France.
F. Pinczower, 83 Sokolow Street, Tel Aviv, Israel.
Antiquariat Pinkus Genossenschaft, Froschaugasse 7, 8001 Zürich, Schweiz—*Kulturgeschichte*.
Librairie Poursin, Cite Noël, 22 rue Rambuteau, 75003 Paris, France.
Dr. Karl H. Pressler, Römerstrasse 7, 8000 München 40, Deutschland.
Pro Libro, Pariser Str. 14, D-1000 Berlin-Wilmersdorf 15, Germany.
Wilhelm Puskas, Weihburggasse 16, 1010 Wien, Österreich.
Librairie Puzin, 30 rue de la Paroisse, 78000 Versailles, France.
Librairie Raoust, 11 rue Neuve, 59000 Lille, France.
Redins Antikvariat, Box 150 49 S-75015 Uppsala, Sweden.
Librairie A. Remy, 25 rue Stanislas, 54000 Nancy, France.
Günter Richter, Breite Strasse 29, 1000 Berlin 33, Deutschland.
Antiquariaat de Rijzende Zon, Poststraat 8, 5038 DH Tilburg, Nederland.
Anne-Marie Robichon, 16 Quai de la Loire, 37210 Rochecorbon/Vouvray, France.
Rogers Turner Books Ltd., 24 rue du Buisson Richard, 78600 le Mesnil-le-Roi, France.
Ludwig Röhrscheid G.m.b.H., am Hof 28, 5300 Bonn, Deutschland.
Librairie A. Rombaut, Lievestraat 14, 9000 Gent, Belgie—*genealogy*.
Nils Sabels Antivariat, Box 1049, 15024 Rönninge 1, Sweden.
Jean-Louis Sainte-Marie, B.P. 24. 6 rue Guileran, 82200 Moissac, France.
Antiquariat und Verlag Georg Sauer, Gerichtsstrasse 7, 6240 Königstein im Taunus, Deutschland.
Gerhard Scheppler, Giselastrasse 25, 8000 München 40, Deutschland.
Ludwig Helmut Schiller, am Birkenrain 28, 7811 St. Peter, Deutschland.
Antiquariat Paul Schindegger, Heidenpoint 26, 8228 Freilassing, Deutschland.

Ferdinand Schöningh, Domhof 4c, 4500 Osnabrück, Deutschland.
Hartmut R. Schreyer, Auf dem Kreuz 9, D-8900 Augsburg, Deutschland.
Libreria Antiquaria Soave, Via Po 48, 10123 Torino, Italia.
Thomas Sonnenthal, Cauerstrasse 20/21, Berlin-Charlottenburg 10, Deutschland.
Sonnewald-Heckenhauer, Waldhof 1, 7947 Mengen, Deutschland.
Antiquariat B.F. Stadelmann, Dieselstrasse 5, 6070 Langen, Deutschland *Kulturgeschichte.*
J.A. Stargardt, Radestrasse 10, 3550 Marburg, Deutschland—*Genealogie und Heraldik.*
Th. Stenderhoff & Co., Alter Fischmarkt 21, 4400 Münster, Deutschland.
Librairie Stendhal, 41 rue Mazarine, 75006 Paris, France.
Jacques Stoven, 53 rue du Mail, 49000 Angers, France.
Stuttgarter Antiquariat, Rathenaustrasse 21, 7000 Stuttgart 1, Deutschland—*16. Jahrhunderts.*
Thélème, rue St. Savournin No. 29, Marseille 13005, France.
Jean Touzot, 38 rue Saint-Sulpice, 75278 Paris, France.
Librairie Valleriaux, 98 Boulevard Voltaire, 75011 Paris, France.
Libreria Antiquaria Andrea Vallerini, Via Dei Mille 7A–13, I-56100 Pisa, Italy —*Italian.*
Josiane Vedrines, 38 rue de Richelieu, 75001 Paris, France.
Wahle et Compagnie S.P.R.L., rue du Méry 14a, 4000 Liege, Belgium—*Belgique.*
R. & I. Wanner-Zander, Kronengasse 35, 5400 Baden, Schweiz.
Elisabeth Wellnitz, Sachsenstrasse 35, 6100 Darmstadt, Deutschland.
Banco Libri s.a.s. Di V. Zanni & C., Via Marsala 6, 40126 Bologna, Italia.

11. LANGUAGES: LANGUES: SPRACHE

Antiikki-Kirja, Kalevankatu 25, 00100 Helsinki 10, Finland—*Finno-ugric linguistics.*
Antikvarijat-Knjižara. Nakladnog Zavoda Matice Hrvatske. Ilica 62, 41000 Zagreb, Jugoslavij—*Slavica; alter deutscher Bücher.*
Librairie d'Argences, 38 rue Saint-Sulpice, 75006 Paris, France—*philologie.*
Libreria Anticuaria Aristeucos, Paseo de la Bonanova 14, G. Barcelona 080 22, España—*Spanish, Catalan, Latin from 15 to 19 centuries.*
Armarium Buchhandlung und Antiquariat, Zum See 10, 2313 Raisdorf Über Kiel, Deutschland—*Slavistik.*
Auvermann und Reiss KG, Zum Talblick 2, 6246 Glashütten, Deutschland—*Roman- istik, Hispanistik.*
Berliner Antiquariat, Rheinstrasse 6, D-1000 Berlin-Friedenau 41, Germany.
Le Bibliophile Russe, 12 rue Lamartine, 75009 Paris, France—*Russe.*
Bouma's Boekhuis, B.V., Turfsingel 3, Groningen, Nederland—*Philology.*
Cankarjeva Zalozba, Kopitarjeva 2, 61001 Ljubljana. Jugoslavija—*Slavica.*
F. Deuticke, Helferstorferstrasse 4, Wien 1, Österreich—*Philologie.*
Bottega d'Erasmo, Via Gaudenzio Ferrari 9, 10124 Torino, Italia—*philology.*
Gerold & Co., Graben 31, 1011 Wien, Österreich—*Philologie.*
Librairie Orientaliste Paul Geuthner S.A. 12 rue Vavin, 75006 Paris, France.
René Gonot, Librairie Saint-Augustin, 99 boulevard Haussmann, 75008 Paris, France—*English.*
J. Grubb's Antikvariat, Nørregade 47, Dk-1165 København-K, Danmark —*Philology.*
Adolf M. Hakkert, Calle Alfambra 26, Las Palmas España—*Philology.*
A. L. Hasbach, Wollzeile 9 und 29, Wien 1, Österreich—*Sprachwissenschaft.*

Antiquariat Iberia, Hirschengraben 6, 3001 Berne, Schweiz—*Espagnole.*
Gunnar Johanson-Thor, AB., Ellinge, 24100 Eslöv, Sverige—*old Swedish.*
Jacques Levy, 46 rue d'Alésia, 75014 Paris, France—*Hebraica.*
Lynge & Son, Silkegade 11, 1113 København, Danmark—*linguistics.*
Martinus Nijhoff B.V., P.O. Box 269, Noordwal 4, 2501-AX 's-Gravenhage, Netherlands.
Libreria Antiquaria Palmaverde, Via Castiglione 35, 40124 Bologna, Italia
— *philology.*
Antiquariat Piermont, Postfach 21 02 32, 5300 Bonn 2; Rolandstrasse 13, 5480
Remagen-Rolandswerth, Deutschland.
Gisela Plähn, Innsbrucker Str. 4, D-1000 Berlin-Schoneberg, Germany—*Rossica,*
Slavica.
G. Postma, O.Z. Voorburgwal 249, 1012 EZ Amsterdam, Nederland.
Libreria Antiquaria Prandi, Viale Timavo 75, Reggio Emilia, Italia—*philology.*
Antiquariaat de Rijzende Zon, Poststraat 8, 5038 DH Tilburg, Nederland
—*Orientalia.*
Rogers Turner Books Ltd., 24 rue du Buisson Richard, 78600 le Mesnil-le-Roi,
France—*études allemandes.*
R. B. Rosenthal, Rua do Alecrim 47-4° Salas D, Lisboa 2, Portugal—*Portugese,*
Spanish.
H. Schmidt und C. Günther, Ubierstrasse 20, 6238 Hofheim, Deutschland
—*Französische.*
Antiquariaat Schuhmacher, Gelderschekade 107, 1011 EM Amsterdam, Nederland
—*Deutsch, English, Français.*
Société Hébraica Judaica, 12 rue des Hospitalières St.-Gervais, 75004 Paris, France.
Librairie-editions Thanh-Long, 34 rue Dekens, 1040 Bruxelles, Belgie—*Vietnamese.*
Thulin & Ohlson, Kungsgatan 9B, 41119 Göteborg, Sverige—*Swedish Childrens*
books.
Wladimir Tiraspolsky, 69 avenue Victor-Cresson, 92130 Issy-les-Moulineaux,
France—*Langues estrangères.*
Zohar, I Nachlat-Benjamin, Tel Aviv. Israel—*Hebrew, Yiddish.*

12. LAW AND CRIMINOLOGY: DROIT ET CRIMOLOGIE: RECHT

Johan Beek, Graaf Van Lyndenlaan 55, 3771 JB Barneveld Netherlands.
Libreria Bonfanti, Via Macedonio Melloni 19, 20129 Milano, Italia.
Robert Cayla, 28 rue Saint-Sulpice, 75006 Paris, France— *manuscrits, autographes.*
Les Chevaux Légers, 34 rue Vivienne, 75002 Paris, France.
Librairie Duchemin, 18 rue Soufflot, 75005 Paris, France.
Bottega d'Erasmo, Via Gaudenzio Ferrari 9, 10124 Torino, Italia.
Livraria Ferin Lda., Rua Nova do Almada 74, Lisboa, Portugal
Luigi Gonnelli & Figli, Via Ricasoli 14 rosso, Firenze, Italia—*manuscripts.*
Libreria Oreste Gozzini di Pietro Chellini, Via Ricasoli 49, 50122 Firenze, Italia
—*jurisprudence.*
Michel Guillaume & Cie., S.A.R.L., Librairie Generale du Calvados, 98 rue
Saint-Pierre, 14000 Caen, France.
Icinimann & Co., Kirchgasse 17, 8000 Zürich 1, Schweiz.
Maarten J. Israel, P.O. Box 8, 1110 AA Dieman, Netherlands.
Librairie J. Joly, 6 rue Victor-Cousin, 75005 Paris, France—*droit ancien et modern,*
periodiques juridiques.
Iuridisch Antiquariaat, L Noordeinde 39, 2514 GC 'S-Gravenhage, Nederland.
Iuridische Boekhandel and Antiquariaat, Kloksteeg 4, 2311 SL Leiden, Nederland.

Keip, KG Wissenschaftliches Antiquariat Hainerweg 46–48, 6000 Frankfurt-am-Main 70, Deutschland—*Wirtschaft und Gesellschaft.*
Herbert Lang & Cie A.G., Münzgraben 2, 3000 Bern 7, Schweiz.
Leonardo Lapiccirella, 3 via Tornabuoni, 50123 Firenze, Italia—*manuscripts woodcut books.*
Libreria Pasquale Lombardi, Via San Eufemia 11, 00187 Roma, Italia.
Jean-Jacques Magis, 47 rue Saint André-des-Arts, 76006 Paris, France.
Manz'sche Verlags-und Universitätsbuchhandlung, Kohlmarkt 16, 1014-Wien, Österreich.
W. Mauke Söhne, Karl-Muck-Platz 12, 2000 Hamburg 36, Deutschland.
Antikvariat Pinkerton, Nansensgade 68, 1366 København-K, Denmark—*crime & detective fiction*
Claude Riccardi, 7 rue Meyerbeer, 06000 Nice, France—*procès.*
R. B. Rosenthal, Rua do Alecrim 47-4° Salas D, Lisboa 2, Portugal—*Portuguese Spanish.*
Antiquariat B.F. Stadelmann, Dieselstrasse 5, 6070 Langen, Deutschland.
Dr. Karl Stropek, Währingerstrasse 122, 1181 Wien, Österreich.
Struppe und Winckler, Potsdamerstrasse 103, 1000 Berlin 30, Deutschland.
René Vigneron, Les Argonautes, 74 rue de Seine, 75006 Paris, France—*autographes manuscrits.*
Alexander Wild, Rathausgasse 30, 3011 Bern, Schweiz.

13. MEDICINE: MÉDICINE: MEDIZIN

l'Ane d'Or, Boite Postale 6, 95450 Vigny, France.
Torsten Baland, Spielhagenstr. 13, D-1000 Berlin-Charlottenburg 10, Deutschland.
Fabrice Bayarre, 21 rue de Tournon, 75006 Paris, France.
Libreria Bertocchi, Strada Maggiore 70, 40125 Bologna, Italia.
Félix Bloch, 10 Route de Rolle, 1162 Saint-Prex, Suisse.
E. J. Bonset, Patrijzenstraat 8, 2040-AC Zandvoort, Nederland—*psychology.*
Bourcy & Paulusch, Wipplingerstrasse 5, 1010 Wien, Österreich.
Alain Brieux, 48 rue Jacob, 75006 Paris, France—*histoire.*
Libreria Antiquaria Brighenti, Via Malpertusoi 40123 Bologna, Italia—*early medicine.*
François et Rodolphe Chamonal, 40 rue le Peletier, 75009 Paris, France.
Cosmos Antiquarian Books, (P.O. Box 30) Market 23, 7240AA Lochem, Nederland —*history.*
Jean Michel de Floesser, 28 rue des Remparts, 33000 Bordeaux (Gironde), France *médecine ancienne.*
Librairie le François, 91 boulevard Saint-Germain, 75006 Paris, France.
Jacques Gabay, 151 bis. rue Saint-Jacques, 75005 Paris, France—*ancienne.*
Winfried Geisenheyner, Postfach 480155, Roseneck 6, D-4400 Münster-Hiltrup Deutschland.
van Gendt Book Auctions N.V., Keizersgracht 96–98, 1015 CV Amsterdam Nederland.
Gilhofer & Ranschburg G.m.b.H., Sternegg 5, 6005 Luzern, Schweiz—*Geschichte.*
Hagelin Antikvariat AB, P.O. Box 3321, 10366 Stockholm, Schweden—*history.*
Heinimann & Co., Kirchgasse 17, 8000 Zürich 1, Schweiz.
Humaniora Antiqua, Herengracht 242, Amsterdam, Netherlands—*psychiatry mental sciences.*
B. M. Israel, B.V., Boekhandel en Antiquariaat, N.Z. Voorburgwal 264, 1012 R: Amsterdam, Nederland.

Heinz Hubertus Kampf, Wasserwerkgasse 31, Postfach 246. CH-3011 Bern, Schweiz
—*alte*.
Valentin Koerner G.mb.H., H.-Sielckenstrasse 36, 7570 Baden-Baden, Deutschland—
16. Jahrhundert.
Carl-Ernst Kohlhauer, Graser Weg 2, 8805 Feuchtwangen, Deutschland—*alte*.
Lange und Springer G.m.b.H. & Co., Antiquariat, Otto-Suhr-Allee 26-28, D-1000
Berlin 10, Deutschland.
Bernard Maille, 3 rue Dante, 75005 Paris, France.
Livraria Eduardo Antunes Martinho, Rua Voz do Operário 7-B, Lisboa 2, Portugal.
Wilhelm Maudrich, Lazarettgasse 1, 1091 Wien, Österreich.
Librairie Monge, 5 rue de L'Echaudé, 75006 Paris, France—*histoire des sciences et
de la médicine*.
Leo S. Olschki—Studio Bibliografico, 52046 Lucignano (Arezzo), Italia.
H. Preidel, Antiquariat Für Medizin, (Postfach 1128), Bismarckstrasse 20, 3007
Gehrden/Hannover, Deutschland—*alte Medizin*.
Libreria Antiquaria C.E. Rappaport, Via Sistina 23, 00187 Roma, Italia.
De Renaissance van het Boek, Walpoortstraat 7, 9000 Gent, Belgie.
Librairie Thomas-Scheler, 19 rue de Tournon, 75006 Paris, France.
Venator, KG., Cäcilienstrasse 48 (im Kunsthaus Lempertz) 5000 Köln, Deutschland.
Dr. Helmut Vester, Friedrichstrasse 7, 4000 Düsseldorf, Deutschland.
"Vieille France", 65 boulevard Général-Leclerc, 33120 Arcachon, France.
Rainer Gerd Voigt, Langerstrasse 2/IV, D-8000 München 80, Deutschland.
J. Vrin, 6 Place de la Sorbonne, 75005 Paris, France—*médecine*.
J. Wristers, Minrebroederstraat 13, Utrecht, Nederland.

14. MUSIC: MUSIQUE: MUSIK UND NOTEN

Antikvarboltok, Muzeum Körut 17, Budapest V, Magyarország
Arioso S.A.R.L., 6 rue Lamartine, 75009 Paris, France.
Berliner Musikantiquariat, Pestalozzlstr. 23. D 1000 Berlin-Charlottenburg 12,
Deutschland.
Bertola & Locatelli Musica, Via Alba 53, 12100 Cuneo, Italia.
Bosworth & Co., Ltd., Dr.-Karl-Lueger-Platz 2, A-1010 Wien, Österreich
—*Musikalien (Noten)*.
Bücherkabinett, Türkenstrasse 21 (Innenhof), 8000 München 40, Deutschland.
Candide, 7 rue Montault, 49000 Angers, France—*musicologie*.
Doblinger Musikhaus und Musikverlag. Dorotheergasse 10, A-1010 Wien. Öster-
reich—*Früh und Erstdrucke*.
Le Libraire Alain Ferraton, Rue Ernest Allard 39, B-1000 Bruxelles, Belgium.
Dan Fog, Graabrødretorv 7, 1154 København-K, Danmark.
Gallini, Via Del Conservatorio 17, 20122 Milano, Italia.
Librairie du Spectacle Garnier Arnoul, 39 rue de Seine, 75006 Paris, France.
Robert Hartwig, Pestalozzistr. 23, D-1000 Berlin-Charlottenburg 12, Germany
—*Musik, Noten*.
Dr. Emil Katzbichler, Wilhelm-ring 7. 8201 Frasdorf, Deutschland.
G.N. Landré, B.V., Muziekboekhandel & Antiquariaat, Anjeller Sdwarsstraat 36
1015 NR Amsterdam, Netherlands.
Leliefeld Muziekantiquariaten, 212 Riouwstraat, 's-Gravenhage, Nederland.
G. de Lucenay, 15 rue Petite-Fusterie, 84000 Avignon, France *musique ancienne*.
Musica Antiqua, Alleen 54, København, Danmark,
Librairie Pugno, 19 Quai des Grandes-Augustins, 75006 Paris, France.
Librairie A. Rombaut, Lievestraat 14, 9000 Gent, Belgie.

269

Libreria S. Agostino, Via S. Agostino 17/A, Roma, Italia.
Schlöhlein G.m.b.H., Schützenmattstrasse 15, CH-4003 Basel, Schweiz
—*Musikliteratur, Musikalische Erst- und Fruhdrucke.*
Hans Schneider, Mozartstrasse 6, 8132 Tutzing Über München, Deutschland.
Manfred Sieg, Fasanenstr. 45, D-1000 Berlin-Wilmersdorf 15, Germany.
Sörhuus Antikvariat AB, Riddargatan 23, 114 57 Stockholm, Sverige.
Musik & Theater Antiquariat Armin Trösch, Rämistrasse 33, 8001 Zürich, Schweiz.
J. Voerster, Relenberg Strasse 20, 7000 Stuttgart, Deutschland.
Karl Dieter Wagner, Rothenbaumchaussee 1, 2000 Hamburg 13, Deutschland.
Madame S. Zlatin, 46 rue Madame, 75006 Paris, France.

15. NATURAL HISTORY: SCIENCES NATURELLES: NATURWISSENSCHAFT

A. Asher & Co., B.V., Keizersgracht 489–491, Amsterdam, Nederland.
Azevedo and Burnay Lda, Travessa de S. Placido 48-B, 1200 Lisboa, Portugal, Portugal.
Dr. W. Backhuys, Ourdorpweg 12, 3062-RC Rotterdam, Netherlands—*zoology, botany.*
Bickhardt'sche Buchhandlung, Karl-Marx-Strasse 168, 1000 Berlin-Neukölln 44, Deutschland.
E. J. Brill, Oude Rijn 33A, Leiden, Nederland.
Brockhaus Antiquarium, Am Wallgraben 127, 7000 Stuttgart 80, Deutschland—*Geographie, Ethnologie.*
Bücher-Schmidt Antiquariat, Torgasse 4, 8000 Zürich, Schweiz—*Zoologie, Botanik.*
Das Bücherhaus, Wiesenstrasse 21, 3012 Langenhagen, Deutschland.
Der Buchfreund [Walter Schaden], Sonnenfelsgasse 4, 1010 Wien 1, Österreich —*Naturwissenschaften.*
Gaston Colas, 84 boulevard Raspail, 75006 Paris, France—*archaeologie.*
F. Deuticke, Helferstorferstrasse 4, Wien 1, Österreich—*Naturwissenschaften.*
Harri Deutsch, Naturwissenschaftliche Fachbuchhandlung, Gräfstrasse 47, 6000 Frankfurt am Main, Deutschland.
Dresdner Antiquariat Paul Alicke, Kurt-Schumacher-Strasse 33–35, D-6000 Frankfurt am Main, Deutschland—*Kochbücher.*
George J. Erdlen, Obermarkt 5, Postfach 1109, 8110 Murnau am Staffelsee, Deutschland—*Botanik, Zoologie, Anthropologie.*
R. Friedländer & Sohn G.m.b.H., Dessauer Strasse 28–29, 1000 Berlin 61, Deutschland—*Botanik, Zoologie, Geologie.*
Librairie Orientaliste Paul Geuthner S.A. 12 rue Vavin, 75006 Paris, France —*archéologie.*
Gsellius'sche Antiquariat, Hertastrasse 16, 1000 Berlin 37, Deutschland.
Dr. Rudolf Habelt, G.m.b.H., am Buchenhang 1, 5300 Bonn, Deutschland—*archäologie.*
Hagelin Antikvariat AB, P.O. Box 3321, 10366 Stockholm, Schweden.
Antiquariaat Junk B. V., Van Eeghenstraat 129, 1071 GA Amsterdam, Nederland.
Kiepert G.m.b.H. Hardenbergstrasse 4–5, 1000 Berlin 12, Deutschland.
A. KOK en Zn, 14–18 Oude Hoogstraat, Amsterdam, Nederland.
Krebser A.G., Bälliz 64, 3601 Thun, Schweiz.
Lange und Springer G.m.b.H. & Co., Antiquariat, Otto-Suhr-Allee 26–28, D-1000 Berlin 10, Deutschland.
S.C. Lemmers, van Bönninghausenlaan 16, 2161 ET Lisse, Nederland.
Wilhelm Maudrich, Lazarettgasse 1, 1091 Wien, Österreich.

Ludwig Mayer Limited, Shlomzion Hamalka 4, Jerusalem, Israel—*archaeology, natural history.*
V.R.I.L.L.E. Editions Pro-Francia, 3 rue Saint-Philippe du Roule, 75008 Paris, France—*archéologie.*
Alois Reichmann, Wiedner Hauptstrasse 18, Wien 1040, Österreich.
Klaus Renner, 8021 Hohenschaeftlarn, Deutschland—*Ethnologie, Archäologie, Anthropologie.*
Antiquariaat de Rijzende Zon, Poststraat 8, 5038 DH Tilburg, Nederland —*ethnology.*
Heinrich Rimanek, Kaiserstrasse 6, 1070 Wien, Österreich.
Librairie Rousseau-Girard, 2 ter rue Dupin, 75006 Paris, France.
Dr. Martin Sändig G.m.b.H., Kaiser-Friedrich-Ring 70, 6200 Wiesbaden, Deutschland.
René Simmermacher, Talstrasse 5, 7800 Zürich, Switzerland.
M. F. Steinbach, Salmannsdorferstrasse 64, 1190 Wien, Österreich.
Technisches Antiquariat, Lauteschlagerstrasse 4, 6100 Darmstadt, Deutschland —*Naturwissenschaft.*
Dr. Helmut Tenner K.G., Sofienstrasse 5, 6900 Heidelburg, Deutschland.
Dr. Helmut Vester, Friedrichstrasse 7, 4000 Düsseldorf, Deutschland.
Wasmuth Buchhandlung & Antiquariat KG., Hardenbergstrasse 9a, 1000 Berlin 12, Deutschland—*Archäologie.*
Robert Wölfle OHG., Amalienstrasse 65, 8000 München 40, Deutschland—*Alte Naturwissenschaft.*
Ch. de Wyngaert, 129A rue R. Vandevelde, B-1030 Bruxelles, Belgium.

16. PERIODICALS: PERIODIQUES: ZEITSCHRIFTEN

Auvermann und Reiss KG, Zum Talblick 2, 6246 Glashütten, Deutschland.
John Benjamins, B.V., Amsteldijk 44, Amsterdam, Nederland—*liberal arts & social sciences.*
Biblarte, Limitada, Rua de Sao Pedro de Alcantara 71, Lisboa 2, Portugal.
Björck & Börjesson, Kindstugatan 2, Postbox 5405, 11131 Stockholm, Sverige.
Dawson-France, S.A., zone Industrielle "la Prairie", 91121 Villebon-sur-Yvette. (B.P. 40), France.
Ex-Libris, 11 rue Victor Cousin, 75005 Paris, France.
Librairie De La Faculté Des Sciences, rue des Ursulines, 75005 Paris, France.
Frederiksberg Antikvariat, Gammel Kongevej 120, 1850 København-V, Danmark.
Hans Höchtberger, Mauerkircherstr. 28, 8000 München 80, Deutschland—*Kunstzeitschriften.*
Christos Katsicalis, Zambakis Bookshop, 14 Massalias Street, Athens 144TN, Ellas —*scientific.*
Kultura, P.O. Box 149, H-1389 Budapest. Fö Utca. 32, Budapest 1, Magyarország.
Lange und Springer G.m.b.H. & Co., Antiquariat, Otto-Suhr-Allee 26–28, D-1000 Berlin 10, Deutschland.
Lynge & Son, Silkegade 11, 1113 København, Danmark—*periodicals.*
Achim Makrocki, Quellenstrasse 14, 3500 Kassel, Deutschland.
W. Mauke Söhne, Karl-Muck-Platz 12, 2000 Hamburg 36, Deutschland.
Librairie Louis Moorthamers, rue Lesbroussart 124, 1050 Bruxelles, Belgie.
Libreria Gia Nardecchia, S.r.l., Piazza Cavour 25, 00193 Roma, Italy—*Italian.*
L. M. C. Nierynck, Verdilaan 85, 4384-LD Vlissingen, Nederland—*early newspapers.*

271

Martinus Nijhoff B.V., P.O. Box 269, Noordwal 4, 2501AX 's-Gravenhage, Netherlands.
Nordiska Antivariska Bokhandeln, Norra Magasingatan 6, Helsingfors, Suomi.
Rudolf Patzer, Mainzer Berg 23, 6739 Weidenthal, Deutschland.
Antiquariat Piermont, Postfach 21 02 32, 5300 Bonn 2; Rolandstrasse 13, 5480 Remagen-Rolandswerth, Deutschland—*Franzosische*.
Alois Reichmann, Wiedner Hauptstrasse 18, Wien 1040, Österreich.
Rönnells Antikvariat, AB, Birger Jarlsgatan 32, 11429 Stockholm, Schweden.
Schmidt Periodicals G.m.b.H., Dettendorf, 8201 Bad Feilnbach 2, Deutschland—*all subjects*.
Swets & Zeitlinger, B.V., Heereweg 347B Lisse, Nederland.
E. von den Velden, Neureuther Strasse 1. 8000 München 40, Deutschland—*Wissenschaften. Fachzeitschriften*.
D. Weil, 1 rue du Dragon, 75006 Paris, France—*anciens et modernes*.

17. PICTORIAL ART: BEAUX-ARTS: KUNST UND GRAPHIK

Theodor Ackermann, Ludwigstrasse 7, 8000 München, Deutschland—*Graphik*.
Marcel Adler, 3 Quai Malaquais, 75006 Paris, France—*beaux arts*.
A. Degli Albizi, Piazza Duomo 22r, Firenze, Italia—*fine arts, old prints*.
Robert Alder, Junkerngasse 41, Bern, Schweiz—*Kunst*.
Aux Amateurs de Livres, 62 Avenue de Suffren, 75015 Paris, France—*beaux-arts*.
Bottega Ambrosiana, Via Vitruvio 47, 20124 Milano, Italia—*fine arts*.
Libreria Antigua y Moderna, Calle De Los Libreros 2, Madrid 13, Spain.
Antikvariat Antiqua, Karlavägen 12, 114 31 Stockholm, Sverige—*Applied Art*.
Arcade Prints, City Arkaden, Østergade 32, København, Danmark—*old prints*.
Librairie-Galerie Arenthon, 3 Quai Malaquais, 75006 Paris. France—*Beaux-arts, estampes*.
l'Art Ancien S.A., Signaustrasse 6, 8008 Zürich, Schweiz—*Graphik und Zeichnungen grosser Meister*.
Art & Print, Kompagnistraede 25, København, Denmark.
Librairie des Arts et Metiers, 20 rue de Verdun, Lormaye, 28210 Nogent le Roi, France.
Axelsen Booksellers ApS., Østergade 44, København, Danmark—*prints*.
Azevedo and Burnay Lda, Travessa de S. Placido 48-B, 1200 Lisboa, Portugal, Portugal.
Torsten Baland, Spielhagenstr. 13, D-1000 Berlin-Charlottenburg 10, Deutschland.
Galerie Gerda Bassenge, Erdenerstrasse 5 A, D-1000 Berlin 33, Deutschland.
Paul Bataille, "Calendal", 14 rue Châteauredon, 13 Marseille, France—*beaux-arts*.
Angel Batlle y Tejedor, Calle de la Paja 23, Barcelona (2), España—*engravings*.
Fernand Beaufils, 169 avenue Victor-Hugo, 75016 Paris, France—*beaux-arts*.
Antiquariat Behrens, Leibnizstrasse 47, D-1000 Berlin 12, Deutschland.
Anton W. van Bekhoven. Ruysdaelplein 5, 1411 RD Naarden, Nederland.
A. Bellanger, 6 et 8 Passage Pommeraye, 44000 Nantes, France—*gravures*.
Berche et Pagis, 60 rue Mazarine, 75006 Paris, France—*Beaux-arts*.
Van Berg Antiquariaat, Oude Schans 8–10, Amsterdam, Nederland—*fine art*.
J. Berger, Kohlmarkt 3, 1010 Wien, Österreich—*Kunst*.
Bergmans and Brouwer Antiquarian Booksellers, Rustenburgerstraat 291, 1073 GE Amsterdam, Nederland—*art & architecture*.
André Bessières, 12 rue Delambre, 75014 Paris, France—*beaux-arts*.
Biblarte, Limitada, Rua de Sao Pedro de Alcantara 71, Lisboa 2, Portugal.

Librairie Auguste Blaizot S.A., 164 Faubourg Saint-Honoré, 75008 Paris, France
—*livres illustrés.*
C.G. Boerner, Kasernenstrasse 14, 4000 Düsseldorf, Deutschland—*alte Graphik; alte
Handzeichmungen.*
Boghallens Antikvariat, Raadhuspladsen 37, DK 1585 København-V, Danmark—*art
books.*
Book Market, Rue de la Madeleine 47, B-1000 Bruxelles, Belgium.
Antiquariaat Hieronymus Bosch, Leliegracht 36 (hk Keizersgracht), 1015 DH
Amsterdam, Nederland—*fine arts.*
Bouquinerie de l'Institut S.A., 12 rue de Seine, 75006 Paris, France—*beaux-arts;
estampes.*
Bice Bourlot, Piazza Castello 9, Torino, 10123, Italia—*Prints, costumes, arts &
crafts.*
Branners Bibliofile Antikvariat ApS, Bredgade 10, 1260 København-K, Danmark
—*illustrated, prints.*
Antiquariat Bremer und Schlak, Kornmarkt 4–5, 3340 Wolfenbüttel, Deutschland.
Librairie-Galerie Bretonne, 1 rue des Fossés, 35000 Rennes, France— *gravures
anciennes.*
Buchantiquariat Britschgi, Rämistrasse 33, 8000 Zürich, Schweiz.
Brocéliandè, rue de la Reine Bérengère, 21, 72000 le Mans, France—*caricature, livres
illustrés.*
Galerie Brumme Frankfurt, Braubachstr. 34, 6000 Frankfurt-am-Main, Deutsch-
land—*alte Graphik.*
Siegfried Brumme, Kirschgarten 11, 6500 Mainz, Deutschland.
Hermann Bub, Postfach 5328, Kürschnerhof 7, 8700 Wurzburg 1, Deutschland.
Das Bücgerfass I, Pfalzburger Strasse 12, Berlin-Wilmersdorf 15, Deutschland.
Buch und Kunst, Münzgasse 16, 7750 Konstanz, Deutschland.
Das Bücherfass II, Hertelstr, 5, Postfach 209, D-1000 Berlin-Friedenau 41, Germany
Graphik.
Das Bücherhaus, Wiesenstrasse 21, 3012 Langenhagen, Deutschland*illus. Bücher.*
Das Bücherkabinett, Poststrasse 14–16, 2000 Hamburg 36, Deutschland—*decorative
Graphik.*
Der Buchfreund [Walter Schaden], Sonnenfelsgasse 4, 1010 Wien 1, Österreich.
Friedrich Burchard, Sonnbornerstrasse 144, 5600 Wuppertal-Sonnborn,
Deutschland.
Burgersdijk & Niermans, Nieuwsteeg 1, 2311 RW Leiden, Nederland.
Arnold Busck, Fiolstraede 24, 1171 København-K, Danmark—*art.*
Giampaolo Buzzanca, Piazzeta Pedrocchi 5, 35100 Padova, Italia—*prints, drawings,
illustrated books.*
Libreria Internazionale C. Caldini, Via Tornabuoni 89/91r., 50123 Firenze, Italia
—*beaux-arts.*
Candide, 7 rue Montault, 49000 Angers, France—*beaux arts.*
La Bouquinerie des Carmes, rue St. Paul 35, 4000 Liege, Belgium—*curiosités.*
Livraria Castro E Silva, Rua da Rosa 31, Lisboa, Portugal.
Librairie Ancienne Chambefort, 26 Place Bellecour, 69 Lyon, France—*beaux arts.*
Librairie Champavert, 2 rue du Perigord, 31000 Toulouse, France—*Beaux-arts.*
Antiquariat "Christo", Alte Gasse 67, Frankfurt M, Deutschland—*bis 1920.*
Aribert D. Claassen, Buch- und Kunstantiquariat, Hardtstrasse 8, 5483 Bad
Neuenahr-aw 1, Deutschland.
René Cluzel, 61 Rue de Vaugirard, 75006 Paris, France—*livres illustrés.*
Antiquariaat van Coevorden, Beukenlaan 3, 8085 Doornspijk, Nederland—*fine arts.*

Gaston Colas, 84 boulevard Raspail, 75006 Paris, France—*beaux-arts.*
Pierre Colas, 38 rue de Vaugirard, 75006 Paris, France—*beaux-arts.*
Libreria Colonnese, 33 Via S. Pietro A Majella, 80138 Napoli, Italia—*prints.*
Jullien Cornic Art Bookshop, 118 rue du Faubourg Saint Honore, 75008 Paris, France.
Librairie de la Corraterie, 20 rue de la Corraterie, CH-1211 Genève, Suisse.
Galerie Gérald Cramer, 13 rue de Chantepoulet, Genève, Schweiz—*éstampes modernes.*
Patrick Cramer, rue de Chantepoulet 13, CH-1201 Genève, Suisse—*éstampes, livres illustrés.*
Gerard Crucis, rue St. Jean 33, 1000 Bruxelles, Belgium.
Librairie Delamain, 155 rue Saint-Honoré, 75001 Paris, France—*beaux-arts.*
Max-Philippe Delatte, 15 rue Gustave Courbet, 75116 Paris, France—*beaux-arts.*
Librairie Denis, 50 rue de la Scellerie, 37000 Tours, France.
F. Deuticke, Helferstorferstrasse 4, Wien 1, Österreich—*Kunst.*
Aniquariaat Deventer, Brink 17, 7411 BR Deventer, Nederland—*fine arts, prints, illustrated books.*
Dresdener Antiquariat, Bautzner Strasse 27, 806 Dresden, DDR —*Kunstwissenschaft.*
Henri Dupont, 141 boulevard de la Liberté, 59000 Lille, France—*gravures, éstampes.*
Eckard Düwal, Schlüterstr. 17, D-1000 Berlin-Charlottenburg 12, Germany —*Graphik.*
Galerie Engelberts, 11 Grand Rue, CH-1204 Genève, Schweiz—*art contemporain, dessins, gravures.*
Paul Eppe, 49 rue de Provence, 75009 Paris, France—*livres illustrés.*
Joseph Fach, Fahrgasse 8, 6000 Frankfurt-am-Main. 1, Deutschland—*Graphik; Handzeichnungen; Gemalde*
Dr. Reto Feurer, Wanningerstrasse 7, D-8201 Obing/Oberbayern, Deutschland.
La Fiera del Libro, Via Marconi 2, 6900 Lugano, Schweiz—*fine arts.*
Librairie Flammarion, 4 rue Casimir Delavigne, 75006 Paris, France—*beaux-arts.*
Gérard Fleury, Librairie François, 1er, 34 Avenue Montaigne, 75008 Paris, France —*livres illustrés.*
Librairie-Galerie Jean Fournier, 44 rue Quincampoix, 75004 Paris, France —*Beaux-arts, estampes.*
Frankfurter Bücherstube, Börsenstrasse 2–4, 6000 Frankfurt-am-Main, Deutschland —*Kunstgeschichte.*
Frankfurter Kunstkabinett, Hanna Bekker vom Rath, G.m.b.H., Börsenplatz 13-15, 6000 Frankfurt-am-Main, Deutschland—*Kunst 20; Jahrhunderts.*
Antiquariat M. und R. Fricke, Poststrasse 3, 4000 Düsseldorf 1, Poststrasse 3, 4000 Düsseldorf 1, Deutschland.
Georg Fritsch, Postfach 883, A-1010 Wien, Österreich—*Kunst.*
Jacques Gabay, 151 bis. rue Saint-Jacques, 75005 Paris, France—*anciennes.*
Librairie Gallimard, 15 boulevard Raspail, 75007 Paris, France—*beaux-arts, livres illustrés.*
Garisenda Libri & Stampe, S.A.S., Strada Maggiore 14/A, 40125 Bologna, Italia —*fine arts.*
Antiquariat Gundel Gelbert, St. Apern Strasse 4, 5000 Köln 1, Deutschland.
Yves Gevaert, rue du Pinson 160, 1170 Bruxelles, Belgium.
Gibert Jeune, 23 Quai Saint-Michel, 75005 Paris, France—*beaux-arts.*
Claude Givaudan, rue du Soleil Levant 3, CH-1204 Genève*livres illustrés.*

Luigi Gonnelli & Figli, Via Ricasoli 14 rosso, Firenze, Italia—*prints and paintings.*
F. Gottschalk, Krugerstrasse 10, 1010 Wien, Österreich—*Kunst, Illustrierte Bücher.*
Antiquariat Götz, Nernstrasse 16, 2800 Bremen 33, Deutschland.
Libreria Oreste Gozzini di Pietro Chellini, Via Ricasoli 49, 50122 Firenze, Italia
  —*fine arts*
Grafik-Antikvariatet, Skomakargatan 24, 111 29 Stockholm, Sverige—*old prints & views.*
Antiquariat Granier G.m.b.H., Welle 9, 4800 Bielefeld 1, Deutschland.
Jochen Granier, Buch und Kunstauktionen, Gadderbaumer Strasse 22, 4800 Bielefeld 1, Deutschland.
Das Graphik-Kabinett, Humboldtstrasse 80, 4000 Düsseldorf 1, Deutschland.
Die Gravüre, Rüttenschneider Strasse 56, 4300 Essen 1, Deutschland.
Galerie Olaf Greiser, Schröderstrasse 14, 6900 Heidelberg, Deutschland.
Hallens Antikvariat, Köpmangatan 4, 11131 Stockholm, Sweden—*prints.*
Hamburgensien-Meyer, Poststrasse 2–4, 2000 Hamburg 36, Deutschland.
Hans Bolliger Bücher und Grafik, Lenggstrasse 14, Zürich, Suisse—*Kunst; Illustrierte Bücher.*
Robert Hartwig, Pestalozzistr. 23, D-1000 Berlin-Charlottenburg 12, Germany —*Illustrierte Bücher.*
A. L. Hasbach, Wollzeile 9 und 29, Wien 1, Österreich.
August Hase, im Trutz 2, 6000 Frankfurt-am-Main, Deutschland.
Elsa Hauser, Schellingstrasse 17, 8000 München 13, Deutschland—*Alte und Moderne Graphik, Alte Drucke.*
Hauswedell und Nolte, Pöseldorferweg 1, 2000 Hamburg 13, Deutschland.
Rudolf Heger, Wollezeile 2, 1010 Wien 1, Österreich—*Kunst.*
Leopold Heidrich G.m.b.H., Plankengasse 7, Wien 1, Österreich—*Kunst.*
Theodor Hennig, Motzstr. 25, D-1000 Berlin-Schöneberg 30, Germany—*Kunst.*
Antiquariat Hennwack, Langenscheidtstrasse 4, D-1000 Berlin-Schöneberg 62, Deutschland.
Jacques Herbinet, 39 rue de Constantinople, 75008 Paris, France—*modernes illustrés.*
Arnold Hess, Galerie zur Krone, Zürcherstrasse 183, CH-8500 Frauenfeld, Schweiz —*Graphik und Ansichtenwerke.*
Theo Hill, Schildergasse 107, 5000 Köln, Deutschland—*Alte und moderne Graphik.*
Hans Höchtberger, Mauerkircherstr. 28, 8000 München 80, Deutschland—*Illustrierte Bücher, Kunstwissenschaft.*
M. und R. Hofer, Münstergasse 56, CH-3011 Bern, Schweiz—*dekorative Graphik.*
Ernst Hoffmann, Weissadlergasse 3, 6000 Frankfurt-am-Main, Deutschland—*Alte Drucke, Dekorative Graphik.*
Jürgen Holstein Antiquariat G.m.b.H., Postfach 68, Feldafingerstrasse 37, 8134 Pöcking, Deutschland—*Kunst.*
Karl Hölzl, K.G., Seilergasse 3, 1010 Wien, Österreich.
Bernard Houthakker, Rokin 98, Amsterdam, Nederland—*drawings, 15 to 18 century, Rembrandt etchings.*
Antiquariaat C. Hovingh & Zn., Kleine Houtstraat 50, 2011DP Haarlem, Nederland—*art.*
Alte Graphik Julia F. Iliu, Barer Strasse 46, 8000 München 40, Deutschland.
B. M. Israel, Prentenkabinet, Singel 379, Amsterdam, Netherlands—*Prints.*
Jacques d'Aspect, "La Legende", 58 rue d'Aubagne, 13001, Marseille, France —*livres illustrés.*
Xavier Jehanno, 4 Place de l'Eglise, 78430 Louveciennes, France.

Jones Antikvariat, Nortullsgatan 3, 11329 Stockholm, Schweden—*fine arts; illustrated books.*

Kaabers Antikvariat, Skindergade 34, 1159 København-K, Danmark—*fine art.*

Antiquariat Gunnar Kaldewey, Poststrasse 3, 4000 Düsseldorf 1, Deutschland.

Sibylle Kaldewey, Poststrasse 3, D-4000 Düsseldorf 1, Deutschland—*Illustrierte Bücher.*

Karl & Faber, Karolinenplatz 5A, 8000 München 2, Deutschland—*Kunst, Graphik.*

Keip, KG Wissenschaftliches Antiquariat Hainerweg 46–48, 6000 Frankfurt-am-Main 70, Deutschland—*Altedrucke.*

E. und R. Kistner, Weinmarkt 6, 8500 Nürnberg, Deutschland.

J. Kitzinger, Schellingstrasse 25, 8000 München, Deutschland.

Antiquariat A. Klittich-Pfankuch, Kleine Burg 12, 3300 Braunschweig, Deutschland—*Dekorative Graphik.*

Rainer Köbelin. Schellingstrasse 99, 8000 München 40, Deutschland—*Dekorative Graphik.*

A. KOK en Zn, 14–18 Oude Hoogstraat, Amsterdam, Nederland—*arts.*

Otto Kolb, Von-Mann-Strasse 2, 8670 Hof, Deutschland—*Stahlstiche.*

Kornfeld & Co., Laupenstrasse 41, CH-3008 Bern, Schweiz—*fine arts; prints & drawings.*

Brigitta Kowallik, Klarissenstrasse 5, 4040 Neuss, Deutschland.

Antiquariat im Kudamm-Karree, Kurfürstendamm 206-208, D-1000 Berlin-Charlottenburg 15, Deutschland.

Jeanne Laffitte, 25 Cours d'Estienne-d'Orves, 13001 Marseille, France—*beaux-arts.*

Librairie Leonce Laget, 75 rue de Rennes, 75006 Paris, France—*beaux-arts.*

August Laube, Trittligasse 19, 8001 Zürich, Schweiz—*Illustrierte Bücher.*

Marcel Lecomte, 17 rue de Seine, 75006 Paris, France—*livres illustrés, beaux-arts.*

Librairie Lefebvre, 1 rue Lucien-Pean, 45750 Saint-Pryvé-Saint-Mesmin, France—*Beaux-arts.*

Lengertz' Antikvariat Gösta Janson, Regementsgatan 6, 211 42, Malmö, Sverige—*illustrated.*

Maurice Lester, 13 bis rue du Cygne (Marché aux Fleurs), 28000 Chartres, France—*gravures.*

Franz Leuwer, Am Wall 171, 2800 Bremen, Deutschland—*Dekorative Graphik.*

Arnold Levilliers, 118 route de Chartres (RN 188), 91400 Gometz-le-Chatel (Essone), France—*gravures, dessins, beaux-arts.*

Librairie des Galeries, Galerie du Roi, 2, 1000 Bruxelles, Belgique—*arts décoratifs, beaux-arts.*

Librairie des Victoires, 4 bis Place des Petits Pères, 75002 Paris, Franc—*livres illustreas.*

Librairie K, 17 rue Mazarine, 13100 Aix en Provence, France—*livres sur l'art.*

Kunstantiquariat Stephan List, Barer Strasse 39, 8000 München 40, Deutschland.

Alexandre Loewy, 85 rue de Seine, 75006 Paris, France—*gravures, dessins.*

Bernard Loliée, 72 rue de Seine, 75006 Paris, France—*surrealisme.*

Librairie Marc Loliée, 40 rue des Saints-Pères, 75007 Paris, France—*livres illustrés.*

A. van Loock, rue Saint Jean 51, 1000 Bruxelles, Belgie—*old engravings.*

Margot Lörcher o.H.G., Meyerbeerstrasse 53, 8000 München, 60, Deutschland.

Margot Lörcher o.H.G., Heubergstrasse 42, 7000 Stuttgart 1, Deutschland.

Christa Lummert, Skalitzer Str. 75, D-1000 Berlin-Kreuzberg 36, Germany.

Buchantiquariat Madliger-Schwab, Postfach 8022, Tiefenhöfe (Beim Paradeplatz) 8001 Zürich, Schweiz.

La Maison du Livre, 24 rue de la Cloche Verte, 16000 Angoulême, France.

Hans Marcus, N. Z. Voorburgwal 284, 1012 RT Amsterdam, Nederland—*old illustrated books.*
Hans Marcus, Ritterstrasse 10, 4000 Düsseldorf, Deutschland—*alte illustrierte Bücher.*
Jean-Claude Martinez, 21 ruc Saint-Sulpice, 75006 Paris, France—*beaux-arts.*
Carla Marzoli, Corso Porta Nuova 2, 20121 Milano, Italia—*Early illustrated.*
Librairie-Galerie Jacques Matarasso, 2 rue Longchamp, 06000 Nice, France —*beaux-arts, livres illustrês.*
Librairie-Galerie Paul Maurel, 27–29 boulevard Albert 1er, 06600 Antibes, France —*livres illustrês modernes; beaux-arts.*
Alain Mazo, 15 rue Guénégaud, 75006 Paris, France—*beaux-arts, livres illustres; gravures modernes.*
Libreria Antiquaria Mediolanum, Via Montebello 30, 20121-Milano, Italia —*engravings.*
R.-G. Michel, 17 Quai Saint-Michel, 75005 Paris, France—*éstampes, dessins.*
Antiquariaat Minerva, Zeestraat 48, 's-Gravenhage, Nederland.
Libreria Mirto, Ruiz de Alarcon 27, Madrid 14, España—*fine arts.*
Libreria Antiquaria Montenegro, Via Dei Gracchi 291/a, 00192 Roma, Italia.
Libreria Antiquaria Moretti, Via Lusardi 8, 20122 Milano, Italy—*illustrated books.*
Kunstantiquariat Otto Moser, Tölzer Strasse 24, 8022 Grünwald, Deutschland.
Otto Moser, Tölzerstrasse 24, 8022 Grünwald, Deutschland.
Galerie Zur Mühle, Billesberger Hof, 8059 Moosinning, Deutschland.
Galerie Annie Muriset, 4 Place du Molard, 1204 Genève, Schweiz—*gravures anciennes.*
Antiquariat Karlheinz Murr, Karolinenstrasse 4, 8600 Bamberg. (Postfach 1037), Deutschland—*Alte Graphik.*
Fritz Neidhardt, Relenbergstrasse 20, 7000 Stuttgart, Deutschland—*Illustrierte Bücher und Graphik*
Librairie Nicaise S.A., 145 boulevard Saint Germain, 75006 Paris, France—*gravures modernes, surrealisme.*
Galerie Nierendorf, Hardenbergstrasse 19, 1000 Berlin 12, Deutschland—*Kunst.*
Dr. Margarethe Noelle Gemälde, Meinekestrasse 11, 1000 Berlin 15, Deutschland.
H.C. Nørgart, Fiolstraede 15, 1171 København-K, Danmark—*prints.*
Librairie Occitania, 46 rue du Taur, 31000 Toulouse, France—*estampes.*
Offermann und Schmitz, Antiquariat, Wittelsbacherstrasse 31, 5600 Wuppertal 2, Deutschland.
Leo S. Olschki—Studio Bibliografico, 52046 Lucignano (Arezzo), Italia—*art and architecture.*
Orangerie-Reinz Galerie, Helenenstrasse 2, 5000 Köln 1, Deutschland—*Graphik und Gemälde.*
Librairie Palladio, 66 rue du Cherche-Midi, 75006 Paris, France—*Beaux-arts.*
J.-P. Parrot, 59 rue de Rennes, 75006 Paris, France.
Hans Pels-Leusden, Kurfürstendamm 59–60, D-1000 Berlin-Charlottenburg 15, Germany—*illustrierte Bücher, Kunstwissenschaft.*
Pierre Petitot, 234 boulevard Saint-Germain, 75007 Paris, France—*art militaire.*
Dott. Ada Peyrot, Via Consolata 8, 10122 Torino, Italia—*illustrated books.*
Annemarie Pfister, Petersgraben 18, 4051 Basel, Schweiz—*Kunst.*
Philographicon, Galerie für Alte Graphik im Antic-Haus, Neuturmstrasse 1, 8000 München 2, Deutschland.
Libreria di Piazza S. Babila, Corso Monforte 2, 20122 Milano, Italia—*old and modern prints.*

Antiquariat Pinkus Genossenschaft, Froschaugasse 7, 8001 Zürich, Schweiz.
Marco Pinkus, ABC Antiquariat, Zähringerstrasse 31 CH-8001 Zürich, Schweiz.
Au Plaisir du Texte, 8 Rue des Fossés St.-Jacques, 75005 Paris, France—*livres illustrês.*
Pont Traversé, 8 rue de Vaugirard, 75006 Paris, France—*Beaux-arts.*
La Porte Etroite, 10 rue Bonaparte, 75006 Paris, France—*beaux-arts.*
Posada Art Books S.P.R.L., rue de la Madeleine 27, 1000 Bruxelles, Belgium.
Antiquariat Constantin Post, Zülpicher Strasse 16, 5000 Köln 1, Deutschland.
Libreria Antiquaria Prandi, Viale Timavo 75, Reggio Emilia, Italia—*fine arts and modern prints.*
Libreria Antiquaria Arturo Pregliasco, Via Accademia Albertina 3 bis, 10123 Torino, Italy.
V.R.I.L.L.E. Editions Pro-Francia, 3 rue Saint-Philippe du Roule, 75008 Paris, France—*beaux-arts.*
La Proue, 6 rue des Eperonniers, 1000 Bruxelles, Belgie—*modern art, surrealism.*
Guy Prouté, 15 rue du 18-Juin, 92210 Saint-Cloud, France—*estampes.*
Robert Prouté, 12 rue de Seine, 75006 Paris, France—*gravures.*
Libreria Antiquaria C.E. Rappaport, Via Sistina 23, 00187 Roma, Italia—*fine arts.*
Reiss und Auvermann, Buch- und Kunstantiquariat, Zum Talblick 2, 6246 Glashütten im Taunus, Deutschland—*Alte Drucke, illustrierte Bucher.*
De Renaissance van het Boek, Walpoortstraat 7, 9000 Gent, Belgie—*gravures et cartes anciennes.*
Ludwig Röhrscheid G.m.b.H., am Hof 28, 5300 Bonn, Deutschland—*Dekorative Graphik.*
Librairie A. Rombaut, Lievestraat 14, 9000 Gent, Belgie—*beaux-arts.*
Jean-Paul Rouillon, Galerie J.P.R., 27 rue de Seine, 75006 Paris, France—*estampes.*
Paul Roulleau, 108 rue Saint-Honoré, 75001 Paris, France—*estampes.*
Ryös Antikvariat AB, Hantverkargatan 21, 112 21 Stockholm, Sverige—*art books.*
Nils Sabels Antivariat, Box 1049, 15024 Rönninge 1, Sweden—*illustrated books.*
Sagot le Garrec & Cie, 24 rue du Four, 75006 Paris, France—*beaux-arts.*
Libreria S. Agostino, Via S. Agostino 17/A, Roma, Italia.
Libreria Salimbeni S.r.l., Via Matteo Palmieri 14R, 50122 Firenze, Italia—*fine Arts.*
Samlaren Antikvariat & Konsthandel, Korsgatan 2, 41116 Göteborg, Schweden—*fine arts.*
Sartoni-Cerveau, 13 Quai Saint-Michel, 75005 Paris, France—*estampes, gravures.*
Gerhard Scheppler, Giselastrasse 25, 8000 München 40, Deutschland.
H. Schmidt und C. Günther, Ubierstrasse 20, 6238 Hofheim, Deutschland.
Kunstantiquariat Monika Schmidt, Türkenstrasse 48, 8000 München 40, und Schloss Haimhausen, 8048 Haimhausen, Deutschland.
Dr. Gerhard Schneider, Rhode-Goldsiepen 12, 5960 Olpe, Deutschland.
Schomaker & Niederstrasser, Bundesallee 221, D-1000 Berlin-Wilmersdorf 15, Germany.
Ferdinand Schöningh, Domhof 4c, 4500 Osnabrück. (Postfach 4060), Deutschland.
Bernd Schramm, Dänische Strasse 26, 2300 Kiel, Deutschland—*Dekorative Graphik.*
Hanno Schreyer, Euskirchenerstrasse 57–59, 5300 Bonn 1, Deutschland—*illustrierte Bücher; alte dekorative Graphik.*
Hellmut Schumann, AG., Rämistraase 25, 8024 Zürich, Schweiz—*Graphik.*
Peter Schwarz, Eisenacher Str. 43, D-1000 Berlin-Schoüneberg 62, Germany.

Tristan Schwilden, Galerie Bortier 5, 1000 Bruxelles, Belgium—*gravures.*
Manfred Sieg, Fasanenstr. 45, D-1000 Berlin-Wilmersdorf 15, Germany.
Rene Simmermacher A.G., Kirchgasse 25, CH-8024 Zürich, Schweiz
—*Kunstwissenschaft; Frühe Lithographien.*
René Simmermacher, Talstrasse 5, 7800 Zürich, Switzerland—*Kunst; illustrierte.*
Boekhandel J. de Slegte B.V., Weversgildeplein 1-2, 8011 XN Zwolle, Nederland.
J. de Slegte, Kalverstraat 48–52, 1012 PE Amsterdam, Nederland—*colour plates.*
Thomas Sonnenthal, Cauerstrasse 20/21, Berlin-Charlottenburg 10, Deutschland.
Sörhuus Antikvariat AB, Riddargatan 23, 114 57 Stockholm, Sverige.
Galerie Stangl, Briennerstrasse 11, 8000 München, Deutschland—*Kunst.*
Antiquariat Michael Steinbach, Demollstrasse 1/I 8000 München 19, Deutschland
—*Kunst.*
M. F. Steinbach, Salmannsdorferstrasse 64, 1190 Wien, Österreich—*Kunst,
Graphik.*
J.F. Steinkopf, Postfach 1116, Marienstrasse 3, 7000 Stuttgart, Deutschland.
Th. Stenderhoff & Co., Alter Fischmarkt 21, 4400 Münster, Deutschland
—*Dekorative Graphik.*
Henk J. Stokking, C.V., Niewe Spiegelstraat 40, 1017 DG Amsterdam, Netherlands
—*old master drawings & prints.*
Jacques Stoven, 53 rue du Mail, 49000 Angers, France—*Beaux-arts.*
Antiquariat Nikolaus Struck, Wilhelmstrasse 5, 5449 Pfalzfeld, Deutschland.
Fl. Tulkens, 21 rue du Chêne, Bruxelles 1, Belgie—*fine art.*
Ukiyo-E Galerie, Citadellstrasse 14, 4000 Düsseldorf 1, Deutschland.
Galerie Valentien, Königsbau, 7000 Stuttgart, Deutschland—*Kunstgeschichte.*
Varia Librairie, rue Soeurs de Hasque 15, 4000 Liege, Belgium.
Galerie Vauquelin, 4 rue Vauquelin, 76200 Dieppe, France—*beaux-arts.*
Martin Veeneman, Noordeinde 100, 's-Gravenhage, Nederland—*art; old prints.*
Venator, KG., Cäcilienstrasse 48 (im Kunsthaus Lempertz) 5000 Köln, Deutschland
—*Dekorative Graphik.*
Christian F. Verbeke, Bloemendalestraat 73, 8030 Beernem (hij Brugge), Belgium.
H. A. Vloemans, Anna Paulownastraat 10, 2518 BE 's-Gravenhage, Nederland
—*modern arts & architecture*
Galerie Vömel, Königsallee 30, 4000 Düsseldorf, Deutschland—*Gemälde,
Handzeichnungen, Graphik.*
Karl Vonderbank, Goethestrasse 11, 6000 Frankfurt-am-Main, Deutschland
—*Moderne Graphik, Kunst.*
Wagner'sche Universitäts Buchhandlung OHG., Museumstrasse 4, 6021 Innsbruck,
Österreich—*Dekorative Graphik.*
Ed. Walz, Lerchenfeldstrasse 4, 8000 München 22, Deutschland—*Graphik und
Zeichnungen des 15.–20 Jahrhunderts.*
Wasmuth Buchhandlung & Antiquariat KG., Hardenbergstrasse 9a, 1000 Berlin 12,
Deutschland—*Kunst, Architektur.*
Antiquariaat Niek Waterbolk, Schoutenstraat 7, 3512 GA Utrecht, Nederland—*fine
arts after 1800.*
Peter Weber, Kunstantiquariat, Eichstrasse 12, 7570 Baden-Baden, Deutschland.
Buch und Kunstantiquariat Friedrich Weissert, Charlottenstrasse 21c, 7000
Stuttgart 1, Deutschland.
Galerie Welz Salzburg, Sigmund-Haffnergasse 16, Salzburg, Österreich—*Kunst;
Graphik.*
Galerie Widmer, Neugasse 35, 9000 St. Gallen, Schweiz—*Kupferstiche.*

Wiener Antiquariat, Seilergasse 16, Wien, Österreich—*Kunst, Graphik.*
Wiener Bücherstube, Eschersheimer Landstrasse 18, 6000 Frankfurt-am-Main, Deutschland—*Dekorative Graphik.*
Arno Winterberg, Buch und Kunstantiquariat, Blumenstrasse 15, 6900 Heidelberg, Deutschland.
Galerie Elfriede Wirnitzer, Lilienmattstrasse 6, Haus Lauschan, 7570 Baden-Baden, Deutschland—*Graphik.*
Walter Wögenstein Singerstrasse 13, Wien 1, Österreich.
Gerhard Zähringer, Hauptstrasse 90, CH-8280 Kreuzlingen, Suisse—*illustrierte Bücher.*
Zentralantiquariat der DDR, Talstrasse 29, 701 Leipzig, DDR.
Buch und Kunstauktionshaus F. Zisska & R. Kistner, Unterer Anger 15, 8000 München 2, Deutschland—*Dekorative Graphik.*

18. RELIGION AND PHILOSOPHY (I): RELIGIONS ET PHILOSOPHIE (I): THEOLOGIE UND PHILOSOPHIE (I)

Alfa Antiquarian Booksellers, P.O. Box 1116, Nijmegen, *and at* P.O. Box 26, 5360 AA Grave, Nederland—*Comparative Religion.*
Bottega Ambrosiana, Via Vitruvio 47, 20124 Milano, Italia.
Rüdiger Barasch, Hähnelstr. 5, D-1000 Berlin-Friedenau 41, Germany.
Anton W. van Bekhoven. Ruysdaelplein 5, 1411 RD Naarden, Nederland.
Herbert Blank, Melonenstrasse 54, 7000 Stuttgart 75, Deutschland—*Philosophie.*
Ton Bolland, Prinsengracht 493, 1002 Amsterdam, Nederland—*Theology, Roman Catholic and Protestant.*
Bouma's Boekhuis, B.V., Turfsingel 3, Groningen, Nederland—*Theology.*
Daniel Brun, Edition et Diffusion M.P., 6 rue Clodion, 75015 Paris, France —*philosophie.*
Bücher-Schmidt Antiquariat, Torgasse 4, 8000 Zürich, Schweiz—*Philosophie.*
Georges Chauvin, 78 rue Mazarine, 75006 Paris, France.
Antiquariaat De Tille B.V., Weerd 11, P.O. Box 233, 8901 BA Leeuwarden, Nederland.
Jürgen Dinter, Antiquariat für Philosophie, Buchholzstrasse 8–10, Köln, Deutschland.
N.G. Elwert Universitätsbuchhandlung, Reitgasse 7–9, 3550 Marburg (Lahn), Deutschland—*Theologie.*
S. Emmering, N.Z. Voorburgwal 304, 1012 RV Amsterdam, Nederland—*Judaica.*
Bottega d'Erasmo, Via Gaudenzio Ferrari 9, 10124 Torino, Italia.
Evangelische Buchhandlung Max Müller, Ernst-Thälmann-Strasse 23, Postfach 229, 9010 Karl-Marx-Stadt, DDR.
Forum B.V., P.O.B. 129, Oude Gracht 206, 3511 NR Utrecht, Netherlands.
Gerold & Co., Graben 31, 1011 Wien, Österreich—*Philosophie.*
Karl Gess, Kanzleistrasse 5, 7750 Konstanz, Deutschland—*Philosophie.*
J. Grubb's Antikvariat, Nørregade 47, Dk-1165 København-K, Danmark—*theology philosophy.*
Gsellius'sche Antiquariat, Hertastrasse 16, 1000 Berlin 37, Deutschland.
Dr. Annemarie Guyer-Halter, Auf Der Mauer 1, 8000 Zürich 1, Schweiz —*Philosophie.*
Bert Hagen, Herenstraat 38, 1015 CB Amsterdam, Nederland—*Theology.*
Jean-Jacques Hankard, 25 rue de la Paix, 1050 Bruxelles, Belgie—*philosophy.*
J.J. Heckenhauer, Holzmarkt 5, 7400 Tübingen, Deutschland—*Theologie.*

Livraria Histórica e Ultramarina Lda [J. C. Silva], Travessa da Queimada 28, 1200–Lisboa 2, Portugal—*Judaica*.

M. L. Huizenga, Oudez. Achterburgwal 156, 1012 DW Amsterdam, Nederland —*philosophy*.

Antiquariat Iberia, Hirschengraben 6, 3001 Berne, Schweiz—*Philosophie*.

Jos. A. Kienreich, Sackstrasse 6 (im Halbstock), 8011 Graz, Österreich —*Philosophie*.

Kreuzberger Antiquariat, Yorckstr. 75, D-1000 Berlin-Kreuzberg 61, Germany.

Akademische Buchhandlung Kuppitsch, Schottengasse 4, Wien, Österreich —*Philosophie*.

Herbert Lang & Cie A.G., Münzgraben 2, 3000 Bern 7, Schweiz.

Dr. Konrad Liebmann, Lortzingstrasse 1, 4500 Osnabrück, Deutschland —*Philosophie*.

Libreria Pasquale Lombardi, Via San Eufemia 11, 00187 Roma, Italia.

Alfred Mader, 67 rue Saint-Jacques, 75005 Paris, France—*philosophie*.

Jean-Claude Martinez, 21 rue Saint-Sulpice, 75006 Paris, France.

S. Matlofsky, Alfasi 7, Jerusalem 92302, Israel   *Judaica-Hebraica*.

Müller & Gräff, Calwerstrasse 54, 7000 Stuttgart-1, Deutschland.

Librairie Nantaise Y. Vachon. 3 Place de la Monnaie, 44000 Nantes, France.

P. C. Notebaart, Postbox 280, 1400 AG. Bussum, Nederland—*theology, humaniora, surrealism*.

Leo S. Olschki—Studio Bibliografico, 52046 Lucignano (Arezzo), Italia.

Libreria Antiquaria Palmaverde, Via Castiglione 35, 40124 Bologna, Italia—*modern first editions*.

Editions A. & J. Picard, 82 rue Bonaparte, 75006 Paris, France.

Anne-Marie Robichon, 16 Quai de la Loire, 37210 Rochecorbon/Vouvray, France.

C. Roemke & Cie., Apostelnstrasse 7, 5000 Köln, Deutschland—*Évangelische Theologie*.

Hans Rohr, Oberdorferstrasse 5, 8024 Zürich 1, Schweiz.

Ludwig Rosenthal's Antiquariaat, Bussumergrintweg 4, 1217 BP Hilversum, Nederland—*Theology, Roman Catholic & Protestant*.

Gerhard Scheppler, Giselastrasse 25, 8000 München 40, Deutschland.

Ludwig Helmut Schiller, am Birkenrain 28, 7811 St. Peter, Deutschland.

Manfred Sieg, Fasanenstr. 45, D-1000 Berlin-Wilmersdorf 15, Germany —*Theologie*.

Thomas Sonnenthal, Cauerstrasse 20/21, Berlin-Charlottenburg 10, Deutschland.

J.F. Steinkopf, Postfach 1116, Marienstrasse 3, 7000 Stuttgart, Deutschland.

Stern-Verlag Janssen & Co., Postfach 7820, FriedrichUstrasse 26, 4000 Düsseldorf, Deutschland—*Geisteswissenschaften*.

Riewert Q. Tode, Dudenstr. 22, D-1000 Berlin-Kreuzberg 61, Germany.

Galerie Valentien, Königsbau, 7000 Stuttgart, Deutschland—*Christlich Archäologie*.

J. Vrin, 6 Place de la Sorbonne, 75005 Paris, France—*philosophie*.

R. & I. Wanner-Zander, Kronengasse 35, 5400 Baden, Schweiz*Literatur*.

Carl Wegner, Martin-Luther-Strasse 113, 1000 Berlin 62, Deutschland —*Philosophie*.

Bernhard Wendt, Hauptstrasse 29, 8084 Inning-Buch/Ammersee, Über München, Deutschland—*Reformation und Gegenreformation Theologie vor 1850*.

Alexander Wild, Rathausgasse 30, 3011 Bern, Schweiz.

J. Wristers, Minrebroederstraat 13, Utrecht, Nederland.

Banco Libri s.a.s. Di V. Zanni & C., Via Marsala 6, 40126 Bologna, Italia.

Zohar, 1 Nachlat-Benjamin, Tel Aviv, Israel—*Hebraica*.

19. RELIGION AND PHILOSOPHY (II): RELIGIONS ET PHILOSPHIE (II): THEOLOGIE UND PHILOSOPHIE (II)

Libreria Alessandria, Via Alessandria 216/a, Roma, Italia—*occult.*

Antiquariaat Antiqua, Herengracht 159, 1015 BH Amsterdam, Nederland —*Philosophy.*

Librairie d'Argences, 38 rue Saint-Sulpice, 75006 Paris, France.

Librairie des Arts et Metiers, 20 rue de Verdun, Lormaye, 28210 Nogent le Roi, France—*histoire religieuse.*

Book Market, Rue de la Madeleine 47, B-1000 Bruxelles, Belgium.

Florence de Chastenay, 76 rue Gay-Lussac, 75005 Paris, France—*demonologie.*

Cité des Vieux Livres, 139 Grande Rue, 25000 Besançon, France.

René Cluzel, 61 Rue de Vaugirard, 75006 Paris, France—*occultism, curiosa.*

Erasmus Antiquariaat en Boekhandel. Spui 2, Amsterdam, Nederland—*Judaica.*

Le Libraire Alain Ferraton, Rue Ernest Allard 39, B-1000 Bruxelles, Belgium.

Paul Goossens, Greenhillstraat 45, 8320 Brugge, Belgium.

Jean-Jacques Hankard, 25 rue de la Paix, 1050 Bruxelles, Belgie—*occult.*

Ernst Hoffmann, Weissadlergasse 3, 6000 Frankfurt-am-Main, Deutschland —*Humanismus.*

l'Intermédiaire du Livre, 88 rue Bonaparte, 75006 Paris, France.

Adolf Kapp, Bahnhofstrasse 17, 7407 Rottenburg, Deutschland—*Katholische Theologie.*

Jacques Levy, 46 rue d'Alésia, 75014 Paris, France—*Judaica, Hebraica.*

Libresso, Antiquariat an der Universität, Binderstrasse 24, 2000 Hamburg 13, Deutschland.

Alfred Mader, 67 rue Saint-Jacques, 75005 Paris, France—*occultisme.*

F. und A. Mehren, Telgenweg 8, 4400 Münster, Deutschland.

Posada Art Books S.P.R.L., rue de la Madeleine 27, 1000 Bruxelles, Belgium —*occult.*

Richard Schikowski, Motzstrasse 30, D-1000 Berlin-Schöneberg 30, Germany —*Astrologie, Okkultismus.*

Peter Schwarz, Eisenacher Str. 43, D-1000 Berlin-Schoüneberg 62, Germany —*Esoterik.*

Société Hébraica Judaica, 12 rue des Hospitalières St.-Gervais, 75004 Paris, France —*Judaica et Hebraica.*

Thomas Sonnenthal, Cauerstrasse 20/21, Berlin-Charlottenburg 10, Deutschland —*Astrologie.*

Sonnewald-Heckenhauer, Waldhof 1, 7947 Mengen, Deutschland—*Theologie.*

Th. Stenderhoff & Co., Alter Fischmarkt 21, 4400 Münster, Deutschland —*Theologie, Philosophie.*

20. REMAINDERS AND OVERSTOCKS: SOLDES: RESTAUFLAGE

Antikvarboltok Csanady Utca 13, Budapest XIII, Magyarország

Dott. Ada Peyrot, Via Consolata 8, 10122 Torino, Italia—*economics.*

21. SOCIOLOGY: SOCIOLOGIE: SOZIOLOGIE

l'Ane d'Or, Boite Postale 6, 95450 Vigny, France.

Antiquariaat Antiqua, Herengracht 159, 1015 BH Amsterdam, Nederland —*Political economy.*

Arno Adler, Hüxstrasse 55, 2400 Lübeck, Deutschland.

Athenaeum Antiquarian Booksellers, Reguliersgracht 50, 1017 LT, Amsterdam, Nederland.
Auvermann und Reiss Kg, Zum Talblick 2, 6246 Glashütten, Deutschland.
Johan Beek, Graaf Van Lyndenlaan 55, 3771 JB Barneveld Netherlands.
Libreria Bonfanti, Via Macedonio Melloni 19, 20129 Milano, Italia—*political science.*
E. J. Bonset, Patrijzenstraat 8, 2040-AC Zandvoort, Nederland—*social sciences.*
Librairie du Camee, 34 rue Serpente, 75006 Paris, France—*metiers; écologie.*
Commerzcabinett, Humboldtstrasse 125, 2000 Hamburg 76, Deutschland.
Matthijs De Jongh, Jeltewei 44–46, 8622 XT Hommerts, Netherlands—*socialism.*
Librairie Jean-Paul Delon, 74150 Marigny-Saint Marcel. TN: 01 29 14, France—*Economie politique.*
Librairie Duchemin, 18 rue Soufflot, 75005 Paris, France—*économie politique.*
Espagnon et Lebret, 1 rue de Fleurus, 75006 Paris, France—*économie politique; historie social.*
A. Gerits Rare Books, Delilaan 5, 1217 HJ Hilversum, Nederland.
A. Gerits and Son Rare Books, Hartenstraat 4, 1016 CB Amsterdam, Nederland—*social sciences.*
Horst Hamecher, Goethestrasse 74, 3500 Kassel, Deutschland.
Antiquariat Hennwack, Langenscheidtstrasse 4, D-1000 Berlin-Schöneberg 62, Deutschland—*Politik*
Antikvaarinen Kirjakauppa Seppo Hiltunen, Viherniemenkatu 3, Helsinki 53, Finland—*political science.*
Humaniora Antiqua, Herengracht 242, Amsterdam, Netherlands.
Maarten J. Israel, P.O. Box 8, 1110 AA Dieman. (Keizersgracht 690, 1017 EV Amsterdam), Netherlands—*economics.*
Juridisch Antiquariaat, L Noordeinde 39, 2514 GC 'S-Gravenhage, Nederland—*economics.*
Karl Marx Buchhandlung, G.m.b.H., Jordanstrasse 11, 6000 Frankfurt 90, Deutschland.
Herbert Lang & Cie A.G., Münzgraben 2, 3000 Bern 7, Schweiz.
Jean-Jacques Magis, 47 rue Saint André-des-Arts, 76006 Paris, France—*economics, politics.*
Livraria Eduardo Antunes Martinho, Rua Voz do Operário 7-B, Lisboa 2, Portugal.
Nansensgade Antikvariat, Nansensgade 70, 1366 København-K, Denmark.
Peter Neser, Kreuzlingerstrasse 11, 7750 Konstanz-Bodensee, Deutschland—*Politik.*
Antiquariat und Verlag Georg Sauer, Gerichtsstrasse 7, 6240 Königstein im Taunus, Deutschland.
Antiquariat Paul Schindegger, Heidenpoint 26, 8228 Freilassing, Deutschland—*Politik.*
Hugo Streisand, Eislebener Strasse 4, 1000 Berlin 30, Deutschland—*Soziologie, Pädagogik, Politik und Staatswissenschaften.*
Struppe und Winckler, Potsdamerstrasse 103, 1000 Berlin 30, Deutschland—*Wirtschaft.*
Riewert Q. Tode, Dudenstr. 22, D-1000 Berlin-Kreuzberg 61, Germany.
H. A. Vloemans, Anna Paulownastraat 10, 2518 BE 's-Gravenhage, Nederland.
J. Vrin, 6 Place de la Sorbonne, 75005 Paris, France—*économie politique.*
Weddinger Antiquariat, Willdenowstr. 5b/E. Burgsdorfstr., D-1000 Berlin-Wedding 65, Germany *Sozialismus, DDR.*
Carl Wegner, Martin-Luther-Strasse 113, 1000 Berlin 62, Deutschland—*Sozialwissenschaften.*

Elisabeth Wellnitz, Sachsenstrasse 35, 6100 Darmstadt, Deutschland—*Politik, Wehrwesen, Geschichte.*

22. SPORTS, GAMES AND PASTIMES: SPORTS ET JEUX: SPORT UND SPIELE

Harvey Abrams-Books, an den Hubertshausern 21, 1000 Berlin 38, Deutschland.
Librairie des Alpes, 6 rue de Seine, 75006 Paris, France—*alpinisme.*
Libreria Alpina, Via C. Coronedi-Berti 4, 40137 Bologna, Italia—*mountaineering.*
Livres Anciens Maurice Bridel, S.A., Avenue du Tribunal-Fédéral 5, 1002 Lausanne, Schweiz—*equitation.*
A. Tavares de Carvalho, Avenida da Republica 46–3°, 1000 Lisboa-1, Portugal —*Chess.*
Librairie des Cimes, Square Steurs 15, 1030 Bruxelles, Belgium.
Librairie Jean-Paul Delon, 74150 Marigny-Saint Marcel. TN: 01 29 14, France —*alpinisme*
Dias & Andrade Lda, Livraria Portugal, Rua do Carmo 70, Lisboa 2, Portugal.
Librairie de Montbel et Cie, 1 rue Paul Cézanne, 75008 Paris, France—*chasse, équitation, vênerie, pêche.*
Paradis des Chercheurs, 245 Chaussée de Charleroi, B-1060 Bruxelles, Belgium —*vieux jouets.*
Pierre Sieur, 3 rue de la Universitée, 75007 Paris, France—*jouets anciens; cartes à jouer.*
Skakhuset [The Chess House], 24 Studiesstraede, 1455 København-K, Danmark —*chess.*
Boekhandel H. de Vries, P.O.B. 274, Ged. Oude Gracht 27-23 Haarlem, Netherlands.

23. TECHNICAL AND EDUCATIONAL: TECHNIQUE ET ERUDITION: TECHNIK

Aux Amateurs de Livres, 62 Avenue de Suffren, 75015 Paris, France—*aéronautique.*
A. Blanchard, 9 rue de Mèdicis, 75006 Paris, France—*mathematique, Chimie.*
Librairie Bourguignat, 10 bis Rue de Chateaudun, 75009 Paris, France—*locomotion.*
Georges A. Deny, rue du Chêne 5, 1000 Bruxelles, Belge.
Dias & Andrade Lda, Livraria Portugal, Rua do Carmo 70, Lisboa 2, Portugal.
Van Dijk's Boekhuis B.V., (Postbox 23), Dieselstraat 1, 8263 AE Kampen, Netherlands—*school & university texts.*
Dresdner Antiquariat Paul Alicke, Kurt-Schumacher-Strasse 33–35, D-6000 Frankfurt am Main, Deutschland—*Automobilen, Eisenbahnen.*
Antiquariat M. und R. Fricke, Poststrasse 3, 4000 Düsseldorf 1, Poststrasse 3, 4000 Düsseldorf 1, Deutschland—*architektur.*
Panayiotis Georgiou & Company, P.O. 622, Athens, Ellas—*encyclopedias, dictionaries.*
Le Grenier du Collectionneur, avenue Orban 238, 1150 Bruxelles, Belgie —*aeronautics, motoring, cycling.*
Gysbers en van Loon, Bakkerstraat 7A, Arnhem, Nederland—*Automobiles.*
Hans-Jürgen Ketz, Scharnhorststrasse 92, D-4400 Münster, Deutschland.
Kiepert G.m.b.H. Hardenbergstrasse 4–5, 1000 Berlin 12, Deutschland —*Geowissenschaften.*
Bouquinerie du Languedoc, 12 rue de l'Université, 34000 Montpellier, France —*livres universitaires.*

SPECIALITÉS   SPEZIALITÄTEN

Antiquariat Gerh. Renner, An d. Unteren Berg (Fuchsfarm), Postfach 1648, 7470 Albstadt 2, Deutschland—*Mathematik*.
Paul Roulleau, 108 rue Saint-Honoré, 75001 Paris, France—*militaria*.
Sartoni-Cerveau, 13 Quai Saint-Michel, 75005 Paris, France—*marine*.
Antiquariat B.F. Stadelmann, Dieselstrasse 5, 6070 Langen, Deutschland.
Technisches Antiquariat, Lauteschlagerstrasse 4, 6100 Darmstadt, Deutschland —*Mathematik: Technik*.
Libreria Santo Vanasia, Via M. Macchi 58, 20124 Milano, Italia—*mathematics, physics, chemistry*.

24. SCIENCE: SCIENCES: WISSENSCHAFTEN

Theodor Ackermann, Ludwigstrasse 7, 8000 München, Deutschland —*Geisteswissenschaften*.
Libreria Alessandria, Via Alessandria 216/a, Roma, Italia.
Bottega Ambrosiana, Via Vitruvio 47, 20124 Milano, Italia.
l'Ane d'Or, Boite Postale 6, 95450 Vigny, France—*sciences humaines*.
Antiquariaat Antiqua, Herengracht 159, 1015 BH Amsterdam, Nederland —*History*.
Björck & Börjesson, Kindstugatan 2, Postbox 5405, 11131 Stockholm, Sverige.
A. Blanchard, 9 rue de Medicis, 75006 Paris, France.
Félix Bloch, 10 Route de Rolle, 1162 Saint-Prex, (Boite Postale 58), Suisse.
Le Bouquiniste, 162 Grand-rue, 86000 Poitiers, France.
Libreria Antiquaria Bourlot, Piazza San Carlo 183, I-10123 Torino, Italia—*old science*.
Alain Brieux, 48 rue Jacob, 75006 Paris, France—*histoire*.
Libreria Antiquaria Brighenti, Via Malpertusoi 40123 Bologna, Italia *early science*.
Brockhaus Antiquarium, Am Wallgraben 127, 7000 Stuttgart 80, Deutschland— *Geistes und Naturwissenschaften*.
François et Rodolphe Chamonal, 40 rue le Peletier, 75009 Paris, France.
Cosmos Antiquarian Books, (P.O. Box 30) Market 23, 7240AA Lochem, Nederland *Biological & geological, chemistry*.
Georges A. Deny, rue du Chêne 5, 1000 Bruxelles, Belge.
Harri Deutsch, Naturwissenschaftliche Fachbuchhandlung, Gräfstrasse 47, 6000 Frankfurt am Main, Deutschland—*Naturwissenschaften*.
Libreria Dotti, Via Della Scrofa 58, 00186 Roma, Italia.
Olivier Encrenaz, 8 rue des Deux-Haies, 49000 Angers, France—*sciences et techniques anciennes*.
Georg Fritsch, Postfach 883, A-1010 Wien, Österreich.
Jacques Gabay, 151 bis. rue Saint-Jacques, 75005 Paris, France.
Garisenda Libri & Stampe, S.A.S., Strada Maggiore 14/A, 40125 Bologna, Italia.
Winfried Geisenheyner, Postfach 480155, Roseneck 6, D-4400 Münster-Hiltrup, Deutschland.
van Gendt Book Auctions N.V., Keizersgracht 96–98, 1015 CV Amsterdam, Nederland.
H. G. Gerritsen, Van Welderenstraat 88, Nijmegen, Nederland.
Gilhofer Buch- und Kunstantiquariat K.G. Bognergasse 2, 1010 Wien, Österreich.
Göttinger Antiquariat, Mauerstrasse 16/17, 3400 Göttingen, Deutschland —*Geisteswissenschaften, Geschichte der Naturwissenschaften*.
Michel Guillaume & Cie., S.A.R.L., Librairie Generale du Calvados, 98 rue Saint-Pierre, 14000 Caen, France.

Dr. Rudolf Hablet, G.m.b.H., am Buchenhang 1, 5300 Bonn, Deutschland—*Altertums Wissenschaft.*

Hagelin Antikvariat AB, P.O. Box 3321, 10366 Stockholm, Schweden—*history.*

Horst Hamecher, Goethestrasse 74, 3500 Kassel, Deutschland—*Geisteswissenschaften.*

Manfred Henke, Motzstr. 59, D-1000 Berlin-Schöneberg 30, Germany.

M. L. Huizenga, Oudez. Achterburgwal 156, 1012 DW Amsterdam, Nederland.

Interlibrum Establishment, Schloss-Strasse 6, Fl 9490 Vaduz, Liechtenstein—*history of science & ideas.*

B. M. Israel, B.V., Boekhandel en Antiquariaat, N.Z. Voorburgwal 264, 1012 RS Amsterdam, Nederland.

Gunnar Johanson-Thor, AB., Ellinge, 24100 Eslöv, Sverige—*old.*

Camille Joyaux, 55 rue de la Scellerie, 37000 Tours, France.

Heinz Hubertus Kampf, Wasserwerkgasse 31, Postfach 246. CH-3011 Bern, Schweiz —*Geschichte der Wissenschaften.*

Hans-Jürgen Ketz, Scharnhorststrasse 92, D-4400 Münster, Deutschland.

J. Kitzinger, Schellingstrasse 25, 8000 München, Deutschland.

Rainer Köbelin. Schellingstrasse 99, 8000 München 40, Deutschland —*Naturwissenschaft.*

Carl-Ernst Kohlhauer, Graser Weg 2, 8805 Feuchtwangen, Deutschland—*alte.*

Kultura, P.O. Box 149, H-1389 Budapest. Fö Utca. 32, Budapest 1, Magyarország.

Georges Lamongie, 2 rue de la Nation, 24000 Perigueux, France.

Dr. Konrad Liebmann, Lortzingstrasse 1, 4500 Osnabrück, Deutschland.

Libreria Luigi Lombardi, Via Constantinopoli 4 bis, 80138 Napoli, Italia.

A. van Loock, rue Saint Jean 51, 1000 Bruxelles, Belgie.

Carla Marzoli, Corso Porta Nuova 2, 20121 Milano, Italia—*history.*

Herbert Meinke, Stubenrauchstrasse 70, D-1000 Berlin-Friedenau 41, Deutschland —*Geographie.*

Librairie Monge, 5 rue de L'Echaudé, 75006 Paris, France—*histoire.*

Rene Munari, 9 rue Bayard, 38000 Grenoble, France.

Librairie Nantaise Y. Vachon. 3 Place de la Monnaie, 44000 Nantes, France.

Leo S. Olschki—Studio Bibliografico, 52046 Lucignano (Arezzo), Italia.

Libreria Antiquaria C.E. Rappaport, Via Sistina 23, 00187 Roma, Italia.

Antiquariat Gerh. Renner, An d. Unteren Berg (Fuchsfarm), Postfach 1648, 7470 Albstadt 2, Deutschland—*alte.*

Rönnells Antikvariat, AB, Birger Jarlsgatan 32, 11429 Stockholm, Schweden.

Librairie Rousseau-Girard, 2 ter rue Dupin, 75006 Paris, France.

Olivier Roux-Devillas, 12 rue Bonaparte, 75006 Paris, France—*anciennes.*

Jörg Schäfer, Alfred-Escher-Strasse 76, 8002 Zürich, Schweiz—*Geschichte der Wissenschaften.*

Librairie "Sciences Nat", 2 rue Andre-Mellenne, Venette, 60200 Compiegne, France —*sciences naturelles.*

Philippe Serignan, 15 rue Joseph-Vernet, 84000 Avignon, France.

Sibrium Libri e Manoscritti, Via Bigli 21, 20121 Milano, Italia.

Libreria Antiquaria Soave, Via Po 48, 10123 Torino, Italia.

Wolfgang Symanczyk, Hubertusweg 32, 4040 Neuss, Deutschland—*Geschichte der Wissenschaften.*

Librairie Thomas-Scheler, 19 rue de Tournon, 75006 Paris, France.

Thulins Antikvariat, AB., 57060 Österbymo, Sverige—*old.*

Libreria Antiquaria Andrea Vallerini, Via Dei Mille 7A–13, I-56100 Pisa, Italy —*Early.*

Jean Viardot, 15 rue de l'echaudé, 75006 Paris, France.
Rainer Gerd Voigt, Langerstrasse 2/IV, D-8000 München 80, Deutschland.
Wagner'sche Universitäts Buchhandlung OHG., Museumstrasse 4, 6021 Innsbruck, Österreich.
D. Weil, 1 rue du Dragon, 75006 Paris, France.
Horst Wellm, Bennigserweg 1, D-3017 Pattensen 1, Deutschland.
Alexander Wild, Rathausgasse 30, 3011 Bern, Schweiz.
Zentralantiquariat der DDR, Talstrasse 29, 701 Leipzig, DDR.

25. TOPOGRAPHY AND TRAVEL: REGIONALISME ET VOYAGES:
TOPOGRAPHIE UND REISEN

Librairie Abbe Girard, 6 rue de l'Abbe Girard, 63000 Clermont-Ferrand, France
voyages; orientalisme.
Jo Charles Abela, 11 rue Pierre-Démours, 75017 Paris, France—*cartes
géographiques anciennes; voyages.*
Robert Alder, Junkerngasse 41, Bern, Schweiz—*Helvetica.*
Librairie des Alpes, 6 rue de Seine, 75006 Paris, France *Alpes, Pyrenes*
Altstadt Antiquariat, rue d'Or 16, CH-170° Fribourg, Schweiz.
Antiquariaat Amaryl, Tuinbouwstraat 74, 9717-JL Groningen, Nederland
—*Northern Netherlands.*
l'Amateur d'Art, 38 rue de Vaugirard, 75006 Paris, France—*Voyages.*
Antiquariat Amelang, Cranachstrasse 45, 2000 Hamburg 52, Deutschland
—*illustrierte Bücher.*
Les Amis du Livre, 9 Valaoritou Street, Athens 134, Ellas—*travel, maps.*
Antiikki-Kirja, Kalevankatu 25, 00100 Helsinki 10, Finland—*Finland and Russia.*
Antiquariat Athenaeum, Narvavagen 23, Box 5852, 102 48 Stockholm, Sverige.
Libreria Anticuaria Aristeucos, Paseo de la Bonanova 14, G. Barcelona 080 22,
España—*Catalonia.*
Arno Adler, Hüxstrasse 55, 2400 Lübeck, Deutschland—*Lübeck, Hansische Gesch-
ichte.*
Atika Books, P.O. Box 1086, Yannai Street 3, Jerusalem, Israe—*Palestine.*
Peter Babendererde, Grosse Burgstrasse 35, 2400 Lübeck, Deutschland
—*Stadteansichten und Landkarten.*
Alexandre Baer [J. Baer & Co.], 2–6 rue Livingstone, 75018 Paris, France—*les
Ameriques.*
Librairie du Bât d'Argent et du Chariot d'Or, 38 rue des Remparts d'Ainay, 69002
Lyon, France.
Paul Bataille, "Calendal", 14 rue Châteauredon, 13 Marseille, France—*voyages.*
Antiquariat Behrens, Leibnizstrasse 47, D-1000 Berlin 12, Deutschland.
Hermann Beisler, Oskar-v. Miller-Ring 33, 8000 München 2, Deutschland.
A. Bellanger, 6 et 8 Passage Pommeraye, 44000 Nantes, France.
Berche et Pagis, 60 rue Mazarine, 75006 Paris, France—*voyages.*
Van Berg Antiquariaat, Oude Schans 8–10, Amsterdam, Nederland—*topography.*
Berliner Antiquariat, Rheinstrasse 6, D-1000 Berlin-Friedenau 41, Germany—*Orts-
und Landeskunde.*
Libreria Antiquaria Berruto, Via San Francesco da Paola 10 bis, 10123 Torino,
Italia—*Italy, Piedmont.*
Antiquariaat G. J. Bestebreurtje, Lichte Gaard 2, P.O. Box 364 AJ Utrecht, Neder-
land—*Voyages & travel.*
Paul Bezzina, 114 Saint Lawrence Street, Vittoriosa, Malta *Malta.*

Bickhardt'sche Buchhandlung, Karl-Marx-Strasse 168, 1000 Berlin-Neukölln 44, Deutschland.

Paul Bisey, 35 Place de la Réunion, 68100 Mulhouse, France.

Björck & Börjesson, Kindstugatan 2, Postbox 5405, 11131 Stockholm, Sverige.

Heinrich Böhringer, Marktplatz 2, 8592 Wunsiedel, Deutschland—*Böhmen, Bayern.*

La Bouquinerie, 89 rue de Lyon, 89200 Avallon, France.

Le Bouquiniste, 162 Grand-rue, 86000 Poitiers, France—*voyages.*

Le Bouquiniste, Via Principe Amedeo 29, 10123 Torino, Italia—*Italy.*

Bouquins, rue de Boigne 13, 73000 Chambéry, France—*provinciana.*

Bourcy & Paulusch, Wipplingerstrasse 5, 1010 Wien, Österreich—*Alpinismus, Austriaca.*

Bice Bourlot, Piazza Castello 9, Torino, 10123, Italia—*atlases & maps.*

Libreria Antiquaria Bourlot, Piazza San Carlo 183, I–10123 Torino, Italia—*Italy.*

Antiquariaat Brabant, Lange Putstraat 14, 5211 KN 's-Hertogenbosch, Nederland.

Antiquariat Bremer und Schlak, Kornmarkt 4–5, 3340 Wolfenbüttel, Deutschland.

E. J. Brill, Oude Rijn 33A, Leiden, Nederland—*Orientalia, biology.*

Klaus Von Brincken, Theresienstrasse 58 und Pacellistrasse 2, 8000 München 2, Deutschland.

Buchantiquariat Britschgi, Rämistrasse 33, 8000 Zürich, Schweiz—*Reisen, Alpinismus.*

Brockhaus Antiquarium, Am Wallgraben 127, 7000 Stuttgart 80, Deutschland—*Africana, Americana, Asiatica, Arctica.*

Galerie Brumme Frankfurt, Braubachstr. 34, 6000 Frankfurt-am-Main, Deutschland—*Landkarten; Topographie.*

Hermann Bub, Postfach 5328, Kürschnerhof 7, 8700 Würzburg 1, Deutschland —*Africana, Suddeutschland.*

Das Bücgerfass I, Pfalzburger Strasse 12, Berlin-Wilmersdorf 15, Deutschland.

Bücherstube am See, Kreuzlingerstrasse 11, 7750 Konstanz-Bodensee, Deutschland —*Badensia.*

Der Buchfreund [Walter Schaden], Sonnenfelsgasse 4, 1010 Wien 1, Österreich.

Arnold Busck, Fiolstraede 24, 1171 København-K, Danmark.

Cachet, Munsterberg 13, CH-4051 Basel, Schweiz—*Helvetica.*

Le Cadre d'Art, rue St. Paul 33, 4000 Liege, Belgium—*gravures anciennes.*

J. W. Cappelens Antikvariat, P.O. Box 350, Kirkegatan 15, N-0101 Oslo 1, Norge —*Scandinavia, Iceland, Greenland, travel.*

Francisco Carrillo, 86 Faubourg Saint-Antoine, 75012 Paris, France—*Espagne; voyages.*

A. Tavares de Carvalho, Avenida da Republica 46–3°, 1000 Lisboa-1, Portugal —*Brazil, Arabia, Persia.*

Giocondo Cassini, Via XXII Marco San Marco 2424, 30124 Venezia, Italia—*Italy.*

Jean Cau, 22 rue Peyras et Bouquinerie Balaran, 52 rue du Taur, 31000 Toulouse, France.

Bouquinerie Cevenole, 10 rue Porte de France, Nîmes (Gard), France.

Jacques Chaminade, 8 rue de l'Isle, 74000 Annecy, France.

Les Chevaux Lêgers, 34 rue Vivienne, 75002 Paris, France—*Bretagne, Provence.*

Librairie I. Chmeljuk, 1 rue de Fleurus, 75006 Paris, France—*Slavisme, Europe de l'Est.*

Cité des Vieux Livres, 139 Grande Rue, 25000 Besançon, France—*histoire locale.*

Aribert D. Claassen, Buch- und Kunstantiquariat, Hardtstrasse 8, 5483 Bad Neuenahr-aw 1, Deutschland.

Librairie Pierre Clerc, 13 rue Alexandre Cabanel, 34000 Montpellier, France
—*Languedoc.*
Bouquinerie Comtoise, S.A.R.L., 9 rue Morand, 25000 Besançon (Doubs), France
—*Franche-Comté.*
Damms Antikvariat A/S, Bokhuset, Tollbodgata 25, Oslo 2, Norge—*Atlases & maps, topography.*
Henri Danigo, 17 rue Marc-Sangnier, 29000 Quimper, France—*Bretagne.*
G. et A. Dargent, 11 rue Alain-Blanchard, 76000 Rouen, France—*Normandie, histoire litterature.*
Librairie des Deux Gares. 76 Boulevard de Magenta, 75010 Paris, France
—*Lorraine.*
Antiquariaat Johan Devroe, L. Vanderkelenstraat 43, 3000 Leuven, Belgium.
Michele Dhennequin, 76 rue du Cherche-Midi, 75006 Paris, France—*voyages anciennes. colonies francaises.*
Gabriel Durance, 5 Allée d'Orléans, 44000 Nantes, France—*régionalisme; voyages.*
N G. Elwert Universitätsbuchhandlung, Reitgasse 7–9, 3550 Marburg (Lahn), Deutschland—*Deutschland.*
S. Emmering, N.Z. Voorburgwal 304, 1012 RV Amsterdam, Nederland
—*Americana (West Indies)*
Frede Engholst, Studiesstraede 35, 1455 København-K, Danmark.
Ex-Libris, 11 rue Victor Cousin, 75005 Paris, France—*Extrême Orient*
Librairie Favereaux, 19ter rue de l'Hôpital-Militaire, 59000 Lille, France.
Fiol, Llibres, OMS 45–A, Palma de Mallorca, 07003, España—*rare books on the Balearic Islands.*
Librairie Gangloff, 13 Auguste Wicky, 68100 Mulhouse, France—*Alsace.*
Louis Gangloff, 20 Place de la Cathédrale, 67000 Strasbourg, France—*Alsace.*
Andre Gauthier S.A., B.P. 373–09, F 75424 Paris Cedex 09, France—*India.*
Jean-Philippe Geley, 229 rue de Tolbiac 75013, Paris, France—*Orientalism; voyages.*
Librairie Orientaliste Paul Geuthner S.A. 12 rue Vavin, 75006 Paris, France
—*Afrique, Egypte, Extrême Orient.*
Gilhofer Buch- und Kunstantiquariat K.G. Bognergasse 2, 1010 Wien, Österreich
—*Austriaca; Bohemica.*
François Girand, 76 rue de Seine, 75006 Paris, France.
Paul Gothier, rue Bonne Fortune 3 et 5, Liège, Belgie—*Belgicana.*
Das Graphik-Kabinett, Humboldtstrasse 80, 4000 Düsseldorf 1, Deutschland.
Die Gravüre, Rüttenschneider Strasse 56, 4300 Essen 1, Deutschland.
Gysbers en van Loon, Bakkerstraat 7A, Arnhem, Nederland—*Dutch.*
Antiquariat Gero Habelt, Königsheimstrasse 12, 5300 Bonn 1, Deutschland.
Hamburgensien-Meyer, Poststrasse 2–4, 2000 Hamburg 36, Deutschland.
Otto Harrassowitz, Taunusstrasse 5, 6200 Wiesbaden, Deutschland—*Oriental.*
V. A. Heck, Kärntner Ring 14, 1010 Wien, Österreich—*Austriaca, alte Landkarten.*
J.J. Heckenhauer, Holzmarkt 5, 7400 Tübingen, Deutschland—*Slavische Länder.*
Leopold Heidrich G.m.b.H., Plankengasse 7, Wien 1, Österreich—*Austriaca; Viennsia.*
P. H. Heitz, Postfach 80, Basel 4006, Schweiz—*Helvetica, Alsatica.*
Serge Helluin, 11 rue Leon-Blum, 80000 Amiens, France.
Theodor Hennig, Motzstr. 25, D-1000 Berlin-Schöneberg 30, Germany—*Berlin.*
Libreria Hesperia, Plaza de Los Sitios 10, Zaragoza, España—*Hispanica, Americana.*
Arnold Heoo, Galerie zur Krone, Zürcherstrasse 183, CH-8500 Frauenfeld, Schweiz
—*Helvetica.*

Livraria Histórica e Ultramarina LDA [J. C. Silva], Travessa da Queimada 28, 1200– Lisboa 2, Portugal—*Africana.*
M. und R. Hofer, Münstergasse 56, CH-3011 Bern, Schweiz—*Helvetica.*
Wilhelm Hofmann G.m.b.H., Bismarckstrasse 98, 6700 Ludwigshafen, Deutschland —*Pfalz und Rhein.*
Eduard Höllrigl, Sigmund Haffner Gasse 10, 5010 Salzburg, Österreich—*Salzburg.*
Karl Hölzl, K.G., Seilergasse 3, 1010 Wien, Österreich—*Alte Landkarten.*
H. Hugendubel, Salvatorplatz 2, 8000 München 2, Deutschland—*Bavarica.*
Alte Graphik Julia F. Iliu, Barer Strasse 46, 8000 München 40, Deutschland.
Interlibrum Estalishment, Schloss-Strasse 6, Fl 9490 Vaduz. Liechtenstein—*Helvetica.*
B. M. Israel, B.V., Boekhandel en Antiquariaat, N.Z. Voorburgwal 264, 1012 RS Amsterdam, Nederland.
N. Israel, Keizersgracht 489–491, Amsterdam, Nederland—*cartography, travel and voyages.*
Antiquariat Ruthild Jäger, Steinweg 17, 2120 Lüneburg-Oedeme, Deutschland —*alte Stadtansichten und Landkarten.*
Xavier Jehanno, 4 Place de l'Eglise, 78430 Louveciennes, France.
Hans-Joachim Jeschke, Winterfeldstrasse 51, D-1000 Berlin-Schöneberg 30, Germany—*Orts- und Landeskunde.*
Gunnar Johanson-Thor, AB., Ellinge, 24100 Eslöv, Sverige.
Antiquariaat R. de Jong, Kruisweg 38a 2011 LD Haarlem, Nederland.
Camille Joyaux, 55 rue de la Scellerie, 37000 Tours, France—*voyages.*
Mme. Juhel-Douet, 3 rue d'Angleterre, 41000 Blois, France.
Kaabers Antikvariat, Skindergade 34, 1159 København-K, Danmark—*maps and prints.*
Libreria Filosofica Kairôs, Studio d'Arte, 11219 Milano-Isola, via Baldinucci 6, 20158 Milano, Italia—*Italian towns, maps, views.*
Dion P. Karavias, 67 Asclipiou Street, 10680 Athens, Ellas—*Greece.*
Christos Katsicalis, Zambakis Bookshop, 14 Massalias Street, Athens 144TN, Ellas.
Librarie Kauffmann, 28 Stadium Street, Athens-132, Ellas—*Greece, Turkey, maps.*
Heinrich Kerler, Platzgasse 26, 7900 Ulm, Deutschland—*Baden-Württemberg.*
Hans-Jürgen Ketz, Scharnhorststrasse 92, D-4400 Münster, Deutschland—*Orts- und Landeskunde.*
Kiepert G.m.b.H. Hardenbergstrasse 4–5, 1000 Berlin 12, Deutschland —*Landkarten.*
Frank Kirkop, 106 Blanche Street, Sliema, Malta—*Malta.*
Antiquariat Klaussner, Professor-Kurt-Huber-Strasse 19, 8032 Gräfelfing (München), Deutschland—*Reisen, Expeditionen.*
Brigitta Kowallik, Klarissenstrasse 5, 4040 Neuss, Deutschland.
Bragi Kristjonsson, Antikvariat, P.O. Box 775, Skolavördustigur 20, Reykjavík, Island—*Icelandicana and norrõna.*
Boekhandel Antiquariaat Kruger, Achter de Hoofdwacht 7, Nijmegen, Netherlands —*maps, prints, atlases.*
l'Invitation au Voyage, 15 Quai Saint-Michel, 75005 Paris, France.
Lagnel-Tastemain, 25 Boulevard Marechal-Leclerc, 14300 Caen, France —*Normandie.*
A. Lanzen, 19 Cathedral Street, Sliema, Malta—*Malta.*
S.C. Lemmers, van Bönninghausenlaan 16, 2161 ET Lisse, Nederland.
Lestringant, 123 rue Général-Leclerc, 76000 Rouen, France—*Normandie.*

Franz Leuwer, Am Wall 171, 2800 Bremen, Deutschland—*Norddeutschland.*
Libri, 20 rue du Pont, 71000 Macon, France.
Louis Loeb-Larocque, 36 rue le Peletier, 75009 Paris, France—*atlases, voyages, topographie.*
Logos Bookshop, 38 Ben Yehuda Street, Tel Aviv, Israel—*Palestine.*
Loose, Papestraat 3, 's-Gravenhage, Netherlands.
Jules Lorieul, Normania, 3 Place du Castel, 50580 Port-Bail, France.
A. Lungelarsen, Øygardveien 16e, Bekkestua, Norge—*Scandinavia.*
Buchantiquariat Madliger-Schwab, Postfach 8022, Tiefenhöfe (Beim Paradeplatz) 8001 Zürich, Schweiz—*Helvetica.*
La Maison du Livre, 24 rue de la Cloche Verte, 16000 Angoulême, France.
Adrien Maisonneuve, 11 rue St. Sulpice, 75006 Paris, France—*l'Orient.*
MAM, P.O. Box 1722, Nicosia, Cyprus—*Cyprus.*
Fernand Martinez, 97 rue de Seine, 75006 Paris, France.
Jean-Claude Martinez, 21 rue Saint-Sulpice, 75006 Paris, France—*Oriental.*
Carla Marzoli, Corso Porta Nuova 2, 20121 Milano, Italia—*Cartography.*
Karna Matchtmeister Bildantikvariat, De Geersgatan 12, 11529 Stockholm, Sweden—*maps, prints & views.*
Henri Metais, 2 Place Barthelemy, 76000 Rouen, France—*Normandie.*
Librairie du Miroir, rue du Miroir 9–11, 7000 Mons, Belgium.
Karl Möhler, Rheinsprung 7, CH-4051 Basel, Schweiz—*Helvetica*
Libreria Antiquaria Moretti, Via Lusardi 8, 20122 Milano, Italy—*atlases and travel.*
Morvran, Boite Postale 22, Brignou en Berrien, 29218 Huelgoat, Bretagne, France—*Bretagne.*
Clemens Müller, Kapellenweg 59, 5600 Wuppertal Barmen, Deutschland
Rene Munari, 9 rue Bayard, 38000 Grenoble, France—*voyages, atlas.*
Antiquariat Karlheinz Murr, Karolinenstrasse 4, 8600 Bamberg, Deutschland—*Städteansichten und Landkarten.*
Henry Müller, Postfach 55, 8405 Winterthur, Schweiz—*Deutchland, Schweiz.*
Gé Nabrink & Zoon, Korte Korsjespoortstraat 8, Amsterdam-C, Nederland—*Orientalia.*
Het Nedersaksische Antiquariaat, Nieuwstraat 50, 7411 LM Deventer, Nederland.
Nordiska Antivariska Bokhandeln, Norra Magasingatan 6, Helsingfors, Suomi—*maps.*
Parsifal [S.A.R.L.], 80 Boulevard Raspail, 75006 Paris, France—*Cartes géographiques anciennes.*
C. P. J. van der Peet, B.V., 33–35 Nieuwe Spiegelstraat, 1017 DC Amsterdam, Nederland—*Africa, Americana, Asiatica, Orientalia.*
Francine van der Perre, rue de la Madeleine 23, 1000 Bruxelles, Belgie.
Albert Petit-Siroux, 45, 46, 47 Galerie Vivienne, 75002 Paris, France.
Philographicon, Galerie für Alte Graphik im Antic-Haus, Neuturmstrasse 1, 8000 München 2, Deutschland.
Editions A. & J. Picard, 82 rue Bonaparte, 75006 Paris, France.
Jean Polak, 8 rue de l'Echaudé, 75006 Paris, France—*voyages.*
Librairie Poursin, Cité Noël, 22 rue Rambuteau, 75003 Paris, France.
Wilhelm Puskas, Weihburggasse 16, 1010 Wien, Österreich—*Austriaca.*
Quartier Latin, 21 rue Albert-1er, 17000 la Rochelle, France—*régionalisme.*
G. Raffy, 85 rue des Rosiers (Stand 83 Marché Biron), 93400 Saint-Ouen (Seine-St. Denis), France.
Librairie Raoust, 11 rue Neuve, 59000 Lille, France—*Flundre-Artois.*

Reiss und Auvermann, Buch- und Kunstantiquariat, Zum Talblick 2, 6246 Glashütten im Taunus, Deutschland.

Librairie A. Remy, 25 rue Stanislas, 54000 Nancy, France.

Ribaux Buchhandlung und Antiquariat, Bahnhofstrasse 2, CH-9001 St Gallen, Schweiz—*Helvetica*.

Librairie Rivares, 3 rue Rivares, 64000 Pau, France—*Pyrenées*.

Anne-Marie Robichon, 16 Quai de la Loire, 37210 Rochecorbon/Vouvray, France.

Hans Rohr, Oberdorferstrasse 5, 8024 Zürich 1, Schweiz—*Helvetica*.

Rönnells Antikvariat, AB, Birger Jarlsgatan 32, 11429 Stockholm, Schweden —*Swedish maps and prints*.

Rosenkilde og Bagger, 3 Kron-Prinsens-Gade, P.O. Box 2184, DK-1017 København, Danmark—*Scandinavica, Arctica*.

R. B. Rosenthal, Rua do Alecrim 47-4° Salas D, Lisboa 2, Portugal—*Africana*.

Librairie Rossignol, 1 rue Jean Daumas, 06400 Cannes, France—*Africana*.

Nils Sabels Antivariat, Box 1049, 15024 Rönninge 1, Sweden.

Samlaren Antikvariat & Konsthandel, Korsgatan 2, 41116 Göteborg, Schweden —*topography*.

Librairie Orientale H. Samuelian, 51 rue Monsieur-le-Prince, 75006 Paris, France —*Orientalisme, Arabie, Arménie*.

Antiquariaat Sanderus, Brugsestraat 88, 8510 Kortrijk, Belgium—*XV-XIX centuries*.

Sartoni-Cerveau, 13 Quai Saint-Michel, 75005 Paris, France—*Voyages*.

Kunstantiquariat Monika Schmidt, Türkenstrasse 48, 8000 München 40, und Schloss Haimhausen, 8048 Haimhausen, Deutschland.

Dr. Gerhard Schneider, Rhode-Goldsiepen 12, 5960 Olpe, Deutschland.

Hartmut R. Schreyer, Auf Dem Kreuz 9, D-8900 Augsburg, Deutschland —*Bavarica*.

Hanno Schreyer, Euskirchenerstrasse 57–59, 5300 Bonn 1, Deutschland—*Alte Landkarten*.

Philippe Serignan, 15 rue Joseph-Vernet, 84000 Avignon, France—*Provence; voyages*.

Rene Simmermacher A.G., Kirchgasse 25, CH-8024 Zürich, Schweiz—*frühe Griechenland Lithographien*.

M. Slatkine et Fils, 5 rue des Chaudronniers, 1211 Genève, Schweiz—*Romanica; Helvetica*.

Boehandel J. de Slegte B.V., Grote Staat 53, 6211 CV Maastright, Nederland.

Boekhandel J. de Slegte B.V., Marktstraat 13, 7511 GC Enschede, Nederland.

Boekhandel J. de Slegte B.V., Weversgildeplein 1-2, 8011 XN Zwolle, Nederland.

J. de Slegte, Spuistraat 9, 2511 BC, 's-Gravenhage, Nederland.

J. de Slegte, Kalverstraat 48–52, 1012 PE Amsterdam, Nederland—*maps, travels*.

Fiammetta Soave, Via Leccosa 4, Roma, Italia—*Roma*.

Sonnewald-Heckenhauer, Waldhof 1, 7947 Mengen, Deutschland—*Slavische Launder*.

Wolfgang Staschen, Potsdamer Str. 138, 1000 Berlin 30, Deutschland—*Stahlstich Ansichten*.

Stavros Stavridis, Panaghitsas 18, Kifisia, 14562 Athens, Greece—*Greece, Cyprus, Turkey*.

J.F. Steinkopf, Postfach 1116, Marienstrasse 3, 7000 Stuttgart, Deutschland.

Th. Stenderhoff & Co., Alter Fischmarkt 21, 4400 Münster, Deutschland —*Staudteansichten, Landkarten*.

Librairie Stendhal, 4 rue de Sault, 38000 Grenoble, France.

Antiquariat Nikolaus Struck, Wilhelmstrasse 5, 5449 Pfalzfeld, Deutschland.
J. G. Sydys, Buchhandlung Ludwig Schubert G.m.b.H., P.O. Box 169, Wienerstrasse 19, 3100 St. Pölten, Österreich—*Austriaca.*
J. A. Telles da Sylva, Travessa Marquês sá da Bandeira, 19-3° Esq. Lisboa 1, Portugal—*Portugese & Spanish travels, Braziliana.*
Bibliographicum E. Tenner, Hauptstrasse 194, 6900 Heidelburg, Deutschland.
Librairie-editions Thanh-Long, 34 rue Dekens, 1040 Bruxelles, Belgie—*Far East.*
Librairie Thomas-Scheler, 19 rue de Tournon, 75006 Paris, France.
Le Tour du Monde, 9 rue de la Pompe, 75116 Paris, France—*voyages.*
Jean Touzot, 38 rue Saint-Sulpice, 75278 Paris, France—*voyages.*
Umea Antikvariat, Västra Esplanaden 6, 90248 Umea, Sweden—*Lapland & Northern Scandinavia.*
Kunstantiquariat Valentien, Niederwall 14, 4800 Bielefeld, Deutschland —*Städteansichten und Landkarten.*
Librairie Valleriaux, 98 Boulevard Voltaire, 75011 Paris, France—*Provinciale et de Paris.*
A.W. Vandevelde, Dweersstraat 6, 8000 Bruges, Belgie—*Flanders, Far East.*
Galerie Vauquelin, 4 rue Vauquelin, 76200 Dieppe, France.
Hendrik van Veldeke, 50 B.10, Guffenslaan, 3500 Hasselt, Belgium.
Christian F. Verbeke, Bloemendalestraat 73, 8030 Beernem (bij Brugge), Belgium.
Jean Viardot, 15 rue de l'echaudé, 75006 Paris, France—*voyages.*
Librairie au Vieux Quartier, Rue des Fripiers 11, B-5000 Namur, Belgium —*gravures topographiques belge.*
Rainer Gerd Voigt, Langerstrasse 2/IV, D-8000 München 80, Deutschland *Ortsbeschreibung.*
Louis Vuille, rue Maison-Rouge 5, 1400 Yverdon, Suisse—*Helvetica.*
R. & I. Wanner-Zander, Kronengasse 35, 5400 Baden, Schweiz—*Helvetica.*
Carl Wegner, Martin-Luther-Strasse 113, 1000 Berlin 62, Deutschland —*Berlinensia.*
Werner Weick, Buch- und Kunstantiquariat, Sternstrasse 2, AM Markt, 5300 Bonn 1, Deutschland—*Topographie.*
Antiquariat H. U. Weiss Bibliotheca Gastronomica, Winzerstrasse 5, CH-8049 Zürich, Schweiz—*Voyages, tourisme.*
Horst Wellm, Bennigserweg 1, D-3017 Pattensen 1, Deutschland—*Orts- und Landeskunde.*
L. und E. Wildner, Stempfergasse 8, 8010 Graz, Österreich—*Styriaca, Austriaca.*
Angelos Zambakis, Le Bibliophile, 14 Massalis, Athens 144, Ellas   *maps.*
Buch und Kunstauktionshaus F. Zisska & R. Kistner, Unterer Anger 15, 8000 München 2, Deutschland.

LIST OF ADVERTISERS

LISTE DES ANNONCES
VERZEICHNIS DER INSERATEN